THE ABINGDON PREACHING ANNUAL 2011

The

ABINGDON

PREACHING
ANNUAL
2011

COMPILED AND EDITED BY
THE REVEREND DAVID NEIL MOSSER, PH.D.

ASSISTANT EDITOR RONDA WELLMAN

Abingdon Press
Nashville

THE ABINGDON PREACHING ANNUAL 2011

Copyright © 2010 by Abingdon Press

All rights reserved.

This book is printed on acid-free paper.

ISBN 978-1-4267-0701-8

ISSN 1075-2250

10 11 12 13 14 15 16 17 18 19—10 9 8 7 6 5 4 3 2 1
MANUFACTURED IN THE UNITED STATES OF AMERICA

To my Perkins School of Theology colleagues

CONTENTS

⟨decorative flourish⟩

Contents

Contents

Contents

Contents

Contents

III. APPENDIX

IV. CD-ROM

The entire print text plus the following are found on the enclosed CD-ROM. (See the ReadMe.txt and 1Intro.pdf files on the CD for instructions.)

Contents

INTRODUCTION

Perhaps you are like many preachers. As you preach week in and week out, you are aware that the work sometimes places you on a lonely path. To repair this homiletical isolation, many preaching pastors assemble with colleagues who share our preaching journey. Sometimes preachers gather weekly or monthly in "study clusters" or "lectionary groups." Yet for many rural preachers, maybe even urban preachers, assembling regularly with other preachers in this fashion is neither convenient nor feasible. Happily, with the Internet we can hear other preachers practice our art. But listening to many sermons tends to be time-consuming—a luxury that few preachers have. Providing preachers a venue by which to delve into texts and ideas with other preachers is the intention behind the 2011 *Abingdon Preaching Annual (APA)*. The APA employs *The Revised Common Lectionary* for half its entries, while sermon series make up the other half. Thus, for each Sunday of the calendar year—January through December—each preachable day's section offers not only a thousand-word sermon on one of the three primary lectionary texts for the day, but also a sermon from a series as well.

The purpose of the APA is to help preachers plan a full yearly schedule for preaching the biblical good news. Each preacher has her or his own method for planning a preaching program for individual congregations. The book in your hands or the CD in your computer allows preachers to sketch a preaching agenda from January through December—or for any segment of the year. Some may use the lectionary exclusively; some the series; others a combination. For any approach by which one plans preaching, the APA can be a useful portion of a planning method.

Perceptive preachers might ask, "For what kinds of preachers has Abingdon Press prepared this book?" The answer would be those who want to be in conversation with other preachers who approach the preaching task with the seriousness that biblical exposition calls forth. Preachers who may benefit from this book may be old or young, novice or experienced, rural or urban. *The Abingdon Preaching Annual*'s intention is to stimulate biblical discourse. We all know that faithful preachers need and want this kind of spiritual and cerebral stimulation.

Each of the sermons in this 2011 edition of the *APA* possesses some superior feature that prompted the editors to place it in this book. Some of the sermons simply provide excellent biblical or historical exegesis of a particular text; others offer an application or a story that may help bring biblical texts to life for congregations. We point the *APA* toward those who desire to see how others use and understand the texts in delivering the biblical message to God's people. However you choose to make use of this book, we trust it will be of assistance to those who want to preach more effective sermons for believers in 2011.

Critics sometimes allege that books like *The Abingdon Preaching Annual* lure preachers into laziness or even plagiarism. Plainly, with the surplus of sermons and preaching helps accessible in print and online, this concern may be valid. However, the task of preaching is so difficult that we can not adequately prepare alone. *The Abingdon Preaching Annual* is one voice among many that preachers listen to with discernment. It offers unique sermon ideas and themes, biblical commentaries, and insights from other pastors' life experiences. Faithful preaching can and does happen when we use our individual gifts in concert with the insights of others.

Naturally we all bring our own gifts in preparing a word for our distinctive congregations. In the *ekklesia* of Jesus Christ, "one size fits all" does not apply. Only in the particularity of God's word spoken in a particular place and time can the church grasp the command of Jesus to "follow me" and live out this command in the world. Each pastor and congregation has an exacting and sacred association that no other person can imitate. Only the pastor as preacher can preach well to her or his individual congregation. In fact, I know many pastors who say that everything else they do—administration, pastoral care, fund-raising, and so on—supports their work of preaching God's word. Therefore, we trust that no authentic preacher would be so lifeless or lacking in zest as to let the enticement for shortcuts weaken his or her effectiveness.

In an earlier time, preachers steadfastly read what other preachers wrote in newspapers, books, and periodicals. In our contemporary world, many shun the reading of sermons, claiming lack of time. Yet to walk through a text and experience it with a sister or brother in the ministry can be one of the most helpful ways to learn. No preacher is ever a finished product. We all continually learn from others and from sharing our own small victories as well as our large mistakes. Through this conversation we and the church are blessed.

In addition to the weekly sermons on lectionary and series themes, each with worship aids intended to help "prime the pump," the *APA* furnishes commentary on lectionary texts not used for the primary sermon. The enclosed CD-ROM includes the full text of the print edition as well as the full lectionary text of each week's readings, and offers search capabilities and hyperlinks for easy navigation. The CD-ROM also provides pre-sermon, offertory, and pastoral prayers for major liturgical celebrations, an extensive annotated bibliography of biblical commentaries to help preachers in their preparation, classical and contemporary prayers and affirmations, and a classic sermon from the past for inspiration.

Finally, I write a word of appreciation to the many preachers who labor under relative anonymity and produce faithful sermons to feed their congregations each week. To them I say a grateful word of thanks.

> But how are they to call on one in whom they have not believed? And how are they to believe in one of whom they have never heard? And how are they to hear without someone to proclaim him? And how are they to proclaim him unless they are sent? As it is written, "How beautiful are the feet of those who bring good news!" (Romans 10:14-15)

David Neil Mosser
FUMC, Arlington, Texas
"Juneteenth" 2009

I. GENERAL HELPS

FOUR-YEAR CHURCH CALENDAR

	2011	2012	2013	2014
Ash Wednesday	March 9	February 22	February 13	March 5
Palm Sunday	April 17	April 1	March 24	April 13
Holy Thursday	April 21	April 5	March 28	April 17
Good Friday	April 22	April 6	March 29	April 18
Easter	April 24	April 8	March 31	April 20
Ascension Day	June 5	May 20	May 12	June 1
Pentecost	June 12	May 27	May 19	June 8
Trinity Sunday	June 19	June 3	May 26	June 15
World Communion	October 2	October 7	October 6	October 5
Thanksgiving	November 24	November 22	November 28	November 27
First Sunday of Advent	November 27	December 2	December 1	November 30

LITURGICAL COLORS

If the gospel can be proclaimed visually, why should it not be? Color helps form general expectations for any occasion. Traditionally, purples, grays, and blues have been used for seasons of a penitential character such as Advent and Lent, although any dark colors could be used. White has been used for events or seasons with strong christological meaning such as the Baptism of the Lord or the Easter Season. Yellows and golds are also possibilities at such times. Red has been reserved for occasions relating to the Holy Spirit (such as the Day of Pentecost or ordinations) or to commemorations of the martyrs. Green has been used for seasons such as the Season after Epiphany or the Season after Pentecost. The absence of any colored textiles from Maundy Thursday to the Easter Vigil is a striking use of contrast. Colors and textures can be used most effectively in textiles for hangings on pulpits, on lecterns (if any), for the stoles worn by ordained ministers, or for ministerial vestments.*

Advent: Violet (purple) or blue

Christmas: Gold or white for December 24-25. White thereafter, through the Baptism of the Lord. (Or, in the days between January 6 and the Sunday of the Baptism, green may be used.)

Ordinary Time (both after Epiphany-Baptism and after Pentecost): Green

Transfiguration: White

Lent Prior to Holy Week: Violet. Black is sometimes used for Ash Wednesday.

Early Holy Week: On Palm-Passion Sunday, violet (purple) or [blood] red may be specified. For the Monday, Tuesday, and Wednesday of Holy Week, the same options exist, although with variations as to which color to use on each day.

Triduum: For Holy Thursday, violet (purple) or [blood] red may be used during the day and changed to white for the evening Eucharist. Then the church may be stripped.

Good Friday and Holy Saturday: Stripped or black; or [blood] red in some churches on Good Friday.

Great Fifty Days: White or gold. Or gold for Easter Day and perhaps its octave, then white for the remainder of the season until the Vigil of Pentecost.

Day of Pentecost: [Fire] red

Annunciation, Visitation, and Presentation of Jesus: White

Commemoration of Martyrs: [Blood] red

Commemoration of Saints not Martyred: White

All Saints: White

Christ the King: White**

---

* James F. White, *Introduction to Christian Worship*, rev. ed. (Nashville: Abingdon Press, 1990), 85–86. Used by permission.

** Laurence Hull Stookey, *Calendar: Christ's Time for the Church* (Nashville: Abingdon Press, 1996), 156–57. Used by permission.

LECTIONARY LISTINGS 2011*
THE REVISED COMMON LECTIONARY

Date	First Lesson	Psalm	Second Lesson	Gospel Lesson
01/02/11	Isaiah 60:1-6	Psalm 72:1-7, 10-14	Ephesians 3:1-12	Matthew 2:1-12
01/09/11	Isaiah 42:1-9	Psalm 29	Acts 10:34-43	Matthew 3:13-17
01/16/11	Isaiah 49:1-7	Psalm 40:1-11	1 Corinthians 1:1-9	John 1:29-42
01/23/11	Isaiah 9:1-4	Psalm 27:1, 4-9	1 Corinthians 1:10-18	Matthew 4:12-23
01/30/11	Micah 6:1-8	Psalm 15	1 Corinthians 1:18-31	Matthew 5:1-12
02/06/11	Isaiah 58:1-9a (9b-12)	Psalm 112:1-9 (10)	1 Corinthians 2:1-12 (13-16)	Matthew 5:13-20
02/13/11	Deuteronomy 30:15-20	Psalm 119:1-8	1 Corinthians 3:1-9	Matthew 5:21-37
02/20/11	Leviticus 19:1-2, 9-18	Psalm 119:33-40	1 Corinthians 3:10-11, 16-23	Matthew 5:38-48
02/27/11	Isaiah 49:8-16a	Psalm 131	1 Corinthians 4:1-5	Matthew 6:24-34
03/06/11	Exodus 24:12-18	Psalm 99	2 Peter 1:16-21	Matthew 17:1-9
03/09/11	Joel 2:1-2, 12-17	Psalm 51:1-17	2 Corinthians 5:20b–6:10	Matthew 6:1-6, 16-21
03/13/11	Genesis 2:15-17; 3:1-7	Psalm 32	Romans 5:12-19	Matthew 4:1-11
03/20/11	Genesis 12:1-4a	Psalm 121	Romans 4:1-5, 13-17	John 3:1-17
03/27/11	Exodus 17:1-7	Psalm 95	Romans 5:1-11	John 4:5-42
04/03/11	1 Samuel 16:1-13	Psalm 23	Ephesians 5:8-14	John 9:1-41
04/10/11	Ezekiel 37:1-14	Psalm 130	Romans 8:6-11	John 11:1-45
04/17/11	Palms: Matthew 21:1-11	Psalm 118:1-2, 19-29	none	none
	Passion: Isaiah 50:4-9a	Psalm 31:9-16	Philippians 2:5-11	Matthew 26:14–27:66
04/21/11	Exodus 12:1-4 (5-10), 11-14	Psalm 116:1-2, 12-19	1 Corinthians 11:23-26	John 13:1-17, 31b-35
04/22/11	Isaiah 52:13–53:12	Psalm 22	Hebrews 10:16-25	John 18:1–19:42
04/24/11	Acts 10:34-43	Psalm 118:1-2, 14-24	Colossians 3:1-4	John 20:1-18
05/01/11	Acts 2:14a, 22-32	Psalm 16	1 Peter 1:3-9	John 20:19-31
05/08/11	Acts 2:14a, 36-41	Psalm 116:1-4, 12-19	1 Peter 1:17-23	Luke 24:13-35
05/15/11	Acts 2:42-47	Psalm 23	1 Peter 2:19-25	John 10:1-10

* This list represents one possible selection of lessons and psalms from the lectionary for Year A (January 1–November 20) and Year B (November 27–December 31). For a complete listing, see *The Revised Common Lectionary*.

Date	First Lesson	Psalm	Second Lesson	Gospel Lesson
05/22/11	Acts 7:55-60	Psalm 31:1-5, 15-16	1 Peter 2:2-10	John 14:1-14
05/29/11	Acts 17:22-31	Psalm 66:8-20	1 Peter 3:13-22	John 14:15-21
06/05/11	Acts 1:1-11	Psalm 47	Ephesians 1:15-23	Luke 24:44-53
06/12/11	Acts 2:1-21	Psalm 104:24-34, 35b	1 Corinthians 12:3b-13	John 7:37-39
06/19/11	Genesis 1:1–2:4a	Psalm 8	2 Corinthians 13:11-13	Matthew 28:16-20
06/26/11	Genesis 22:1-14	Psalm 13	Romans 6:12-23	Matthew 10:40-42
07/03/11	Genesis 24:34-38, 42-49, 58-67	Psalm 45:10-17	Romans 7:15-25a	Matthew 11:16-19, 25-30
07/10/11	Genesis 25:19-34	Psalm 119:105-112	Romans 8:1-11	Matthew 13:1-9, 18-23
07/17/11	Genesis 28:10-19a	Psalm 139:1-12, 23-24	Romans 8:12-25	Matthew 13:24-30, 36-43
07/24/11	Genesis 29:15-28	Psalm 105:1-11, 45b	Romans 8:26-39	Matthew 13:31-33, 44-52
07/31/11	Genesis 32:22-31	Psalm 17:1-7, 15	Romans 9:1-5	Matthew 14:13-21
08/07/11	Genesis 37:1-4, 12-28	Psalm 105:1-6, 16-22, 45b	Romans 10:5-15	Matthew 14:22-33
08/14/11	Genesis 45:1-15	Psalm 133	Romans 11:1-2a, 29-32	Matthew 15:(10-20), 21-28
08/21/11	Exodus 1:8–2:10	Psalm 124	Romans 12:1-8	Matthew 16:13-20
08/28/11	Exodus 3:1-15	Psalm 105:1-6, 23-26, 45c	Romans 12:9-21	Matthew 16:21-28
09/04/11	Exodus 12:1-14	Psalm 149	Romans 13:8-14	Matthew 18:15-20
09/11/11	Exodus 14:19-31	Exodus 15:1b-11, 20-21	Romans 14:1-12	Matthew 18:21-35
09/18/11	Exodus 16:2-15	Psalm 105:1-6, 37-45	Philippians 1:21-30	Matthew 20:1-16
09/25/11	Exodus 17:1-7	Psalm 78:1-4, 12-16	Philippians 2:1-13	Matthew 21:23-32
10/02/11	Exodus 20:1-4, 7-9, 12-20	Psalm 19	Philippians 3:4b-14	Matthew 21:33-46
10/09/11	Exodus 32:1-14	Psalm 106:1-6, 19-23	Philippians 4:1-9	Matthew 22:1-14
10/16/11	Exodus 33:12-23	Psalm 99	1 Thessalonians 1:1-10	Matthew 22:15-22
10/23/11	Deuteronomy 34:1-12	Psalm 90:1-6, 13-17	1 Thessalonians 2:1-8	Matthew 22:34-46

* This list represents one possible selection of lessons and psalms from the lectionary for Year A (January 1–November 20) and Year B (November 27–December 31). For a complete listing, see *The Revised Common Lectionary*.

Date	First Lesson	Psalm	Second Lesson	Gospel Lesson
10/30/11	Joshua 3:7-17	Psalm 107:1-7, 33-37	1 Thessalonians 2:9-13	Matthew 23:1-12
11/06/11	Revelation 7:9-17	Psalm 34:1-10, 22	1 John 3:1-3	Matthew 5:1-12
11/13/11	Judges 4:1-7	Psalm 123	1 Thessalonians 5:1-11	Matthew 25:14-30
11/20/11	Ezekiel 34:11-16, 20-24	Psalm 100	Ephesians 1:15-23	Matthew 25:31-46
11/24/11	Deuteronomy 8:7-18	Psalm 65	2 Corinthians 9:6-15	Luke 17:11-19
11/27/11	Isaiah 64:1-9	Psalm 80:1-7, 17-19	1 Corinthians 1:3-9	Mark 13:24-37
12/04/11	Isaiah 40:1-11	Psalm 85:1-2, 8-13	2 Peter 3:8-15a	Mark 1:1-8
12/11/11	Isaiah 61:1-4, 8-11	Psalm 126	1 Thessalonians 5:16-24	John 1:6-8, 19-28
12/18/11	2 Samuel 7:1-11, 16	Psalm 89:1-4, 19-26	Romans 16:25-27	Luke 1:26-38
12/25/11	Isaiah 52:7-10	Psalm 98	Hebrews 1:1-4 (5-12)	John 1:1-14

* This list represents one possible selection of lessons and psalms from the lectionary for Year A (January 1–November 20) and Year B (November 27–December 31). For a complete listing, see *The Revised Common Lectionary*.

II. SERMONS AND WORSHIP AIDS

JANUARY 2, 2011

❧❧❧❧

Epiphany

Readings: Isaiah 60:1-6; Psalm 72:1-7, 10-14; Ephesians 3:1-12; Matthew 2:1-12

Rise and Shine
Isaiah 60:1-6

An atheist was upset with me. It started when I wrote a response to an article in the local paper about the growing number of people with no religious affiliation who consider themselves spiritual. I gently suggested that spirituality without God is empty, and that what many people who claim to be spiritual without going to church really want is to be spiritual without taking any responsibility. I implied that some use their lack of faith in the church as an excuse to not give money to the needy or work for social justice. I argued that true spirituality leads people to feed the hungry, listen to the lonely, and join with others who are doing the same.

What I wrote made perfect sense to me, but a self-described "hard-core atheist" in Colorado sent an e-mail informing me that I am "painfully ignorant." He helpfully pointed out that those who attend church can be just as greedy, cheap, and unfeeling as those who don't. This is not news to a Baptist preacher.

One of the disadvantages of e-mailing preachers is that it's easier for us to send a sermon than a thoughtful response. So I attached a sermon on why it makes sense to believe in God, and the debate was on.

My atheist friend responded with a lengthy rebuttal that led to an exchange of opinions on heaven, hell, prayer, faith-healing, easy answers, difficult questions, astronomy, awe, skepticism, curiosity, the death penalty, black holes, quantum gravity, warped space-time, fifteen billion years of evolution, Carl Sagan, Jerry Falwell, which one of us had the worse experience in Sunday school, subservient wives, and wives who aren't subservient at all.

3

As you would guess, neither of us has changed the other's mind. My atheist pen pal wanted verifiable proof—"no evidence, no belief" is how he put it. Ultimately, I had to admit that what I hold is impossible to prove. I believe that once in a while I see a glimmer of light. It's not much to go on as tangible proof.

Isaiah cannot prove he has seen a flash of light in the middle of a stormy night. The prophet lives in dark times. Palestine is forever being overrun. Wars between the countries to the east and west bring those foreign armies to Israel. When battles take place Hebrew parents watch their children be carried away. The days are even darker because the people's hearts are far from God. No one pays attention to anyone who thinks God matters. An enemy army has wiped out Jerusalem, the temple, and the economy of once-proud Judah. The tiny remnant of Israel, those who were not killed or carried off to Babylon, is again threatened with destruction.

In the middle of the night, the prophet sees a light. "Rise and shine," Isaiah shouts. "Get out of bed. God is here." Jerusalem is in ashes, ruin, and despair, but just when it looks as if the sun will never rise again, dawn is about to break.

"Your sons will return from far away, and your daughters will be carried in their mothers' arms again," Isaiah continues. "The sight of the exiles coming home will make your face break out in a grin, your heart pound, and your eyes light up. The whole world will come riding camels and bringing gifts. People will march in from the South and sail in from the West. They will bring gold and frankincense, and they will bow down and worship God's light" (author's paraphrase). Isaiah saw that one day the darkness would be overcome by the coming of the light.

The world is still dark with ignorance, hatred, and death. We know that during this new year children will starve, terrorists will strike, and armies will retaliate against the innocent. Hard workers will lose their jobs, sick people will die, and drunk drivers will commit murder. Preschoolers will be abused, women will be molested, and older adults will be mistreated. Wealthy people will find it hard to give, lonely people won't find the friends they need, and lost people won't find their way home.

If it's not dark for you this minute, be grateful even as you recognize it will be dark again. The day always turns into night. The dark shadows of the past never go completely away. Not all your dreams will come true. You won't always love your job. Your family will have problems you haven't imagined. Someone will leave too soon and you'll be praying for a sunny day.

When life seems hard we need to remember that no matter how dark it gets, there's a flickering light that tickles the retina just enough to give us hope. The light shines on, into, and through us. Some of the places we go are shadowy. Some of the people we know haven't seen any light in a long time. We are the lights in our homes, neighborhoods, schools, workplaces, and church. God's light illumines everything we do—the way we treat our employees, serve our employers, and speak to one another. We are candles that keep others from cursing the darkness, candles on birthday cakes that celebrate life, flashlights that make emergencies less terrifying, searchlights looking for those who've lost their way, lighthouses leading sinking ships to shore, and traffic lights pointing out when to go and when to stop.

Do you remember singing, "This little light of mine, I'm gonna let it shine"? Who can forget "hide it under a bushel, no!" Like most children's church songs with motions, it was fun to sing. Our greatest joy comes in shining our little light. Light is the joy of a doctor giving sight to the blind, a lawyer protecting someone who is innocent, and a follower of Christ shining light where there was only darkness. Joy comes in being what we are meant to be, doing what we are meant to do, and shining as we are meant to shine.

This child of light whose birthday we just celebrated—who Isaiah dreamed was coming, who the magi traveled so far to see—took on the darkness so we could see the light. It's hard to explain and we can't prove it, but if we look carefully we may see a flicker of hope even in the darkest night. (Brett Younger)

Lectionary Commentary
Matthew 2:1-12

The truly wise leave their minds open to possibilities further out and deeper within. They imagine more than they can explain. In most of the Gospel stories, Jesus goes looking for people, intrudes into their lives, moves into their villages and homes, but in Matthew's story of the magi, they come looking for Jesus. No one travels farther to see him. They come looking for wisdom.

Ephesians 3:1-12

When people look for a new church to join, they often count people their own age, look over the budget, or time the sermons. The measure of a church in this passage is how "through the church the wisdom of God in its rich variety might now be made known to the rulers and authorities in the heavenly places" (Ephesians 3:10). The story of Jesus carries not only the obligation to live and share the gospel but also the "boldness and confidence" (v. 12) to carry out that obligation. (Brett Younger)

Worship Aids

Call to Worship

Welcome to the celebration of Epiphany, the day we remember that the light has come. We may not see Jesus sitting on his mother's lap, as did the magi, but we find Christ in the word of forgiveness and the hope of the table. There we worship.

Invocation

God, our light and salvation, teach us to walk as children of the light, to give our praise and prayers. Even as the magi worshiped the Christ Child, may we give ourselves in celebration, knowing that all we are and have belongs to you, through Jesus. Amen.

Pastoral Prayer

God, we pray for those who live in the darkness of fear, bigotry, and hatred, for those who are hungry and sick, for all who are hurting and lonely. We pray that your goodness will shine even in the darkest corners, through Jesus Christ, the light of the world. Amen. (Brett Younger)

Claimed and Marked

First in a Series of Two on Baptism

1 Peter 2:9-10

The melancholy strains of "Auld Lang Syne" fade away. Our football orgy isn't quite over, but even the most ardent fans are weary. The holiday season closes down and life returns to normal. The one thing we can say for certain is that the New Year is now. It is a time of new beginnings.

How do we start a new year? There are so many places we can legitimately begin. The temptation to draft a list of resolutions is almost overwhelming. We take secret vows to try harder and do better at keeping our resolutions. Good intentions aren't a bad thing; nor are well-intended vows at self-reform. Yet the struggles remain. Our best efforts are just not good enough.

At the point of our weakness, the Christian faith invites us to reconnect with God. We are embraced by the grace of God, God's radically free and wholly unmerited redeeming love. At the crossroads of grace and beginnings, the beginning of this year of our Lord 2011 once again beckons us to the sacrament of baptism. It is literally a grace-filled beginning.

Baptism is that sacred moment in which we acknowledge God's embrace of love. It is God's great divine claim of love for all people. You are mine, says the Lord; come what may—good or bad—you are mine. I claim and love you! The Heidelberg Catechism (1563) states: "What is your only comfort, in life and in death? That I belong—body and soul, in life and in death—not to myself but to my faithful Savior, Jesus Christ."

The actor in baptism is God! Baptism does not depend on the person (young or old), on the parents, or on the pastor, and depends even less on the church. It is God who claims and says this one is mine from creation.

Acts 18:8 records that the whole house was baptized. All those in it, children and adults. Baptism does not depend on your response, your knowledge, or your faithfulness. It is God's act of love on your behalf— an outward and visible sign of the inward and spiritual grace of God. Our earliest records of the Christian church demonstrate conclusively that children were brought for baptism; to be marked, that is, claimed, as Christian disciples. A baby has done nothing to earn God's love, and that is precisely the point. Baptism declares God's great "I love you!" regardless of who you are. It is that sacred moment in the life of the community of faith where grace is most visibly demonstrated. Here is radically good news. God claims us with a great love long before we can even remotely begin to earn such love.

Scholars assert that 1 Peter is possibly, in part, a baptismal address. This marvelous little and often-forgotten book, tucked in the back of the New Testament, was written for grace-filled beginnings! Where the culture represents starting the new year with grim determination to do better, the Christian faith asserts that better takes place only when we understand that we are claimed in God's grace.

The church would do well to let the power of the text speak. We are "chosen" (1 Peter 2:9). We are "God's own" (v. 9). We do not proclaim our own righteousness, nor are we smart enough to accept Jesus. We proclaim God's "mighty acts" (v. 9). Once we didn't even matter; now we do because we are God's! Once mercy was a desperate longing and a distant hope; now in Christ we "have received mercy" (v. 10). The sacred act of holy baptism calls us to embrace the very depth of meaning in this text. It demands that our new beginnings rest not in ourselves but in God. We are the claimed!

Consider well the truth of a baby. A baby has not and cannot earn our affection or love. But just ask any new parents if they love their child. The response will be overwhelming. One new father exclaimed to me that his whole life was changed before he even met his daughter. So too God claims, and baptism is the outward and visible sign of that claiming.

We are also the marked. Our baptismal liturgy speaks of someone being baptized and "marked as a Christian disciple." The order is significant: first the claiming, and then the marking. We are claimed by God and marked as Christian disciples.

Out in west Texas, marking is better known as branding, and a brand is an important thing. There are the "Double Springs Ranch" and the "Lazy J" brands, just to name two. The big ranches brand their herds so that everyone knows to whom the cattle belong. Those *marks* are a form of claiming and identification.

Human beings have brands as well; we know what marking is all about. To be sure, they are not usually burned into the skin, but they are there nonetheless. Youth gangs often have a special sign or kind of clothing. Sports fans have their colors and logos. Businesspeople speak in studied terms of the "branding of a product." We are marked by the groups we associate with and by our lifestyle choices. Go to any high school, and the students can tell you about the various groups of nerds, jocks, kickers, preppies, and the like. Adults do the same. There are unwritten dress codes that abound in our work and social settings. All of this branding is an effort to note and proclaim who and whose we are. The mark calls us into a different future, a future as a follower of Christ.

The passage from 1 Peter fairly screams of a marking (or branding). Chosen race, royal priesthood, dedicated nation, God's people—the marking or branding is explicit. Christians are different! They are God's. How do you begin the New Year? Are you claimed by God? Yes! Are you marked by God? Through baptism the answer is again an emphatic yes!

Let us remember two clear points of focus about baptism: In baptism we are claimed. In baptism we are marked. (Mike Lowry)

Worship Aids

Responsive Call to Worship (Revelation 22:17, 20-21)
The Spirit and the bride say, "Come."
And let everyone who hears say, "Come."
And let everyone who is thirsty come.
Let anyone who wishes take the water of life as a gift.
The one who testifies to these things says, "Surely I am coming soon."
Amen. Come, Lord Jesus!
The grace of the Lord Jesus be with all the saints.
Amen.

Pastoral Prayer
Great and gracious God, we come to you this morning in such thanks-giving and joy for this, your new year. The glory and honor are yours, O Lord.

We take joy in the morning of possibilities as a gift from your hand. We receive the opportunities of new beginnings as a boon of your favor. We embrace the dawn of a new life in the blessing of life with you.

Guide us, Lord, we pray, to open our hearts to your love, our minds to your wisdom, and our lives to your service. Help us to see in the least, last, and lost among us your presence.

Challenge us, Lord, in this new year, to rise to a higher level of faith-fulness. Prod us to reach out with a wider expression of your love. Drive us to a closer walk with you in all we do and say. We pray this day in the name of the great triune God—Father, Son, and Holy Spirit. Amen!

Benediction
Go now with the God of grace and love. Go now with the God of power and might. Go now with the God of wisdom and courage. Go now into this new year with the sure and certain knowledge that God goes with us this day and on all days; Father, Son, and Holy Spirit. Amen. (Mike Lowry)

JANUARY 9, 2011

Baptism of the Lord

Readings: Isaiah 42:1-9; Psalm 29; Acts 10:34-43; Matthew 3:13-17

The First Step
Matthew 3:13-17

We don't think about it much, but for most of us, one thing that brings us to church on Sunday is the fact that we were baptized. Some of us were baptized without being given any choice in the matter. Cries at the baptismal font are not interpreted theologically. Some of us were baptized because we turned ten years old and decided that we were sick and tired of not getting to drink the grape juice. Some of us went to a worship service where the minister made us cry and invited us to be baptized. Some of us have never been baptized because we've never seen any reason why we should be. Some of us haven't been baptized, but we've had to work hard to avoid seriously considering it.

It's good that we learn the meaning of our baptisms after the fact. None of us fully knew what we were doing on the day we were baptized. Years later, as we make our way slowly into faith, the purpose begins to unfold. We discover what our baptisms mean after the event rather than before. That's how it was for Jesus too, at least in Matthew's Gospel.

The story skips from Jesus as an infant to Jesus as a thirty-year-old, and we don't have a clue as to what happened in between. One day Jesus puts down his hammer, takes off his tool belt, hangs a "Closed" sign on the door of the carpenter's shop, and asks, "What does God want of me?" Jesus heads south and finds his cousin John, standing in the muddy Jordan in his camel-hair baptismal robe, smelling of locusts and honey. Jesus gets in line and waits his turn. He wades out into the water, right next to real live sinners like you and me.

While three Gospels tell the story of Jesus' baptism, only Matthew records the curious conversation prior to the baptism. Jesus is eager to be baptized, but John hesitates. They stand hip-deep in the river and engage in a fervent theological debate concerning who should baptize whom. The first time Jesus speaks in Matthew's Gospel, it is to say that he needs to be baptized, because baptism will help him learn who he's meant to be. Jesus leans back into the water because he believes that God is calling him to a different kind of life.

When Jesus stands up, the waters of the Jordan dripping down his face, he sees the Spirit descending like a dove to rest upon his soggy head. The Spirit comes, not as an all-consuming fire of judgment, but with the flutter of hopeful wings. A voice says: "You are my child. I love you. I'm delighted with you."

Then Jesus goes into the desert for forty days to think about what it means to be God's child. Jesus spends all the days and years that follow that afternoon in the Jordan discovering the meaning of his baptism. Jesus gives everything—his dreams and deeds, his labors and his life itself. Jesus gives himself to God's people, takes his place with hurting people. Baptism was Jesus' commissioning to ministry.

During the week before his death, the leaders of the temple challenge Jesus: "By what authority are you doing these things?" (Matthew 21:23). Jesus answers with a reference to his baptism: "Was the baptism of John from heaven or not? I was baptized. That's why I do the things I do." In the waters of baptism, Jesus heard the Spirit calling him to speak the truth and live with grace.

So Jesus doesn't die of old age. He dies because he takes his baptism seriously. When Jesus cries on the cross, "It is finished," it is his baptism that is complete.

Baptisms, like most beginnings, find meaning long after the event. Beginning is often easy, while finishing is often hard. The significance of any decision takes a while to emerge. Moments of initiation are meaningless until we are true to the promise of that beginning. We're handed a map, but then we have to take the trip. It takes our whole lives to finish the journey we begin when we're baptized.

So what does it mean to us to live out our baptisms? If we are true to our baptisms, we cannot make ourselves comfortable, cannot do only what will be appreciated, and cannot be satisfied with the way things are. Our baptisms demand that we struggle with what's right and what's wrong, what's important and what's not.

The children of God tell the truth in a world that lies, give in a world that takes, love in a world that lusts, make peace in a world that fights, serve in a world that wants to be served, pray in a world that waits to be entertained, and take chances in a world that worships safety. The baptized are citizens of an eccentric community where financial success is not the goal, security is not the highest good, and sacrifice is a daily event.

Baptism is our ordination to ministry, our vow to live with more concern for the hurting than for our own comfort, and our promise to take issue with ideas with which everyone else agrees. Baptism is the commitment to share our time with the poor and listen to the lonely.

What did it mean when you were baptized? The meaning of your baptism is seen in what you think, feel, and do this day. Have you done anything today that you wouldn't have done if you had not been baptized? We are forever answering the question "Why was I baptized?" (Brett Younger)

Lectionary Commentary
Isaiah 42:1-9

Ministers who love to preach on justice may be delighted on the first reading of this text. Isaiah's inspiring poetry calls for justice for the nations, opening the eyes of the blind, and bringing out prisoners from the dungeons. A second reading, however, may lessen the sense of delight. The servant brings justice by enduring suffering. That makes it harder to hear.

Acts 10:34-43

Peter visits in the home of a Roman centurion, an officer of the occupying army. Cornelius wants to join the church. The law-abiding Jewish Peter may have wanted to send the question to a committee, but he's caught the absolute joy of what God is doing and what the church is supposed to be. Peter almost explodes with the good news: "The gospel is for everybody. God plays no favorites." (Brett Younger)

Worship Aids

Call to Worship
God calls each one of us by name because we are God's children. God invites us to the hard, joyful way of baptism. In worship we find the foundation for our lives in Christ and learn the meaning of our baptisms.

Invocation

God, we gather today in the presence of baptismal waters. We come to remember our baptisms and move toward the completion of what you are doing in our lives. On this day, whether for the first time or the thousandth time, may we hear Christ calling us to follow. Amen.

Pastoral Prayer

God of all creation, when your spirit descended on Jesus at his baptism, you called him your beloved child. We worship as your beloved children. In giving ourselves in worship, may we learn more of what it means to love Christ. Amen. (Brett Younger)

Filled with the Spirit

Second in a Series of Two on Baptism

Acts 19:1-7; Mark 1:8

There are two days in my life that stand out clearly with the grace and joy of God's love. On those days, my two children were baptized. There before the altar of God, I remembered that every child has two fathers; I am blessed to be their earthly one. In baptism we remembered that they were claimed by God as God's chosen and beloved. In baptism we acknowledged that they were marked as Christian disciples. Our children's baptisms were sacred moments in their lives and in the life of the community of the faithful.

There are many special sacramental moments, sacred means of grace, if you will, in which we experience the outward and visible sign of God's love and experience the inward and spiritual grace of God's presence. They are means of grace wherein we come to know and live with Christ through the Holy Spirit. Baptism is always first and foremost about what God does in us in order to work through us. It is not an inoculation against sin and all things bad. Baptism is instead an outward and visible sign of the indwelling of the Holy Spirit.

Today I invite the congregation to examine a little-used text from the book of the Acts of the Apostles in order to understand the very nature of baptism. There is a connection that we often ignore between baptism and the indwelling of the Holy Spirit. Let's consider the impact of the text.

The apostle Paul encounters some disciples. We do not know what takes place between the lines of verses 1 and 2 of the nineteenth chapter of Acts. Something sparks Paul to inquire if they received the Holy Spirit when they became believers. While we should engage due caution in speculating, it is clear Paul senses something is missing. They report receiving John's baptism of repentance. They had an awareness of sin and the need to be spiritually cleansed, forgiven, by God. Repentance is important. Paul in no way criticizes the need for repentance. He simply indicates that the experience of repentance alone is not the full experience of the gospel. The baptism of John is a pre-Christian act of human repentance. They had not connected that action to new life in Christ.

We know the experience of pre-Christian baptism (even by some who are Christian). How often has the Christian life been experienced as a dull duty of living righteously? We can have just enough faith to be miserable and not enough grace to experience the gospel (good news). All too many people know just enough Christianity to be repulsed by a sense of grim judgmentalism. Garrison Keillor, of *Prairie Home Companion* fame, pokes gentle fun at such a restrictive version of the Christian faith in speaking about a church he names "Our Lady of Perpetual Responsibility."

Baptism becomes a full completion of repentance and new life as it submits to the lordship of Christ. Acts 19:5 is clear about the explicitly Christocentric connection of new life in the Spirit: "On hearing this, they were baptized in the name of the Lord Jesus." The full nature of the Holy Trinity is engaged in baptism.

It is important to note that this is not a second baptism. Nor is this a claim that baptism does not count unless it is accompanied by a certain ecstatic set of emotions. Emotions do not govern the validity of baptism. Nowhere does the text lead to the conclusion of a baptism differing from the orthodox understanding of "one" baptism (Ephesians 4:5: "one Lord, one faith, one baptism").

The passage continues with three actions taking place. The now baptized disciples of Jesus receive the Holy Spirit, speak in tongues, and prophesy. Distance from the New Testament text has accumulated meaning on those actions like barnacles on a ship. We need not run down every rabbit trail; however, the essence is clear. They experience the presence and power of God as Father, Son, and Holy Spirit coursing through them. They experience ecstatic praise (speaking in tongues is a praise language), and they speak for God (the truest meaning of the word *prophesy*; prophecy is not about predicting the future!).

Taken in the full sense of the passage, baptism ushers the believer into the Spirit's presence. Baptism enables and invites us to live with an active sense of the Holy Spirit in our lives. We don't have to rely solely upon ourselves or our own power. God, as Holy Spirit, is with us moment by moment, day by day. The tragedy of so much Christian living is that we live as functional atheists. Remembering our baptism is a call to re-engage with the Spirit that has been present all along! At baptism the Holy Spirit is poured in us through the profession of Christ. God in Christ really is with us in the Holy Spirit. Thus the prayer "Come, Spirit, come" is in some sense a prayer for what is already the case. In praying we reawaken our awareness to the God who is acting in us and through us.

Baptism is about so much more than ogling over cute babies and visibly moved adults. It is about a proclamation of the Spirit's presence. In addition, the baptism of the Spirit is given not for private enjoyment but for public praise. It is no mistake that the church is a community of the Spirit (Acts 2; 2 Corinthians 13:13; Philippians 2:1). In baptism we are filled with the Spirit as individuals and as a community! (Mike Lowry)

Worship Aids

Call to Worship (Psalm 98:1, 4)

O sing to the LORD a new song,
for he has done marvelous things.
Make a joyful noise to the LORD, all the earth;
break forth into joyous song and sing praises.

Prayer of Confession

Gracious Lord, we come to you in this new year mindful of our failures and shortcomings. The possibility of new life with you stretches before us, and we are still nursing old grudges and painful hurts. Lead us to lay aside our pride and forgive our slowness to forgive others. As we enter this new year, we confess our failure to fully remember the poor and needy among us. Let us again see you in them. We acknowledge our idolatrous tendency to worship money and things. We have embraced the human spirit over the Holy Spirit. Forgive us such false obsessions and free us for newness of life in, with, and through your spirit. Receive our confession and open us to this new year, this year of the Lord 2011; in your grace and by your love we pray. Amen.

Words of Assurance

"If we confess our sins, he who is faithful and just will forgive us our sins and cleanse us from all unrighteousness" (1 John 1:9). Receive now the grace of God that passes all our understanding. In the name of God, you are forgiven.

All: In the name of God, you are forgiven. Amen and amen! (Mike Lowry)

JANUARY 16, 2011

Second Sunday after the Epiphany

Readings: Isaiah 49:1-7; Psalm 40:1-11; 1 Corinthians 1:1-9; John 1:29-42

Come and See
John 1:29-42

How would your life be different if you were not a Christian? For some of us who have lived surrounded by Christian people, it's hard to imagine, but what if you had no interest in God? How would your life be less or more or just the same?

What would you miss about church? I would never sing out loud in public were it not for church on Sunday. Which of your friends would not be your friends? If you had never met the people you have met in Sunday school, how great a loss would that be? How would your family change? How would you spend your time differently? Would you be home reading the *New York Times* right now? What do you do because you are a Christian that makes you happy? Which religious activities could you do without? What would be easier if you weren't a Christian? Do you feel good about the time you spend helping strangers? Do you wish you still had all the money you've given away? Have there been experiences you would hate to have missed—hope-filled books you are glad you read, experiences of God's grace in worship, times you've cared for hurting people? If you were not a Christian, would your life be less interesting?

Every once in a while the disciples thought about how different their lives would have been if they had never met Jesus. It started so quietly. John the Baptist is standing with two of his students when Jesus walks by. John says, "That's the one. You know how cocky I can be, but I'm not worthy to tie his sandals."

The two disciples are understandably curious. They start following Jesus. He turns and asks, "What are you looking for?" They answer nervously,

"We thought we would see where you're staying." In other words, "We don't have anything better to do, so we're wondering what you're doing." Jesus offers the invitation that will change their lives: "Come and see."

They stay with Jesus all day because he's interesting. They have no idea what they are getting themselves into. They don't know that they will end up leaving behind their nets, boats, homes, friends, work, and retirements. They will end up changing their ideas about almost everything.

Andrew goes to get his brother. "You have to come and see this guy," he says. Simon is dragged along, going more so that his brother will leave him alone than out of any great faith. When Jesus meets Simon, he says, "Your name is going to be Rock." The often-confused Simon is anything but a rock, but everything is starting to change. Most of the time, we move toward God in small steps taken as much out of curiosity as out of faith.

So what are we looking for? What are we looking for in worship today? Why did we come to church? Some of us are here because our parents didn't give us a choice. For some of us, our mother's voice telling us to go to church somehow lodged in our minds, and we can't get rid of it. Some of us are here because it's easier to come than to argue with our spouse about it.

Most of us didn't come with great expectations. The religious reasons we have for being here are mixed at best. We're interested in thinking about how we could live better lives, but only up to a point. If we're in worship today for no good reason, that's okay. Lots of people find their way by accident.

Jesus says, "Come and see." The disciples stumble along, following without knowing where they are going, discovering well after the fact that they have wandered onto a path that leads to grace. "Come and see," Jesus says, and in John's Gospel the disciples soon taste water turned into wine, watch in horror as Jesus clears the temple, and listen with amazement to Jesus' words to Nicodemus, that the spirit of God blows wherever it wills. They stumble onto a way of life they have never imagined.

What are we looking for? Deep in our souls, we are looking for something to believe in and hold on to, something important enough to live for, and something big enough to claim our passions. We are looking for challenge and purpose. We are looking for God.

What begins with curiosity becomes a step toward grace. The emptiness we feel from time to time is God calling us to the paths that lead to meaning. God lets us know that we can look beyond our computers and coffee cups into the enchanted possibilities of grace. God is the one who makes us long for something that lasts. God draws us toward life even when we don't recognize what's happening.

"Come and see" is how the disciples' story begins. It's a wonderful line and a great way to start a story. "Come and see" is the invitation to explore, discover, and travel without knowing exactly where we are going, but to know that if we catch a glimpse of God, we will also catch a glimpse of who we can be. Come and see. Come and look for places where we've never been. Come and see what it means to hope, believe, and follow.

We are in church to open ourselves to God, who will lead us to new places. The people who follow Jesus end up doing the things Jesus did. They care for the hurting, listen to the lonely, feed the hungry, pray for the brokenhearted, bandage those who are wounded, do more than is expected. They look for God and find extraordinary lives.

The spirit of adventure is what calls us to worship. We come to seek the meaning of life, join with people on the journey, and ask God to help us see where grace invites us. We are here to look at the gifts we've been given and the needs of the world. We come to this place to discover the possibilities.

If we worship God, if we share our lives with other people looking for God, we will see beyond what we have assumed. If we look for God, we will find that God is looking for us, offering life. (Brett Younger)

Lectionary Commentary
Isaiah 49:1-7

The God of all creation speaks to the world through a people "deeply despised, abhorred by the nations, the slave of rulers" (Isaiah 49:7). The defeated Israelites are the messengers of God's blessing to the Babylonians who took them into exile. The second of the servant songs reminds us that the church needs to listen to the voices of those who don't seem powerful. God still speaks through the oppressed.

1 Corinthians 1:1-9

The church at Corinth understood that Paul wasn't always happy with them, but then he would catch them off guard by sending a letter that started out sweet. Paul was feeling sentimental when he wrote: "I always thank God for you and for what God's grace means to you and me. Grace becomes the words on our lips and the hope in our hearts. God calls us to share our lives, our ministry, the church." (Brett Younger)

Worship Aids

Call to Worship

God has claimed us and we have to respond. We come to praise our Creator, listen to God's word, and set our hopes on things that matter. In our perplexity, God offers direction. In our weariness, God offers strength. In our boredom, God offers wonder.

Prayer of Confession

Loving God, we confess that we don't expect nearly enough from life, and we are slow to accept great adventures. We call ourselves disciples, but we keep our distance from anything that seems hard. Give us the courage to follow more closely, through Jesus Christ, who shows us the way. Amen.

Words of Assurance

"Ask, and it will be given you; search, and you will find; knock, and the door will be opened for you" (Matthew 7:7). Direction, strength, and wonder—free gifts from the God who claims us, who awaits our response in praise.

Benediction

God is always inviting you to come and see. Open your eyes, open your mind, open your heart, and open your hands. Follow Christ. You may be surprised where God leads. (Brett Younger)

How We Are Defined: Our Personal History

First in a Series of Three on Defining Relationships

Matthew 1:1-17

It has long been recognized that our identity is molded within a social context. In his book *Childhood and Society*, psychoanalyst Erik Erikson suggests that a child, "at every step, derive[s] a vitalizing sense of actuality from the awareness that his individual way of mastering experience (his ego synthesis) is a successful variant of a group identity" (Erik H. Erikson,

Childhood and Society [New York: W. W. Norton & Company, 1963], 235). Who we become is a complex interaction of influence and synthesis.

Defining Jesus is even more complex, a task central to the Gospels. The pivotal point of the Gospels is in a question from Jesus to his disciples: "Who do people say that I am?" (Mark 8:27). The Gospel of Matthew begins defining Jesus through genealogy. Jesus' ancestry is traced to the patriarch Abraham and emphasizes that Jesus is "the son of David, the son of Abraham" (Matthew 1:1b). Jesus is first defined through God's covenant with Abraham and through the kingship of David.

Ancestry is part of how each of us is defined. A common question when people discover my last name, Flanagan, is whether I am related to the founder of Boys Town, Father Edward J. Flanagan. Most of my information about our relationship is anecdotal. My grandfather, also named Edward John Flanagan, and my grandmother Ruby shared stories of being married by Father Flanagan, identified as a cousin to my grandfather. My great-grandparents emigrated from the same area of Ireland. Therefore, I proudly claim a distant relationship to the founder of Boys Town.

I am also proud of my heritage on my mother's side of the family. My great-great-grandfather, Abner T. Griffith, was among the first settlers of the town of Cozad, Nebraska. He homesteaded the land on which I was raised, which my family continues to farm today. A carpenter by trade, he built the first schoolhouse in Cozad and was among the town's first teachers.

Just as my identity is shaped by my ancestry, Matthew begins to define Jesus through his ancestry. Matthew's genealogy is told only through Joseph and the patriarchs of Joseph's lineage. For Matthew, the foundation of Jesus' identity is the Hebrew covenant of Abraham.

Maintaining the purity of the covenant is important throughout Hebrew literature. When it comes time to find a wife for Isaac, Abraham sends his servant to his home country, saying, "You will not get a wife for my son from the daughters of the Canaanites, among whom I live, but will go to my country and to my kindred and get a wife for my son Isaac" (Genesis 24:3-4). Isaac's wife, Rebekah, is the daughter of Abraham's nephew Bethuel. Rebekah is similarly adamant that her son not marry a Canaanite. Jacob marries his cousins, Leah and Rachel, who are the daughters of his uncle, Rebekah's brother Laban.

The covenant community remains an issue in the early Christian church. Peter and Paul disagree about whether one must be circumcised to be a Christian. Covenant relationship is a defining factor throughout scripture.

While cultural heritage is a large part of who we are, the cultural purity desired by the Hebrews seems more difficult in today's melting pot. America is becoming more diverse in every way, including ethnically and religiously. Our defining ancestry and historical influence are less linear today than in the time of Jesus. The flattening of the world has introduced other defining factors. One such contemporary feature is generational influence. Research is showing that generational factors may be the most significant factor in identity.

Authors William Strauss and Neil Howe have contributed greatly to our understanding of generational theory. They believe a common collective persona can be defined about every twenty years. Each generation has an identifiable *weltanshauung,* or worldview, which is usually formulated by significant events. The GI generation, for example, born between 1901 and 1924, is defined by their experience of the depression and World War II. The boomers, born between 1943 and 1960, experienced social upheaval and the war in Vietnam. The millennials, or the Y generation, born since 1982, have been heavily influenced by the Internet, cable TV, and 9/11. Generational research suggests that we may have more in common with those of our era than we do even with our families.

Generational theory was not available for the Gospel writers. They define Jesus through his ancestry, as well as through his roles as carpenter, Rabbi, teacher, healer, and certainly as a Jew. When Jesus asks his disciples who others say he is, Peter's response is "John the Baptist; and others, Elijah; and still others, one of the prophets" (Mark 8:28). Jesus then personalizes the question to Peter, "But who do you say that I am?" Peter answers him, "You are the Messiah" (v. 29). Peter's response reflects as much about Peter as it does about Jesus.

If we are asked to describe ourselves, how do we do it? How do others define us? Who and what has shaped our identity? Part of who we are is determined socially, but there is also a part for which we are responsible. Through this complex interaction of social influence and personal synthesis, we Christians strive to discover the will of God for our lives. (Dan L. Flanagan)

Worship Aids

Call to Worship

We are the product of God's covenant with Abraham.
As God promised, Abraham has become the ancestor of many nations.

While products of that covenant, we are also of a different generation. **We are both and more. Who we are is a gift of God.**

Prayer

Creator God, you have made each of us unique. Our DNA is more than biology. We share faith history. We share family history. We have personal history. We are complex and we are yours. In this time together, may we discover more of who we are in the light of your love. Amen.

Benediction

Strengthened by our covenant history, share the blessings of God with everyone you meet. (Dan L. Flanagan)

JANUARY 23, 2011

Third Sunday after the Epiphany

Readings: Isaiah 9:1-4; Psalm 27:1, 4-9; 1 Corinthians 1:10-18; Matthew 4:12-23

Steps in the Right Direction
Matthew 4:12-23

The crucial moments in which we choose directions for our lives aren't usually marked with caution signs, bright red flags, or even the feeling that we are about to make a big decision. Some of the decisions that matter most slip by without our even noticing. Some of the choices that seem small are bigger than the ones that appear big. Because the sacred is present in the ordinary, we can't be sure that any decision is unimportant. Because life is holy, every moment matters. Every day and hour is crucial.

Jesus is walking beside a lake one afternoon when he sees two men in a rowboat waiting for unsuspecting fish to wander into their nets. It's hard to believe what happens next. Jesus offers them a job with no pay, and they accept: "Follow me, and I will make you fish for people" (Matthew 4:19). Why should they follow someone who uses such tortured metaphors?

Had the sales pitch been, "Come and make more money than you could ever make fishing," then it might make sense. But this invitation and response seem unlikely. Four fishermen drop what they are doing and head off to God-knows-where, to lives they can't imagine.

People always try to explain away big-fish stories, and this one is no exception. Some commentators suggest that young men often left their occupations to become students of a rabbi. They say it sounds more unlikely to us than it would have to people in the first century.

We read the story and assume that this isn't the disciples' first encounter with Jesus. Surely they knew Jesus before this. But Matthew doesn't seem to feel any need to explain why they would follow Jesus.

The disciples' instant acceptance of Jesus' peculiar invitation is as dramatic as any moment we will ever encounter. On occasion, we face big decisions about family, jobs, and faith. We stand at a fork in the road and have to choose. We have moments when we feel that we have to act in a particular way for reasons that we cannot completely explain. We feel the need to sacrifice something we would rather keep in order to follow. We have taken a few big risks. But most of the time, it isn't that dramatic. We don't drop everything to start a new life very often. The calling of the disciples is more spectacular than what happens to us most days.

Most of my life is routine. I go to work each morning. I always have a list of things to do. There are phone calls to return, e-mails to respond to, and meetings to attend. There are a dozen administrative details to take care of. The urgency in what I do is usually the urgency of keeping up. Most of it doesn't feel holy. My day is filled with pleasant people. I receive too much credit for what I do. My work is enjoyable, but it's not spectacular.

My life doesn't feel as adventurous as that of the disciples, leaving their nets and following Jesus into the unknown. There are women and men who live each day in danger because of their faith. There are people who do astonishing, heroic works. Maybe someday we will do something spectacular. For now, most of us feel called to less-dramatic discipleship. Most days, we answer God's invitation from within the situation in which we find ourselves.

Maybe Jesus' disciples had days when their lives didn't seem sensational, as they walked up and down Galilee from village to village, through Samaria to Jerusalem and back again. Maybe they had days when they thought things were going too slow. On those days, perhaps their faithfulness was more modest.

We tend to forget the importance of details in the journey of faith. We focus on dramatic conversions, overwhelming encounters with God, and powerful moments of prayer. We search for peak experiences and end up assuming that some people are born with a spiritual talent that we just don't have.

But God is in the details. God calls us every hour of every day. God invites us to be friends, practice kindness, and pray for our daily bread. We live out our faithfulness in worship, work, and study.

The routine, everyday ways in which we follow Jesus, the way we read scripture, welcome strangers, and love the people with whom we live are all crucially important.

The difference between the saints of the church and most of us is not some spiritual talent that we don't possess, but the way the saints' everyday habits, disciplines, and practices have prepared them to live extraordinary lives.

God is at work in a variety of unspectacular ways. God is present in every way that grace is shared, hope is proclaimed, and healing comes. Love spreads word by word. The bucket fills drop by drop. Wrongs are righted one by one.

Our calling is to be faithful, to live God's grace on routine days in ordinary ways. If we pay attention, then we will see that even as unsurprising a life as most of us think we live is extraordinary: taking a child to school; hugging someone you love good-bye; eating lunch with a friend; trying to do a decent day's work; talking to a neighbor; coming to worship. There is no event so commonplace that God is not there. Every moment and every word have possibilities.

Slowly but surely our priorities change. On the day they first followed Jesus, the disciples were brash, impulsive, stubborn, and they smelled of fish. They had to learn day by day how to be the church.

We grow in faith, not only in memorable, never-to-be-forgotten moments, but also in forgettable moments when we decide to pray instead of turning on the radio, to do better with the next hour than we did with the last, and to give something that we would rather keep. We become faithful as we confess a misspent hour, an unnecessary word, or a wasted opportunity. We start to follow again and again.

In every moment, God offers us another opportunity to take a step in the direction of Christ, to begin anew to live with purpose, hope, and love. (Brett Younger)

Lectionary Commentary
Isaiah 9:1-4

When Isaiah wants to speak to our deepest longings, the prophet chooses *light* as the symbol, because he knows how dark the world can be: "You live in darkness, but take hope, for a light is shining. Your despair will become joy. Your oppressors will be driven away." The hurting people in Zebulun and Naphtali, the two northernmost tribes, cut off from Israel by the Assyrians, must have said, "But that doesn't look like the world." Isaiah's response is, "It will one day."

1 Corinthians 1:10-18

Paul's "I give thanks to my God always for you" in 1 Corinthians 1:4 is the setup for "Now I appeal to you" in verse 10. The church has a propensity for division. People tend to fall into discord. Only by "the same mind and the same purpose" (v. 10) that come in the "foolishness" of the cross (v. 18) can the church learn to say, "I belong to Christ." (Brett Younger)

Worship Aids

Call to Worship
God who is with us every step of the journey, may we come as saints who live each day with faith. May we see the holiness of a moment of genuine worship, the singing of our commitment, the partaking of the supper shared in the love of Christ. Amen.

Invocation
God, in every age you have called men, women, and children to be your disciples. We believe you have invited us to join the great company who follow you. Give us a vision of the next step and the strength to fulfill the ministry to which you call us. Amen.

Benediction
The Spirit calls each one of us to take another step in Christ's direction. Remember God's presence and draw strength from understanding that the one who calls you to take the next step will be with you every step of the way. (Brett Younger)

How We Are Defined: Our Choices

Second in a Series of Three on Defining Relationships

Luke 23:1-3

The words of Shakespeare ring true today. In *Julius Caesar* Cassius says to Brutus, "Men at some time are masters of their fates: The fault, dear Brutus, is not in our stars, but in ourselves" (Shakespeare, *Julius Caesar*, act 1, scene 2). We are responsible for who we become.

Researchers Jeremy Burrus and Neal Roese at the University of Illinois report that 75 percent of the respondents to their research project believe in fate, but 85 percent believe that fate and individual initiative are intertwined in determining outcomes. Respondents are more likely to see fate in events of the distant past. For more recent events, however, they believe choice can change the outcome (Karen Lawrence, "Does Fate or Personal Choice Rule Our Lives?" suite101.com, September 17, 2008).

Our choices impact our futures. They shape our character and the way others perceive us. Our choices have a role in defining who we are.

Our earliest social affiliations begin to label us. Those roles become peer-defined in school. Some of us are jocks, others prom queens, others nerds or geeks. Throughout life we tend to associate with people of similar interests, and our identity is shaped by those relationships.

Whom we choose as life partners also defines us. It is interesting how, if we know both partners in a relationship, we tend to think of them as one, even before marriage. Our choice of spouse or significant other influences later choices, such as residence, career, and lifestyle.

A 1995 movie, *Before Sunrise*, features a conversation between two young people who meet while traveling through Europe on a train. Celine is a French college student and Jesse a touring American. The train pulls into Vienna where Jesse is to board a plane to America. Jesse convinces Celine to leave the train with him and spend the next few hours before his plane departs walking the streets of Vienna so they can get to know each other. "If I don't ask you this," says Jesse, "it'll haunt me the rest of my life." He proposes that Celine too might look back upon this time as a missed opportunity. He is suggesting that this decision in Vienna will have a significant impact on their futures.

Scripture contains stories of moral choices with significant consequences, such as the relationship between King David and Bathsheba. David's inappropriate sexual behavior with Bathsheba and his role in the death of her husband, Uriah, help shape his future and result in consequences for his children.

Our choices always carry consequences, reflect who we are, and lay groundwork for who we become. We will see how swimmer Michael Phelps is treated during the 2012 Olympics and beyond following his public use of marijuana. Phelps's story, tragic at some level like King David's, reflects the character required to shape a positive identity.

Americans have witnessed a host of public figures affected by questionable choices. Sexual relations with an intern taint the image of former president Bill Clinton. The allegations of steroid use have significantly affected the images of baseball players Barry Bonds, Roger

Clemens, Mark McGwire, and Alex Rodriguez, and may keep them out of the Baseball Hall of Fame.

Our character is transparent in our actions. Our persona is defined by whether we behave selfishly or in the interests of others. Involvement in the community, service organizations, and church paints a picture of who we are. Our moral compass is reflected by our decisions to serve others or to serve our own self-interests.

Our choice of career also defines us. We are judged by the effort we are willing to expend to achieve in school and as an adult. The public perception of a career's importance is beyond our control, but the passion with which we pursue our careers and perform well certainly defines us.

There are some things over which we have no control, such as our genetic line. However, our choices also impact who we are, affect our self-image, and shape our character and public persona.

Jesus does everything he can to avoid personal labels, and he attempts to radically change his defining culture. The chief priests seek to protect that culture and rid themselves of Jesus. "He stirs up the people by teaching throughout all Judea, from Galilee where he began even to this place" (Luke 23:5). Jesus is in constant conflict with the Pharisees and scribes because he brings a different *weltanshauung* (worldview). He teaches that we are not limited by heritage or by our choices. Our bad decisions are forgiven, and we become new beings by God's grace.

The message of Jesus is countercultural. "You have heard that it was said, 'An eye for an eye and a tooth for a tooth.' But I say to you, do not resist an evildoer. But if anyone strikes you on the right cheek, turn the other also" (Matthew 5:38-39). "You have heard that it was said, 'You shall love your neighbor and hate your enemy.' But I say to you, Love your enemies and pray for those who persecute you" (Matthew 5:43-44). "Follow me, and let the dead bury their own dead" (Matthew 8:22). Jesus offers a radically different life, one not tied to the past but defined by a new life offered through God's grace.

Jesus would not allow himself to be defined by cultural categories. Jesus heals those considered to be defiled such as lepers and a woman with a flow of blood. He raises the dead. He and his disciples break sabbath laws to meet human need. Jesus relates to women and children. He eats with tax collectors, and his own disciples would fail the "smell test" for high character in their culture. Jesus is blind to cultural definitions, and his inclusive ministry levels the playing field.

Pilate understands Jesus only within a cultural framework. "Are you the king of the Jews?" asks Pilate (Luke 23:3). "You say so," responds Jesus (v. 3). Pilate fails to understand who Jesus is. The Jewish leaders fail to understand him, and for most of the Gospel story, even his own disciples fail to understand who Jesus is.

We are defined biologically, socially, and by our choices, but Jesus refuses such parameters and attempts to change the cultural understandings that define people. Who Jesus is can be found in his relationship with God. As his disciples, we too are defined by faith and not by the world. (Dan L. Flanagan)

Worship Aids

Call to Worship

We come to worship our Creator.
Our week has been hectic as we strive to please.
We live with expectations from others and from ourselves.
May we find peace today in the one who created us.

Prayer

Gracious and loving God, our lives are defined in many ways. We may be parents or children, responsible for others or to others, members or non-members. Who we are is often a result of our choices. Help us to use this gift of decision wisely and to enhance our relationships with you. Amen.

Words of Assurance

God promises that our past is not the way we shall be defined. We are defined by the grace of God. We are defined by forgiveness. (Dan L. Flanagan)

JANUARY 30, 2011

❧❧❧

Fourth Sunday after the Epiphany

Readings: Micah 6:1-8; Psalm 15; 1 Corinthians 1:18-31; Matthew 5:1-12

A Lovely Walk
Micah 6:1-8

I am in a covenant relationship. My husband and I have been married for thirteen years. I will grant you that many others have been married for longer than that, but one thing I am reminded of in this relationship is that we do not always communicate well. It is not that we are not talking; we just don't talk at the same rate or exchange information in the same way. Part of our difficulty lies in the fact that he is male and I am not.

Often, when I have been thinking about an issue or problem, I forget that my husband has not been privy to my thoughts. He comes in from the garage and I, in my haste to share my latest understandings or hopes or plans, bombard him with words—and forget to mention the subject. He listens, trying to understand me, and finally says, "What is the subject? What are we talking about?"

In the book of Micah, the Lord is more structured and methodical. The Lord tells Israel everything that is on God's mind. The Lord gives exact, historical details of what the Lord has done for them. The Lord reminds the people how God has never left them, not one time. The Lord brought them up out of Egypt, redeemed them from a life of slavery, gave them leaders, and protected them! There is no question of the Lord's presence and action in their lives.

Yet the nation Israel has forgotten they are in a covenantal relationship; they have gone astray and not repented. The Lord demands their loyalty and love; they are estranged from the Lord. God reminds Israel of the Lord's saving acts that they may again enter into right relationship.

31

The Lord reminds them of what has been done on their behalf and how they thrive when they follow the Lord's ways.

The Lord understands the people. God knows that they will try to make God happy, and that they will try to do so in ways that they have been told are wrong. The Lord recognizes the traditional burnt offerings and also the unacceptable offering of the firstborn as attempts to return to the Lord. How many times have the people been told not to imitate the abominable practices of the Canaanites who sacrifice their own children? The people just forget; in their desire to reestablish their covenant with Adonai, they show they still have attachments to heathen rituals.

I see faint reflections of these dynamics in my covenant relationship with my husband. I do not doubt that my husband loves me and wants me to be happy. What I do doubt sometimes is his memory. I think I have been perfectly clear in my feelings and desires. I have even been overwhelming in providing details on how to load the dishwasher or where to find the thermometer. He doesn't get it. He can't find it. I go to the closet and pull out the thermometer from exactly where I said it would be. I know he looked because the closet is in slight disarray; he tried to please me. But the next time I need the thermometer, he will have to ask where it is again. My husband also has a tendency, like the Israelites, to make up for his shortcomings with gifts and generosity in small things. If I really needed a thermometer and he couldn't find it, he would go out and buy, not one thermometer, but at least two! "I wasn't sure if you wanted a digital readout with batteries or if you wanted an old-timey one, so I got both!"

Israel began by offering year-old calves and upped it to thousands of rams, rivers of oil, and finally the firstborn. They wanted to please, even offering what they did not have the authority to give.

Drawing from my own experience of male and female approaches to life, it seems as if Israel was more masculine than feminine in its approach. Men are generally more concerned with plans, processes, and solutions, while women tend to focus on emotions and relationship. Israel wanted to know what to do; what should the plan of action be? (I am applying some observations to the text here, not attempting to stereotype the sexes.)

Generally speaking, women want to discuss problems more, get more details, and relate personal history as to how they would feel if someone hurt their feelings or did not seem to appreciate what had been done for them. It is a valid problem-solving procedure. They relate what would make them feel better and apply that knowledge to the problem at hand.

Often, men, once they understand a problem, want to take action to solve it. They don't ignore emotions and relationships but focus more on action than feeling. This is also a valid approach to problem solving. In the biblical scenario we are exploring, it is the approach Israel takes—Israel takes action to solve the problem of its broken relationship with the Lord.

The answer the Lord gives Israel is perfect—short, concise, and full of action verbs with emotional connections. As such, it addresses both masculine and feminine understandings and priorities of action and relationships. The Lord tells Israel exactly what to do, what to love, and how to walk! Do what is just. Love kindness. Walk humbly.

Today, as New Testament people, we may think that these requirements have been replaced by the cross. Yet, as long as injustice, poverty, and oppression exist in our world, we need to be reminded of the Lord's words. Do justice. Love kindness. Walk humbly.

Three small phrases perhaps, but they carry the weight of the Torah and the New Testament alike. O mortals, human beings, why should we try to offer more than what is asked for when, even now, we cannot give the minimum the Lord has required? (Raquel Mull)

Lectionary Commentary
1 Corinthians 1:18-31

The letter to the believers in Corinth addresses the quarrelsome nature of the community. The different factions try to outdo one another or prove themselves more worthy through standards different from those Paul taught. Paul explains the true wisdom of God and how Christ is the power of God on earth. The community is reminded that not everyone will understand or accept this, but that they have staked their lives on it.

Matthew 5:1-12

The scriptures known as the *Beatitudes* begin Jesus' Sermon on the Mount. Speaking to crowds of people that include the demon-possessed, epileptics, the sick and paralyzed, as well as the poor, Jesus offers a new lifestyle based on God's will. To people who have more reason than most to mistrust, bear grudges, hold resentment, and seek retribution, Jesus promises salvation. (Raquel Mull)

Worship Aids

Call to Worship

We want to please you, O Lord.
We are human beings with flaws and imperfections.
Yet you love us.
Assure us of your love as we offer our praises in song and prayer.

Invocation

Come to us, Lord. Give us the eyes to see you in one another's faces. Let us hear your love in one another's voices as we sing, pray, and laugh together. Quiet our beings that we might know your voice in our midst. Amen.

Benediction

Go into a world that needs to hear you. Let your words and actions point to the one whom we serve. (Raquel Mull)

How Are We Defined? By Faith

Third in a Series of Three on Defining Relationships

Mark 3:31-35

To live as a Christian is to live within the call of Christ. Dietrich Bonhoeffer suggests the first call that every Christian experiences is the call to abandon the attachments to this world (Dietrich Bonhoeffer, *The Cost of Discipleship* [New York: Macmillan, 1977], 66–67). As was true of Jesus, Bonhoeffer's countercultural stance cost him his life.

Christ's call to discipleship is a call to redefine ourselves. If Christ is our foundation, we no longer identify with the way culture defines us genetically, socially, or through our choices. "There is no longer Jew or Greek, there is no longer slave or free, there is no longer male and female; for all of you are one in Christ Jesus" (Galatians 3:28).

Christ's invitation to discipleship has power. Simon, Andrew, James, and John were actively engaged in fishing, James and John with their father. But when Jesus invited them, "immediately they left their nets and followed him" (Matthew 4:20). They left behind the familiar and comfortable to follow a stranger into an unfamiliar lifestyle. The Gospels celebrate those who said yes. How many refused Christ's invitation?

Regardless of the pain it may bring, most of us are quite comfortable with who we are. I am proud of my heritage and for the most part happy with my social identity and status in life. Even if we are dissatisfied, however, change is difficult. Abused women, for example, often hesitate to change their relationships because the familiar, even when it is tragic, feels more comfortable than the unknown. Working to form a new identity often means challenging those who appear to be more powerful. Change is risky.

Doing something against the grain can also appear peculiar. In the movie *Field of Dreams*, Ray Kinsella peers at the baseball field he carved out of his cornfield and says to his wife, "I have just created something totally illogical.... Am I completely nuts?" Acting counter to his upbringing and community expectations, Ray steps into the unknown on faith. Ray is about to lose his farm but chooses to listen to a voice calling him into a radically different future. Simon, Andrew, James, and John must have felt similar power in the call of Christ.

The call to discipleship is not a call to comfort. On the contrary, it is a call to risk. It is a call to become vulnerable. Jesus is clear about the risk involved. "If any want to become my followers, let them deny themselves and take up their cross and follow me. For those who want to save their life will lose it, and those who lose their life for my sake, and for the sake of the gospel, will save it" (Mark 8:34-35). The call to discipleship is a call into an absolutely new life, a totally new identity.

Christ's call to become his disciple is strangely alluring. Even Peter, the one who identifies Jesus as the Messiah, seems disappointed that being a disciple is not about rewards. "Look, we have left our homes and followed you" (Luke 18:28). "Truly I tell you," says Jesus, "there is no one who has left house or wife or brothers or parents or children, for the sake of the kingdom of God, who will not get back very much more in this age, and in the age to come eternal life" (Luke 18:29-30). The call to be a disciple of Christ is a call to change focus. The focus of the Christian life is not this world but the world to come. Christianity is a counterculture.

Peter is probably not fully aware of what it means to identify Jesus as the Messiah. Immediately following Peter's confession, the Gospel of Mark says Jesus predicts his rejection by the religious leaders and his death and resurrection. This is not Peter's understanding of the Messiah. He rebukes Jesus, prompting a sharp reply: "Get behind me, Satan! For you are setting your mind not on divine things but on human things" (Mark 8:33).

Jesus offers a harsh assessment of human things. He teaches that we should hate this life and keep our eyes on the eternal. Jesus' peace is of a different nature. "I do not give to you as the world gives" (John 14:27). The apostle Paul also suggests Christian citizenship "is in heaven" (Philippians 3:20) and not of this world.

Jesus suffers at the hands of those whose authority he challenges. Jesus' ministry is a sign of hope that the world can be different. The world can become more like God's kingdom, but it requires those grounded in the eternal to challenge the status quo. To be grounded in the eternal provides hope for transformation.

The divine/human struggle is present in the nature of the Christ. The divine presence experienced through Christ is a sign of God's hope for human nature. Things can be different if our foundation is in the eternal.

The power of the "force" in the *Star Wars* movies has Christian implications. When Obi-Wan begins training Luke Skywalker as a Jedi knight, his first lesson is to help Luke trust his grounding in the "force" (read *faith*) rather than in what he sees. Han Solo calls the Jedi success simple "luck," to which Obi-Wan responds, "In my experience, there's no such thing as luck."

While the world wants to define us in human terms, Christianity is an "otherworldly" religion. Our identity is formed not by this world but by our faith, the invisible. Christ offers us a new definition of who we are.

When Jesus' mother and siblings are announced by one of his disciples, Jesus says, "Who are my mother and my brothers?" (Mark 3:33). Looking at those who sit around him, he says, "Here are my mother and my brothers! Whoever does the will of God is my brother and sister and mother" (vv. 34-35). Jesus offers a new definition of family and a new definition of who we are as his disciples, grounded in the eternal, the will of God.

If we are grounded in faith, our social affiliations and personal choices become reflections of our attempt to seek the will of God. We can be defined by bloodline, peer groups, and bad choices. Or, we can choose to respond to the call to discipleship and be shaped by faith.

Dietrich Bonhoeffer could have chosen otherwise, but he stood strongly in faith and against the Nazi terror. Living the way the world defines us may be comfortable. Christ calls us to be grounded differently, to live out our faith, transformed by God and transforming the world. (Dan L. Flanagan)

Worship Aids

Call to Worship

We come before you, O God, uniquely created.
We are members of the human family, hungry to discover the spiritual.
Our lives are woven together genetically, socially, and by our own choices.
But we long to discover who we really are through you.

Prayer

We seek to be grounded in you, O God. Move us through the maze of worldly concerns to touch the ground of our very being. We know that our citizenship is not of this world. We know that we are called beyond the world to reside in the eternal. May we come to know you and to live from our spiritual foundation. Amen.

Benediction

May our lives reveal God's grace. In the physical world, live by the Spirit of God. (Dan L. Flanagan)

FEBRUARY 6, 2011

❧❧❧

Fifth Sunday after the Epiphany

Readings: Isaiah 58:1-9a (9b-12); Psalm 112:1-9 (10); 1 Corinthians 2:1-12 (13-16); Matthew 5:13-20

A Truth about Sin
Isaiah 58:1-9a (9b-12)

One characteristic I notice about children is their complete, and many times unsolicited, honesty, until they are taught some social norms. I can remember walking into the grocery store with my preschool-age son. We had gone through the ritual of "Can I have some of that cereal I saw on TV?" and "If I'm real good, can I have a toy?" dialogue and were walking in relative silence. I was thinking about dinner, and my son was staring at shelves to see what he "needed."

Suddenly, a man in a wheelchair, with no legs, entered the aisle. Anticipating an outburst from my son, who did not understand the phrase "politically correct," I glanced down, hoping that he would be so busy checking out the frozen foods that he wouldn't notice the man wheeling toward us. Maybe the man would be so busy checking out the frozen foods, he wouldn't notice us! Hope, hope, hope.

Not so. They both looked down the aisle at each other at the same time! *Oh, no,* I thought, *here it comes!* Some totally insensitive remark from my four-year-old, which I knew was going to embarrass me and the man.

My son opened his mouth and took a breath, still staring at the man with no legs in the wheelchair. I squeezed and jerked on his hand. Then came the words I knew were going to embarrass us all: "Hey, stop; leggo my hand; you're hurting me! Mommy!"

The man's eyes went from my son to me. I was absolutely right in knowing that I would be embarrassed. The words I had feared—"Where are his legs?" or "What is wrong with him?"—were not the words that

39

ultimately caused embarrassment. It was my ineffective, wrong response of avoiding the truth as I tried to control the conversation and the response.

The man had probably been in other situations where he was the first amputee some kid had seen. He handled the whole thing better than I did. I blushed, let go of my son's hand, and apologized to both of them.

Sometimes the truth is hard to hear, but kids especially don't have a problem telling people they are fat, or missing their legs, or even that they are nice. It is not that we don't know the truth; we may not want to acknowledge it. We live in a state of denial. The man knew his legs were gone. The fat person has probably been told before that she is overweight.

In Isaiah 58, the prophet tells the people something they probably already know and don't want to hear. They are rebellious and do not have the right attitude in their hearts and minds to make their fasts acceptable.

Their worship is unrighteous because the Israelites participate in only the outward actions of worship; they show up at the right times with others to worship and pray. But what about the rest of the week? Do they seek the Lord's presence and blessing on Tuesday or Thursday? How do they seek God's face?

Jesus addressed similar problems. In Matthew 6, Jesus gives instructions on how to fast, pray, and give. Don't bring attention to yourself, that others will praise you and think you are perfect and wonderful, above reproach and judgment.

Now, centuries later, has anything changed? The television tells us that we should look like movie stars—thin and attractive. It is acceptable to be in debt as long as you can make your monthly payments and have the right car in your driveway. If we make sacrifices at all, they should be relatively small so as not to create too much discomfort. It is acceptable to turn away or cross the street in order to avoid the homeless, smelly people. If you are in church on Sunday morning for worship, it is not necessary to go to Sunday school. After all, you plan to be in your pew again next week, unless, of course, you have company.

I fear we are in need of an Isaiah—someone who is bold enough to "shout out" without holding back, to remind us of our sins. I use the word *remind* because we probably already know we are sinning—we may just hope that, since everyone else is doing it, we are not too bad. We may be pinning our hopes on the fact that we do the right thing most of the time and may even hesitate before breaking any of the ten commandments. That's ironic, because the first command is to honor the Lord and keep the commandments! I suspect we know in our heart of hearts that we have much in common with those Israelites and first-century believers!

Or perhaps we need a four-year-old. My little boy did not have a clue what he had done to merit a jerked arm and a painfully squeezed hand. The man in the wheelchair did, and I did. I had tried to hide the truth, to control it so that I would not be embarrassed. I was wrong.

So the next question is easy to ask and hard to answer. What are we going to do about it? I believe the first step is to be honest and look at ourselves. In the grocery store, I began with an apology—to my son, to the man, and to God. The issue is not how much we sin; it is when and why. Do we really think that God doesn't notice, that God allows our standards to be set by the television and popularity contests? Do we really think God can't handle the truth?

May the Lord, who never abandons us, forgive us through grace and love when we abandon God and God's ordinances. (Raquel Mull)

Lectionary Commentary
1 Corinthians 2:1-12 (13-16)

Corinth was a cosmopolitan city consisting of Greeks, Romans, and Jews, as well as people from Syria, Egypt, and Asia Minor. Apollo's temple sat in proximity to those of Hera, Octavia, Venus, Fortuna, Hermes, Heracles, and Poseidon. Paul was concerned about the boundaries between the Christian community and the other societies. Paul proclaims that his ordinary preaching brings results through the power of God, revealing God's wisdom through that power. Only the spirit of God can explain the gifts bestowed upon us by God.

Matthew 5:13-20

Salt and light are easy metaphors to understand and explain to people from a wide variety of cultures. Matthew writes to a group of believers from many backgrounds and nations who evidently are questioning which laws and ordinances are really necessary to follow. Is this another case in which people are looking to do the bare minimum instead of remembering that a Christian is called to sacrifice and give generously when establishing the kingdom of God? We take a similar attitude when we ignore or discount the Hebrew Scriptures, which Jesus took great care to know, teach, and follow. When we are called to follow Christ, let us remember our full heritage and common roots. (Raquel Mull)

Worship Aids

Call to Worship

Creator, we have left our homes and warm beds to be in your presence.
We gather in your name to worship and praise you.
May this first day of the week...
be only one of many days in which we sing your praises and worship you.

Invocation

God of wisdom and righteousness, your standards and expectations of us have not changed. Fill us with the desire to know your truth and to follow your commandments. Amen.

Benediction

Go, as a forgiven and holy people, to do the will of the one who loves us unconditionally. (Raquel Mull)

Where Are Your Seeds?

First in a Series of Four on the Kingdom of God

Matthew 13:1-23

The kingdom of God, as offered and explained by Jesus Christ, is not what people are expecting. They assume the kingdom will be ushered in with majesty, power, and authority. They expect a show of grandeur, abundance, and excess. They do not think a Jewish carpenter will show up with a ragtag group of mavericks following him around, professing a life of simplicity, peace, tolerance, and love. As soon as he arrives on the scene, Jesus defies everyone's expectations.

One might imagine that Jesus was viewed as unbelievable or unfathomable. A Nazarene is performing miracles and claiming to be the Son of God? It makes sense, then, for his message to match his persona. Both Jesus and his message were countercultural to his listeners and to us today. Jesus' parables offer simple yet rich and practical lessons for his disciples, those gathered around him, and for us about the kingdom of God. Jesus' images are of farming, seeds, merchants, and pearls—everyday or familiar images for the first listeners. Jesus meets his listeners where they are.

In the first parable of this discourse in Matthew, we meet a sower going out to plant seeds. The sowing method is not efficient. Some seeds are intentionally placed where they will get the nutrients, water, and sunlight they need for health and growth, but seeds also fall in a variety of other, less nurturing locations. Clearly Jesus wants everyone to pay attention. He even goes so far as to say, "Listen!" (Matthew 13:3) at the beginning of this important story. Jesus privately explains the parable to his disciples. They are going to need to remember the fate of each seed when they are the sowers responsible for propagating the kingdom of God in the world's mission field.

The time the disciples have with Jesus is short. They see and participate in miracles and healings. They hear and bear witness to Christ's countercultural message of a kingdom of peace and devotion rather than of tyranny and war. Soon they will watch their leader and friend endure unbelievable suffering and death. The future of the church and the furthering of the kingdom will depend upon the seeds the disciples sow. They will need to remember Jesus' words about seeds so they can focus their energy on sowing seeds in fertile ground to maximize their efforts.

Undoubtedly, as the disciples discern and digest the meanings of Jesus' parables, this one will stay with them. They will learn to watch and recognize new converts as they embody the behaviors of the seeds sown in varying types of ground. Some seeds will fall along the path and be swallowed up by birds. These seeds represent those who hear the lessons of Christ but do not seek to understand, thus they are vulnerable to being whisked away by other interests.

Other hearers mirror the seeds that fall on rocky ground. These seeds are alluring because they soak up the sun and rain and quickly put forth signs of growth and life. However, their growth is deceiving because the rocky soil provides no healthy depth for the roots. The new life dies under the heat of the sun without support from good roots. Similarly, some hearers of the word will eagerly soak up the message of salvation and be drawn in by the promise of eternal life. When the challenges of a life modeled after Christ arise, immature faith, without discipleship and conviction of the heart, is not enough to survive the hardships. These "one-shot wonders" appear promising at the outset with their energy and enthusiasm, but, unfortunately, that is the best they have to offer.

Last among the undesirable fates for seeds is falling among thorns. These seeds resemble the hearers who have probably shown up simply to see what the commotion is all about. These are the folks who follow fads;

if there had been a counterpart to a tabloid magazine in Jesus' day, these people would have read it.

The disciples need to be prepared to encounter each of these types of ground. Seeds falling to non-nurturing soil can serve as distractions from the larger goal: kingdom propagation. Jesus knows that not all the seeds the disciples sow will bring forth fruit. They need to focus their efforts on sowing seeds in rich, lush, fertile soil. Jesus' attempts to educate the disciples will hopefully keep them on track and encourage them in their work.

Jesus' parable of the sower and the seeds provides a powerful message for the first disciples as it does for us today. The parable suggests some significant questions about our discipleship. What kind of soil are we? Where has the seed of the kingdom of God fallen in our lives? How do we work to provide the best conditions for God's seed to grow within us individually and as a community? How do we keep our soil fresh and healthy? The parable also offers us some of the same consolation it offers the disciples. In our missional efforts, it is our job to sow seeds. We may not always know where they will land or what their fate might be. Only God truly knows the fate of each seed and how it will turn out.

Our task is clear. First, we are to sow seeds. Some will land in fertile, healthy ground. These are the seeds that will bear fruit and give life. Second, we are to look inward and examine our own soil. God wants to grow something magnificent in our lives. It is our responsibility to make sure God's seeds land in fertile, ready, healthy soil in order to best fulfill their full potential.

A sower went out to sow seeds. What does your soil look like? Amen. (Victoria Atkinson White)

Worship Aids

Invocation

As the sower gathered his seeds before planting in his field, we gather our hearts together to worship. We turn our focus to the Great Gardener of our souls. Feed us, nurture us, and shine your light upon us. Amen.

Prayer of Confession

We confess that we do not always offer you good soil in which to plant your seeds, O God. We ask that you till up that which separates us from you so that we may grow to love you more. Amen.

Words of Assurance

Trust that God is already and always working to prepare you to receive the seed of faith, and nurturing your soul for magnificent growth. Hallelujah!

Benediction

May your eyes seek out fertile soil so that God may sow seeds of abundance in your life. Ponder anew what role you will play in increasing the yield of the kingdom of God. Go forth; there is work to be done until the harvesttime. Amen. (Victoria Atkinson White)

FEBRUARY 13, 2011

❧❧❧❧

Sixth Sunday after the Epiphany

Readings: Deuteronomy 30:15-20; Psalm 119:1-8; 1 Corinthians 3:1-9;
Matthew 5:21-37

Aleph
Psalm 119:1-8

Psalm 119 is written in praise of Torah, God's law or teaching. Psalm
119, the longest chapter in the book of Psalms, is an alphabetical acrostic that contains praises, laments, meditations, petitions, and assurances
of God's presence. The 176 verses are divided into twenty-two sections,
each named after a letter of the Hebrew alphabet. Some Bibles show the
letters as the subtitles for the divisions.

Hebrew letters differ from the English alphabet because each has a
name that is itself a word. Each letter is also a picture or symbol, representing an object, animal, or thing. When people read Hebrew, not only
do they understand the sounds of the letters, they know the words they
are reading. They also have the added dimension of seeing how the
images interact!

The first letter in the Hebrew alphabet is *aleph,* which means "master."
Aleph is the first and master of the other twenty-one letters. As such, the
first verses of Psalm 119 remind us of the blessings we receive when we
keep God's laws.

These pointed reminders of blessing and promise need to be repeated
many times for us mortals. The author of 1 John writes in chapter 5 that
"the love of God is this, that we obey his commandments. And his commandments are not burdensome" (v. 3). It would be nice to think that
second-century C.E. life was filled with fewer temptations, making the
commandments less of a burden, but we know that people throughout
history have struggled to follow God's ordinances. Those who find them
light to carry are the saints among us.

I have difficulty obeying some of the laws, especially the one dealing with covetousness. My daughter, the mother of our two beautiful grand-daughters, lives in another state. Her father and I have been divorced for many years, but our relationships with each other and our respective new mates have improved since we are now grandparents. Or so I thought.

One day, my daughter called and explained what they were going to do when they visited her father for four days. Four days! They don't visit us very often, and they never stay for more than two days! We make the seven-hour trip every other month to ensure that our four- and six-year-old granddaughters know their *shimmy* (Navajo for my mother's mother) and *hosteen* (Navajo for old man). My feelings were hurt, and jealousy's ugly head rose quickly and strongly. I hung up the phone and cried on Hosteen's shoulder. I decided not to talk to my daughter again that day.

By the next morning, I was much better and had gotten things into perspective. I called my daughter and thanked her for giving me some time to get my house in order. I reassured her that her family is very important to us; visits to us are not a condition for us to be part of their lives. I had reminded myself of the reasons her father is not able to visit them as frequently as we can. I remembered that the girls would be on summer vacation, and we would be at a yearly conference. I had moved from the jealous woman to the loving mother and grandmother. But it was not easy. It took time and effort, and in all honesty, I didn't even think about the commandment "Thou shalt not covet" (Exodus 20:17 KJV).

What I did was read Psalm 119:1-4, and I discovered, to my complete astonishment, that I was happy. I had obeyed the commandment and, in doing so, enabled my daughter and her family to be with her father without guilt or worry. We were both free because I finally followed God's command.

As I mentioned, *aleph* is the first letter and the master of all other Hebrew letters. It is first and considered by Jewish theologians to actually be made in the image of God. In fact, the first two letters of the Hebrew alphabet spell "father," which is an example of God at the beginning of all things.

Psalm 119 begins by reminding us that we need to conscientiously choose to walk in God's ways. It does make a difference in our relationships, all of them; our relationships with God as well as with our fellow human beings.

The second half of today's lection is a prayer seeking God's help in keeping the commandments of the Lord. Originally this was written in regard to Torah and all of its 613 laws, but we still need help to obey even the two greatest commandments! Our situation has not changed. We are still tempted, and we still forget the Lord's laws. Even knowing some of the consequences, we forget. Shame is not easy to live with. We feel guilt when we recognize we have done something wrong, but shame is what we feel when we believe something is wrong with us as people.

The God of creation made us in God's own image and did not want shame to be a part of our lives. The idea that we are not good enough or will never be right is an attack on our faith. God promises we will be heirs because God sees us as sons and daughters. When we follow God's commandments, never taking our eyes off them, shame will not rest on us. Knowing we are keeping our relationship with God first prevents doubt from creeping into our prayers and enables us to fulfill our destiny as God's children.

God wants to be first; in the Hebrew alphabet and in our lives. God has given us the pattern to live through God's Son, Jesus. Let us remember the laws and why we need to follow them. It is not just happiness and blessings; it is love. It's the love we have for God and the love we are to have for others, which, as promised, becomes stronger when we diligently keep God's precepts. (Raquel Mull)

Lectionary Commentary
Deuteronomy 30:15-20

Deuteronomy is the fifth and last book of the Torah. Today's lesson concludes a covenant in Moab between the Israelites and the Lord. Moses, about to die, gives the Israelites, about to enter the Promised Land, a choice. Obedience to God's commands means life and prosperity, while any other path is death. The choice is black and white, no gray areas here. The covenant requires a witness, and Moses is backed by the witness of heaven and earth.

Matthew 5:21-37

Jesus reminds the listeners of four laws from Torah concerning different subjects. In each case, he offers a radical reinterpretation of the law followed by an example of his new viewpoint. Jesus, who comes to establish the kingdom of heaven on earth, expands the laws by teaching that anger can kill; that not only are bad oaths prohibited, but all oaths should be avoided. We tend to be legalistic to excuse our behavior. We say, "I didn't actually commit adultery with her because we did not have a physical relationship." Jesus understands our weaknesses and helps us to prevent sin by offering tight boundaries for our values and actions. (Raquel Mull)

Worship Aids

Call to Worship

We gather as family and friends in the name of the Lord.
Hear our voices as we sing and pray together.
Keep our thoughts from drifting and wandering,
and let our lives be a reflection of your laws and precepts,
All: freeing us to love everyone we meet.

Prayer of Confession

Creator God, we forget. We forget that we are made in your image, and we sometimes let Hollywood and commercials tell us what is beautiful. We forget to love others and to forgive as you forgive. We even forget how to ask for forgiveness when we have broken your laws. Help us to remember your Son died for our sins. Help us to repent of our sinful ways. Loving God, forgive our prideful ways, and let us grow more into your likeness. Amen.

Words of Assurance

Jesus the Christ died on the cross and was resurrected so we would have forgiveness and be perfect in your sight, Lord. Even in our humanness, may we remember we are co-heirs with Christ and have been promised eternal life. (Raquel Mull)

Weeds and Seeds

Second in a Series of Four on the Kingdom of God

Matthew 13:24-30, 36-43

Those of us who call suburbia home tend to spend a lot of money on our yards. We use the glib phrase, "The grass is always greener in someone else's yard," which is of course about envying our neighbors' possessions. When taken at face value, however, that phrase can send us racing to the home improvement store. We want our grass to be green and mowed in crisscross patterns. We want well-manicured shrubs and pruned trees. We dump money into the right color of mulch and annual flowers that last only a few months. In suburban America, our yards are a great source of pride and status. Often a person's yard and its maintenance can suggest what goes on within the walls of the house. If the grass is too high, someone may be sick, or perhaps they are away on vacation, or they might have gotten into some financial trouble and are working extra shifts at work. If there are dead patches in the lawn, that can indicate visiting grandchildren who left a wading pool on the grass too long, or the patches can speak to efforts to conserve water and not using the sprinklers as often as the neighbors. We take our little plots of land seriously. We invest time, money, and sweat equity into them so that they are healthy and beautiful.

One could say something similar of our farmer in today's passage. He takes care of his land. The text implies that he prepared it so that the seeds he sowed would bring forth a bountiful yield. But all does not go as planned. An enemy comes in the night and sows weeds among the good seeds. The results are devastating. Weeds grow up among the crops, to the amazement and disappointment of the sower and his slaves. The slaves' first intuition is to offer to pull up the weeds for the health of the crops, but the sower knows better. The sower chooses to risk the life of the crops alongside the weeds until harvesttime, rather than risk the slaves' endangering the life of even one plant by mistakenly pulling one up when trying to destroy the weeds. It is an interesting gamble.

Do you remember picking dandelions as a child? Perhaps you even secretly offered up wishes before you blew the almost translucent seedpods into the air and watched them take flight in the wind. Certainly this is fun for children, but now my blood pressure rises at the sight of dandelions. With all the backbreaking effort I put into my lawn, dandelions are the last things I want to see. One small plant can hold a myriad of feathery seedpods waiting to overtake and infiltrate my luscious green grass. Simply mowing the plant down does nothing to fix the problem; only a shovel will do. You have to battle the roots to truly conquer a dandelion, but at what cost? Digging up a dandelion also means you dig up some of the lush green grass you have worked so hard to grow. Dandelions place us in a position similar to that of the sower in our parable.

Notice that the sower has faith in his crop. He knows he has done good work. He has prepared the soil and carefully planted good seeds. He has faith that his crops will do well and bring forth a productive yield despite the work of the enemy or the growth of the weeds. Interestingly, this parable follows the one in which Jesus talks about the fate of seeds that fall outside good soil. We know from that parable that good soil is the ideal location for the seeds of the sower. We learn from this parable that landing in good soil does not guarantee a life without challenges. Good soil is as attractive to weeds as it is to seeds. But the farmer has faith that his plants will produce fruitful yields even in the presence of the weeds.

So the weeds are given a reprieve. They grow alongside the good seeds until it's time to harvest. This is where the parable makes us uncomfortable. We do not like thinking about the violence involved in the gathering and burning of the weeds. The fact that it comes from the mouth of Jesus makes it all the more difficult to comprehend. Here is the self-professed Son of God proclaiming a message of death and destruction, violence and hellfire. While the fate of the weeds is frightful and devastating, a clear message prevails regarding where we should focus our energy and efforts. We are to sow good seeds in healthy soil. We are to sow the kind of seeds the sower planted. We need to have the same kind of faith so that when and if the enemy comes in the night to sow weeds, we will be confident that our yield will not be affected.

The weeds are fated to be burned whether they are pulled up or gathered at harvest. The fire awaiting the weeds should light a metaphorical fire under us to focus our efforts toward sowing seeds in good soil, seeds that will be healthy enough to endure the potential sabotage of weeds sown in the darkness.

Jesus' message is clear that both healthy plants and weeds will be present until harvesttime. Hearers of his word will live next to those who choose to reject Jesus' word until the end of time. The focus of our efforts must be on sowing seeds of health, seeds that can withstand threats with confidence, seeds that will produce good fruit until the harvest.

How green is your lawn? How much time and energy do you invest in preparing the soil for the seeds God wants to sow in your life? Are you providing God good soil in which to plant seeds? How will you respond to the dandelions that may land in your life or the weeds that crop up in the night?

The closing of this parable is key: "The righteous will shine like the sun in the kingdom of their Father. Let anyone with ears listen!" (Matthew

13:43). Jesus invites us to take seriously the work we do and the lasting consequences it will have. So, what are you sowing? (Victoria Atkinson White)

Worship Aids

Invocation

Pull the weeds of distraction from our garden of faith in this time of worship so that we may better hear your word, sing your praises, and adore you this day. Amen.

Prayer of Confession

Forgive us when we have sown weeds among your seeds. Let us not be as weeds to others, but rather plants of shelter, nourishment, and strength. Help us to grow to become the fruitful bounty you would have us be. Amen.

Words of Assurance

Rest in the assurance of God's patience and love. Know that the fruit God plants and nourishes is fruit that will last.

Benediction

Go forth, knowing that the weeds will always be among us. Discipleship is not an easy path, but the yield is most definitely worth it. Trust in your God-given strength to stand firm until the harvest. Amen. (Victoria Atkinson White)

FEBRUARY 20, 2011

❧❧❧

Seventh Sunday after the Epiphany

Readings: Leviticus 19:1-2, 9-18; Psalm 119:33-40; 1 Corinthians 3:10-11, 16-23; Matthew 5:38-48

Hei—Breath of God
Psalm 119:33-40

Psalm 119, an alphabetical acrostic, praises Torah, God's law. It contains praises, laments, meditations, petitions, and assurances of God's presence. The 176 verses are divided into twenty-two sections, each named after a letter of the Hebrew alphabet.

In today's text, the subtitle is *hei*, the fifth letter of the Hebrew alphabet. The picture associated with this letter is a window because the letter actually has three sides, similar to our *n*. According to the Talmud, God created the universe with the letter *hei*. *Hei* has creative power.

When the Holy Spirit dwells within a person, that person takes on a new identity; the old person passes away and new life is given. It is *hei* God breathes into Adam to change him from a bit of dirt into a living, breathing human being. God shared breath with Adam and continues to do so with us. The *hei* has life-changing and life-giving qualities.

I am sure we can look around our congregations and see what changes are reflected in people's lives when God breathes *hei* into them. I know a young woman, who would not even talk on the phone to order a pizza, whose life has been transformed through *hei*. Her confidence and self-esteem grow daily. Through patience, encouragement, some mentoring, and encouraging her to take advantage of opportunities for growth, I have seen a life reborn. The patience and encouragement as well as the giving of time to be with this young mother are also gifts of *hei*, the Spirit.

Our small town recently hosted the American Cancer Society's Relay for Life event. This young woman, because of her involvement with the event and her growing self-confidence, went out to ask for money and door prizes from businesses and made announcements over the loud-speaker. She even surprised herself! What a joy to witness the change in her life and the life of her family as she is less dependent upon others and moves out of her comfort zone to do ordinary and extraordinary things. This is *hei*.

In the Hebrew Scriptures, Abram is one of the earliest patriarchs whose life is recounted for our faith and instruction. Abram and his wife, Sarai, had wanted children for many years. The couple even tried to take "control" of the situation and at eighty-six years of age, Abram fathered Ishmael, the ancestor of modern-day Arabs, by Hagar, Sarai's servant. Later, God renewed his covenant with Abram, promising that the land of Canaan would remain in the possession of Abram's family forever and that Abram would have a son of his own (Genesis 17). At this time, God gave the couple new names—Abram became Abraham, and Sarai became Sarah. Scripture says God talked to Abraham and promised a son through his wife, Sarah.

When God changed their names, God essentially added a letter—*hei*, the breath of God. It was only after the names were changed and *hei* was added to their lives that they were able to give birth to a new life through their son, Isaac.

Psalm 119:33-40 reflects Abram's life. The story of the renewal of the covenant comes right after Ishmael is born, right after Abram sins by not trusting God. The author of this psalm begins this stanza by asking for instruction to know God's statutes and for the desire to follow the law once he understands it.

Abraham and Sarah had to wait another fourteen years before Isaac was born. Even with *hei*, they still made mistakes, but their faith that God would not forsake them remained strong. They were willing to move out of their comfort zones many times to be obedient. When they did make mistakes, they confessed and returned to the Lord's way. "Turn away my eyes from looking at worthless things, and revive me in Your way" is the translation from the New King James version of verse 37. *Revive* is a verb meaning to restore life. The NRSV uses the phrase "give me life." Either way, this is a petition for a renewed desire to follow the Lord's path, for *hei* to be imparted into a person's being, and for guidance and wisdom to follow the right direction.

The last verse of our text is another request for revival, this time for righteousness. We have the righteousness of Christ, but, like Abraham and other humans, we forget and lean on our own wisdom, desires, and needs to determine our course. We need *hei* to revive righteousness in our lives.

My young friend is growing in her faith, her courage, and her self-confidence. She is willing to take on new challenges and experiences, much like Abraham and Sarah. Her life is an example, not only for her children but also for others as to the power of *hei*. I do not hesitate to tell her that life has many surprises in store for her, both good and bad. I hasten to assure her that she has the inner strength to do what is necessary for her family and for her relationship with God. She has *hei*—the breath of life! (Raquel Mull)

Lectionary Commentary
Leviticus 19:1-2, 9-18

When one reads the word *holy* in the Bible, it means "set apart" and defines the process by which that happens. Too often, we think of *holy* as the final product of blameless lives, pure and completely free from sin. We are reminded this day that we are holy because we belong to the one who is blameless and pure. Our lifestyles and choices make us different from the rest of the world because we have been set apart. The values and principles set forth by God for the people to follow are what set us apart.

Matthew 5:38-48

Again, Jesus takes a law from the Hebrew Scriptures and offers a reinterpretation of it. He offers an antithesis on the subjects of retaliation and enemies. Torah did not encourage retaliation but did set boundaries regarding it: don't take a whole life for the loss of one eye. Matthew, in discussing enemies, seems to refer not only to personal enemies but also to persecutors of the church. He even offers the reward of being the children of "your Father in heaven" (Matthew 5:45). The idea of holiness, set apart from the general society, is also stressed here. (Raquel Mull)

Worship Aids

Call to Worship
Creator, we hear your voice in the wind and the thunder.
Creator, whose breath gives life to the world,
we hunger to be in your presence.

Made in your image,
All: make us ready to come to you with renewed hearts and without
shame.

Offertory Prayer

Let us come, with our gifts, tithes, and offerings, in an attitude of thanksgiving. May our guilt be assuaged by the Creator's grace and not by our
own deeds. Amen.

Benediction

Go with the breath of *hei* in your soul, words of love on your lips, and a
willingness to follow the Creator's commandments. Amen. (Raquel Mull)

Good Things

Third in a Series of Four on the Kingdom of God

Matthew 13:31-32

In remembering Christmases and birthdays past, doesn't it feel as if
there were more gifts to be opened, that the piles of presents seemed
larger? Perhaps the gifts were larger in size and so it appeared as if there
were more of them. As a parent of a young child, I know my daughter definitely thinks bigger is better. A bigger cookie is better than a smaller
cookie, and a bigger gift is bound to be better than a smaller gift. But with
age comes wisdom, at least in the gift department. A smaller velvet box
can mean an engagement ring to a young woman in love. A flat business
card–sized envelope for a teenager can mean a gift card for a favorite
store. A business envelope to new parents might mean a savings bond for
their child's college fund. Good things can come in small packages.

So says Christ in the parable of the mustard seed. Jesus insinuates that
no one expects much of the "smallest of all the seeds" (Matthew 13:32),
but when planted, it grows so large that birds are able to nest in its
branches. What begins as seemingly insignificant can, with nourishment,
care, and time, become something amazing. Good things can come in
small packages.

The mustard seed parable challenges our hierarchical preferences and
invites us to expect the unexpected with Jesus. If the kingdom of God is
like a small seed becoming a great tree, what might that mean for us?

What might that mean for those we see as less than we are? Good things can come in small packages.

To Jesus' listeners, this parable was more than unexpected. It was countercultural. They were expecting the kingdom of God to come blazing into their lives with power, authority, and influence. They were expecting grandeur and excess, clout and control. They were certain that something big was coming with the kingdom of God. With the eyes of children waiting for the gift of a lifetime, they were anticipating something really big.

But here comes Jesus, a simple Jewish carpenter, telling stories and traveling around with his buddies. Jesus' message is not what his listeners want to hear. In fact, Jesus' ushering in of the kingdom of God is so different from what everyone is expecting that Jesus is forced to use parables like this one to help people understand. In a clever twist, it is Jesus' crafty use of stories that will stay with the disciples when he is gone.

Jesus knew that the kingdom of God, like a mustard seed, would grow gradually. There would not be a "growth spurt" until long after Jesus was gone. The disciples would need his encouragement, his wisdom, and his stories to remind them that Jesus knew what was coming; he knew the challenges they would face. Like a mustard seed faced with droughts, floods, and scorching heat, the seed would prevail and a fruitful plant would grow, just as Jesus promised.

The disciples became a band of friends who left everything they knew and loved to follow Jesus. They gave years of their lives to him. After the Crucifixion, they could have scattered in fear or they could cling to a parable such as this one and remember that mustard seeds turn into great bushes under the right conditions. What might happen to the kingdom of God under the right conditions?

Jesus' message holds words of hope. With this parable he leaves a legacy for the disciples and offers hope to everyone hearing the story. The widow with her small children hears the voice of Christ and dreams of a day she will not struggle. The paraplegic lies on the outskirts of the crowd and listens to Jesus' words and wonders how he too might make a difference in the world. The social outcast hears about Jesus' parable of the mustard seed, shakes her head in agreement, and says, "I knew it! I can be more than they think I am!"

Good things come in small packages. Good things come in unexpected packages. According to Jesus' parable, no one expects much of the mustard seed, but from it grows a plant large enough to shelter animals. No one would likely come to expect much out of the disciples after Jesus' death. They were a group of mavericks who gambled on an individual who suffered the most gruesome and humiliating of all public deaths. Yet from these disciples grew the church that took root and grew across the world.

With its small size but enormous impact, the mustard seed holds hope for us all. With our human frailties and misgivings, we each fall short and sometimes feel quite small. This parable, however, shows that even the kingdom of God allows for times of growth spurts and pruning. Once small and hesitant about its growth, the kingdom of God is still bearing fruit and will continue far beyond our life spans. Thanks be to God for that!

So, were the piles of gifts from Christmases and birthdays bigger when we were little, or have we become wiser in valuing that which comes in smaller wrappings? Size matters in this story of Jesus. Watch out! Good things come in small packages. Amen. (Victoria Atkinson White)

Worship Aids

Invocation

God, we come to worship you, knowing that you need and desire each one of us. Remind us that we play a part in your kingdom no matter who we are or where we are in our journeys. Call away the distractions of our busy lives so we may better worship you.

Prayer of Confession

Gracious Lord, we confess that sometimes we doubt that mustard seeds can grow to be majestic and amazing. Help our unbelief so that we may channel our doubt into a deeper understanding of you and who you desire for us to be in this world.

Words of Assurance

Good things come in small packages. Do not doubt the faith within you. A mustard seed, when fully grown, changes the landscape of its field. You too, in the fullness of God, can change the world. Amen. (Victoria Atkinson White)

FEBRUARY 27, 2011

❦❦❦

Eighth Sunday after the Epiphany

Readings: Isaiah 49:8-16a; Psalm 131; 1 Corinthians 4:1-5; Matthew 6:24-34

What Would Jesus Say?
Matthew 6:24-34

Imagine that the Lord Jesus Christ is our speaker. Imagine that our church invited the Lord Jesus to be our guest preacher. What would Jesus say? In today's Gospel lesson, the Lord Jesus speaks directly to us.

First, the Lord Jesus says we cannot serve two masters. Jesus says we cannot serve God and wealth. When I graduated from college, several of my friends and I made a decision to serve God, some in full-time ordained ministry and others as active church members. I also remember one acquaintance who told me, "I'm going to make lots of money." He had made his decision. I do not know what happened to him, but I do know that my friends who decided to serve God have been blessed in ways more important than material wealth. But more important than serving one master is serving the right master. As Christians we have one master: our Lord Jesus Christ.

Second, the Lord Jesus said not to worry about what we eat, what we drink, or what we wear. This message was countercultural. During the time of Jesus, there was no refrigeration. No one could keep food items such as fish, meat, ripe fruits and vegetables, and milk longer than a day or two at most before the food spoiled. Consequently, people in the first century worried about what they would eat and drink, especially if there was a food shortage.

The Lord Jesus was not suggesting that we neglect our need to eat and drink, especially in times of scarcity. His concern was that in our worries about what to eat and what to drink, we tend to become obsessed with material things and forgo or forget our spiritual connection with God.

When we forget God, we become greedy. We develop a "me first" attitude so that the widows, the orphans, the sick, the aliens, and the poor are shoved aside, ignored, neglected, and forgotten. The prophets and the Lord Jesus were always clear that God cares for the marginalized and the poor; and those who belong to God and follow the Lord Jesus Christ are to care for them as well.

In his first sermon in Nazareth, Jesus read from the prophet Isaiah (61:1-2):

> The Spirit of the Lord is upon me,
>   because he has anointed me to bring good news to the poor.
> He has sent me to proclaim release to the captives
>   and recovery of sight to the blind,
>   to let the oppressed go free,
> to proclaim the year of the Lord's favor. (Luke 4:18-19)

When Jesus told his family and longtime friends in Nazareth that in that moment of his preaching, God's word was being fulfilled, they got angry at him and attempted to throw him off a cliff. What a response to Jesus' first sermon in his home synagogue! His message was truly countercultural.

What the Lord Jesus was saying to his first-century listeners, and what he is saying to you and to me today, is that we are to trust God completely for everything. We are not to worry about what we eat, what we drink, and what we wear. Jesus gives the example of how God feeds the birds and clothes the lilies of the field with such beautiful colors. If God feeds the birds and clothes the flowers, how much more will God do for the people of God! The Lord Jesus states that God, our heavenly Father, knows what we need. God knows that we need to eat, to drink, and to be clothed. God will provide abundantly for those who trust in God and serve God. Indeed, the prayer the Lord Jesus taught his disciples includes a petition regarding our need to eat: "Give us this day our daily bread" (Matthew 6:11).

Jesus says that our only concern should be to "strive first for the kingdom of God and his righteousness, and all these things will be given to you as well" (Matthew 6:33). In other words, we should put Christ above all.

Seeking God's kingdom means we put the Lord Jesus Christ first in our lives, in our relationships, and in our choices. Seeking to do what is right means we love our families, our friends, our acquaintances, our enemies, and strangers in the spirit of the living Christ. Seeking God's kingdom means we live in the spirit of the living Christ.

A young man joined the Navy upon completing high school. When he retired from the Navy, he got a good job with a state agency. A few years later, he decided to serve God full-time. He made the decision to serve one master, the Lord Jesus Christ. He is happier than ever before and ever more blessed by God. He trusted God and God blessed him. You do not have to wait until you retire to serve the Master.

Throughout your life, you will make decisions about your life and how you will live. You have goals and dreams you want to accomplish. You prepare to reach your goals and dreams. Sometimes, however, circumstances force changes in your life. You may not reach your goals and dreams, or you may have to change them. Whatever your goals and dreams are, never forget your relationship to the Lord Jesus Christ. Jesus Christ is your lifelong companion, ready to help you, guide you, and bless you. If you belong to the Lord Jesus Christ, then "strive first for the kingdom of God and his righteousness, and all these things will be given to you as well" (Matthew 6:33). (Roberto L. Gómez)

Lectionary Commentary
Isaiah 49:8-16a

When things do not go our way, we groan and moan. Yet most of us are truly blessed. In this passage from Isaiah, God reminds the people how they have been sustained and blessed through God's intentional and direct relationship with them. In moments of hardship, we forget God and God's blessings for us, yet in this passage from Isaiah, God says the people will not be forgotten. The Lord has inscribed (tattooed?) the names of God's people on God's hands. The important lesson here is God's enduring love.

1 Corinthians 4:1-5

First, Paul invites the faith community to think of themselves as servants of Christ and stewards of God's mysteries. Christians are called to service. It is one of the hallmarks and signs of faithful discipleship. When a natural disaster such as an earthquake, flood, hurricane, or tornado occurs, thousands of people respond to help in some way, whether through prayer or physical help to reconstruct churches and homes. Second, Christians are called to accountability. When all is said and done, Christians are accountable to God. Paul sets the bar high for

Christian service and stewardship, but then reminds us that it is God who finally judges us. (Roberto L. Gómez)

Worship Aids

Call to Worship

We live in a noisy world full of familiar and strange voices.
Every voice says something different.
We live in a state of confusion, not knowing what to think or what to do.
Whom should we listen to?
Our Judeo-Christian faith offers its own voices.
Our faithful voices speak and sing in harmony, reminding us of God's love, joy, peace, and justice.
The living Christ speaks to us.
In our time of praise and worship, let us pause and listen to the Lord Jesus Christ.

Opening Prayer (Unison)

Dear God, we grow deaf from excessive noise day and night. At home, our stereos and televisions blare. As we drive to and from work, we are overwhelmed by boom boxes in cars idling next to ours. At night, the sirens of the police, the medics, and the firefighters sometimes seem to go on and on. Yet in the loudness of these sounds, you call, you beckon, you whisper to us, faithfully and lovingly. We have only to listen. We have only to focus on your voice as a baby listens to its mother's voice. Help us to hear your calming voice of care and hope, love and support, renewal and direction. Amen.

Benediction

Dear God, as we return to our homes, to work, to school, and to all the places you lead us to during this new week of life, help us to pause during the busyness of the day; help us to have the discipline to overcome distractions; and help us to listen to your voice of hope and direction, renewal and strength, joy and peace, and above all, your love. We pray in the name of God our Father, Jesus the Christ, and the Holy Spirit. Amen. (Roberto L. Gómez)

Obsession

Fourth in a Series of Four on the Kingdom of God

Matthew 13:44-46

Have you ever witnessed someone becoming a parent? Often, we first encounter young people with strategic career goals and dreams for what they will master before reaching a certain age. Money is spent on vacations, entertainment, or housing projects. Then the prospect of a baby comes into the line of sight and things begin to change. Money goes toward a nursery, diapers, clothing, and toys for someone yet to arrive. Parents-to-be even start to make long-term financial plans, assuming their child will go to college and perhaps graduate school. This is just the buzz of activity before the baby comes. Once parents meet their child, a bond is formed that creates a carnal parental instinct matching none other. Priorities change. It is almost as if with parenthood comes a new set of lenses through which one views life. Parenthood, at least in the beginning, is all-consuming. That once seemingly rational person becomes single-mindedly and overwhelmingly devoted to the health, welfare, and success of their child.

I sense a similar consuming notion in today's scripture text. Our first character joyfully sells everything he has to buy a field, which is worthless to everyone else but priceless to him. Who does that? Who gives up everything he knows and loves for something buried in a field? Did he get a peek at that treasure? Did he make sure it would be worth it? It seems like a big risk.

In the next verse, the merchant does something similar, although it appears at first that he knows what he is doing. He searches for pearls for a living. He is used to looking for the most beautiful and rare of gems. He has experience; he is an individual on a mission. We do not expect anything out of the ordinary for him, except for the fact that it is Jesus telling the story, so his hearers know something is coming. The merchant finds a pearl of great value. One could assume this is the one he has been searching for throughout his career. Upon finding so great a gem, he, like the treasure-finder of the first story, sells all he has to possess this pearl.

Something consumes the characters in these parables. Something overtakes them so that they become single-minded. They are able to think of nothing other than the treasure that they feel they must possess to be complete. They have to have the prize in front of them.

What value that treasure and that pearl must possess to provoke seemingly irrational actions by those seeking them. Amazingly, Jesus seeks us with the exact same obsession. Jesus sees us as the treasure, the pearl, with which he must be in relationship. He is willing to give up everything to be with us. Not long after Jesus first shares this parable with the disciples, he does just that—Jesus sacrifices his life for us.

Remember our initial thoughts about becoming a parent and that all-consuming obsession that can take over at the sight of a new child. Or perhaps you can relate to the obsession of falling in love. Did you feel that you just had to be around someone or you couldn't focus, couldn't think, couldn't breathe? Did you love that person so much your heart might burst inside your chest? Did your skin ache until you got to hold her or him? That is the same passion, the same desire with which Jesus seeks us. Jesus sees so much value, so much love, so much potential, and so much of himself in us that he can't help but chase after us as if we were the greatest treasure the world has ever known.

Truth be told, that is what we are. We are God's greatest treasure. We are the children of God, created in the image of God. We are priceless simply because we have been born in the image of God. So of course Christ seeks relationship with us, just as the farmer sought after the treasure in the field or the merchant went after the pearl. Why wouldn't Christ want a relationship with us?

Too often, we fail to see our true value. We judge ourselves as not good enough, not worthy, and unlovable. We think we need to achieve something or complete a task or attain a certain status before we are worthy of the kind of all-consuming love Jesus has. We sell ourselves short. We get in our own way of having the kind of relationship Jesus wants with us. We hinder ourselves from that which we were created to be and do.

The treasure was created to evoke joy and happiness and purchase things of value. The pearl was created to be admired and loved and enjoyed. We have been created to worship and love and adore God. Yet we keep ourselves from being in unity with Christ by focusing on false treasures and fake pearls. This only makes Christ work harder to find ways to be in relationship with us and embrace the treasure that we are.

When the pearl is found, the merchant celebrates and changes the course of his life to have that precious pearl. When the treasure is found, the farmer sells everything he has to claim that land, to explore his treasure. Christ has found us and seeks to be in relationship with us. Christ, like the merchant or farmer, has already given up everything so that we may be found worthy to be in relationship with him. Worthiness is not the issue. Willingness is. Like the treasure and the pearl, you have been found. Will you embrace your master when he seeks to embrace you? Amen. (Victoria Atkinson White)

Worship Aids

Invocation

God, we treasure this time of worship with you and we offer our lives up to you in song, prayer, adoration, and reflection. Help us to center ourselves to better hear and know you through this service. We know that you constantly seek a better relationship with us. We come now seeking you. Amen.

Prayer of Confession

God, we confess that so often we do not see what you see, especially when we look in the mirror. You have created us in your image, but we do not treat ourselves or others as we should. Help us to see one another as you see us. Amen.

Words of Assurance

God sees! God knows! God treasures you!

Benediction

Go forth, knowing that you are sought out by God. Know that you are a treasure, not buried in a field, but discovered and coveted by God. Live life knowing that you are a priceless gem, beautifully and wonderfully made. Amen. (Victoria Atkinson White)

MARCH 6, 2011

Transfiguration Sunday

Readings: Exodus 24:12-18; Psalm 99; 2 Peter 1:16-21; Matthew 17:1-9

Shone Like the Sun
Matthew 17:1-9

The Gospel lesson from Matthew tells us of an extraordinary event several of the disciples experienced: the transfiguration of Jesus. Matthew states that Jesus took Peter, James, and John to the top of a tall mountain. A bright cloud covered them. Jesus was transfigured so that his face shone like the sun and his clothes became white. Moses, representing the law tradition, and Elijah, representing the prophetic tradition, appeared with Jesus. Then the disciples heard God's voice tell them that Jesus was his beloved Son and that they should listen to him. The disciples were extremely frightened and fell on the ground. Jesus walked to them, touched them, and told them to get up and not to be afraid.

What are we to understand from Matthew's testimony about this event? Simply put, that Jesus is indeed the Messiah, the Christ, and the beloved Son of God.

Many of the first-century readers or listeners of Matthew's Gospel knew that Moses had gone up to the mountaintop to be in the presence of the Lord God. They knew that when Moses came down, his face shone brightly, so brightly that he had to wear a veil to shield his face.

Matthew tells his audience that Jesus had a similar experience, actually a greater one. So great was this experience that even Moses and the great prophet Elijah paid homage to Jesus as the Son of God. God gave Moses the ten commandments and took Elijah to heaven, but God said that Jesus was his beloved Son.

I heard the Transfiguration story as a child, and over the years I wondered about the disciples' experience. What was it like and what did it mean for them? Then, some years ago, I unexpectedly got an answer to my questions about the transfiguration of the Lord Jesus Christ.

One night, I woke up with a sharp pain in my back and felt nauseated. The pain worsened, and I went to the emergency room. As I waited to see a doctor, the pain became excruciating. I felt lonely and weak with pain.

After I was x-rayed, the chief resident in nephrology spoke to me. He showed me the X-ray picture and pointed to what he said was a kidney stone. Since the stone was moving I did not need surgery. I told him that I could not stand the pain. The doctor said my pain would get worse. He told the nurse to give me a shot of morphine. That was when I had one of the most extraordinary experiences in my life. I suppose some of it was the effect of the morphine. For me, it was an incredibly fantastic gift of God.

I remember lying in the bed in the emergency room. Suddenly there was an extremely bright light, a vertical light about seven feet tall. Although the light was intensely bright, I could look at it. There was a lovely, warm golden glow to it. It was an awesome sight, but I was not afraid. I felt safe. To my amazement, I heard this intense bright light speaking to me: "Roberto, Roberto. You are going to be all right. You will get well. I have much work for you to do." Deep in my heart, I knew it was Jesus Christ speaking to me! Then it was over.

I told no one about my experience. I thought, *If I tell anyone I'll end up in a psychiatric ward.* Six years later I was taking a class on Christian spirituality. I read Saint Teresa of Avila's writings. As I read her life story, I was happily surprised and blessed to read her first experience of the risen Christ.

> One feast day of St. Paul, while I was at Mass, this most sacred humanity in its risen form was represented to me completely, as it is in paintings, with such wonderful beauty and majesty....
>
> The splendor is not one that dazzles; it has a soft whiteness, is infused, gives the most intense delight to the sight, and doesn't tire it; neither does the brilliance, in which is seen the vision of so divine a beauty, tire it. It is a light so different from earthly light that the sun's brightness that we see appears very tarnished in comparison with that brightness and light represented to the sight, and so different that afterward you wouldn't want to open your eyes.... It is a light that has no night; nothing troubles it. In sum, it is of such a kind that a person couldn't imagine what it is like in all the days of his life no matter how powerful an intellect he might have. God gives it so suddenly that there wouldn't even be time to open your eyes, if it were necessary to open them. (Teresa of Avila, *The Book of Her Life* [Washington, D.C.: Institute of Carmelite Studies, 1976], 28.3, 28.5)

I was overcome by Teresa's description of her experience. It reminded me of my experience. Saint Teresa had experienced the risen Christ in all his glory: the brilliant, warm light of love and life. I was not alone in having such an experience. The risen Christ had been revealed to her and to me! I wept with joy. I felt great peace in my life and God's gracious providence touching my life again and again.

It occurred to me that the disciples had a similar experience at the Transfiguration. The Son of the living God, Jesus Christ, was revealed to them. No wonder Peter wanted to build three edifices to commemorate the occasion.

What does my experience mean to me? It means that Jesus Christ died for me to break the power of sin and death over me. It means that after three days Jesus Christ arose. It means that Jesus Christ now lives forever. It means that through Jesus Christ, God loves me, even me, and has a plan for my life!

If you are in pain, if you are lost, if you are living in fear, if you are overcome with problems, if you are drowning in a sea of sin, if you are in darkness and without hope, the Lord Jesus Christ has not forgotten you. The Lord Jesus Christ is waiting to appear in your life and bless you, renew you, fill you with faith, hope, and love. The Lord Jesus Christ in all his glory is waiting to give you new life. The Transfiguration reminds us that in a world of darkness and no hope, the Lord Jesus Christ is the living light and hope for humankind. Those who in faith open their lives to the Lord Jesus Christ find eternal light and a life of hope. Won't you open your life to Jesus Christ, God's beloved Son? (Roberto L. Gómez)

Lectionary Commentary
Exodus 24:12-18

My seminary professor of Old Testament would speak often of God's awesome glory. I caught a hint of that when I saw the Grand Canyon and Mount Olympus. However, it was not until I saw the mind-blowing photographs that the Hubble space telescope took of galaxies and stars that I began to understand a bit more of God's awesome universal glory. Yet God's majesty and glory are revealed in the particularities of our lives. Every time I baptize an infant or celebrate Holy Communion, I am reminded of God's awesome glory in those grace-filled moments of life. Just as Moses went up the mountain and experienced God's awesome glory, we too can experience God's awesome and majestic glory as we live in God's grace.

2 Peter 1:16-21

Years ago, I was emotionally and spiritually burned out, struggling with a congregation in a downward tailspin. The congregation was in a continuing crisis of faith and so was I. My ministry and my family were suffering. In one last act of a smoldering faith, I went to a meeting of clergy friends. The invited speaker had experienced Christ in a powerful, life-changing encounter fueled by the Holy Spirit. He told us about his experience of the majesty of the risen Christ. He was a transformed individual sharing God's love with us. My spirit was touched, healed, and transformed. I left the meeting a changed pastor, renewed and refreshed to serve God. Second Peter 1:16-21 tells us of the early Christian church proclaiming the majesty of our Lord Jesus Christ. As we experience the risen Christ, we too become eyewitnesses of his majesty. (Roberto L. Gómez)

Worship Aids

Call to Worship

The Lord Jesus Christ beckons us to follow him.
We follow him gladly and joyfully.
The Lord Jesus Christ reveals the awesome glory and majesty of God.
We are awestruck and dumbfounded by the beauty and power of God's presence and so we praise God with all our might, mind, and spirit.

Opening Prayer

Dear God, we all look for and want a powerful mountaintop experience to rejoice in your awesome glory and majesty. Yet we often do not make it to the mountaintop with so many distractions and obstacles in life. Remind us that you are not in the earthquakes or the howling winds, but that your voice is a gentle, loving whisper of hope and grace. Amen.

Benediction

May the light of the transfigured Christ shine upon you, guide your journey, and bless you with God's warmth, joy, and peace as you proclaim the love of Jesus Christ by word and deed. Amen. (Roberto L. Gómez)

Jesus' Stimulus Package: Making Ourselves Rich in the Sight of God

First in a Series of Four on the Parables from Luke

Luke 12:13-21

The reader finished the Gospel reading for the day, Luke 12:13-21, and concluded with the words: "This is the word of God for the people of God." The congregation responded: "Thanks be to God." An older gentleman stood, hands holding firmly to the back of the pew in front of him, and said: "I don't know about the rest of ya, but before I say 'thanks' to God for these words, I've gotta think long and hard about 'em." He then sat down and a stunned silence descended upon the congregation.

Perhaps for the first time, the rest of the folks in church that morning were confronted with the reality that the old man named—we really do have to let the words of Scripture sink into our minds and hearts if they are going to have any influence in our lives.

In today's reading from Luke, we find Jesus warning the listeners against all forms of greed. It is what I would call Jesus' stimulus package for making ourselves rich in the sight of God. It is a reading that demands more than an interpretation or exegesis; these words examine and interpret us. For the scriptures we just heard moments ago call us to do one specific thing if we are to allow them to give us a rich insight into God's ways; they call us to guard against all forms of greed.

Who are the greedy? Is it just the rich folks? Is it just the huge, multinational finance conglomerates that prey on the naïveté of the public? Or can it be anyone? Can it also be the small vendor on Main Street who struggles to put food on the table? Could it even be the street person who strives to secure a few coins for the next pack of smokes? Jesus' warning seems to include everyone, no exceptions.

To be greedy means putting self first no matter what our station is. It means to use possessions to better one's life at the expense of others' lives. The man with the barns catered only to himself. He couldn't see the needs of others as his own wants got in the way. Who among us doesn't have to guard against this tendency? Every effort, investment, dream, and longing was valued in direct proportion to his hunger to please himself. While he was getting rich in his own eyes, he was actually becoming impoverished in the presence of God.

71

A larger question might be: In what ways do we adapt to Jesus' stimulus package? What would provide significant stimulus for us to avoid greed?

First, we need to realize that wrestling with greed will always be a part, a nagging part, of our Christian walk. Admitting to ourselves that we are greedy and confessing this is a tremendous first step.

Second, ask God's help. Our first line of defense is God. Without God's help and the guidance of the Holy Spirit, we cannot creatively and genuinely deal with greed.

Third, inventory the ways we judge what we need versus what we want. Another way of putting this is that we need to be transparent stewards, stewards who let God be seen in our actions. Remember the rich man in the story and his inventory: "I will do this: I will pull down my barns and build larger ones, and there I will store all my grain and my goods" (Luke 12:18). "My, my, my" was his litany of greed. Notice the emphasis? His inventory was about what he wanted, not what he needed. God couldn't be seen because it was all about the rich man.

By admitting our selfishness, genuinely seeking God's help, and focusing on needs over wants, we may be able to better guard against greed. Thus empowered, we can begin to see the needs of others!

Greed turns us away from God and other people. It is like having a bank account full of money and a life bankrupt of generosity and compassion. This is why greed is, first and foremost, a spiritual matter that manifests in our actions, actions that will ultimately lead to our demise. If the rich man in Jesus' story had heard these words, I wonder if he would have changed his mind about building larger barns. Maybe not. Perhaps his lust for ownership was too great.

Let us go no further than the inventory of our own lives, asking, "Am I making myself rich in the sight of God?" Like the old man in the worship service, we need to think long and hard about these words. But let's not take too much time and accept the fool's stimulus plan. (Mike Childress)

Worship Aids

Call to Worship
God calls us away from the rigors and demands of the world
    to focus our thoughts on things that last.

We respond to God's call with courage and joy,
   strengthened to be God's servants.
Our worship is a witness to our response. Amen.

Prayer of Confession

Gracious God, you have given us the law of Moses and the teachings of Jesus to direct us in the way of life. You offer us your spirit, so that we can be born to new life as your children. Give us the vision and courage to choose and nurture life, that we may receive your blessing. Amen.

Words of Assurance

By our confession, God readily and willingly forgives us.
By God's grace and the help of the Spirit, our words of confession are not offered in vain.
All: We will do what is necessary that God's justice and righteousness are evident in our lives. Amen. (Mike Childress)

MARCH 9, 2011

Ash Wednesday

Readings: Joel 2:1-2, 12-17; Psalm 51:1-17; 2 Corinthians 5:20b–6:10; Matthew 6:1-6, 16-21

On Repenting
Matthew 6:1-6, 16-21

Thirty-five years ago, a small independent movie became unexpectedly famous. The movie was about a washed-up boxer who gets one more chance to make it. The movie was *Rocky.* The boxer, Rocky Balboa, is a tired, older boxer who has taken too many punches and lost too many fights. His career is over. Then, the world champion, Apollo Creed, offers Rocky a title fight. The champion is using Rocky as one more easy-to-beat opponent, a loser being set up for a loss.

Although everyone knows that Rocky has no chance against the champion, Rocky agrees to the fight. To have a chance to put up a decent fight, Rocky has to overcome many demons: low self-esteem, inconsistency in his workouts, distractions, and bad health habits. In other words, Rocky has to repent of his past just to have the smallest chance to put up a good fight.

Rocky wants so much to fight well that he repents and works as he has never worked before. Fortunately, a few people support and believe in him. Still, it takes all of his courage and will to prepare. Finally, the fight takes place and Rocky succeeds, but only because of his determination to repent and to overcome his background.

Although the world may see us as winners, as leaders, as first-class people, there are moments when we feel, privately, like the old Rocky, especially when it comes to our Christian faith and to spiritual matters. All of us go through experiences that pull us away from God. We might still attend worship, but the truth is that there are times in our lives that we are distracted from our faith.

Matthew 6 addresses our spiritual struggles as we practice our faith. We may think and feel we are doing right, but the truth is that we often miss the mark of faithful obedience to the Lord Jesus Christ.

When we no longer feel that we are children of God, our self-esteem suffers. Our Christian living becomes inconsistent, we are easily distracted from the faith, and over time we develop bad and unhealthy spiritual habits. We become spiritual losers. No one may know how we feel spiritually, but we know and God knows.

When we forget that we are children of God, we feel tremendous loneliness, impotence, and a blandness that covers everything we do. We feel lost and dislocated. We feel unloved and disconnected, sometimes even from those who love us and are close to us. We may feel immense guilt, but sometimes we get so out of touch that we mentally suppress the guilt feeling that could motivate us to repent.

Yet God is merciful and always, as long as we are alive, willing to give us one more chance. It may be that God reaches out to us through an illness, an accident, or a misfortune. It may be that God reaches out to us through a family member or a friend or even a stranger. It may be that God reaches out to us through a song, a Bible reading, a Sunday school lesson, or a sermon. It may be that God reaches out to us while we are on a church project or mission. But God does reach out and give us another chance to remember we are God's beloved children.

When God reaches out to you, perhaps even right now, do you want to be a child of God? Do you want it so much that you are willing to repent of your bad thoughts, your bad attitudes, your bad habits, your distractions, and your negative will? Are you willing to turn back to God and let God be God in your life? Are you willing to experience the love, the joy, and the peace of being a child of God? Are you willing to open your mind and your heart to the presence of God in your life so that all evil thoughts and habits are eliminated and your spirit is made not only clean but also new with the blood of the Lord Jesus Christ?

That is what Ash Wednesday is about: repenting, turning to God, and letting the Lord Jesus Christ wash us clean of all sin and evil so that we can be God's children. God wants us to want to be his children, and God gives each one of us another chance, but we have to do our part: we have to repent and be truly sorry for our mistakes and sins and evil thoughts and bad actions. If we truly repent, then there is new life for us. The Lord Jesus Christ said, "I am the way, and the truth, and the life" (John 14:6).

Being truly alive is being part of God's family, being a child of God. How do you become a child of God? You repent and let God be God of your life. (Roberto L. Gómez)

Lectionary Commentary

Joel 2:1-2, 12-17

The prophet Joel speaks of a dark, stark day of judgment for those who live wayward lives. It is a day of reckoning, of holding people accountable for their sins of commission, of omission, and, as someone said, of "no mission." We love our freedom to do what we want, when we want, and the way we want. Yet Holy Scripture, in this case Joel, vividly reminds us that while we may be free, we are accountable for our thoughts, intentions, and actions. If we have wronged others, then our judgment will be harsh and the punishment will be severe. But God is willing to give us one more opportunity to change, to repent, to return, and to ask for mercy. We may have forgotten God and hurt those around us, but if we recognize our wrongdoing and come to God with a contrite heart and a broken spirit, God will forgive us and give us new life. Even as the Day of Judgment nears, there is hope for salvation.

2 Corinthians 5:20b–6:10

During World War II, the German air force bombed the city of Coventry in England and destroyed the city's electric power station. Several days later the German air force bombed Coventry's cathedral. Without electric power, the firefighters could not operate the water pumps. The people of Coventry watched their magnificent cathedral burn to the ground. After the war, the people of Coventry built a glorious new cathedral next to the ruins of their old cathedral. In the space of the old cathedral there is a statue of a man and a woman kneeling, facing and embracing each other. The statue is called *Reconciliation*. The people of Coventry invited Christians from Germany to join them for a service of reconciliation and for the dedication of the statue.

God's grace truly had a part in bringing together these two former enemies. Such is God's grace revealed in the Lord Jesus Christ, with power to overcome hatred, bigotry, broken trust, anger, and other divisive obstacles between God's children. (Roberto L. Gómez)

March 9, 2011

Worship Aids

Call to Worship

Advent, Christmas, Epiphany, and now, suddenly, it is the beginning of
Lent. Ash Wednesday has arrived.
We know the Lord Jesus Christ overcame death, and he lives.
We forget that he prepared for his suffering and death for our sake.
**God, help us to meditate on your Son's sacrifice
of suffering and death for us.**
Remind us that he became the sacrificial Lamb for our sake.
**In the days that follow, may we take time to reflect
on your pain for us,**
your tears of disappointment and sadness for us,
your hopes and dreams for us, and your willingness to forgive us.

Opening Prayer

Dear God, as we start this season of Lent, help us to reflect on our relationship with you. We know you love us and take care of us as your precious children. Yet we often fall short of the mark. We are easily led
astray by worldly temptations. We forget you and your word for us. We
strike out on our own and get lost in a world of spiritual poverty and
material obsession. Thank you for your patience with us. Help us to
remember your Spirit of grace, peace, and joy that we may choose to be
your obedient people. Amen.

Benediction

As we start this season of Lent, let us remember that God requires contrite hearts and broken spirits. Let us remember who we are: God's children, rebellious and confused, yet seeking love and direction. May God
bless us with love, with the peace of Jesus Christ, and with the communion of the Holy Spirit. Amen. (Roberto L. Gómez)

The Power of God in Small Things

Second in a Series of Four on the Parables from Luke

Luke 13:18-21

What's Jesus up to, anyway? Has he nothing better to do on a sunny
sabbath afternoon than to give gardening and culinary tips? No, Jesus is

simply drawing attention to the obvious and unveiling what is not so obvious. In our text, Jesus gives the people two short but vividly clear pictures of what the reign of God is like in this world. He paints two exceptional scenes on the canvasses of his hearers' minds, hearers who are eager to see just how Jesus is going to deal with what we all find curious and mysterious—what is "the kingdom of heaven" or the "reign of God" really like?

The mustard seed was not the smallest seed known in Jesus' day (the cypress seed was the tiniest). However, the mustard plant, not the cypress, was well known as a nesting and eating place for birds. Its little black seeds provided great nutrition. Its height of almost twelve feet provided protection against predators.

Jesus' use of this little seed was a clear picture for his audience about what powerful things happen when God and people share a relationship. Yes, powerful things happen, but they begin in small ways.

A single idea can grow into a concept that includes hundreds, thousands, even millions of people. One act of kindness can have a ripple effect that touches the masses. A comment of affirmation or encouragement can change a person's, or a people's, life.

As a young boy, I remember watching my neighbor, Mr. Deffenbaugh (not his real name), get out his seed catalog every mid-winter and order his garden seed for the coming year. Like clockwork, this annual ritual never failed to occur. The catalog was crammed with all kinds of seeds, each with its accompanying picture of expected results. Mr. Deffenbaugh would order tomato seeds—Better Girl, Big Boy, Rutgers, and German Reds.

As I recall my neighbor's annual ritual and Jesus' words, I look back and see something that maybe Mr. Deffenbaugh saw in those tomato seeds—in every seed was a plant and on every plant would grow a botanical treasure. Now I don't know if he ever thought that or not, but what I do know is that every year our neighborhood could depend on going to Mr. Deffenbaugh's to get delicious tomatoes!

Jesus' point: In every seed there is a plant. But Jesus isn't talking about mustard or tomatoes. Jesus is talking about seeds planted in the hearts and minds of people.

Christians are seed planters. The seeds we plant yield eternal fruits. Such seeds develop on God's calendar, God's watch, and with God's intended purpose.

I suppose one way to understand or make sense of this is to make some bread. I love making bread. It's one of my favorite things to do when I have the time. Sourdough is my favorite bread to make. It's more time-consuming, but worth the extra effort. I mix flour, warm water, salt, sugar, evaporated milk, eggs, instant potato flakes, and oil in my stainless-steel bowl, and I have a delectable treat.

But, wait. The main ingredient is missing. Leave out the leaven and you don't have bread. All you end up with is a lump of heavy, bland-tasting dough that only makes a good doorstop.

Another important aspect of bread-making, the fermentation period, is an extraordinary and necessary step of successful bread-making. The most extraordinary aspect, though, is not the time it takes to work but how much leaven or yeast it takes to affect the batch of bread. It is the smallest of all the ingredients yet the most potent of them all. It takes only a tiny portion—like the old Brill Cream commercial—"a little dab'll do ya."

Just a little bit of grace goes a long way in God's realm. The transforming power of leaven in bread makes the bread more enjoyable, more delectable. The transforming power of grace makes life more enjoyable, more delectable. So when are we to use this leaven? Anytime, anyplace, with anyone, under any circumstances. Everybody is always hungry for this bread! Everybody is always hungry for grace.

But like the leaven in bread, the leaven of grace (and all the gifts of the Spirit) takes time to do its work. Even without the constraints of the natural world, the leaven of the Spirit needs God's time to work. For example, we can forgive someone, even ourselves, but we must be willing to allow the healing to come on God's watch and God's calendar. Just as the writer of Ecclesiastes notes: "Everything that happens in this world happens at the time God chooses" (3:1 GNT).

Just as we have to wait for the dough to rise and the bread to bake, we are to wait and allow forgiveness to come on God's terms and work in its marvelous and wondrous process, without expecting immediate gratification or reciprocity.

This waiting is part of the power of transformation. This is the leaven's effect in Jesus' parable. Yes, by the end of the two parables, it is obvious what Jesus is up to. What are you and I up to? (Mike Childress)

Worship Aids

Call to Worship
Have you not heard?
Heard what?

Have you not been told?
Told what?
How Jesus of Nazareth went to towns and villages teaching how small things in God's realm are valuable.
We come to worship the God who, through Jesus' example, still calls us to serve in small but powerful ways to make this a better world. Amen.

Prayer of Confession

Almighty God, as the church, we are part of your redeeming work in the world. Yet we know that often we withdraw from taking our place in your healing of many who seek to be released from their diseases. Forgive us. Empower us to step up and take our place in your redeeming work. In the power of your Holy Spirit we pray. Amen.

Words of Assurance

God's redeeming love we still seek. For this Jesus came. This love still travels among us and has claimed us yet again, this morning!
We give thanks to God, to whom all power and glory be given. Amen.
(Mike Childress)

MARCH 13, 2011

❧❧❧

First Sunday in Lent

Readings: Genesis 2:15-17; 3:1-7; Psalm 32; Romans 5:12-19; Matthew 4:1-11

Life Instead of Death
Romans 5:12-19

When I was young, one of my duties was to take care of my younger brothers. When one or both made a mess, I was responsible for cleaning it up. I hated cleaning up after them, and they messed up often when they were under my care. We all have been called upon to clean up someone else's mess from time to time. Sometimes those messes are small and can be taken care of quickly, but sometimes the messes are huge and take lots of time and energy to clean up. Messes can happen anywhere, in any kind of situation. In the business world, some CEOs specialize in fixing businesses that were ruined by a former CEO. Messes happen in school districts, in hospitals, in city government, and in any enterprise that involves human beings.

The lectionary lesson for today is about the man who made the biggest spiritual mess of all time. The first man, Adam, messed up big-time when he and his wife disobeyed God. Their sin caused them to be kicked out of Paradise and to eventually suffer death. Adam's spiritual mess was so big that it has affected all of his descendants, meaning all of us here today, you and me. We are all born into a sinful condition, separated from God, and destined to die. Saint Augustine put it grimly: "When a man is born, he is already born with death, because he contracts sin from Adam" (Gerald Bray, ed., *Ancient Christian Commentary on Scripture: New Testament VI: Romans* [Downers Grove, Ill.: InterVarsity Press, 1998], 137).

Moses offered a response to Adam's mess by introducing the concept of law and the ten commandments. Before the idea of law, the concept of sin was vague. With the concept of law, sin became crystal clear. However, while law defined sin, it did nothing to help humanity overcome sin. Adam's mess was defined but not cleaned up.

The point that Paul makes in Romans 5:12-19 is that the Lord Jesus Christ cleaned up Adam's mess. Indeed, Paul refers to Jesus as the second Adam who came to undo what the first Adam did. Whereas Adam was disobedient, the Lord Jesus Christ was perfect in his obedience to God. Oecumenius, an ancient church father of the sixth century, said the following:

> Christ's obedience was greater than Adam's disobedience in the follow-
> ing sense. Death, which originated with the sin of Adam, had our coop-
> eration in the sins which we all committed, and so it was able to gain
> control over us. For if men had remained free of all wrongdoing, death
> would not have been in control. But the grace of Christ has come to us
> all without our cooperation and shows that the grace of the resurrection
> is such that not only believers, who glory in their faith, will be resur-
> rected, but also unbelievers, both Jews and Greeks. (Gerald Bray, ed.,
> *Ancient Christian Commentary on Scripture: New Testament VI: Romans*
> [Downers Grove, Ill.: InterVarsity Press, 1998], 145)

Paul reminds us of how Adam messed up spiritually so that the world is now in a state of sin and spiritual death. But Paul does not stop there, he goes on to proclaim the good news that the second Adam, the Lord Jesus Christ, broke the power of sin, brought new life, and cleaned up Adam's mess.

What does this mean to you and to me? It means that there is hope for us. It means that we do not have to be mired in sin; we no longer have to wallow in a life of despair and isolation from God's love, joy, and peace. It means that while we may never be perfectly obedient, the one who was perfectly obedient has paid the price for us, has forgiven us, and has worked to reconcile us with God.

Paul's letter to the Romans also offers the following:

> For while we were still weak, at the right time Christ died for the
> ungodly. Indeed, rarely will anyone die for a righteous person—though
> perhaps for a good person someone might actually dare to die. But God
> proves his love for us in that while we still were sinners Christ died for
> us. (Romans 5:6-8)

A young man lived a disordered life that kept him far from God. He met and married a Christian young woman. She loved God, prayed daily, and was faithful in attending church. She invited him to attend worship and he refused, but one day, out of curiosity, he went to church with his wife. To his surprise he liked it. He began attending church. Then he had a personal encounter with the Lord Jesus Christ that changed his life. He realized he had been spiritually dead but now was alive in the Lord Jesus Christ. His family life greatly improved. He has become a servant of the Lord Jesus. His life is now one of much happiness and blessing.

The Lord Jesus is the Lord of the living and comes to give you life in abundance. Open your mind and heart to the Lord Jesus. Let the Lord Jesus break the power of sin over you. Let the Lord Jesus free you from the hold of sin over your soul and mind. Come to the Lord Jesus and live the life God wants you to live. (Roberto L. Gómez)

Lectionary Commentary
Genesis 2:15-17; 3:1-7

We all struggle with temptation. Genesis 2 and 3 remind us that the first man and woman, Adam and Eve, were both tempted, even when God gave them a specific, direct rule. Sadly, Adam and Eve gave in to their first temptation. Their story also illustrates that giving in to temptation has consequences, although we may never think about them as we are being tempted. Temptation is a reality in our daily lives. How we learn to cope with and overcome temptation is one of the great challenges in life; it requires spiritual discipline. The Lord Jesus Christ promised his followers the Holy Spirit, who gives us gifts and the grace to learn and live spiritually disciplined lives.

Matthew 4:1-11

In a parable Jesus said that a house built on sand would not last; only a house built on rock would survive storms. In his own life, Jesus demonstrated that his life was built on a solid, eternal foundation—God's love. Before he starts his ministry, Jesus goes into the desert and faces his temptations of material hunger, attraction to fame, and lust for power. Satan directly challenges Jesus. Jesus deals with and overcomes Satan's temptations because his life is based on God's love. The good news is that Jesus invites us to have such a relationship with God, one based on love—true, holy, and eternal love—that will be our solid foundation during the storms of life. (Roberto L. Gómez)

Worship Aids

Call to Worship

People of God, hear the Lord's call
   to worship, serve, pray, share gifts, and proclaim the good news.
We hear the Lord's call to ministry, and we try to follow,
   but the temptations of material gain, fame, and power are so strong
   and attractive,
   we go astray.
If we ask, God will give us the Holy Spirit
   to remain faithful and to overcome the most powerful and attractive
   temptations.
Come, Holy Spirit, fill our hearts with your fire and power
   and bind us to God's love for faithful discipleship.

Opening Prayer

Dear God, as we start this holy season of Lent, we marvel at your holy
patience with us. We lament our lack of faith and discipleship. We know
you love us. We know about our call to faithful discipleship. Yet we stumble easily, we lose our way, and we fail to be your obedient children. We
come to worship recognizing our spiritual weaknesses and asking for
mercy. We remember your forgiving Spirit. Therein is our hope. We
praise you and worship you. Amen.

Benediction

We came to worship God, who gives us new life. We do not have to live
like Adam, separated from God and living a life of physical, emotional,
and spiritual deprivation. The Lord Jesus Christ blesses us with his
redeeming grace, and the Holy Spirit showers us with abundant spiritual
gifts as a people of God. We can go forth, knowing that God is at our side,
blessing us each moment. Amen. (Roberto L. Gómez)

Something Worth Celebrating

Third in a Series of Four on the Parables from Luke

Luke 15:1-10

I recall growing up and hearing my parents talk about a fellow my dad
worked with. The man worked hard. He was always at the job on time,

rarely took days off, and accepted every offer of overtime work. He went to church faithfully, paid his taxes, and worked hard so his children could have the necessary things for school in order to succeed. But he had a problem. He was an alcoholic who took his anger out on his family, violently and abusively. The community was shocked when this family's problem was exposed. It seemed a foregone conclusion that his wife would divorce him and take the children, or that the family would just move as far away as possible to avoid ridicule, embarrassment, and isolation.

But something extraordinary happened. The man began the journey of recovery. In those days alcoholism wasn't seen as the illness it is known to be today. Alcoholics Anonymous (AA) was basically unknown and only slightly supported in our hometown. But the man got on board with AA and the results were amazing. No more drunken displays of violence, no more hiding from the problem but accepting it as something to work through. Everyone in town who knew the family was overwhelmed by the changes. The man's countenance and carriage all demonstrated that a major life-changing experience had taken place. His closest friends, coworkers, and church members all celebrated his new life direction. As he put it on one occasion, "My life has been saved."

In 1985, when my wife and I were in seminary, my parents made their first visit to Louisville, Kentucky. During their stay, my wife planned a shopping excursion to downtown Louisville. Our entourage of about ten people, including our toddler daughter, arrived at the downtown mall and began what we thought would be a simple outing. Our daughter would prove otherwise. In one of the huge department stores, we split into two groups and agreed to rendezvous at the store's rear entrance in precisely one hour. We all completed our shopping and met up at the store exit—everyone but our four-year-old daughter. Each group thought that she had been with the other group.

Frantically we began our search. An all-points bulletin had been sounded throughout the store, even out in the mall area. Running down each and every aisle proved unproductive. She was nowhere to be found. We stopped person after person, showed them her picture, and asked if they had seen our daughter. By this time, a few of us were in tears. Then, as several of us stayed put in the middle of the store, to intercept her should she come through the store, a little hand reached out and touched me on the kneecap. She had been hiding for more than a half hour under a carousel of children's dresses. She peeked out and laughed. Well, you can imagine our response. No one could keep their hands off of her. We had found her at last. Our worst fears had not happened. A huge roar of applause and adulation filled the department store over the recovery.

Some may be quick (and correct) to point out how easy it is to celebrate those we love, especially when they have been lost or in trouble, but what about those whom we don't especially love? How do we celebrate them?

According to the parable in Luke, Jesus has no problem eating with those the writer describes as "tax collectors and sinners" (Luke 15:1), the unlovable of their day. I believe Luke wants us to see something truly extraordinary about those with whom God keeps company and about God through Jesus' life. So we have to ask, whom would Jesus welcome in our own day and time? Who are the hated and despised among us today? Terrorists? People of other religions? People different from us? I suspect that many of us would be just as shocked as the Pharisees to discover whom Jesus would befriend. If Jesus' life is the model for our lives, and if the central purpose of the church is to welcome sinners and eat with them, then how prepared are we to live the life of faith?

What happened in my dad's friend's life and losing our daughter on a shopping trip are not just personal stories about losing something or someone precious to us. They, like the parables, speak to a much larger concern. Such episodes happen all over the world each day. Has a false security—that nothing like that can happen to us—prevented us from seeing the value of finding people where they are in life and joining God's search party? Real people, the good and the bad, still get lost or lose their way in this life. How do we know this? We have only to visit our own lives to know this truth.

One of the best ways I've heard of describing the church's central purpose of joining God's search is a story about a little girl who was lost. In her book *Traveling Mercies*, Anne Lamott tells how the little girl was frightened, but a policeman stopped to help her. He put her in his car and drove around the neighborhood until she finally saw her church. "You could let me out now. This is my church, and I can always find my way home from here." Lamott concludes, "And that is why I have stayed so close to mine—because no matter how bad I am feeling, how lost or lonely or frightened, when I see the faces of the people at my church...I can always find my way home" (Anne Lamott, *Traveling Mercies* [New York: Random House, 2000], 55).

May God give us the strength, the insight and foresight, and the faith, to join God's search and not exclude any person in our daily living. In our sometimes frantic, anxious, even selfish moments of living, may we be reminded of those around us like the man in my hometown, our daughter lost on a shopping trip, or the little girl needing a policeman's help. May we stop, turn, and remember that there are those who are being left behind or forgotten, and may we hear God calling us to go back and find them where they are. This will be something worth celebrating! (Mike Childress)

Worship Aids

Call to Worship
Welcome, sojourners.
Welcome!
Sometimes it is more difficult to cross a busy intersection than to travel cross-country.
Sometimes it is harder to forgive a neighbor than to welcome a stranger.
But God teaches us that we should welcome the stranger as we would welcome Jesus Christ.
However far we have come this week,
    we bring the gift of ourselves—our minds, our compassion, our love, and our devotion.
Let us continue our journey together.

Prayer of Confession
O God, you have called us to live as Christ lives. It is difficult. We confess to you and to ourselves how often we fall short of Christ's example. Cleanse and renew us, that we may know the joy of your presence and be bearers of your light, through the grace of Jesus Christ. Amen.

Words of Assurance
Hear the good news! God has forgiven each one of us
    and calls us to take our parts in the drama of redeeming love.
Praise God, who accepts and uses our very human lives
    in the unfolding story of salvation and new life! (Mike Childress)

MARCH 20, 2011

Second Sunday in Lent

Readings: Genesis 12:1-4a; Psalm 121; Romans 4:1-5, 13-17;
John 3:1-17

We Know...Nothing
John 3:1-17

You are a day or two from graduation, and the registrar grabs you and
tells you there is a math class you signed up for and forgot to attend, but
you have to pass the class to graduate and you have to take the final to
pass and you have not been to class all semester and you run to find your
place in a chilly, hard seat in a room as cold as a morgue. The professor
glides toward you like the grim reaper, the exam in his hand as good as a
scythe, and you look at the exam and it could be hieroglyphics or the
extra-credit question for Honors Chinese for all the sense you can make
of it, and you look up to see all the other students staring at you, laugh-
ing at you. Your chest heaves, your heart all but stops, you feel incredibly
vulnerable, exposed...and then you wake up. Night terrors, they are
called, and all of us have them.

I do not know for sure, but I imagine that is something of what
Nicodemus experienced that night he came to see Jesus.

The story is a familiar one, perhaps too familiar. How many times have
we read or heard this story? How many sermons have been preached on
this nocturnal encounter between Jesus, the up-country Rabbi, and
Nicodemus, the representative of religious education, authority, and tradition? Many times, I would venture to say, and rightly so. It is one of the
crucial stories in John's presentation of his Gospel. There is no way that
any one sermon can do it justice: there are just too many important
details in this text. Every word makes a difference. But sometimes we just
race by as we read and hear, imagining that we already know what Jesus
is saying here and to whom. Let's slow down.

Nicodemus, a ruler or leader of the Jews—a Pharisee, himself a teacher and a powerful one too, a recognized religious authority—comes to Jesus by night.

Why "by night"? My father, a weekend preacher, opined that, as both men were busy, perhaps night was the only time they could meet. A New Testament professor said the meeting time indicated Nicodemus's caution: What would other officials, and even the common folk, think of him if Nicodemus were discovered conversing with Jesus? Could be. There could be other explanations as well.

In the Gospel of John, however, "night" tells more than time. The evangelist uses "night," and also "darkness," to reveal something deeper and truer than a clock could. Night is a metaphor as well as a marker, and in John, many people are in the dark (John 13:30).

"Rabbi," Nicodemus says, "we know that you are a teacher who has come from God…" (John 3:2).

Who is "we"? Other Pharisees? Members of the Sanhedrin? Closeted believers? Possibly. Or maybe Nicodemus uses the cover of "we know" for what is far more likely the truth of the matter: "I don't know." Nicodemus is "in the dark," does not know who Jesus is or what Jesus' words and miracles mean. They must mean something—"No one can do these signs that you do apart from the presence of God" (John 3:2)—but Nicodemus cannot make sense of it all.

It turns out Nicodemus is much like Jesus' other followers, those who saw him command the wind and sea and exclaimed, "Who then is this?" (Mark 4:41). Nicodemus, in the dark, comes with a protest of knowledge that belies the truth: "I do not know who you are." He is trying desperately to fit Jesus into his view of things—to fit Jesus into the long line of teachers, prophets, whatever—one more in the sequence.

Jesus' response sounds like an answer even though Nicodemus has yet to ask a question. Jesus says, "No one can see the kingdom of God without being born from above" (John 3:3). It is with that statement most sermons on this text begin and end, an evangelistic word offered (sometimes arrogantly and almost always condescendingly) to unbelievers, atheists, skeptics, pagans.

But look at the titles Nicodemus holds. In verse 10, Jesus calls Nicodemus a "teacher of Israel"—like preachers and Christian educators are teachers of the church.

In verse 1, Nicodemus is called a "leader of the Jews," which is to say an elected official, an administrative officer. He has responsibilities in the day-to-day operation of the synagogue and Jewish governance—not altogether dissimilar to our trustees, or church council, or other elected officers.

In verse 1, Nicodemus is identified as a "Pharisee," which is to say he is recognized as a faithful person. The Pharisees studied, tithed, prayed, made God a part of their everyday lives. Does that sound like anyone you know?

Jesus says to Nicodemus—not to an atheist or nonbeliever, not to a skeptic or pagan, but to a faithful Pharisee, to a leader of the Jews, to a teacher of Israel—unless you are born again, you will not see the kingdom of God.

Familiar as this text is, and as comforting in a way, if we look deeply, we find it to be frightening as well, for we are the ones who so often come to Jesus saying, "Lord, I know who you are...I know what you want." When I say such a thing or think such a thing, I prove only that I too am in the dark, that I do not know at all.

I am unprepared for the exam, I admit it. I have missed too many classes, and maybe you have too. I look at this book and it might sometimes be hieroglyphics, advanced Chinese. I do not understand the first thing, can't answer the first question, and the final exam is looming. And yet in Jesus we just might have the opportunity to experience God's grace. God help my unbelief. (Thomas R. Steagald)

Lectionary Commentary
Genesis 12:1-4a

The covenant history begins here with the call of Abram. It is not the first covenant God has formed with the earth or its people, but in this story God sets apart Abram and his descendants for specific responsibilities in the world.

The "faith" of Abram is often highlighted in sermons on this text, but the critical Lenten theme of mortification is given slight attention. The command, "Go from your country and your kindred and your father's house" (Genesis 12:1), is a terrible summons—and foreshadows the not dissimilar mandate, "Take your son, your only son Isaac, whom you love...and offer him there as a burnt offering on one of the mountains" (Genesis 22:2). The call to faith is always a call to loss as well as to gain, and the harsh edges of God's will are no sharper anywhere than in this text.

Romans 4:1-5, 13-17

Abram was not yet a father (at least with Sarai) when God changed his name to *Abraham*, meaning "father of many nations." It was a name bigger than Abram's experience or imagination (like a suit of clothes he would have to grow into), and Abram dared believe that what God said was true.

"Nevertheless" is shorthand for faith: believing in the face of evidence to the contrary. Abraham went where God directed him, and he believed what God told him. When age, experience, and conventional wisdom might have told him to stay at home and forget raising a family at his age, he obeyed and trusted as a kind of "nevertheless." (Thomas R. Steagald)

Worship Aids

Opening Sentences (based on Psalm 121)

I will lift up my eyes to the hills.
From where will my help come?
Our help comes from the LORD,
who made heaven and earth.

Invocation

O Lord, keeper of Israel and guardian of our souls, you neither slumber nor sleep but are ever vigilant to keep us from all evil. Lead us through the wilderness of our days to the fullness of your promises. Through Jesus Christ, our Lord. Amen.

Benediction

Now let us go from this place into the world, and may we who share in the faith of Abraham, who are blessed to be heirs of the covenant and rich on account of God's promises, be a channel of blessing to others. Amen. (Thomas R. Steagald)

When the Church Makes a Difference

Fourth in a Series of Four on the Parables from Luke

Luke 12:49-56

I recall a friend telling me years ago about a minister giving a retirement sermon at the end of a long and successful ministry. When the minister reached the end of his sermon, he paused, looked out over his large con-gregation, and proceeded to apologize for having done the gospel a disserv-ice by trying to make ministry too easy. Now, I am not too sure that's the way I would have wanted to end a sermon on my retirement Sunday. It took a lot of courage to say that. Moreover, it took a lot of faith. Perhaps the minister had asked himself something that all of us must at some time ask: Is the church making a difference in its community, in its mission life? Is it the kind of difference with which God is pleased?

Do we reflect our vision of the church: a community of people who make a difference because we follow the one who came to make a differ-ence and did so? Jesus intended to make a difference, and God still intends for the church to do the same.

Perhaps the retiring minister was disappointed that he did not chal-lenge the church enough to light and feed faith's fire. A church commu-nity can die, in fact needs to die, when it doesn't kindle faith's fires. It needs to die to the things that entice us to believe that faith is easy and part-time. It needs to die to those things that minimize the disciplines of faith and magnify simplicity and casualness. I wonder if that minister had realized that, although the church had lots of members, its faith had not really grown spiritually under his leadership.

A church that makes a difference in people's lives is a church that kin-dles and rekindles its members' faith in God and challenges them to live out Jesus' teachings of justice and peace. As a pastor, it is sometimes tempting to think that if I try hard enough, I can give you faith, the kind of faith I want you to have. But I cannot do this. Jesus couldn't give peo-ple faith either. God cannot give people faith. It is something that has to be worked out, struggled with, developed, and shared.

I think that we don't really want a growing faith because it costs time, energy, and our very lives. It can even cost us friends and family members. When was the last time you differed with a loved one? Didn't it hurt? Do you recall the last time you had to stand firm on what you believe in direct contradiction with what your spouse or child or mom believes? A growing faith cannot help but make a difference in our lives, and sometimes that affects those closest to us. Jesus knew this to be true; and it still is the truth today. When Jesus told the crowd he was bringing fire and division, I think he was telling them that the faith in God that costs something, that moves us and inspires us to struggle, is the kind of faith God wants us to have.

A church that makes a difference in people's lives helps us understand and deal with this. But I want to say something that may not sit too well with us: we cannot build this kind of faith by attending worship just one day a week for an hour. Sunday churchgoing alone will not grow the kind of faith Jesus came to live and die for. When we encourage people to think that an occasional visit is all they need for a life of faith, we yield "sour grapes." When we allow people to think that faith requires no life commitment to God, we destroy our churches. If this is the church with which we are satisfied, then we offer nothing to God that can help make a difference in this world.

The church that makes a difference in people's lives does all it can to offer God's physical and spiritual nourishment. This takes commitment beyond Sunday morning. When we prepare to discern God's will and to pay the cost in time, energy, and devotion to give all of ourselves to making a difference, that's when we can actually do something about that which is destroying people's lives.

Think of it. Jesus, a simple carpenter, lived in a town most people despised—Nazareth. He was a carpenter who left his trade and became an itinerant preacher, proclaiming the good news of God's love and grace. He was a person who believed in the power of God to change people and situations, who believed that what he was doing would help God change the world, help God save the world.

What a faith! This is the kind of faith God wants to help us develop. This kind of faith makes a difference and must be developed within the church.

Let us work, let us give, let us pray for the church to be a community that learns how to interpret the times of our generation and then goes about making a difference in this world. Let us seek God's help in doing all we can to rekindle the fires of faith. (Mike Childress)

Worship Aids

Call to Worship

Come now and worship the Lord our God, maker of heaven and earth!
Gathered and grateful, we honor the Lord.
Come now and celebrate new life in our Lord Jesus Christ!
Gathered with open hearts and open minds, we worship our God.

Prayer of Confession

Loving God, we confess we have made a mess of our lives. Holding tightly to our hurts, we covet past injuries. We fail to admit our own brokenness.

Grant us the courage to let go of every crippling emotion that keeps us from you and others. Grant us the peace to face with grace all of life. Amen.

Words of Assurance

God has called us and will lead us.
Through Christ, we trust that God loves us and will always be with us.
Arise, then, people of God! We are free.
Our future is open and assured by the love of our Redeemer. Amen.
(Mike Childress)

MARCH 27, 2011

Third Sunday in Lent

Readings: Exodus 17:1-7; Psalm 95; Romans 5:1-11; John 4:5-42

Three Times a Loser
John 4:5-42

There is a hunger deep in every heart, a deep craving for forgiveness and hope, a sense that our best days are not all behind us, that God has not given up on us even if we have in some ways given up on ourselves. I believe we all crave some token of God's presence in what often seems a godforsaken world.

Our Gospel lesson for this morning, the "Woman at the Well," is such a token, I think. It is a familiar text and just as important in John's telling of his Gospel as last week's story of Nicodemus. The two stories are a couplet, in fact, mirror images of each other, meant to be read side by side. One cannot help noticing the many similarities and differences too.

Look at the characters of the two stories: "Nicodemus" and "the woman." She is not named, which is significant. If the designation makes her anonymous in one way, it also makes her representative. We cannot excuse ourselves from this story by imagining that what Jesus said or did applies only to her.

In addition, obviously, unlike Nicodemus she is a woman. That Jesus talked to women at all, even taught women, scandalized the Pharisees, who were known to thank God they had been born men.

She is a Samaritan, moreover, while Nicodemus was a Jew. Jews had no dealings with Samaritans (think apartheid or Jim Crow). Jews considered Samaritans half-breeds, pagans, heretics, and apostates. Samaritans, like all persecuted peoples, considered themselves the true witnesses to God, the builders of God's true temple on Mount Gerizim. Jews and Samaritans hated each other both racially and religiously.

Nicodemus is a three-time winner and insider: he is a Pharisee, a leader of the Jews (meaning an elected official), and he is a teacher of Israel. The woman is as outside as Nicodemus is in: not only because she is a woman, and a Samaritan woman besides, but she is a sinful Samaritan woman at that—married and divorced so many times she doesn't even bother with the ceremony anymore—ostracized by the other women, by the other *Samaritan* women; that's when you know it is bad.

Nicodemus, whatever his reasons, comes to Jesus by night. Jesus comes to the woman by day. She draws her water when no one else does—is she slovenly? Afraid of the other women's reproaches? Jesus had come to Samaria on purpose. Most Jews avoided that part of the world. Jesus sits down at Jacob's well; he is there when the disgraced woman arrives. This could be awkward. Grace, it seems, always is.

One last difference: Nicodemus doesn't get it. He says he knows that Jesus is a "teacher who has come from God" (John 3:2), but even the way he makes the assertion tells you that he knows little or nothing. The woman, on the other hand, does get it: "Sir, I see that you are a prophet" (4:19). She says that in response to Jesus when he reveals to her the sin and brokenness in her life.

Jesus does not tell her anything she does not know about herself—prophets generally tell people what they already know—but the way Jesus tells her the truth, without the least bit of condescension, and the fact that he is talking to her at all in spite of her sin and shame, reveals to her that he is something special. Something different. Not the typical prejudiced Jew. Not the typical judgmental rabbi. Not the typical self-righteous religious leader. Not the typical man.

No surprise, then, that later, when their conversation turns to the coming of the Messiah—and the woman says, "I know that Messiah is coming" (4:25), and Jesus says, "I am he" (v. 26)—she believes him. She goes back to town, finds the ones who have shunned her, and says, "He cannot be the Messiah, can he?" (v. 29). Even the way she asks the question tells you she believes it to be so.

Nicodemus leaves confused. The woman leaves, what, liberated? Saved? "[He] told me everything I have ever done," she says (v. 29). What an interesting line from the lips of this sinful Samaritan woman.

Despite the culture of affirmation that characterizes our day, most people already know that they are flawed, that their lives are full of misdeeds and missed opportunities, that they have fallen short not only of the glory of God but also of their own expectations. I once heard a sociologist of religion put it this way: Everyone, believer and nonbeliever alike, believes in sin. Not everyone, however, believes in forgiveness.

Jesus does. He looks at the woman at the well with compassion and says, in effect, "You are a mess." She knows she is a mess. Everyone knows she is a mess. If Jesus couldn't see it, he would be the only one. But to be sure, Jesus sees.

Jesus sees that we are a mess too. Not like her, exactly, but like her in many ways. We need what only Jesus can provide: grace that does not ignore our sin but is greater than our sin, forgiveness that does not pretend what we have done or left undone is any different than what it is—sin—but he forgives us anyway.

That is what Jesus means to the woman at the well, grace greater than her sin. That is why she feels liberated, saved, so excited that she is compelled to share it, to tell someone.

I think we all hunger for the presence of Jesus. Not for false affirmation, but for proof of God's presence in our lives—forgiveness and hope, bread and wine, the water of life.

"If you had asked me," Jesus said to the woman, "I would have given you living water." She said, "Sir, give me this water" (4:15); and Jesus did. And Jesus will. There are holes in your bucket, but not to worry; the water Jesus gives is healing water, restoring water, more than you can lose in a lifetime, welling up to eternal life. (Thomas R. Steagald)

Lectionary Commentary
Exodus 17:1-7

There was too much water at the Red Sea, not enough water in the wilderness; it is always something, of course. A teacher of mine once said, "When people do not know what went wrong, they will decide *who* went wrong." That seems to be the case with the Israelites and Moses. The same teacher said, "When people do not know what to do, they will do what they know." Indeed. The Israelites know how to do slavery. They know how to complain. They long for the very bondage from which they have been freed, and they blame Moses for their "predicament." It is through this suffering, however, that they will learn obedience and trust until they find their truest freedom at last in the land God will show them.

Romans 5:1-11

I have people in my church who "boast in [their] sufferings" (Romans 5:3), but not always as Paul means here. For some, in other words, the "suffering" is the object of the boasting itself, whereas for Paul the sufferings show forth the love and mercy of Jesus. The sufferings, related to the privations Paul experiences on account of the gospel, provide rich new access to the presence of God. In this Lenten season, the idea of "suffering for Jesus" in some way—whether through voluntary mortifications or unimagined circumstances—is a powerful entry into this text, and a helpful corrective to "prosperity theology" on the one side and narcissism on the other. (Thomas R. Steagald)

Worship Aids

Call to Worship
O come, let us sing to the Lord!
Let us make a joyful noise to the rock of our salvation!
For the Lord is a great God,
A great King above all gods!

Collect
O God, whose love has been poured into our hearts by the Holy Spirit, look upon our emptiness in mercy and compassion, and provide those gifts we need to be strong and faithful in your service through Jesus Christ, who suffered the loss of all things for our sake. Amen.

Benediction
The Lord is our God. We are God's people. In God's hands are the depths of the earth, and in God's heart is provision for the depth of our need. Amen. (Thomas R. Steagald)

The Model of Prayer

First in a Series of Four on Great Prayers of the Bible

Matthew 6:9-15

Growing up in a noncreedal denomination, there were very few instances in my home church when the congregation collectively spoke during our worship services. We rarely even read the responsive readings printed in light and dark in the back of our hymnals. We did, however, recite the Lord's Prayer from time to time, and I remember the power of those words ringing through our small country church. It was as if a light switch had suddenly been turned on as the entire community of faith spoke those familiar words together.

Since my childhood in that little church, I have spoken those words many times in many different groups of believers, feeling each time that sense of community and awe at the power of the voices united in prayer. Yet, as is the danger of any tradition, I realize that at times I am lost in that warm and fuzzy feeling of reciting the prayer alongside my sisters and brothers in Christ. Many times, the very words that Jesus gave as the model for prayer become merely words spoken or sung as part of our worship service.

Jesus' instructions on which the Lord's Prayer is based are found in Matthew 6:9-15 (see also Luke 11). The instructions are found in the Sermon on the Mount, a series of teachings by Jesus on various matters of faith. Much of the sermon is an admonition on taking faith to a new level, beyond what the most pious of the day were doing. Although many of the Pharisees and priests were hyper-religious, Jesus encouraged believers to attain a new level of sincerity and humility in their faith. The beginning of chapter 6 covers the importance of humility and genuineness in offering and prayer. It encourages believers to avoid what must have been common prayer practices of the day, the loud, showy prayers of the Pharisees and the overly wordy prayers of some of the Gentiles. Jesus gave a model for the personal prayer of the believer.

Finding materials for further study on the Lord's Prayer is not difficult. Entire books, Bible studies, and sermon series have been committed to those five verses in Matthew. The prayer's recitation is perhaps one of the most acceptable ecumenical practices among Christians. The prayer is an acknowledgment of God's sovereignty and power and of our own need for the sovereign God to be involved in our lives.

The words remind us not only of God's participation in our daily lives but also of the importance of forgiveness—God's forgiveness of us and our forgiveness of others. Even the very first words remind us that the God of the universe has a familial connection to us. Jesus offers a model for prayer, understanding our human need for direction in the best way to connect to our God, and foreshadowing God's desire for a new kind of relationship with creation.

As significant as this model of prayer is for believers today, I think that it's important to point out several things about the passage. First of all, Jesus never calls it the "Lord's Prayer" or instructs the group to recite the words together in a communal worship situation. Even in Luke, when the prayer model is given in response to one of the disciple's inquiry on how to pray, it is intended as a model and not as the actual words they should speak. I am not suggesting that we not recite the Lord's Prayer together as believers. However, I think that Jesus, because of the religious practices he observed, would have been leery of communal recitations, even of his own teaching. Jesus was concerned about understanding and practice, not the parroting of his words.

Second, the warnings about prayer given by Jesus earlier in chapter 6 are significant in relation to the Lord's Prayer. Jesus warns against words that are merely loud or numerous and encourages an attitude of reverence and repentance in his model for prayer.

As we look at great prayers of the Bible, the Lord's Prayer easily tops the list for Christians. Jesus' instructions on prayer struck our founding parents of faith so significantly that those instructions are a powerful part of our Christian tradition today. It is important, however, to remember that these words are more than a group recitation or theme song. They are also not magic words that need to be spoken exactly in order for genuine prayer to take place. They are words exemplifying God's desire for communication with us.

I have encountered many believers, from children to adults, who do not know how to pray, and even who wonder about the necessity of prayer. Like me, these same people have probably recited the Lord's Prayer dozens of times, and yet have missed Jesus' intended message. It is about attitude. It is about acknowledging that God is bigger than we are. It is about seeking God's will even as it sometimes transcends our own understanding. It is about communicating every part of who we are to our Creator, from our everyday concerns to our need for forgiveness and to forgive. We are challenged every time we pray, individually and communally, to consider this model, not merely as an equation for faith but as a way to balance our own human desires and needs as we seek providence.

Tradition is a great thing. As believers, our Christian traditions transcend generations and connect us to those very believers who first followed Jesus. Of the many traditions no longer shared in our denominationally separated world, the Lord's Prayer is one of the best ecumenical practices. Its words are recognized and remembered regardless of geography or denomination. As powerful as the tradition is, we must be careful not to relegate the words of Christ to mere tradition. These words are instructions on how we can best communicate with our Creator. (Tracey Allred)

Worship Aids

Pastoral Prayer

Our God, we come to you this day, praising you for our lives and our world. You are our Creator and friend, and we acknowledge your abiding love in our presence. As we enter this time of worship in our community this morning, we have much on our minds. (*Speak the praises and concerns of the people.*)

We also recognize our individual need to communicate with you even as we enter this time of community. We offer these individual words to you as well. (*Give a few moments of silence for individual prayer.*)

Oh, Christ, we acknowledge the imperfection of our motives and our words, but we seek you this day as we pray using the words you gave . . . (*Repeat Lord's Prayer together.*)

Children's Message—The Recipe

Bring ingredients for a cake. Ask children how they would use them to make a cake. Have a couple of children share what they would do. Explain that there are many ways to make a cake and many different uses for the ingredients and tools you brought. Show them a recipe for cake. Explain that although you don't always need a recipe for a cake, a recipe is necessary if you don't know how to make a cake.

Read aloud the Lord's Prayer from Matthew. Explain that Jesus was instructing the crowd on how to live a Christian life. Because many of them did not how to pray, and because some of their leaders were not offering them the best example, they needed instructions. In many ways, this prayer is like a recipe for a cake.

Benediction

Now, go in peace and wisdom, ready to embrace the world with the words of Christ planted firmly in your heart. Amen. (Tracey Allred)

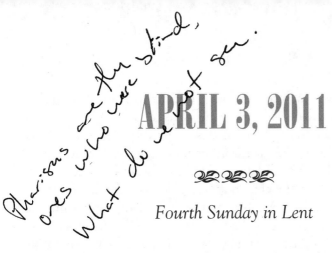

APRIL 3, 2011

Fourth Sunday in Lent

Readings: 1 Samuel 16:1-13; Psalm 23; Ephesians 5:8-14; John 9:1-41

There Are None So Blind . . .
John 9:1-41

In *Rinkitink in Oz*, the tenth of L. Frank Baum's books about the "over the rainbow" land and its people, the father of Rinkitink's companion, Prince Inga, gave to the king and his son three magic pearls as they began the journey the book comprises. One pearl conveyed strength, one victory, and the third wisdom. The first time it was consulted the third pearl said, "Never question the truth of what you fail to understand, for the world is filled with wonders" (*Rinkitink in Oz* [Sioux Falls, S.D.: NuVision, 2008], 12).

But of course, people often prove more foolish than wise. The Pharisees in the story of the man blind from birth questioned the truth of this "sign"—Jesus' healing of a blind man—but before we get too critical, let us confess that we can be just like them.

I once heard a leadership speaker say: "When people do not know what to do, they will do what they know." Here's support for this maxim from Kathleen Norris: "In feeling rejected, I learned to reject, and became far too good at it; I have declined to accept even many of the good things that might have come my way in life" (*Acedia and Me: A Marriage, Monks, and a Writer's Life* [New York: Riverhead, 2008], 155). One could surmise (or confess) that many individuals and groups have learned to reject what they do not understand about religion and spirituality; to disregard that from which they themselves feel excluded; to dismiss experiences they have not shared firsthand. Feeling apart from the "moment" (or experience or insight), at a loss to understand or explain it, and not knowing otherwise what else to do, they do what they know: reject, disregard, dismiss.

When testimony is embraced, everyone is enriched. When testimony is not received or welcomed, everyone feels diminished. Think of Thomas, not believing the word of his closest spiritual friends. But think also of those who shared the glad word of Jesus' resurrection. Thomas's doubt of them, his dismissal and distrust, must have cut them deeply.

In Acts 11, conversely, the church at Jerusalem receives the testimony of Simon Peter as he relates the pouring out of the Holy Spirit onto the Gentiles at Cornelius's house in Joppa. The leaders of the church are dubious about the whole matter at first, especially Peter's part in it: "Why did you go to uncircumcised men and eat with them?" (Acts 11:3). Ironic, isn't it, that Jesus had not only eaten with sinners, he had spoken to Samaritans and women, and even Samaritan women?

Peter simply offers his testimony and "they were silenced. And they praised God, saying, 'Then God has given even to the Gentiles the repentance that leads to life'" (11:18). Everyone was enriched.

Not so in John 9. By the end of this story, all the key players are impoverished (except Jesus, who disappears and remains "off-camera" for most of the chapter, his longest absence in the four Gospels). Why? Because the Pharisees and the man's parents and neighbors were unable to receive the formerly blind man's testimony. When people do not know what to do, they will do what they know.

Nor is this the only lens by which to view this healing story. The same leadership consultant I mentioned above maintains that when a system does not know "what" went wrong, they will figure out "who" went wrong—in a hurry, with a vengeance (Dr. Gil Rendle lecture, Myers Park United Methodist Church, Charlotte, North Carolina, March 9, 2009). The anxiety of a system "failing," or of its realizing it has inadequate categories to deal with a given situation, will force the system into retreat or defense. It is the nature of systems, really: couples, families, congregations, nations, or any other kind of relational grouping—even a religious magisterium like the Pharisees.

It is no surprise that when there is a crisis forced by new experience or unanticipated novelty, when something from outside or beyond the normal frames of reference impinges on the system, in short, when something goes out of whack, members of the system will be inclined to whack the "who" that system deems at fault. Accusing, blaming, scapegoating—all of that stuff routinely occurs when the system is forced to face its limits, or when it endures anxiety produced by its own incapacities or ignorance.

Anxious, first of all, are the neighbors of the blind man. They cannot decide whether it is the man or "someone like him" (John 9:9). Even his initial testimony and subsequent protestations do not assuage them.

Ignorance, evidenced in the healing story itself and turned into a powerful metaphor by the evangelist, besets the religious authorities with terrible anxiety. They are the teachers of Israel but do not know what is happening. As the man moves from blindness to sight, first the crowds and then the Pharisees move from sight to blindness. They still see in one way, but they do not see at all in another, more important way. In the course of this story, they play "whack a mole" with the healed man, with his report about Jesus, with his family, and then with the man again. A penultimate exchange between the Pharisees and the formerly blind man allows us to see another spiritual solstice: the layperson is the teacher and the rabbis are those in need of education.

There are none so blind as those who will not see. There are none who see so clearly as those whose eyes have been opened. (Thomas R. Steagald)

Lectionary Commentary
1 Samuel 16:1-13

You really have to feel sorry for King Saul. David is the chosen, while Saul is the rejected. Yes, maybe he deserves it after all, but there are merits on his résumé as well as demerits. Saul has worked long, hard, and more or less successfully to secure the kingdom of Israel and protect it from its (mostly) Philistine enemies. If Saul's sanity suffers as a result, if he has presumed to offer priestly sacrifice, he has in fact been among the prophets. He has been both prophet and king—almost a trifecta—but he is rejected for his instability, impatience, and impertinence.

Saul is one of the most tragic figures in scripture; still, God is more concerned with the nation than its current leader, and God's commission to Samuel is for the sake of the future, not the past. David's surprising accession says much about God's grace, even as Saul's fall and fate say more than we perhaps wish about God's judgment.

Ephesians 5:8-14

Like the Gospel of John, Ephesians is rife with images of darkness and light. In the passage before us we see both the *objective* aspect of redemption ("once you were in darkness, but now in the Lord you are light" [5:8]) and what we might call the *subjective* aspect of redemption or the ethical consequence of our salvation ("Live as children of light. . . . Try to find out what is pleasing to the Lord" [vv. 8, 10]). Much atonement theory has historically been preached on the transactional nature of Jesus' death and resurrection, but Ephesians allows us to explore the transformational nature of Christ's atoning work. (Thomas R. Steagald)

Worship Aids

Call to Worship

The Lord leads me in right paths for the sake of the divine name.
Even when we walk in the darkest valleys, we fear no evil.
The Lord provides for us even when we are surrounded by enemies.
Goodness and mercy are ours every day;
God's provision never ends.

Collect

O God, who by the light of Jesus Christ has made visible all things, dispel every shadow from our hearts and disperse every dark thought from our minds, that we may all the more visibly love you and all the more ably serve you. So may your heart be refreshed and our lives blessed; through Christ our light. Amen.

Benediction

Be careful how you live, not as unwise people but as wise, making the most of the time that has been given to us in these evil days, giving thanks to God at all times for everything in the name of our Lord Jesus Christ. Amen. (Thomas R. Steagald)

Praising God for the Unexpected

Second in a Series of Four on Great Prayers of the Bible

Luke 1:46-55

My husband and I volunteer in the university ministry at our church. It has been an appropriate ministry for us; we have been in that transitional phase of life for many years as my husband trained to be a physician. It is an exciting life stage as students not only grow in their faith but also seek God's will for their vocations and relationships. We've watched as many fervently seek God's plan for their lives, and then celebrate as God reveals direction. As exciting as it is to watch God working in their lives and to hear their great plans, we are often reminded, as people significantly beyond college age, that God's plans are usually revealed in small snippets and are often much different than we would ever imagine. The challenge, then, is to wholeheartedly seek God's will, celebrating God's participation in our lives when the journey takes an unexpected turn.

If ever there was a biblical character who personifies the unexpected nature of God's will, it is Mary, the mother of Jesus. We often relegate her story to Christmas, somewhere between Elizabeth and the shepherds, but her story is a powerful example of one who sought God's will and celebrated despite the unexpected nature of her journey.

Although the details are scarce, we learn primarily from Luke that Mary is a young woman betrothed to a man named Joseph. She is visited by an angel who reveals that she has found favor in the eyes of the Lord and will give birth to a child who is the Son of God. The scenario certainly seems unlikely to Mary, since she is a virgin, but she responds with obedience. After hearing the news that her elderly, barren cousin Elizabeth is also expecting a baby, she visits Elizabeth (perhaps witnessing Elizabeth's miracle is a step in accepting her own). As Elizabeth's unborn child responds to the Christ Child in Mary's womb, the miracle of her role as the mother of the Christ is confirmed.

Perhaps the most significant part of this story is Mary's reaction, found in Luke 1:46-55, as she praises God for the great things God has done for her. The reality is that as she speaks those words of praise, her life is taking a scary turn. She is pregnant and unmarried, a combination that could lead to her execution. Even if her life is spared, she is still unsure how her fiancé, Joseph, and her family will react to her news. Mary's explanation of her pregnancy and the angel's visit no doubt seem unlikely to those around her. Beyond the effect of her news on her life and reputation, as scary as having a new baby was to a young woman, the prospect of having a baby that would be the Savior of the world must have seemed beyond belief. Yet, unlike many who had gone before her, Mary does not hide, bargain, or even try to talk God out of her calling. Mary praises God, thanking God for the great things that are happening in her life and for the mercy God offers God's people.

I am certain my reaction would have been different. In my own life, like the college students with whom I work, I spend a lot of time praying for God's will. I pray for wisdom, purpose, and discernment. The reality, however, is that I am actually praying that God will bless the direction I have already chosen for myself. I am mindful that my five-year plan is nothing without God's hand on it, but still not quite faithful enough to let go of the road map altogether and allow God to truly direct me. Perhaps saddest of all, when God throws me what I like to call a "curve-ball," praise is not my first reaction.

Mary's acceptance and thanksgiving of her own surprise calling produce a powerful example of just how we might embrace our own journey of faith. The reality is that God has a plan for each of us, just as God had a plan for Mary. In Jeremiah 29:11, God acknowledges that there is a providential plan for each of us. There will be times in our spiritual journeys when God's plan seems the sensible next step. There will be other times, however, when God's plan is surprising, even undesirable. Our challenge is to not only follow God into the unknown but also to praise God for every opportunity and blessing.

In this series, we are looking at great prayers in the Bible. Last week, we studied the Lord's Prayer, the very model for prayer that Jesus gave. As you think about prayer in the Bible, Mary's song, commonly called "the Magnificat," may not come to mind. However, with her simple act of praise, Mary personifies the attitude with which we should each approach our lives. She praises God when she is scared and unsure of her next step. Although Mary is not mentioned much after the birth narrative, I imagine that she approached much of her life as the mother of Christ with that same attitude, even to the cross.

When we choose to praise God instead of bemoan or negotiate God's will for our lives, we acknowledge our humanness and God's wisdom. We acknowledge our dependence on the one who created us and knows us better than we know ourselves. We humbly allow God to work in our lives in the way that only God knows is best. In my own journey, God has demonstrated this again and again. God's plan will take us in directions we never would have imagined...all we have to do is praise! (Tracey Allred)

Worship Aids

Invocation

O Creator God, we come into your presence this day with praise and thanksgiving. We praise you for this place and for time to worship you with our brothers and sisters in Christ. We invite you into our presence. Abide with us and bless all that takes place. To you, we offer this time of worship. Amen.

Call to Worship (based on Psalm 100)

We shall enter his gates with thanksgiving
    and his courts with praise.
Give thanks to him, bless his name.
For the LORD is good;
    his steadfast love endures forever,
    and his faithfulness to all generations.
Give thanks to him, bless his name.

Benediction

Go in peace, praising God for your journey of faith and embracing God's call in all our lives. Amen. (Tracey Allred)

APRIL 10, 2011

Fifth Sunday in Lent

Readings: Ezekiel 37:1-14; Psalm 130; Romans 8:6-11; John 11:1-45

Meditating on Dry Bones and Resurrection
Ezekiel 37:1-14

Five and a half weeks ago, we crossed our foreheads with ashes and entered into this intentional period of fasting, prayer, and repentance. Many of us are beginning to feel the weight of the season of Lent. Indeed, if our Lenten commitments are to produce much spiritual fruit at all, they are probably heavy enough to weigh us down at this point. Our lectionary texts during Lent help us feel that weight, but they also direct us through the spiritual work we should be doing. After all, abstaining from candy or television is not because candy and television are bad by themselves (although overuse of either is certainly bad). We are preparing the way of the Lord and learning to walk in Jesus' footsteps as he makes his way to the cross. We are nearing Holy Week, when Jesus will show us the cost of following him. How interesting that before we enter into that week of the narrative, the lectionary takes us to the raising of Lazarus and also tells us of the resurrected multitude in Ezekiel's valley of dry bones! Why do we get resurrection before the Crucifixion?

It is true that we are simply following the narrative of Jesus' life, and in that narrative, Jesus raises Lazarus just before entering into Jerusalem. However, we need to look a little deeper to see why these two passages, John 11 and Ezekiel 37, are paired for this Sunday in the Christian year. Why now? Why this pairing? What are we to learn from these passages that will prepare us for Holy Week and the cross?

The Ezekiel passage seems fairly Lent-appropriate to me. The imagery is thick and hard to miss. A prophet stands in a dry valley. I imagine the wind blowing dust around, tossing Ezekiel's threadbare robes and possibly giving him a bit of a chill. He is surrounded by dead bodies so dry that they are now simply a pile of bones. The prophet enters the disturbing site of a mass grave, perhaps even more disturbing because no one bothered to bury these bodies. When many people hear this story, they know it is a story of resurrection and hope, so they mentally check in somewhere around the "Can these bones live?" (Ezekiel 37:3) part... but let us follow the prophet, who says that God led him all around the many bones. We are told later that these are the slain of Israel. That means these are the people to whom Ezekiel has been speaking all along. In other words, these are the people who did not listen. To take it one step further, this is the result of Ezekiel's message— not repentance and forgiveness, but failure, stubborn sinfulness, hard-heartedness, and, ultimately, death and decay. I cannot imagine what it must have been like for Ezekiel to be led all around knowing that the very purpose of his ministry was to keep this from happening. Despite his own faithfulness, he was faced once more with the reality and end result of human sinfulness.

Just as God led Ezekiel "all around" (37:2) to survey the scene, we too must meditate on this reality. When we follow in our minds the course of human sinfulness, we see that it leads to death and decay. Our truest repentance will come out a deeper knowledge of where our hard-heartedness leads us. For our own edification, we must sit and meditate on where the course of our lives will go without divine grace. We must walk with Ezekiel all around the valley, because a major part of witnessing the story of God's redemption is seeing just how much we need it. Those of us who have been staring into the darkness of our souls during the Lenten season know that we really do need God's resurrection.

The second reason for hearing these stories at this point in the Christian calendar has nothing to do with us or our sin. Purely external to us, it has everything to do with learning that it is God who brings life out of death and that God is the one acting for our redemption. Our knowledge of God's identity is often tied to God's action for (or in some cases, against) humanity. God says repeatedly in the Old Testament, "You shall know that I am the Lord," and it is always related to divine activity toward humanity.

When we witness the type of resurrection offered in our lectionary texts, we see God's promise of restoration to God's people after they have completely cut themselves off from God's love. We see a Savior who has the power to overcome death and yet weeps over the deaths of those he loves. We see a God who pulls us up from the depths but who gently makes us see to what depths we have sunk. Part of the story shows us who we are, but the rest shows us who God is.

I see these stories of resurrection as God's way of giving us strength for the rest of the journey. Jesus beckons us to follow him, but the journey to the cross is daunting. For the past five weeks, we have been following Jesus as he instructs/warns us about his eventual suffering and death. However, when faced with the reality of taking up our crosses to follow, we quickly realize there is nothing within that equips us to do it. At this point, the Lord gently reminds us that it is not about us. The spiritual work we do during Lent was never intended to be what sustains us and what brings us the new life we need. Rather, our spiritual work is meant only to help us clear the path so that we can see God's work in and for us. It is God who will strengthen us to follow Jesus. It is God who will bring resurrection where there was only death and decay. It is God who can breathe new life into our mortal bodies. Amen. (Amber Essick)

Lectionary Commentary
John 11:1-45

It is interesting to note several similarities between the story of Lazarus's resurrection and the story of resurrection in Ezekiel. Ezekiel and Jesus have both been called to a place where their prophetic messages have failed. Ezekiel was faithful to his calling but could not convince God's people to repent. This resulted in the people's utter destruction. Jesus preached in Judea but was unable to evoke faith. Some were so opposed to his message that he barely escaped being stoned. Ezekiel notes that the bodies were very many and very dry. Jesus' beloved friend Martha also notes that her brother is . . . very dead. She warns that after four days his body likely will give off a terrible odor.

The prophet's message failed, and he was led around to view the results of that failure. Jesus preached in Judea and barely escaped stoning before he went beyond the Jordan to continue his ministry. Lazarus's death brought Jesus back to that hostile territory in order to glorify God and himself. Both Ezekiel and Martha were pulled aside for a catechetical moment prior to God's performing the miracles. Finally, in both stories, God makes it clear that redemption comes only from above, and it comes when all hope for healing has been lost.

Romans 8:6-11

This passage comments on the futility of living life apart from God's spirit. Not only are humans incapable of pleasing God, but we find ourselves hostile to God as we live lives directed toward the gratification of our own urges and appetites. We are shown here how obeying our appetites can lead from misguided thinking to the inability to please God and eventually to hostility toward God. Submission to God involves surrendering our appetites and our attention to the Spirit. Finally, this is more than just a head game; God will enliven our minds as well as our mortal bodies through the indwelling of the Holy Spirit. This last sentence reminds the reader to stop short of demonizing the body itself. God will not redeem us from our bodies; God will redeem our minds *and* our bodies. (Amber Essick)

Worship Aids

Call to Worship (based on Psalm 130)

Out of the depths I cry to you, O LORD.
Lord, hear my voice!
If you, O LORD, should mark iniquities,
Lord, who could stand?
But there is forgiveness with you,
   so that you may be revered.
I wait for the LORD, my soul waits.
   And in God's word I hope.
My soul waits for the Lord more than those
   who watch for the morning,
   more than those who wait for the morning.
O Israel, hope in the LORD!
For with the LORD there is steadfast love
   and with him is great power to redeem.

Prayer of Response

O Lord God, we set our minds on you this day. We ask for your strength because in us is only weakness. We hope for your light to shine on us because our lives are hopelessly darkened by sin. We watch for you because only you can give us new life as you teach us how to die to self. In the name of the Creator, Redeemer, and Sustainer we pray, one God, now and forever. Amen.

Benediction

May Christ, who dwells within us, give us strength to wait and watch for him. Amen. Go in peace. (Amber Essick)

Confession and Prayer

Third in a Series of Four on Great Prayers of the Bible

Psalm 51

It is said that confession is good for the soul. Although I know this is true, I'm not sure that my five-year-old son would agree. Confession is a challenge for him. For example, he recently gave himself a haircut. It was one of those discreet little trims that led us to wonder for several weeks why his hair looked a little different, but was only revealed by the barber at his next cut. Once discovered, my son acknowledged his sin, but mysteriously had no recollection of how or when it had happened. We got the whole story only much later, as we pieced his mumbled accounts together. Had he not been "exposed" by the barber, we may have never known. Truth be told, my son hoped that he would never get caught, and only reluctantly, halfheartedly confessed after he was discovered.

It's easy to laugh at his childhood mischief, but I think my son's attitude mirrors many of our attitudes toward confession. As we discuss great prayers of the Bible, however, we cannot overlook the importance of genuine confession in the prayer life of the believer.

Perhaps no one in Scripture learned a more humbling lesson about the importance of confession than David. God sought out David to be Israel's king after Saul's failure. God led Samuel, an unexpected leader, to anoint David (1 Samuel 16). Although young and inexperienced, David proved to be up to the job. He was a valiant soldier, a beloved military leader, and would be remembered as the greatest king of Israel.

David was, as Acts 13:22 put it, a man after God's own heart. Even in his greatness, however, David failed miserably from time to time. Perhaps one of his greatest failures occurs in 2 Samuel 11. While his soldiers are away fighting, David lusts for and commits adultery with the wife of one of his soldiers, Uriah. When the wife, Bathsheba, becomes pregnant, David tries to trick Uriah into thinking that the child is his. This attempt fails when Uriah proves to be above David's tricks. David then sends Uriah to the front lines of battle where Uriah is killed, allowing David the opportunity to marry Bathsheba. Needless to say, the Lord is not pleased with David's actions and sends Nathan to confront David. In 2 Samuel 12, Nathan approaches David with a parable of a rich man who has wronged another. David is enraged by the story until he realizes that the story is about him. Indeed, David is the sinner, and the penalty of his sin will be great. David grieves and seeks forgiveness.

Psalm 51 is attributed to David as his prayer of confession after Nathan's confrontation. It is a powerful example as David pleads for mercy and cleansing after acknowledging his great sin against God. Psalm 51 has been on the lips of many since David. It is a powerful prayer that brings full circle the realization, repentance, and redemption of the sinner. Like David, we have all failed God miserably at times. Sometimes we realize our sin right away, like Peter after his denial of Jesus. Other times, like David, our sin must be pointed out to us. Whatever the situation, we realize our need for repentance and confess our sins to God. We seek not only God's forgiveness but also a clean heart and a right spirit. We also acknowledge our need to be broken in our sacrifice to God.

The words in Psalm 51 are powerful, but true confession is about more than saying the right words. Confession must be an attitude of utter repentance and humility. When David realized his sin (it did not take much for him to connect the dots after Nathan's parable), he sought God's forgiveness. David fell to his knees, grieved his failures, and cried out to God. This was not very kingly behavior, but David cared only about confessing and being forgiven.

This is what God requires of us as well. It is not enough to say that we're sorry and then go on with our lives without true change taking place. When we truly confess our sins to God, it should be a gut-wrenching, wholehearted acknowledgment of our sin and plea for forgiveness. Whatever our words, the result of our confession should be life change. There is an important thing to remember, however, regarding our personal confessions. Just as David learned, confessing our sins to God does not always equal a free pass on consequences. There may be times when God offers unexplainable mercy, but more often than not, we will still have to face the earthly consequences of our sins. David lost his child and peace in his family. Our own consequences vary, but it is important to realize that God's forgiveness is worth far more than earthly consequences.

We are challenged to exercise and promote confession as a regular spiritual practice. Although David's situation was steeped in sin, God wants confession to be part of our everyday lives as well. We are not to wait until we are in some type of huge, sin-filled situation like David's before we confess. Confession should be part of our regular prayer lives as we acknowledge our imperfections and tendencies toward sin as human beings. It is also important not to exercise confession like my son, confessing our sin only after getting caught. God already knows the whole story. We cannot hide our sins any more than David did. God wants us to realize our sins and seek clean hearts. (Tracey Allred)

Worship Aids

Call to Worship

O God, we thank you for your mercy and love.
We are mindful of our failures,
    and our need to seek you in all circumstances.
Lead us on the path to confession,
    as we seek a right relationship with you. Amen.

Prayer of Confession

O God of love and mercy, we enter your presence today seeking your forgiveness for our many sins and shortcomings. We seek your face as we confess all the ways we have failed you. We acknowledge our sins before you. (*Allow a few moments for silent confession.*)

Words of Assurance

Thank you, O God, for creating a clean heart in me and restoring my soul. In you alone my sins are washed way, and I am made whiter than snow. Amen.

Benediction

Go in peace, aware of both our shortcomings and our need for forgiveness. Seek our God of mercy and love in all we do. Amen. (Tracey Allred)

APRIL 17, 2011

❧❧❧

Palm/Passion Sunday

Palm Readings: Matthew 21:1-11; Psalm 118:1-2, 19-29
Passion Readings: Isaiah 50:4-9a; Psalm 31:9-16; Philippians 2:5-11;
Matthew 26:14–27:66

Make Room for the Coming King
Matthew 21:1-11

It is Palm Sunday. Our Lord comes. Yet Jesus does not come as we expect, not as we would like him to come. Today we mark the end of Lent; we make final preparations to commemorate Christ's passion. Our work during Lent has been to clear the spiritual path so that Christ's presence in and with us may become more recognizable. As we hear the story of Jesus' entry into Jerusalem, we must reflect on what it really means to welcome Jesus into this passion week.

The narrative leading up to Jesus' triumphal entry is an awkward mix of Jesus' instruction on the nature of the kingdom of heaven and the disciples' misunderstandings and jockeying for power. Jesus teaches them to become like children in their faith, but they fight like children for their master's favor. Jesus tells them that the kingdom is about suffering and service, and then they ask to be first in glory. Peter asks about the limits of forgiveness, only to be told that he must forgive from the heart without limits. The rich young man approaches Jesus hoping the kingdom is about *doing*, only to find that it is about *emptying*.

This awkwardness bleeds over into today's text as Jesus enters Jerusalem. The crowd traveling with him sets up a king's entry, but Jesus comes in on a donkey. Others go to purchase their sacrifices, but Jesus walks in, pronounces judgment on those buying and selling, challenges the priests and scribes, and then leaves the city for the evening. One thing is clear: Jesus does not come to us on our terms. Jesus comes on his own terms.

Yet, he comes. Jesus could have resisted this royal processional, but he permits it, even participates in it. He comes on a donkey instead of riding in on a warhorse, yet he comes. Although there is a great deal of misunderstanding involved in this parade, Jesus still allows them to offer him praise. So there is a bit of a dance going on here, isn't there? How do we welcome our king this week without falling into the trenches of misunderstanding? We cannot expect with the crowd a glorious assumption of military, political, or religious power. Jesus clearly means to suffer and serve rather than to rule and reign. We must not, however, sit back and critically second-guess the incorrect expectations of the crowd—that is not a helpful view of this passage, and it certainly is no way to welcome our Lord.

Instead, let us consider afresh what Jesus' entry means. Jesus has come as Jerusalem's king to bring salvation, but salvation means more than relief from an oppressive regime. Jesus enters Jerusalem to free the people from themselves. You see, the oppressive Roman state is not the only thing wrong with this picture. In fact, political liberation does not even seem to be on Jesus' radar. Those who suffer often fail to see beyond their immediate complaints. Oppression can be overwhelming, but it is just one small symptom of a fallen world.

Jesus comes to make many wrong things right, and he does not overwhelm military power with greater military power in order to do it. Jesus comes to bring salvation from oppression . . . and from shame, hate, selfishness, greed, fear, death, lust, and anything else that corrupts God's creation. Jesus' salvation reaches far beyond our urgent, gnawing needs. He does not simply bow to us and our needs; Jesus saves us from the shortsightedness of our own perceived needs.

Jesus' entry also signifies divine judgment. We pretend that it is only those religious leaders who are being judged, but Jesus' judgment falls on us all. We are so misguided that we contribute more to the problem than to the solution. Our desires lead us far from celebrating Jesus' kind of kingdom, so his judgment also falls on us. In this sense, Jesus' coming to town is not good news to us. It thwarts our own plans for salvation.

What we often resist seeing about the kingdom is that every step of the way Jesus must wrestle with his own people and their agendas. Resistance to the way of peace, self-sacrifice, and service is so strong that his own disciples will eventually desert him, and his own people will kill him. The folks in this story do not prefer God's judgment, and neither do we. Now, no one wants to think about divine judgment on Palm Sunday, when a crowd happily fills the streets and the singing of "Hosanna" fills the air. But if we truly seek to prepare the way of the Lord, and if we really want to follow Jesus' footsteps, we must prepare our own hearts by accepting God's judgment of our intentions and plans. Otherwise we stand in the way when Jesus enters.

Friends, let us allow God to break down our resistance and bring us into the kingdom. Here are a few practical ways to follow Jesus this week:

Offer forgiveness freely and from the heart. It may be that you have been withholding forgiveness from someone who has deeply offended you. Or perhaps you need to work on forgiving those little everyday offenses that creep up. Become a good forgiver, without keeping count, as Jesus instructed Peter.

If you love money or possessions, as did the rich man who approached Jesus, let go of your money or stop obsessing so much over it that you spend too much time holding on to what you think is yours. Obsession over money can also signify a love of money. Let go as Jesus told the rich man to do.

There are other dreadfully practical ways to welcome Jesus as well. Be a peacemaker; love and pray for your enemies; go an extra mile with someone; stop striving to be first or best or most powerful. You may say that these practical instructions amount to being nice to others and being a good person but carry very little spiritual weight. We would all prefer merely to contemplate the mystery of God's coming near and follow Jesus' journey with a spiritual devotion to the suffering servant.

It is true that many of these instructions don't seem spiritual in themselves. We must do them, not because of their own spiritual weight, but because our hearts are very small. We clutter them daily with concern for ourselves, misplaced loves, and hurt feelings. We must make room for Jesus in order to welcome him properly. Somehow this practical work done with spiritual attention prepares the way of the Lord as nothing else can. It changes us. It makes room in our hearts that Jesus can fill with the kingdom of heaven. This is the way to make straight the path of the Lord: self-emptying. There is no other way to let Jesus' message sink in, and there is no other way to follow our Lord than to walk in his footsteps.

Jesus' life was one of self-emptying and service to God and humanity, and so we make our lives in his likeness. If there was ever a week to get this right, this is it. If there was ever a point in the Christian narrative to step out of the way and let the story of divine love continue, this is it. Let this work be the homage you pay to the king as he comes. Amen. (Amber Essick)

Lectionary Commentary
Isaiah 50:4-9a

The speaker in this passage is an unnamed servant of the Lord who remains confident in God's ability to sustain and deliver. That the prophet in this text speaks in the first person is rare in chapters 40–55 (often referred to as Second Isaiah). The servant challenges the adversaries to contend and confront, suggesting a refusal to back away from the prophetic calling.

Those who abuse the prophet do so by means of beatings, plucking out of the beard, insults, and spitting. It is unclear whether such treatment amounts to state-sponsored torture or, more likely, the equivalent of routine run-ins with opponents or personal enemies. Either way, such efforts were employed in the ancient world to shame one publicly. Typically, such public humiliation demanded a corresponding action to restore the victim's honor. Still, God's servant insists that justice and vindication are near. The sentence "Let us stand up together" in verse 8 is reminiscent of judgment rather than retaliation.

The image of setting one's face like flint, which is among the hardest of rocks, reinforces the idea that the harsh treatment has not left the servant ashamed. Likewise, the servant is convinced that the adversaries will suffer the same fate as a moth-infested garment. This suggests delayed vindication, as the enemy is gradually worn away, rather than any immediate confrontation.

Philippians 2:5-11

This famous and oft-quoted passage from Paul's Epistle to the Philippians is part of a larger, dual appeal to steadfastness and unity. In 2:2-4, Paul makes a connection between achieving unity and acting humbly, and then in 2:5-11 enjoins the believers in Philippi to embody Jesus' mind-set in pursuit of unity. Paul demonstrates Jesus' mind-set by including a poetic narrative with several scenes: Jesus was unwilling to exploit his divine status; Jesus emptied himself; Jesus took the form of a slave and was born in human likeness; Jesus humbled himself to the point of death by crucifixion; God exalted Jesus to the loftiest position.

Notice that Jesus gave up what was his to assume that which he was not, and in the end he was given that which he did not seek. The logic seems to be that if God in Jesus acts in such a humble manner, then those who claim to seek after God should do likewise. Not all scholars agree that 2:5-11—whether in part or in whole—is an early Christian hymn. Even so, it is appropriate to consider this passage in the context of early Christian worship. In so doing, one can see how framing and narrating God's saving act in the person of Jesus forms the heart of the Christian message as proclaimed in the church's worship.

Matthew 26:14–27:66

This lengthy Passion narrative includes several poignant moments of betrayal, commitment, and suffering. In the hours leading up to his crucifixion, Jesus is disappointed by the inability of his friends to pray, betrayed by a friend for a handful of money, and publicly rejected by a friend who had only a few hours before boldly claimed: "Even though I must die with you, I will not deny you" (Matthew 26:35). The remorseful responses of those who betray or deny Jesus in this passage also range from regret to weeping to suicide. Contrast the examples of the disciples with the examples of Gentiles, women, and a little-known rich man. Ironically, it is the Gentiles standing around the cross who recognize Jesus' true identity. The female disciples who had followed Jesus end up protecting his body. It is the wealthy Joseph of Arimathea who places Jesus' body in his own family's tomb.

Jesus' rejection of the sword at this critical juncture in his ministry serves as a reminder that any attempt to realize the kingdom of God by violent means is in and of itself a betrayal of Jesus and his mission. Jesus reminds the unnamed disciple (identified as Peter only in John's Gospel) that use of the sword perpetuates use of the sword, but more important, suffering is part of God's plan as expressed in the Hebrew Scriptures.

The trials described in Matthew's Gospel highlight the breakdown of just and legal procedures. Jesus is arrested, interrogated, tortured, condemned, and crucified within a matter of hours. Notice the interesting exchanges between Jesus and those who wish to execute him. Jesus is reluctant to speak of himself or his identity, yet his opponents identify him as "Messiah" and "King of the Jews." Such misunderstanding of Jesus' identity is prominent throughout Matthew's passion narrative.

Interestingly, it is in Matthew alone that midday darkness, an earthquake, and the resurrection of saints occur (though darkness also surrounds the hour of Jesus' death in Luke). Such theophanic occurrences illicit the centurion's statement, "Truly this man was God's Son!" (Matthew 27:54), and terrify all those present at the crucifixion. Also, the tearing of the temple curtain, mentioned in several of the Gospel accounts, is never explained in any of them. Perhaps while other events needed commentary, this did not require an explanation for the original hearers. (Amber Essick)

Worship Aids

Call to Worship (based on Psalm 118)

(With two people leading, the right side of the congregation reads the text in roman type, and the left side responds with the text in bold type.)

O give thanks to the LORD, for God is good;
   God's steadfast love endures forever!
Let the people say,
   "God's steadfast love endures forever."
Open the gates of righteousness,
   and the righteous shall enter through them.
Blessed is the one who comes in the name of the LORD.
   Hosanna in the highest!
The LORD is God,
   and God has given us light.
You have taken the stone the builders rejected,
   and you made it the cornerstone.
We shall give you thanks
   because you have answered us and become our salvation.
This is the LORD's doing.
   It is marvelous in our eyes.

Pastoral Prayer

Lord, we watch and wait for you to come. We confess that we still think of your kingdom as grand and glorious when you have shown us time and time again that it comes to us in the humble, the obscure, and the small. Teach us your ways, O Lord. When we seek honor, show us how to humble ourselves. When we go ahead of you, remind us that we are to follow. In the name of our Lord Jesus Christ, who lives and reigns with you and the Holy Spirit, we pray. Amen.

Silent Meditation

This is the day that the Lord has made. Jesus calls us all to follow him into his passion week. May our hearts be set on him as we become the people he has called us to be. (Amber Essick)

Prayer in the Hard Times

Fourth in a Series of Four on Great Prayers of the Bible

Matthew 26

I've heard it said that there is no such thing as a foxhole atheist, meaning that in one of life's most difficult places, a military foxhole, for instance, even someone who claims disbelief in God will believe. The same might be said of another of life's difficult places, the hospital bed. During my time in church ministry and as a hospital pastoral care volunteer, I have spent quite a bit of time in hospitals and have observed that during life's scariest times, prayer is accepted even by those who otherwise might not believe. As believers, hopefully our prayer lives are more consistent. Our God seeks to be in communication with us in all areas of our lives. In 1 Thessalonians 5:17, Paul calls us to pray continually. Yet, even for believers who spend regular time in prayer, there is something different about those times of urgent, desperate prayer when we face scary situations and uncertainties. This week we conclude our series on great prayers of the Bible by discussing praying during the hard times.

Because prayer is a common response in both believers and nonbelievers in times of difficulty, examples abound in scripture. As Jacob approaches his meeting with Esau, he spends time in prayer, even wrestling with God over his difficulty (Genesis 32). Moses often cries out to God as he faces hardships while leading the people out of Egypt. As a matter of fact, Moses is in almost constant communication with the Lord as he journeys. As Samson stands blinded and tied to the pillars at the feast of the Philistines, he cries out to God. Jonah even prays to God in his misery from inside the giant fish. The list could go on and on.

Perhaps the most powerful example in scripture of praying through difficulty is Jesus' prayer in the garden just before his arrest. Through Jesus' example, we can learn some key things about our own prayer in the hard times of life. Jesus' prayer in the garden is found in each of the Gospels. (The accounts from Matthew 26 and Mark 14 are nearly identical.) Separating himself to pray was nothing new for Jesus. His prayer in

Gethsemane, however, is different. He has just celebrated the passover with his disciples. He knows that the time is approaching for his death. The scripture even suggests that Jesus knows that Judas has already betrayed him.

After the dinner, he goes to the garden at Gethsemane to pray, accompanied by the inner circle of Peter, James, and John. As it is late, Jesus asks the disciples to stay awake and pray with him. It is a request they are unable to fulfill, and they fall asleep on three occasions through the evening, no doubt deeply disappointing Jesus. Jesus then cries out to God. In his humanness, he is fearful of what is about to take place, and he earnestly calls to God to allow the cup to pass. With each request, however, Jesus acknowledges that it is God's will and not his.

For me, of the many painful scenes in the last hours of Jesus' life, this scene in the garden is one of the most poignant. Jesus Christ, the Savior of the world, desperately cries out to his Father God, his *Abba*, to spare his life, while knowing that this cup that he prays will pass is the very reason he was born. Even as Jesus prays, feeling the conflict of fear and acceptance, his closest friends do not surround him with outstretched hands. Instead they sleep, while one of their own prepares to betray him. The prayer scene ends with Jesus' arrest. Immediately he knows that the cup will not pass from him, and we know that the ultimate sacrifice is about to be made for humankind.

Although examples of praying through the hard times are prevalent in scripture, there are none as revealing and instructive as Jesus in the garden. Jesus is perfect and truly innocent. He did not cause this painful situation, and yet Jesus has access to God's perfect plan and its outcome.

Our own difficulties are never so simple. As part of fallen creation, we are not exempt from evil and difficulty in the way that the Son of God could have been. Yet, even through Jesus' most difficult moment, we can learn much about our own prayers in the difficult times of life. First of all, as Jesus approaches this scary situation, he seeks God. Jesus does not spend more time teaching, doing miracles, or even resting physically for what is ahead. He wholeheartedly seeks God in his time of difficulty. We are called to do the same. Many times, we intend to pray, and even believe in prayer's power and necessity, but we do not take the time to do it.

Second, Jesus is honest in his prayer. He prays that he will not have to go through what he is about to go through. We are called to do the same. As we call out to God, we should allow ourselves the freedom to speak our minds and our hearts. God knows our thoughts already, but there is comfort and power in speaking the truth as we pray, even if it reveals our own fears and weaknesses.

Finally, Jesus accepts that his will may not be God's. Even as Jesus pleads for his life, he realizes that it may not be God's will for that to take place. As we seek God and pray wholeheartedly in mind and heart, we can acknowledge that our design may not be God's. God's plan for our difficulty may not be even close to our own, and yet we are called to accept God's love and mercy in whatever form it comes. In many ways, I think that Jesus' time in prayer prepares him for what comes next. As we seek God in all situations, we are better prepared to accept God's will for our lives. (Tracey Allred)

Worship Aids

Pastoral Prayer
(*Depending on the tradition in your church, consider opening the altar or chancel rail for those who are praying regarding a particular personal difficulty to approach and pray.*)
Almighty God, you are the God of our beginnings and our endings. You know us better than we can know ourselves. We call out to you to participate in all areas of our lives. Today, we acknowledge that there are those among us who are going through great difficulty. We lift their needs to you. (*Allow time for silent prayer.*) We thank you for hearing our prayers and for allowing your will to be done in each situation. Amen.

Words of Assurance (based on Psalm 18)
I love you, O LORD, my strength.
The LORD is my rock, my fortress, and my deliverer.
God is the shield and the horn of my salvation.
I call to the LORD, who is worthy of praise, and I am saved.

Benediction
Go now in peace, believing that God desires participation in all of our lives, embracing us in times of both joy and pain. Amen. (Tracey Allred)

APRIL 21, 2011

❧❧❧

Holy Thursday

Readings: Exodus 12:1-4 (5-10), 11-14; Psalm 116:1-2, 12-19;
1 Corinthians 11:23-26; John 13:1-17, 31b-35

Keepers of the Feast

Exodus 12:1-4 (5-10), 11-14; 1 Corinthians 11:23-26;
John 13:1-17, 31b-35

Tonight we gather for a distinctive event in the life of the church.
Holy Week is valued by us partly because we get to come together more
often. Remembering the last week of our Lord's earthly life is not an individual act. It is an act of the community to remember together. We have
confessed our own brokenness, entered into a season of fasting and prayer
(Lent), walked with our Lord as he approached this week, and even welcomed him into Jerusalem with our "Hosannas." But tonight is the night
when Jesus takes his disciples into the upper room to teach them a final
lesson and draws them to him one last time. So we come together to celebrate that unique meal together as did the first disciples.

Jesus and the disciples are in Jerusalem (with the rest of the Jewish
world) to keep the Passover feast. Passover celebrated God's final deliverance of Israel from Egyptian bondage. God took the life of each
Egyptian firstborn but passed over the homes marked with lamb's blood.
The Old Testament reading includes God's instructions for preparing and
eating the Passover meal: roast an unblemished, year-old lamb over fire
(either one lamb per household or two households should share it). The
whole community killed and cooked their lambs the same night and ate
them with quickly made, unleavened bread and bitter herbs. They were
to eat the meal with shoes on, cloaks fastened, and staff in hand. The
required posture for eating the Passover meal calls to mind the sense of
anticipation associated with departing Egypt. Notice the communal language in this passage: families share; no one keeps leftovers; the whole

host of Israel eats at the same time. This was a communal remembrance of God's salvation.

How fitting, then, that according to the reading from 1 Corinthians, Jesus chooses this feast, on this night, to become the sacred Communion celebrated by his church. What formerly marked the old covenant of deliverance now marks the new covenant in Jesus' body and blood. Christ becomes the Paschal Lamb inasmuch as he says that his body is broken for us, and his blood is the new covenant for us. Again, we are invited to celebrate this meal in remembrance of God's saving act in Jesus. As the apostle Paul puts it, "As often as you eat this bread and drink the cup, you proclaim the Lord's death until he comes" (1 Corinthians 11:26).

Something else also happens on this final night of Jesus' life. Jesus dons the clothes of a household slave and washes the dirt from his followers' feet. Not only is the God-person stooping to humanity, but during the feast celebrating freedom from slavery, Jesus takes on the role of a slave in order to teach his disciples a vital lesson about what it means to follow. Life in this new covenant is a life of service. It is a life in community. It is a life of giving up our own way to walk the Christian path together.

When reading about our Lord's last night with his disciples, two things stand out. The first has to do with the acts themselves. The second has to do with the meaning they carry. First, the acts of footwashing and Communion are important simply because they were given by Jesus and handed down as part of the church's tradition. Not only do they retain their original significance, but the elements of the Lord's Supper have been touched and handled by generations upon generations of saints. They have been passed down like a carefully guarded recipe. God's people have come again and again to eat of this bread and drink of this cup. How interesting that God uses everyday elements like food and drink or the washing of feet to nurture our faith and to proclaim a message about salvation. These mundane acts must be repeated daily. Likewise, we must regularly partake of the spiritual food Christ offers here at the table. Christ has made us keepers of this tradition, this feast, so that the church will be marked by it throughout the ages.

Tonight we must also hear the meaning behind the Lord's Supper and the washing of feet and let those meanings sink into our hearts. "Do you know what I have done to you?" he asks (John 13:12). For a moment, Christ, our teacher and Lord, becomes a slave at the feet of his disciples. Jesus does this out of love for them. Because he loves them in that way and tells us to follow his example, he ordains that our love for one another should be a sign to the world of our identity in Christ.

If anyone in that upper room failed to grasp the significance of Jesus' riding into town on a donkey, the blinders were taken off at this point. Mutual love and service is what life in the kingdom of God is about. We are to carry on the tradition of serving one another in love. Though it is meant as an outward sign of the Christian life, it accomplishes an inward work as well. An act of service for my Christian brother or sister is spiritual work because it produces humility and generosity in me and gratitude in the one I serve.

The Lord's Supper is also rich with meaning. Christ, in the celebration of the Eucharist, draws us to himself. This meal is a proclamation of Jesus' sacrificial death. Not only is Christ's body broken and his blood spilled for us, it is given to us as spiritual food. The elements of bread and wine allow us to receive Christ in a material, physical way and be nourished in him.

Tonight, Christians everywhere stand around this table to participate in this family meal. We come together to be marked once again as God's people. We celebrate the intimate supper Christ had with his disciples on the night he was betrayed. Christ stands with us and offers us the chance to be known to the world by the love we have for him, for one another, and for the world. Christ charges us once again to keep the tradition that has been handed down to us. The table is set. So, let us keep the feast. Amen. (Amber Essick)

Worship Aids

Pastoral Prayer

O Lord, we draw near to you this evening. Teach us the meaning of service. Draw us into your loving embrace. We freely take what you offer us this night: a space at your table and an invitation to serve one another as you have served us. Amen.

Words of Assurance

In God's invitation to feast, we are redeemed. In Christ's call to the table, we are nourished. In the Holy Spirit, who is present in the fellowship of the saints around us, we are called to serve one another in love. Come and take all that God offers this day. Amen.

Responsive Reading (based on Psalm 116)

I love the LORD, because God has heard my voice and my supplications.
Because God has inclined the divine ear to me,
therefore I will call on the LORD as long as I live. (Amber Essick)

Upper Room Christians in a Temple Church

First in a Series of Three on Worship Sites

John 2:13-25

Where can God be found? Where in this world might we hope to find truly sacred space? Where can we turn our attention to enter most fully into the holy presence of our Lord and Savior? The simple answer is *church*, but, interestingly, the majority of worshiping Christians report that they do not experience God most fully in their churches. Story after story relates occasions where people have their transformative experiences of God on retreat, at camp, with a close friend, in a hospital, or in the wee hours of the morning. So often, the significant encounters we have with God happen in the world rather than in the church. This calls into question the very nature and existence of the church. Why are we here? What is this place we call *church* actually for?

In the earliest days of our pre-Christian roots, the Hebrew people carried "the church" with them. Called the *Mishkan* in Hebrew and translated as "tabernacle" in English (from the Latin word for *tent*), this holy place housed the ark of the covenant—in an area referred to as the holy of holies—and established the gathering place for worship of God. The early Hebrews believed that God dwelt in the holy of holies, present to the whole people through the priests. There was no place on earth more revered and respected than the tabernacle. Also called "the tent of meeting," the tabernacle was the spiritual center for the "chosen of Israel."

Once in Israel, the tabernacle was replaced by the temple of Solomon—an incredible edifice that established Jerusalem as the holiest city of the holiest God. Offerings were made in the temple, and it was a center for worship and praise on the festival celebration days. Priests led daily morning prayer. Men gathered in the courtyards and antechambers, while women gathered in the women's court. A constant flow of people to the temple characterized the lives of the Hebrew people—gathering to give glory and honor to God. For the majority of the "chosen people," the temple was where God lived—a tradition carried metaphorically today, when we refer to the church as "God's house."

Yet it is fascinating to note as we survey the writings of the poets, historians, law-keepers, scribes, and prophets that the turning-point encounters with God happen on the mountains, in the plains, and on the lakeshores. The temple may have been God's house, but apparently God was seldom home. Fringe sects of Judaism (as well as early sects of Christianity) rebelled against the idea of any structure "containing" God, opting instead for an all-embracing "the earth is the LORD's, and the fullness thereof" (Psalm 24:1 KJV) worldview.

Perhaps the most significant difference between the temple of the Hebrew people and our Christian churches today is that the focus of "going to temple" was to turn one's attention completely to God. The temple experience wasn't about the worshiper, but about the worshiped. All honor, glory, praise, adoration, supplication, intercession, and thanksgiving was directed to God. People in worship were humble, appreciative, and felt unworthy to be in the presence of such greatness. Many Christians today attend church, not for what they have to give to God, but to receive God's blessing, instruction, guidance, and encouragement. The focus of much modern worship is us, rather than God.

Apparently, Jesus was much more a tabernacle than a temple kind of guy—he carried God with him. Church didn't happen just in temple or synagogue, but it happened wherever two or more were gathered, at any time of day or night. The rules and regulations were given as gifts to the people of God, not as legalistic rules and limitations. Healing on the Sabbath was as acceptable as healing any other day of the week. Teaching on the lakeshore or mountainside was as binding and true as any teaching in the temple or synagogue. Sacred space had little to do with location, but everything to do with relationship.

The amazing and wonderful tales of transformation in our four Gospels take place in homes, on streets, in fields, and on the road. No more wondrous a story of transformation has occurred than the story of Jesus' last night in a small, unassuming upper room, where Jesus celebrated the Passover meal (synoptic) or engaged in footwashing (John) with his closest friends and followers. In that humble setting, Jesus took ordinary bread and everyday wine and turned them into powerful and enduring symbols of the centrality of Christ to our lives—each time we eat bread or drink from the cup, it is to be for us an occasion for remembrance, remembrance of Jesus Christ.

Ultimately, the message is clear—church isn't the place we go in order to meet God. The place we go is anywhere we are equipped to be the church for the world, filled with God's spirit. Sacred space is where we find it—sometimes in a building, but always in the faith shared with our friends in Christ, wherever they may be. (Dan R. Dick)

Worship Aids

Call to Worship

Enter, friends, and feel God's presence.
We gather in God's holy presence!
Enfold yourselves in the redeeming love of God.
We celebrate the wondrous gift of God's love!
Prepare yourselves to share God's love with others.
By God's spirit, and with God's help,
   we promise to spread God's love to everyone we meet!
All: Amen.

Pastoral Prayer

Gracious and merciful God, we seek you in this place, forgetting sometimes that you constantly seek us. Remind us that when we leave this place, we do not leave you behind, but we leave with you, to share you with others in the things that we say and do. Keep us mindful of your presence, that we may always, and in every way, honor and glorify your holy name. Amen.

Benediction

Go forth from this place to be the church in the world. Be for others a sacred space—a place where people can find comfort and care, hope and joy, acceptance and forgiveness, kindness and love. Amen. (Dan R. Dick)

APRIL 22, 2011

☙☙☙☙

Good Friday

Readings: Isaiah 52:13–53:12; Psalm 22; Hebrews 10:16-25;
John 18:1–19:42

The Voices of Good Friday
Isaiah 52:13–53:12; Psalm 22; John 18:1–19:42

There are readings and days during the Christian year that need little or no exposition. Today is such a day, and these readings are such readings. This liturgical journey we've been on since Advent is in many ways a familiar one. We know how to do Christmas. Epiphany is nice. Think of something meaningful but not too difficult to abstain from during Lent. Then it's Palm Sunday; Easter. The story rolls on into Pentecost and beyond.

But today we pause to observe and contemplate the suffering of our Lord. The assigned lectionary passages for this day are among the most familiar in all of scripture. We hear of God's suffering servant in Isaiah. We hear the cry of dereliction in Psalm 22. We hear Peter's denial, Pilate's exasperation, and Jesus' calm commitment to the path before him in John. I fear, however, that in our attempts to grasp the meaning and import of such passages, we may be silencing the texts themselves. It may be simpler to fill our ears with theological words or exegetical explanations rather than listening to the texts themselves, so for the next few minutes, join me in listening to the voices of Good Friday.

Listen to one of God's choice servants. His humanness is indiscernible. He is utterly familiar with rolled eyes and pointed fingers. He knows the absence of eye contact and the distance of avoidance. He is told that God has forsaken him. He bears the shortcomings of those who hate him. He swallows the rejection he is offered. He is taken before justice only to have it turn away. His innocence is a curse, his purity a burden. He provides no rebuttal, yet he calls out in a deafening and defiant silence. His future is unlike his past. His demise is inextricably tied to the righteous-ness of those who taunt and ridicule. Somehow his death is their gain. Are you listening?

Hear the voice of another servant. She admits that God is holy and enthroned on the praises of the people. She tells of how her ancestors trusted for generations and experienced deliverance instead of shame. She recalls a time when God safeguarded her every move, but not now. Not anymore. She laments God's absence. She wonders aloud why God stepped away in her moment of greatest need. Countless naysayers and enemies are nearer to her than the God of her ancestors. There is neither saliva in her mouth nor flesh on her bones. Her groans fall on deaf ears. Death is certain. Yet she hopes for deliverance, for a future unlike the past. She longs to see the face of God again, but her life is in God's hands. Are you listening?

We also hear a confused voice on this day. He is quick to draw his sword, but slow to acknowledge the one for whom he draws it. He joins himself to slaves and the police, opting for anonymity and warmth. "I am not one of his disciples," he retorts again . . . and again. There is resentment in his voice. There is fear in his voice. A cock is crowing. Are you listening?

Hear another confused voice. He is trying to understand the situation. He can't decide whether to follow the voice of reason or the cry of the crowd. He's interrogating the accused about being "the King of the Jews." He insists he's in control of the situation, yet he's inquiring about truth. He finds no fault with the accused. He's less insistent about being in con-trol as the situation deteriorates. He releases a bandit. "Here is the man!" "Here is your king!" What is truth? He knows he's lost control. Are you listening?

Hear one last voice. "I am the one you are looking for." "Put your sword away." "My kingdom is not of this world." "Everyone who belongs to the truth listens to me." Are you listening?

These are voices of rejection, suffering, confusion, pain, innocence, abandonment, anguish, searching, blaming, injustice, confidence, and silence. These are the voices of Good Friday. Are you listening? (John I. Essick)

Lectionary Commentary
Hebrews 10:16-25

The author quotes Jeremiah 31:33-34 as the words of the Holy Spirit in order to connect the idea that God has inscribed the law on the hearts of the people with the conviction that past sin has been completely for-given. In light of this news, the author exhorts his "friends," by means of the "let us" refrain, to pursue authentic worship, hope, and mutual encouragement. It should be noted that understanding the final phrase of verse 20, "through his flesh," is notoriously difficult. The question centers on whether the phrase explains further the curtain (that is, the veil) or the "new way" provided by Jesus. Finally, "the Day approaching" in verse 25 refers to the *Parousia* (Greek for "coming," "appearance," or "arrival"), which demands an end-time urgency of each generation of Christ's fol-lowers. (John I. Essick)

Worship Aids

Responsive Prayer (based on Isaiah 53:1-5)

Who has believed what we have heard?
And to whom has the arm of the LORD been revealed?
He had no form or majesty that we should look at him...
He was despised and rejected by others.
But he was wounded for our transgressions...
And by his bruises we are healed.

Words of Repentance

Lord have mercy, Christ have mercy.
Kyrie eleison, Christe eleison.

Benediction (Unison; based on Hebrews 10:16-25)

Let us go now, holding fast to our hope, provoking one another to good deeds, and encouraging one another, for Jesus has opened a new and liv-ing way for us. Amen. (John I. Essick)

Sinners in the Synagogue

Second in a Series of Three on Worship Sites

Matthew 6:1-6

Who should be in church? A 2008 poll of mainline Protestants in the United States indicated that almost two-thirds would prefer that we not allow "sinners" into our churches. Think about that for a minute. Were we to prohibit sinners from church, who would come? Our scriptures clearly state that things like borrowing and lending money at interest, gossip, bearing false witness, judging others, and cutting one's hair are all sinful—forget the "big sins" like murder or blasphemy. Were we to exclude sinners from the church, no one—including our pastoral leaders—would ever set foot inside our sanctuaries.

Obviously, the best place for a sinner is inside the church, not outside. For sinners to know God, to experience God's grace and love and hope and promise, we need to include them in our circles of fellowship. We need to understand that even the best of us fall into sin from time to time. Churches should be centers of grace, acceptance, forgiveness, and love, not citadels of judgment, intolerance, ostracism, and exclusion. Jesus points this out when he focuses on the hypocrites in the synagogues who present themselves as holy men, when in fact they are no better than those they condemn.

The synagogue was not a consecrated space like the temple in Jerusalem, but it was a gathering place set apart for worship, prayer, study, and religious instruction. The synagogue resembles in many respects the modern Christian congregation. It is a place made holy by the respect and religious convictions of those who gather to better know God. Also, like the modern Christian congregation, participants in the synagogue often turned their attention from God and made a show of their religion before others. For Jesus, this was the height of hypocrisy—to draw attention to oneself in a space dedicated to the honor and glory of God.

The passages from Matthew's Gospel where Jesus instructs his audience in appropriate behavior before God underscore the fact that actions speak louder than words. What we say we believe is less important than how we live our beliefs in the world. When our faith extends beyond our beliefs to our actions, we put ourselves at risk—standing up for what we believe in can be dangerous.

On this Good Friday we remember Jesus crucified—put to death not only for what he taught but also for what he did. But what Jesus did was not to draw glory to himself—see how often he instructs people he has healed to silence—but to point to the power of God to heal and to transform. Jesus did nothing for personal acclaim but gave all in service to God.

Another way of saying this—one that Jesus himself used—is that we will be known by our fruits (Matthew 7:16). Our fruits are those outward and visible signs of our inward and spiritual beliefs. They are the indisputable evidence of the "love, joy, peace, patience, kindness, generosity, faithfulness, gentleness, and self-control" (Galatians 5:22-23a) that God places in each heart.

When we gather together as God's people—whether in synagogue or in church—we gather to be made more holy. The place itself where we gather is not holy, but it becomes a sacred space as we engage in the deepest practices of our faith—prayer, study, worship, and praise—that form us in the image of God and empower us to be the body of Christ. We gather in our brokenness and sin to be made whole—to be forgiven, to be instructed, and to be equipped to live our faith in the world.

When "church" is only a place we go to, a building on a lot, an "X" on a map, it limits our vision of what it means to *be* the church. We often believe that our church building is sacred and special. If it is, it is because we share faith there. When we learn to take our faith with us beyond the walls of the church, an amazing thing happens. Our homes become sacred spaces. Our work provides us with sacred space. A bench in the park, a path through a forest, a cabin in the woods, a beach on a lakeshore—any and all places can become sacred space.

In these dark hours when we remember Christ crucified and buried, we reflect on what life is like when all that is sacred and holy is gone. Even our churches can feel empty and bereft—without the presence of Jesus the Christ, nothing feels right. It is a wonderful blessing and assurance to know that our feelings of Christ's absence—and they do come from time to time—will pass, and that by God's grace we might be transformed in our faith so that we never stand as hypocrites, but faithfully as witnesses ready to bear fruit and take our stand as the body of Christ in the world. (Dan R. Dick)

Worship Aids

Prayer of Confession (Unison)

God of grace and light and life, receive us as we are, rough edges and all. We are not the people we ought to be—we lose our patience, and we miss opportunities to be kind. We forget to be thankful, and we take so much for granted. We often behave in ways that are a far cry from what we say we believe. Forgive us for our failings and strengthen us to be better. Guide us, inspire us, be patient with us, and love us, we pray, in Jesus' holy name. Amen.

Words of Assurance

We are a "good news" people, and the good news is this: God loves us as we are, but will never leave us alone. By God's grace, and the love of

Christ, and the power of the Holy Spirit, we are a new creation in Christ, getting better day by day!

Benediction

Let us bear bountiful fruit—to share the sweetness of God's grace, the nourishment of Christ's love, and the satisfying fullness of God's Holy Spirit—to feed a world starving for acceptance, peace, and meaning. Amen. (Dan R. Dick)

APRIL 24, 2011

❧❧❧❧

Easter Sunday

Readings: Acts 10:34-43; Psalm 118:1-2, 14-24; Colossians 3:1-4; John 20:1-18

Losing Jesus?
John 20:1-18

The last few days have seemed like an eternity as we've reflected on final meals, footwashings, betrayals, brutal beatings, crucifixion, and preparation of Jesus' body for burial. After all of that—and because of all of that—we long for this day when we gather to celebrate the resurrection of Jesus as God's triumph over sin and death, and what a glorious day it is! The stone is gone, and we even stuck our heads into the tomb for good measure. Jesus is no longer in the tomb, nor has he been taken. "He is risen! He is risen, indeed."

Countless sermons have been delivered on this passage and rightfully so. It contains a series of powerful gospel moments: an apostolic footrace, linen wrappings without the corresponding corpse, a weeping woman, angels, and a risen but unrecognizable Lord. Often lost in these narrative elements, however, is Mary Magdalene's troubled refrain: someone has taken away my Lord. She expresses a concern for the location of Jesus' body no fewer than three times throughout this passage.

Mary first reports the body's disappearance to Peter and the other disciples. This first Easter proclamation is filled with blame, doubt, and uncertainty. Her words prompt Peter and the other disciple to go and see for themselves. Similarly, in tear-laden words, Mary reports to the two angels that "they" have taken away my Lord, never once stopping to inquire of the divine messengers regarding Jesus' location.

On a third occasion, in the presence of Jesus himself although she mistakes him for a gardener, Mary wonders aloud about the location of the corpse. In an interesting narrative twist, Mary seeks clarification from the supposed gardener: "Sir, if you have carried him away, tell me where you have laid him, and I will take him away" (John 20:15). The anxious uncertainty that motivates Mary's remarks and questions is somehow anchored in her ignorance of the Resurrection. She has yet to encounter the risen Lord. It is almost as if the absence of his body exacerbates her grief. Mary Magdalene's frantic search for Jesus suggests that finding a corpse on Easter morning is preferred to the absence of Jesus' body altogether. She has found her treasure yet she does not recognize its form. She is holding on to the crucified Jesus so tightly that she is unable to grasp the resurrected Lord.

Mary's frantic search ends abruptly when Jesus calls her by name. Her eyes and heart are opened to his presence as she hears the familiar voice of her rabbi, her teacher. Although the text does not say, it is not difficult to imagine Mary reaching out to embrace Jesus or falling at his feet. Her mind must be filled with relief, confusion, and sundry questions at this point. Her Easter morning is indeed a serendipitous one.

Returning to the text, however, it is striking that immediately after Mary realizes it is Jesus who stands before her, she is forbidden to cling to him: "Do not hold on to me, because I have not yet ascended to the Father" (20:17). She is then instructed to deliver a message to the brothers: "I am ascending to my Father and your Father, to my God and your God" (v. 17). (Are we to hear echoes of Ruth's memorable speech in these instructions by Jesus?)

What! You can't be serious! What kind of tragedy is this? It isn't enough that Mary is mourning the torture and crucifixion of her teacher, now her own expectations in the wake of his death and subsequent resurrection are frustrated as well. Why is Mary being told that she is about to lose Jesus yet again? Granted, she is not losing Jesus to death, but she is losing him to the Father.

Next week's Gospel reading reveals that Jesus was quite content to let Thomas "hold" on to him by placing his hands in the wounds; why not Mary? Are we to think that Jesus ascended after meeting Mary only to descend again before meeting Thomas? Did Jesus simply change his mind in the days between the appearances to Mary and Thomas? Scenarios and explanations such as these seem quite unlikely, so perhaps this Easter morning we should question more deeply Jesus' response to Mary on that first Easter morning if we wish to learn something of what Jesus' resurrection inaugurates for us and within us.

Earlier in John's Gospel, after the footwashing (14:18-19), Jesus informs those present that in a short while the world will no longer see him, but he goes on to say that he will be visible to his followers. Two chapters later, Jesus again promises that "I will see you again, and your hearts will rejoice" (16:22). Is it possible that Mary has mistaken Jesus' appearance to her on Easter morning by associating it with the promises made in 14:18-19 and 16:22?

If this is the case, then Jesus' admonition against holding on to him functions as an instructive correction with regard to resurrection and postresurrection life. Things are not as they were. Jesus' abiding presence will not "appear" as it did before. Instead, Jesus' presence will permanently "appear" in the form of the Spirit. In this way, then, John's Gospel, unlike Acts, paradoxically interrelates resurrection and ascension. Just as John associates Jesus' glorification with his crucifixion, so in 20:1-18 we find that Jesus' resurrection should not be separated from his ascension.

Mary Magdalene mirrors many of our concerns and wishes on this Easter morning. Resurrection seems so unlikely, so distant—although it is ever so near. Like Mary, we are frantically searching for whatever shred of proof or foothold of new life we can find. Yet this passage insists that we not expend energy trying to hold on to Jesus or worrying about losing him, for only when we release him to God do we receive the permanent indwelling of the Holy Spirit. (John I. Essick)

Lectionary Commentary
Acts 10:34-43

Peter's speech appears in the midst of an account of how even the Gentiles are included in God's saving work carried out via the life, death, and resurrection of Jesus. In these words delivered by Peter, we can see the core of the *kerygma*, or proclamation, of some of the earliest Christian sermons. In many ways, verses 34-43 are a summation of Luke's Gospel. In addition, the content of Peter's speech is in keeping with other speeches and sermons delivered in the opening chapters of Acts.

The following list outlines a few of the sermonic elements in Peter's speech: (1) God is not partial; (2) God's message of peace came by Jesus; (3) Jesus is Lord of all; (4) News of Jesus spread throughout Judea; (5) God was with Jesus, as evidenced by the many healings Jesus performed; (6) Peter and the other apostles are witnesses to these events; (7) "They" put Jesus to death by crucifixion; (8) God raised Jesus on the third day; (9) We have been commanded to proclaim that Jesus is the judge of those living and dead; and (10) Those who believe receive forgiveness of sins in the name of Jesus. Notice that God's saving action in Jesus forms the heart of the earliest Christian *kerygma*.

Colossians 3:1-4

These verses serve as a transitional introduction to a lengthy section of ethical instruction. Drawing on baptismal imagery, the text calls attention to a new beginning in Christ, a new way of thinking and seeing. This new beginning requires that we no longer set our minds on the things of earth, which amount to those things that have not been raised with Christ. It is Christ (mentioned no fewer than four times in the passage) who resides in the highest realm and occupies the place of honor. Verses 3 and 4 reveal in a rather cryptic fashion that those who have been raised with Christ are somehow hidden with him "in God." Thus, believers paradoxically participate in a hidden heavenly reality while simultaneously working to set their minds on that reality, and what is now hidden will be revealed in a future eschatological moment. The remainder of chapter 3 consists of practical instruction on how to seek the things above. (John I. Essick)

Worship Aids

Call to Worship

He is risen!
He is risen, indeed!
We have come to encounter the risen Lord.
May our eyes adjust to the light of his resurrection.
We have come to worship the risen Lord.
May our hearts recognize him as the Savior of the world.

Responsive Reading (based on Psalm 118:1-2, 14-24)

This is the day that the LORD has made;
   let us rejoice and be glad in it.
The stone that the builders rejected
   has become the chief cornerstone.
This is the LORD's doing;
   it is marvelous in our eyes.
The LORD is our strength and our might;

God has become our salvation.
We shall not die, but we shall live,
  and recount the deeds of the LORD.
We thank you that you have answered us
  and have become our salvation.
All: This is the day that the LORD has made;
  let us rejoice and be glad in it.

Benediction (based on Colossians 3:1-4)

Sisters and brothers, having been raised with Christ, leave this place seeking the things that are above and setting your minds on things that are above. (John I. Essick)

"Sanctuosity"

Third in a Series of Three on Worship Sites

1 Corinthians 6:12-20

We gather this day to celebrate a miracle. Jesus who was dead is now alive! The Lord and Savior of the world has overcome the "rulers and authorities" (Colossians 2:15) to offer eternal life to all. This is an amazing story, an amazing gift.

Look deep inside. Reflect for a moment. As you examine your heart and mind, what you most deeply value and revere, do you see Christ? You are the body of Christ—or at least a member of it. If there is no Christ inside, there can be no Christ for others. "Or do you not know that your body is a temple of the Holy Spirit within you, which you have from God...?" (1 Corinthians 6:19). Christ is alive! A time to rejoice. But if Christ is not alive within you, then where will Christ live?

We are a resurrection people. This day, among all others, is a day to rejoice, to celebrate, to give thanks, and to appreciate the greatness of our God. This is Easter. Jesus, who was killed upon the cross, is alive! From the depths of darkness and despair comes a grand and glorious light. Our beaten, defeated, and crucified Lord has defeated all the powers of evil and darkness. Jesus is alive!

As Christians we come together on this day to rejoice. Indeed, this is a wondrous day—a day to be grateful to be alive. Our Lord is Lord over death and destruction. Our faith is a faith that prevails over every obstacle. The light of Christ dispels all darkness. How great is that?

Yet it cannot stop here. Jesus lives again to establish God's kingdom for all time. We are the people of God, gifted, graced, and called to be the body of Christ for the world. When we say yes to the Christian faith, we are making a commitment to be Christ for others. We are a holy people set apart for holy work. What was begun in the earthly ministry of Jesus Christ is entrusted to us to continue. God is deeply interested in what we will do next.

We call this room in which we gather a *sanctuary*. Historically, a sanctuary is a holy space, designated for the worship of God. In various ages and places, sanctuaries were dedicated to worship, to protection, and to consecration. But the sanctuary of the Lord—the holy place where God dwells—is defined not merely by bricks and mortar but by the people who proclaim, "Jesus Christ is Lord." *Sanctuary* cannot become a place we use to escape the world, but it must be a holy orientation to all of God's creation. *Sanctuary* is not just where we go but must become a valid description of who we are.

A contemporary hymn pleads, "Lord, prepare me to be a sanctuary, pure and holy, tried and true" (© 1982 Whole Armor Publishing Company). But is this what we truly want? To be a sanctuary—a holy place set aside for the worship and commitment to God—requires that we give our whole lives to serving God. This is an incredible pledge.

The Easter miracle is that Jesus is alive, not just as a special historical event, but for all time. The evidence of this miracle in the world today is us—God's people, the church as witness to the reality of Christ's redeeming love. By our words and actions, we prove God's grace is real. Christ is alive, but only to the extent that he is alive in the hearts and minds of his people.

Consider for a moment, we are the body of Christ. We are the ongoing gift of love and grace and forgiveness and compassion in the world. We are to dedicate ourselves to peace and justice, mercy and acceptance. If those outside Christian community are to ever know Christ, they will come to know him through us.

What a humbling responsibility! This is why we are the church. There is no other reason for our existence together—as the Christian church—than to be Christ for others. Too often, we are very clear on what we receive from the church, but we are less clear on our responsibility to be the church for others.

The sanctuary is a holy place. It is, and has always been, the sacred space where we seek God. It is the place where we gather together to worship God, but it also becomes an aspect of our identity as the people of

God. Other people, who are hurting and struggling, and who ache to know love and acceptance, need sanctuary as well. They may never enter our churches, but they will come to us. Will they find sanctuary? Will they find grace in us? Will they receive love and acceptance from us? Will they encounter the risen Christ in our words and our actions?

Jesus lives! Jesus lives in us! The incarnate Word of God, the Savior of the world, the living, breathing body of Christ is present in the world today—present in us. Each of us is a temple of God—a holy sanctuary. May we honor and glorify God in the way we treat others—sharing the teachings of Jesus and extending to everyone we meet his healing love and care.

We are an Easter people! We believe in the risen Lord. Let us go forth from this place to be Christ for the world. Hallelujah! Amen. (Dan R. Dick)

Worship Aids

Invocation (Unison)

We come to a tomb seeking Jesus. We come expecting a corpse, but instead we find a savior. We look to tend to a body, but we experience a miracle. Jesus Christ is alive! The Spirit of the living God meets us and calls us to new life, to new hope, and to a renewed belief. Not only do we receive the gift of the resurrected Christ, we also receive a challenge—to tell the world: Jesus Christ is alive and Jesus Christ is Lord. Hallelujah! Amen.

Pastoral Prayer

Forgive us our doubts and fears, O Lord. Our Savior reigns! Death is defeated, suffering is but a fleeting dream, our future rests with Christ Jesus. Help us, O Lord, to share this Easter miracle with others. Empower us through your Spirit to live the good news. Fill us with gratitude and joy, grace and thanksgiving that we might bless everyone we meet with the love of Christ. As you have graced us with the miracle of Easter, enable us to be an Easter people, spreading your gift throughout the world. Amen.

Benediction

Jesus Christ is risen! The miracle has happened. God's love reigns supreme. Go forth from this place to share God's love with everyone you meet. You are Easter people. Live each day in the assurance of God's amazing power. Amen. (Dan R. Dick)

MAY 1, 2011

❧❧❧

Second Sunday of Easter

Readings: Acts 2:14a, 22-32; Psalm 16; 1 Peter 1:3-9; John 20:19-31

The Liturgy of Resurrection
John 20:19-31

We have just come through Lent and Holy Week, periods of serious spiritual labor. Lent is similar to the work required to prepare a plot of land for gardening: there are weeds to pull, clumps of grass to remove, and rocks to clear. In like manner, Lent requires the backbreaking and tedious labor of clearing ourselves of pride, pulling out weeds of selfishness, and trimming away the accumulated clumps of self-centeredness. Lent, then, was our season to work the soil of our souls and clear away the debris that distracts our minds and clutters our hearts. I don't know about you, but my liturgical legs were pretty tired when resurrection finally rolled into town last week. I was ready to throw off the discipline of Lent and the anxiety of Holy Week and replace them with a more relaxing and relief-filled resurrection: "The Lord is risen!"

Yet today's reading from John 20, the infamous "doubting Thomas" passage, calls to us to say: "Wait. There is work to be done. There is gardening yet to do." This point is driven home by the fact that this reading is the Gospel lesson for the Second Sunday of Easter in all three years of the lectionary cycle. Whereas the spiritual work of Lent could be conducted in a more private manner, the work of resurrection life is more communal, more public. Many readers of this passage have noted traces of early Christian liturgy or worship.

Some Protestants bristle at the idea of "liturgy" because we mistakenly equate it with rote repetition, heaping up empty phrases like the Gentiles in Matthew 6, or we associate it with a formal style known as "liturgical worship." Liturgy, however, is not confined to one worship style. The word *liturgy* (*leitourgia*) carries the idea of "public work" in service of the state or in a religious context, the people's "work" or "service" to God. In this sense, all worship is liturgical. But the idea of liturgy as our "public work" of worship returned to my mind as I contemplated this passage.

If we simply stop with the spiritual work demanded by Lent and Holy Week, then all we've accomplished is spiritual brush removal. But the Lord is risen! That changes everything. Jesus' resurrection plows to the depths of us to plant and reap new life. Resurrection ensures that the church's soil does not lie fallow. We've cleared the ground of our souls; we now need to move on to realize the goal of the people's work: planting and harvesting in the garden of Jesus' resurrection. If we turn to John 20:19-31 with the spectacles of public work or the people's worship, we can identify several species of plant life that should spring forth from the fertile soil of resurrection at work within us.

The first thing we notice is that the disciples are already in the habit of assembling on the Lord's Day (first day of the week). Despite their fear and confusion, these earliest disciples find it necessary to gather as a community. Could it be that Thomas's conspicuous absence from the assembled disciples impacts his ability to believe? Even the decision to gather is part of our liturgy as the people of God, an act of worship. If we wish to probe the meaning and reality of the risen Lord, it is going to happen most fully when we are gathered for the work of worship.

In this liturgy of resurrection, as the disciples are gathered, Christ appears—bearing the marks of his passion. Don't miss that. Jesus, from the beginning, exposes his wounds for the sake of those present, effectively allowing them to find their faith again. Both Sunday appearances involve a physical confrontation with the actual marks of the passion. We would do well to consider the same invitation to embrace the eucharistic marks in our own liturgies as often as we gather for worship. One could make a good theological case, I believe, that the church was being formed as those disciples handled the body that was broken for them. This Easter liturgy does not call us to forget or discard the marks of suffering. No. Our liturgical work is to live into and out of those marks by filling ourselves with the bread of life and drinking deeply of the cup of salvation.

We also notice in this passage the giving of a blessing: "Peace be with you" (John 20:19, 21). Peace is the fulfillment of Jesus' earlier promises. Scholars point out that Jesus' statement is not a wish or hopeful intention; it functions grammatically as a statement of fact. The liturgy of resurrection requires that, as followers of Christ, we work for and proclaim peace.

Another aspect of our resurrection work involves apostolic mission. Only here does John have the disciples commissioned by Jesus as "apostles," or "sent ones," entrusted with the salvation message of resurrection. In John's Gospel, the Father sends the Son to serve as both the model and the ground for the Son to send the disciples. Our liturgy of resurrection will always involve a divine mission and, as Jesus continues, divine empowerment.

Jesus gives the Holy Spirit to the disciples by breathing on them. In liturgical terms, the Holy Spirit empowers them to complete the commission just delivered and ensures the power over sin to follow (what is often called "absolution"). "Receive the Holy Spirit," Jesus utters as he breathes on them (20:22). It is not difficult to imagine why ancient baptismal subjects were often breathed upon in baptism. We see that the church's work in worship and witness are indistinguishable aspects of liturgy.

In one of the more complicated and puzzling statements from the resurrected Jesus, we read that the forgiveness and retention of sins somehow falls on our shoulders. Notice that John doesn't spell out how all this forgiveness business works, only that this power is exercised in light of the resurrection. Such power has been used and abused throughout the church's history, but in the end we must be aware that what we do matters. Our forgiveness matters. Our spiritual work, like that of the trinitarian God, is in and for the world, for the healing of all nations.

Finally, our call to liturgical work finds us confessing, with Thomas, that Jesus is both Lord and God. Our work is complete. We have transformed from a fearful and anxious group gathered in an out-of-the-way place into a liturgical body wherein peace, mission, and forgiveness are the norm, a realm where the resurrected Jesus is proclaimed as the Lord of all. (John I. Essick)

Lectionary Commentary
Acts 2:14a, 22-32

This reading from Acts includes a portion of Peter's Pentecost sermon to some of the Israelites who had gathered in Jerusalem for the Feast of Weeks, or Pentecost (celebrated fifty days after Passover). More specifically, Peter's proclamation is the gospel-filled answer to those asking, "What does this mean?" We notice that Peter insists that God's redemptive work in the crucifixion and resurrection of Jesus is in complete and utter continuity with God's previous saving actions in the Old Testament. Furthermore, the identification of Jesus as the risen Messiah—of which Peter and the eleven were witnesses—constitutes the core of the early apostolic preaching.

1 Peter 1:3-9

The first catholic (general) Epistle of Peter was likely written in the second half of the first century to an audience somewhere in modern-day Turkey. The Epistle lacks the customary thanksgiving, yet that absence is overshadowed by the insertion of a glorious section on the dignity of the Christian. Verses 3-4 in particular focus on the nature of the Christian's identity in light of "the resurrection of Jesus Christ from the dead." The result of the resurrection is a rather distinguished existence for Christ's followers, complete with an incorruptible inheritance that is housed in heaven. Thus, the seminal event in the new birth of each believer is the new life experienced by Christ himself. The completion of this new life is nothing less than the "salvation" of our souls (v. 9). (John I. Essick)

Worship Aids

Call to Worship
The peace of Christ be with you.
And also with you.
Lift up your hearts.
We lift them up to the Lord.

Responsive Reading (based on Psalm 16)
Protect me, O God, for in you I take refuge.
You are my Lord; I have no good apart from you.
The LORD is my chosen portion and my cup; you hold my lot.
I keep the LORD always before me;
    because he is at my right hand, I shall not be moved.
Therefore my heart is glad, and my soul rejoices;
    my body also rests secure.
You show me the path of life.
In your presence there is fullness of joy;
    in your right hand are pleasures forevermore.

Benediction (1 Peter 1:3)

Go now, in the great mercy of our God and Lord, who has given us a new birth into a living hope through the resurrection of Jesus Christ from the dead. (John I. Essick)

Bloodthirsty or Blood-bought?

First in a Series of Three on Proverbs

Proverbs 1:8-19

I can still remember my mom saying, "Choose your friends carefully, for you are who your friends are." How interesting that the first group of sayings Solomon includes with his kingly book of wisdom addresses the role of friends. We know that Solomon was not always very good about his choice of friends, particularly women. Is this a case of "Do as I say, not as I do"?

Recently, my younger son asked me to attend a father-son retreat with the theme "Passing the Baton." I found the metaphor very interesting. As parents, we run the opening leg of our children's lives, and they hear and watch us. Proverbs 1:8-9 says, "Hear, my child, your father's instruction, and do not reject your mother's teaching; for they are a fair garland for your head, and pendants for your neck."

In adolescence, the child moves from listening and observation to running with the parents. In a relay race, both the runner of the first leg and the runner of the second leg run a short distance together, during which time the baton is passed. But there is a complication—the power of peers. Parents teach and warn, but they know that despite their best efforts, they eventually will be trumped by the pull of friends. As a result, most parents end up relying on another proverb, 22:6: "Train children in the right way, and when old, they will not stray."

If only that were always true! Is there anyone among us who wouldn't like to redo some teenage and young adult actions with the wisdom we have gained through consequences and "hard knocks"? As the saying goes, "Youth is wasted on the young."

In Proverbs 1, the innocence of the child is put to the test through temptation. As James writes, "One is tempted by one's own desire, being lured and enticed by it; then, when that desire has conceived, it gives birth to sin, and that sin, when it is fully grown, gives birth to death" (James 1:14-15).

The power of the counterpart to the parents' teaching is that it appeals to selfishness and willfulness deep within. The father and mother warn of it, because they know its power from experience! The adolescent will need to learn the skill of resistance. Again, James gives practical application: "Submit yourselves therefore to God. Resist the devil, and he will flee from you. Draw near to God, and he will draw near to you" (James 4:7-8).

Note the double strategy! Defensively, we use our willpower to fend off the temptation, but the success rate is mixed at best. Resistance must also have an offensive dimension: the nurture of our commitment and a growing relationship with God. When both the defensive and offensive strategies are employed, the chances for staying in range to receive the baton are much greater.

The enticement of the friends in Proverbs 1 is to participate in violence (vv. 11-14). The church has yet to deal with the pervasiveness and the intoxication of violence in our society, and so has not prepared adequately our children, youth, and young adults to resist it. Instead, we find ourselves co-opted by violence. We build our athletes for greater punishment of one another (stronger, bigger, faster, more aggressive), which forces everyone to play at a more aggressive and violent level. But the result is escalating risk and feeding insatiable gladiatorial thirst. In mixed martial arts, for example, fighters are trained to punch with enough force to break the bones of eye sockets and to drop people with the force and recoil of a car crash. Astonishingly, mixed-martial-arts fighting is being marketed to children.

Now consider illegal and more lethal realms. Gang members say that there is a greater high in beating someone senseless or to death than in drug abuse or sexual intercourse. In fact, all three are related. Violence is highly addictive, and particularly for young men, violence and testosterone levels are connected. But the example of gangs invites us to consider something else, the power of violence in groups. The tempters in Proverbs 1:11-12 say: "Come with us, let us lie in wait for blood; let us wantonly ambush the innocent...let us swallow them alive." In school days we formed circles around combatants and started the mantra "Fight, fight, fight." Most of those fights would never have happened without an audience.

Connected to this violence is quick, ill-gotten gain. Verses 13-14 say: "We shall find all kinds of costly things; we shall fill our houses with booty. Throw in your lot among us; we will all have one purse." The group commits to sharing the ill-gotten wealth together, which assumes trust and care for one another, contrary to what formed the group in the first place. Eventually, however, selfishness betrays the group's unity (vv. 15-19). The net catches the one who built it. A life of violent destruction eventually becomes self-destruction.

By contrast, consider the nonviolent approach of Jesus. He chose to become the victim of the world's violence at its most vicious level, and chose not to retaliate. Jesus taught "turning the other cheek," and Paul taught "not repaying evil for evil" as a way of life. It was misunderstood by Roman society ("behold how they love each other") as weakness, but in the end, nonviolence has shown its ability to win. From Jesus to the martyrs to Gandhi to Martin Luther King, Jr., to Mother Teresa, the case for world-changing nonviolence has been made. As followers of Jesus, we are called to resist our world's natural and growing thirst for blood and instead witness to the blood of Christ as the world's salvation and redemption. (Will Cotton)

Worship Aids

Call to Worship

We gather in joy to praise you, O Lord. You have called us friends, and we are being reconciled with you and one another. Break down any walls we have created and free us to receive and share your love with everyone we meet. Through Jesus Christ our Lord. Amen.

Prayer of Confession

We confess to you, O Lord, that we have chosen complacency over prayerful action in our violent, fractured, and war-torn world. Forgive us, and by your Spirit, empower us to be agents of justice and peace in our daily lives, both individually and together as the church. Amen.

Words of Assurance

We worship a God of infinite patience and love. God's love for us will overcome our complacency and fill us with the power to transform the world. Thanks be to God. Amen.

Planning Help

Photos, a re-enactment of the passing of the baton, or an interview with a track coach would be effective. Intoxication with violence could be addressed through "impact scenes" from a sport or from movies. Recommended hymns are "Let There Be Peace on Earth" and "The Way of the Cross Leads Home." People could also share favorite proverbs they learned as children that are not in the book of Proverbs. (Will Cotton)

MAY 8, 2011

Third Sunday of Easter

Readings: Acts 2:14a, 36-41; Psalm 116:1-4, 12-19; 1 Peter 1:17-23;
Luke 24:13-35

Easter Perspective
1 Peter 1:17-23

One of the blessings of medicine is good eye care. When our vision becomes compromised by age or disease, we are fortunate to be able to go to the ophthalmologist or optometrist and take care of the problem. Often the doctor prescribes eyeglasses or contact lenses, which correct our vision so we can see clearly. Good vision gives us the right perspective and enables us to function well. However, when we first try out a new prescription, we may find that it takes awhile to get used to the corrected vision. At first things can seem a little strange, as though we are not seeing clearly. Gradually, our eyes adjust to the correction of the new lenses and we are able to see well.

The Easter season is a time of adjusting to a new vision. God has done an incredible work. The tomb has been emptied. Death has been defeated. On the Sunday of the resurrection, our hearts fill with joy and our voices soar with the hymns of new life. A new world has been born, a new vision has been given, and a new way of living has been prescribed. The church is invited to wear its Easter lenses as it looks out upon the world and responds to the challenge of living in light of the resurrection.

We live from the perspective of Easter. Perspective is important. The right perspective can bring joy and happiness; the wrong perspective can lead to disaster. A little boy and a little girl, brother and sister, were shopping with their mother in a large department store. The mother needed to have some time for her shopping so she took the children to the soda fountain, bought them ice-cream cones, and told them to stay there till she came back. Well, the children were fascinated by the elevator and could not resist the temptation to ride it one more time. So, with ice-cream cones in hand, they jumped off their stools and went to ride the elevator.

They were enjoying their up-and-down ride, but the little boy's ice cream was melting faster than he could eat it. Finally it was dripping down the cone and onto his hand despite his best attempts to eat the delicious treat before it melted. At one floor the elevator stopped and an elegantly dressed woman in a full-length fur coat got on. She stood in front of the children waiting to be taken to her floor. The little boy was desperately trying to deal with his melting ice cream. Seeing the back of the lady's fur coat, he gently began to wipe the sticky, melting ice cream on her coat. His sister said, "Be careful, Billy, or you will get fur in your ice cream." Now that illustrates perspective. What is a solution to one is to another a way to damage an expensive garment. It's all in the perspective.

Easter people live with the perspective of the resurrection. God has won the victory over death. The worst that can happen to us has been overcome by God taking Jesus from the tomb. That is our perspective. This vision challenges us to live boldly and daringly. "You have been born anew, not of perishable but of imperishable seed, through the living and enduring word of God" (1 Peter 1:23). In other words, you have a new perspective. Live from this perspective. Dare to "love one another deeply from the heart" (v. 22).

The early church had to get used to its Easter lenses. It must have seemed strange to live from the perspective of love in a world that was used to living in alienation. It must have been disorienting to include the outcast and the marginalized in the fellowship of the church. But this is what the Easter community did, and its witness was powerful. The world stood in awe as it watched a community of love live its life with redemptive acts of service and inclusion. Such a community was a new reality that embraced a way of living that others had never imagined.

The story continues as Easter people put on their new lenses and dare to live the way of love in a world of alienation and hurt. We are people of new perspective. We have seen what God has done in Jesus Christ. We no longer live in fear; rather, with radical love we go forth to practice the perspective of love as we follow the way and example of our risen Lord.

The church has to put on its Easter glasses and see life from the perspective of the resurrection. We are the people who dare to live the hope that other people believe can never be realized. From the Easter perspective, we live the "as if" principle. That is, we live "as if" the world has more love than it does, "as if" there is more hope than people are willing to embrace, "as if" the kingdom of God can reign on the earth today.

Our Easter glasses also give us the holy boldness to ask "What if?" What if every child had a warm, safe place to sleep? What if there was enough food for every person on this earth? What if we all lived from a sense of abundance rather than scarcity? What if today all the killing of all the wars stopped?

It all starts with vision, with perspective. Have the right perspective and you live the right life. Our perspective is Easter. "Through him you have come to trust in God, who raised him from the dead and gave him glory, so that your faith and hope are set on God" (1 Peter 1:21). We are the people of Easter whose vision has been forever corrected by what God has done in Jesus Christ our Lord. (Chris Andrews)

Lectionary Commentary
Acts 2:14a, 36-41; Luke 24:13-35

The texts for today show the early community of faith trying to come to terms with the Easter faith. What would it mean to live as a community of people whose lives were centered in the resurrection? It may be helpful to try to read these texts with a first-Easter attitude. Easter is a fantastic event that we may have compromised by familiarity. What if we had never heard the Easter story? These texts were addressed to people who were unacquainted with the tradition of the church and the witness of the apostles. The Emmaus walk in Luke is the story of two disciples gradually coming to realize that Jesus is alive. In Acts, Peter brings the news of Easter to people who don't already know of the resurrection. In each text, when eyes are opened and people realize the truth that Christ is alive, there is a distinctive change in energy and attitude. (Chris Andrews)

Worship Aids

Call to Worship

Return, O my soul, to your rest,
    for the Lord has dealt bountifully with you.
I love the Lord, because he has heard
    my voice and my supplications.
All: Let us offer praises of thanksgiving,
    for the Lord has blessed us abundantly.

Prayer of Confession

Forgive us, Lord, for our limited vision. We confess that we have been timid in the face of challenge and that in our spirits we have failed to follow the way of Easter. Sometimes we live as if death rather than life were the last word. Lift our hearts and our minds to the Easter heights that we might join the mighty chorus of apostles and prophets in witness to your glory, grace, and strength. We pray through Jesus Christ our Lord. Amen.

Words of Assurance

Hear the Easter news as if for the first time. Christ is risen from the dead! See with new light and new life. All things are now possible. Hallelujah!

Benediction

We are the people of Easter. We have been given a new perspective. Let us show the world resurrection power through deeds of love and mercy. May our vision be clear and our hearts bold as we let Christ shine in our lives. Amen. (Chris Andrews)

You Can Learn a Lot from an Ant

Second in a Series of Three on Proverbs

Proverbs 6:6-11

Proverbs puts a high value on industry. The feature character of Proverbs 6:6-11 is "the sluggard" (v. 6 NIV), taken from the slug, a most lifeless and unattractive creature. Interestingly, in eighteenth-century British worship services, they had among the ushers one who was the "sluggard waker." The usher used a long wooden wand with a brass knob or fork on the end (for men) or a foxtail (for women) to strike firmly those who fell asleep during the sermon. What a great tradition! My favorite sluggard passage is Proverbs 26:14: "As a door turns on its hinges, so a sluggard turns on his bed" (NIV). The writer of Proverbs invites the sluggard in each of us to consider the ant.

First, the ant doesn't need an authority to tell it what to do. "It has no commander, no overseer or ruler, yet it stores...and gathers" (6:7-8 NIV). When our parents used to ask us, "Why didn't you wash the dishes or clean up your room?" we said, "You didn't tell me." In the ant kingdom, there are different levels of authority, even among the worker ants, and discipline is carried out on those who don't do their work. The ant, by instinct, has motivation. What motivates you? Maybe a better first question is "Who motivates you?" Some are highly motivated because the virtues of hard work were modeled for them by parents and coaches. Those who grew up on farms know the cost of laziness; they have been trained in the value of hard work through lots of practice. These folks had a motivating community. To watch the ant is to watch a functional motivating community at its best.

Jesus' great strategy was calling forth the greatness in people and then creating a body that would do the same. Consider the difference between our world's ways and what should be the church's ways. In the world, if you are down and distressed, you are isolated. If you are underperforming, you are threatened and belittled. If you are sick or hurt, you are cast aside and even blamed for your problems. But by the "Jesus standard," we encourage the down and distressed, exhort people to do better in performing, love people into healing, and walk with people in their weaknesses. Furthermore, we are motivated by passion-filled mission: make disciples of Jesus Christ and transform our world. We have a purpose for being on planet Earth, and we give our lives to fulfill that purpose. As followers of Jesus Christ, we are highly motivated.

The next lesson from the ant is the value of preparation. "It stores its provisions in summer and gathers its food at harvest" (6:8 NIV). There are people who hit it big without great preparation, but they are rare exceptions. Successful business owners, great teachers, and Olympic athletes all require extensive and sacrificial preparation. It is in the preparation phase that depth of character, holy motivations, and resilience in tough times are built. Yet we often doubt the value of the preparation, feeling that it's time wasted, time we could be "playing the game" or "making a difference." But I find that I am just now enjoying the benefits of practices and lessons that were communicated to me twenty years ago, things I thought were both irrelevant and unnecessary at the time.

Now I wish I had stored more of those lessons. According to Jesus' instructions (Acts 1:4), the first act of the church was to wait, preparing for God's next history-making move by the power of the Holy Spirit. So much of what individuals and churches do is reactionary, wasting precious time and resources and becoming more hyperactive and scattered. The period of change we are in is both rapid and unpredictable. What if, while we do the necessary work of learning how to reach the world, we also grow deeper and store up the spiritual resources required to navigate a long and challenging chapter in the church's life?

Still, that work of reaching the world is necessary and urgent. And so we come to the third lesson from the ant, how to avoid our favorite vice: procrastination. Is there anyone who isn't addicted to the adrenaline of doing things at the last minute? Mark Twain allegedly wrote, "Never put off until tomorrow what you can do the day after tomorrow." Our passage says: "A little sleep, a little slumber, a little folding of the hands to rest—and poverty will come on you like a bandit and scarcity like an armed man" (Proverbs 6:10-11 NIV). We indeed can sleep away, dream away, TV away, and excuse away most any opportunity. Procrastination is pervasive, isn't it? My dad has this little "Tuit" button that he keeps in his front desk drawer. It simply means "Get to it now."

Workers in the United States put in more hours weekly than those in any other industrialized country. We are overcommitted and sleep-deprived. Our problem is not that we are lazy overall, but rather that we are lazy about some of the most important things. We may work hard on the job, but not on relationships with our family, friends, or with God. We may do so much busywork that we are never able to do the holy work we were created to do. In other words, as busy and overtired as we are, we could well be relational and spiritual sluggards. In our calendar-driven, technology-driven world, the problem could be epidemic.

Can we learn from the lowly ant, who acts decisively on its own inner authority, drawing on its storehouse of food and energy? Motivated within by the power of the Holy Spirit and armed with a storehouse of spiritual knowledge and power, we too can wake up, get up, and change the world. (Will Cotton)

Worship Aids

Call to Worship

You are the people of God, blessed with holy love.
We are blessed to be a blessing
   so that we might make God's love real in
   our homes, our church, and our community.
You are God's workmanship,
   formed in the divine image and growing in grace.
We rejoice to do God's work:
   sharing the gospel, offering hope, and changing our world. Amen.

Prayer of Confession

Lord, you call us to a life of purpose and fruitfulness, but we instead have chosen lives of distraction and busywork. We are scattered and lost, in need of your direction. By your grace, teach us new priorities and give us strength to carry them out. Amen.

Words of Assurance

Through the love of God, the redeeming work of Jesus, and the power of the Holy Spirit, we already have the power, the authority, and the energy to change the world. Join in praise and celebration!

Planning Help

A video of an ant farm in action or a children's sermon that reviews the roles of the ants in the colony could be used. Hymn suggestions are: "I Am Thine, O Lord" and "Breathe on Me, Breath of God." (Will Cotton)

MAY 15, 2011

Fourth Sunday of Easter

Readings: Acts 2:42-47; Psalm 23; 1 Peter 2:19-25; John 10:1-10

Experience the Living Christ
Acts 2:42-47

No one can make the case that the Christian faith is theoretical. It is not a system of thought, a bank of words, or a collection of ideas. Ultimately the Christian faith is about living in relationship and community. The Easter legacy is the church of Jesus Christ.

Try as we might to clean up Christianity, this faith of ours always brings us back to the same place—the church. What Jesus leaves on this earth to continue his work is the church. I know people who like the idea of religion, but they don't want the church. Some folks enjoy the warm, pleasant feelings that come from spiritual thinking, but they don't want the church. Some are excited by the idea of love, but they don't want the church. Some people certainly want heaven for eternity, but they don't want the church for today.

That is a problem because, like it or not, if we are going to follow Jesus, we are going to be involved in the church. The church is often called the "bride of Christ." Someone said, "I love Jesus. I just wish he wouldn't bring his leprous bride every place he goes." But church and Jesus go together like "love and marriage" or "horse and carriage."

So just pause and reflect for a moment. Easter has come. The tomb has been emptied. The Lord has appeared to his disciples, and the announcement has gone forth: "He is alive!" Jesus is alive! Where do we find him for ourselves? Where do we experience his aliveness in personal ways? The answer is through the fellowship of the redeemed, in the quarters of the church, in the embrace of the manifestation of the body of Christ.

What I am saying elevates the church to a status that some may not appreciate. In today's passage, we get a glimpse of the church in its earliest moments, and it is a beautiful thing to behold. The people are united, everyone is attentive to the teaching of the apostles, no one misses a service or a Bible study, there are enough volunteers for every task, folks are giving generously to support the church, and people are lining up to join. This is going to be a megachurch!

If you know your Bible and the story of the church, though, you know this way of life does not last. Soon the church will be dealing with all sorts of unpleasant matters. For example, today's text is from the second chapter of Acts. By the fifth chapter, folks are dropping dead in the church for lying about their financial support. We're talking about lying about their pledge. Hello!

Is this the church? Yes, this is the church. This is the "holy, catholic church" we affirm and believe in. This church is the aftermath of Easter. Do you want to experience the living Christ? Go to the church. Oh, I know there will be frustration. The church likes to "major in the minors," quarreling over the most foolish things. It seems, at times, to enjoy poor health and to love complaining. I know all this. But I also know that if you want to find Jesus, it will be in his church.

I think of my own life. Both my parents were alcoholics, both died by their own hands through suicide. We lived from day to day in a volatile world of economic uncertainty—and the church came. The local Methodist church showed up with food, clothes, and, most of all, kindness. They welcomed me into their fellowship. They made me part of their choir. They said I was important to them. I had nothing to offer in return, but they did not care about that. They offered a new economics, the economics of grace. All I knew was that I was one lost young fellow, and these good people put the arms of Jesus around my life and sent me in a new direction of hope and meaning and purpose. I had found Jesus, or Jesus had found me, and life was forever changed.

The Christian faith is never theory. It is not about religious thinking. The Christian faith is about relationship. In the midst of the comings and goings of our lives, the risen Christ appears, community happens, and the church takes shape. Easter has come, and Easter continues. Easter continues in the imperfect, grace-filled community we call *church*. Remember this the next time you are tempted to give up on church. If you want to experience Jesus, this is the place and the people, for in spite of their imperfections and idiosyncrasies, the church is where the living Christ lives.

Give thanks for your church and your place in it. There is no better place to find what you are looking for, which is the touch of the Master's hand in your life. I know because I have experienced it. Thanks be to God for church! (Chris Andrews)

Lectionary Commentary
1 Peter 2:19-25; John 10:1-10

Each of today's passages makes a reference to the *shepherd*. Christ as the Shepherd is a rich metaphor for the church. His caring love has guided the community of faith as a shepherd tends the flock. We are the sheep and he is the shepherd of our souls. In his care we are safe and well.

The question naturally forms as to where the shepherding love of Christ can be experienced in today's world. The answer is in the community of faith. Through the hymns, scriptures, fellowship, and service of the church, people come to know the shepherd's voice, understand the shepherd's ways, and experience the shepherd's grace. (Chris Andrews)

Worship Aids

Call to Worship
Christ has called us to this time of worship.
We open our lives to Christ's grace.
Bring to Christ your hurts and hopes.
We have come to be shaped by the Spirit of Christ into the body of Christ.

Prayer of Confession
O Lord, we confess that we have often failed in our witness to your love. We have been timid when we should have been bold. We have caused division in the human family. Our sin is ever before us as we have rejected the stranger and taken shelter in our fears. Forgive us, we pray. Once more we ask that you make us into a community worthy of the name of Jesus. Lead us, Lord, that we might bring our lives to the noble work of transforming the world to live your will in all things. Amen.

Words of Assurance
In the name of the risen Christ, you are forgiven.
In the name of the risen Christ, you are forgiven.
Thanks be to God.

Benediction

Go forth into the world to be the transforming presence of Jesus. At work, at home, at play, may the grace of Christ sustain your witness. You are the church, the body of Christ. Go in the strength of Christ and know that because of you others will come to know the love of Jesus. Amen. (Chris Andrews)

There Is Nothin' Like a Dame

Third in a Series of Three on Proverbs

Proverbs 9:1-18

In a midweek Bible study on Proverbs, we shared favorite wisdom sayings folks had learned. There were, of course, traditional ones: "A stitch in time saves nine," "He who laughs last laughs best," and "To the early bird goes the worm." But my favorite one was from a former Kansas ranch boy who said, "Always drink upstream from the herd." The class just roared. It's common sense, of course, as are most of the biblical proverbs. But if common sense is so common, why did our folks have to drum it into our heads as kids, and why do we need to learn what should be "common" again and again?

The ninth chapter of Proverbs contrasts Dame Wisdom with Dame Folly. The concept of "the two ways" is a popular teaching tool throughout Middle Eastern and Eastern religions. Jesus used it as well: the wide and narrow gates (Matthew 7:13), the wise and foolish builders (Matthew 7:24-27), and the wise and foolish bridesmaids (Matthew 25:1-13), to name a few. Choosing between two obvious alternatives should be easy. But in the case of right living, it isn't easy at all.

Dame Wisdom calls out to those who lack judgment, "Let all who are simple come in here!" (Proverbs 9:4 NIV). That's easy enough, except for one problem: you have to admit that you are simple, that you lack judgment. As I once heard in a conference, "One of the most dangerous things is not knowing what you don't know." The economic, political, medical, and moral problems in our society are paralyzing because those on opposite sides cannot admit they "lack judgment" or that they don't know. Wisdom requires humility and admitting that we don't have it all together. But the pressure around us is to look all-wise and self-sufficient. In our attempts to look wise, we show ourselves foolish.

Once we have admitted we are simple and lack judgment, Dame Wisdom calls us to follow that up with action, letting go of that which is foolish. Is there anything more difficult than letting go of a way of thinking or behaving that we have followed for years? Doesn't that very thing challenge teachers and professors, salespersons and marketers, psychologists and physicians, politicians, and even preachers and parishioners? Even if what we are thinking and doing isn't working, we hang on to it because we are afraid of what we don't know. You do catch the irony, don't you?

So there we have it. The way of wisdom requires us to admit that we are simple (needy) and lack judgment; and we follow that up by letting go of our old ways. That's easy enough, but there is a problem, a competing voice for our attention and desires. The invitation is the same: "Let those who are simple come here!" But the approach and the delivery system are very different. Dame Folly is loud and carefree. Her ways are seductive: easy fixes, fast money, instant gratification, fuzzy ethics, and freedom from accountability.

"Stolen water is sweet; food eaten in secret is delicious" (Proverbs 9:17 NIV). The place in our souls that Folly calls to is different, appealing to what Paul calls our "carnal mind" (Romans 8:7 KJV; "mind that is set on the flesh" NRSV), our selfishness. As James writes in his letter, we are "lured and enticed" by our own desires, and the end is the same every time (1:14-15).

That is the second half of Dame Folly's bargain. "But little do they know that the dead are there, that her guests are in the depths of the grave" (Proverbs 9:18 NIV).

The thing is, we knew it from the beginning. We knew it was all glitz, promising a whole lot of something for nothing, but we hoped maybe this time we could get away with it. Casinos, racetracks, and bookies exist to do one thing, to rip off gamblers hand over fist. People win sometimes, but we choose to ignore (we do not forget) why the gambling industry exists. Likewise, the pornography industry exists to prey on those who might become addicts, and to make enormous amounts of money off them. Short-term gain and pleasure are traded for distracted lives and broken relationships.

Let's not fool ourselves. Dame Folly can be quite attractive, and each of us falls into her ways, even though we end up feeling guilty, stupid, and robbed. They don't call her Folly for nothing! In the words of Paul, "I do not do what I want, but I do the very thing I hate.... Wretched man that I am! Who will rescue me from this body of death?" (Romans 7:15, 24).

Dame Wisdom points us to the way out of our dilemma in Proverbs 9:10: "The fear of the LORD is the beginning of wisdom, and the knowledge of the Holy One is insight."

Paul's answer is the same, "Thanks be to God through Jesus Christ our Lord!" (Romans 7:25). Dame Folly calls us to self-centeredness and self-indulgence for the purpose of insatiable and short-lived self-satisfaction. Dame Wisdom calls us to God-centeredness for the purpose of healing and transforming the world, soul-satisfaction that lasts a lifetime and beyond. Answering the call of wisdom might even lead to longer life. Actuarial tables tell us that wise living strongly outlives foolish living. There are exceptions, of course, which Dame Folly celebrates on billboards. But following her ways is a whole lot like "drinking downstream from the herd." The good news is, even if our days do not outnumber the days of those who follow Dame Folly, the life we experience in following Dame Wisdom will be of far superior quality and inner joy (not to mention clean water). So which way will you choose this day or even this moment? Amen and amen. (Will Cotton)

Worship Aids

Call to Worship (based on Proverbs 3:5-6; 9:10; 3:8)

Trust in the LORD with all your heart, and lean not on your own understanding.
In all your ways acknowledge the LORD, and God will make your paths straight.
The fear of the LORD is the beginning of wisdom.
It will be healing for your flesh and refreshment for your body.

Prayer of Confession

Lord, you invite us to choose what is wise, but we willfully choose that which is foolish. We are drawn to what is loud, glitzy, and temporarily satisfying, rather than following your still, small voice. Forgive our blindness of mind and heart, and free us to truly follow you. Amen.

Words of Assurance

God waits. God hopes. God celebrates when we choose Dame Wisdom. Thanks be to God.

Planning Help

Show images of "too-good-to-be-true offers." A children's sermon could be offered about making wise and foolish choices. Recommended hymns are "'Tis So Sweet to Trust in Jesus" and "I Want a Principle Within." (Will Cotton)

MAY 22, 2011

Fifth Sunday of Easter

Readings: Acts 7:55-60; Psalm 31:1-5, 15-16; 1 Peter 2:2-10; John 14:1-14

A Peculiar People
1 Peter 2:2-10

The scripture lesson for today is a call to a new way of living. It is a call to be a "holy priesthood" (1 Peter 2:5), a different people who "long for the pure, spiritual milk" (2:2). It is a fitting text as the glow of Easter recedes. It is a reminder that we are called for special work and have been made, by God's gracious action in Jesus Christ, into a new people. Today's text culminates in a strong call to the people of faith. We are "a chosen race, a royal priesthood, a holy nation, God's own people, in order that [we] may proclaim the mighty acts of him who called [us] out of darkness into his marvelous light" (v. 9).

In older translations of this verse there is an interesting variation on the wording. The King James Version renders the phrase "God's own people" as "a peculiar people." While I enjoy the clarity of newer translations, there is an intriguing meaning in being designated "a peculiar people."

The word *peculiar* is not one that we wear easily. Most of us want to be normal and fit in. Who wants to be peculiar? There is a town in west-central Missouri named *Peculiar*, and I have often wondered how it feels to folks born and raised there to say they are from a place called Peculiar. I once served a church that was named *Strange*. The name Strange United Methodist Church was and is something of a joke in the ministers' association.

Strange and *peculiar* are terms we would rather apply to people other than ourselves. Yet this is exactly the label the text asks us to wear. When one considers the call of Christ to live as a disciple in today's world, there may not be a more fitting label. We Christians are strange, and we are peculiar. We love our enemies, we care for the forgotten, and we believe that the last shall be first. There is a new world, an alternative community that rises out of the pages of the New Testament, which you and I inherit.

God offers the church as an alternative community for the world's redemption. This fellowship operates under a new economics that believes people matter as much as profits. This community has a new vision that sees every life as an image of God. Here, in this fellowship, a dynamic of inclusion thrives in a world that has made exclusion a fine art. That is our call.

Christians are different. We practice the ethic of grace in a world that lives by an ethic of law. We embrace cooperation rather than competition. We live aware of the gracious hand of God rather than from a sense that we must have more and more to be happy. This is true because we long for the "pure, spiritual milk" that Christ offers. This diet makes us a different people, a peculiar, strange people, who dare to live the life of love in a world in love with alienation, competition, and winning.

I heard about a mythical village where disturbing things began to happen. The people of the village were going insane. Slowly, madness was taking over and no one knew the cause. After careful observation, the villagers realized that their insanity was tied to the food they were eating. Something was wrong with their diet and it caused insanity. The village elders gathered to find a solution. In the end they concluded they had little choice but to eat the bad grain and go crazy. It was better to be crazy and alive than sane and dead. So, this is the word they prepared to bring to the people.

But just before the elders were to address the villagers, someone came running from another village with an announcement. A warehouse of good grain had been discovered. People who ate this grain did not go crazy. They remained sane and sound. The only problem was, there was not enough grain for everyone. So the elders gathered again and considered this news. They decided to appoint a special group from the village whose job would be to eat a different diet of good grain. Then, when all the other villagers had become insane, this group could remind them of what sanity was. Because, the elders knew, if enough people are crazy then crazy can begin to look normal.

Our culture has poisoned itself with a bad diet. Racism, sexism, and militarism have been our food. Consumerism, anxiety, and speed have become the staples of our diet. We have bought it all, raced it all, tried it all, and gone mad in the process. In our collective insanity, we must live fearful lives, we must regard the stranger as an enemy, we must send our young to die in war, and children must be denied health care and access to good water and food. There is no question that this is the way we must live for we have bought into a corporate insanity that says, "This is the way life is."

Then there is the church, the community that eats a diet of prayer, scripture, and love. This is the different diet that many have not known about, but we do. From this diet we live the peculiar and strange lives that show what the kingdom of God looks like, that demonstrate what servant love is, that claim every life as a precious gift.

The world looks at the church and says, "You're crazy." But the church knows better, for it lives a sanity born of love and grace. It points to a new way and invites others to the table where the food of love and redemption is served.

You, Church, are one strange-looking, peculiar-acting community. You are beautiful to behold as you "proclaim the mighty acts of him who called you out of darkness into his marvelous light" (2:9). Continue to yearn for the pure, spiritual milk, the special diet of love and grace. By this you show the world a better way, a different way, a way of sanity that is the way of Christ. (Chris Andrews)

Lectionary Commentary
Acts 7:55-60; John 14:1-14

The texts from John and Acts offer assurance—Jesus' words that our hearts should not be troubled and Stephen's calmness before the stoning mob are each based upon the Christian assurance of the adequacy of God's love. As the Easter community lives in light of the resurrection, there will be moments when we wonder if the way of Christ is the correct way. We face possible ridicule and even persecution because of the gospel message. Yet the people of faith hold fast to their conviction that Christ is the salvation of the world and that his way is the only way to true life. We do this with a confidence born out of a relationship of love that nothing can destroy.

The text from John is often used at funerals. Understandably so because these words are the soothing assurance that there is nothing that can separate us from God's love. Stephen's action before the mob is testimony to the strength derived from such conviction. Note that

Stephen's witness is so powerful that Saul, the young man watching the coats of the members of the mob, would later be convinced that Christ was the source and way of salvation. (Chris Andrews)

Worship Aids

Call to Worship

Turn from the world and be embraced by the love of Christ.
Like lost children, we seek our true home.
Know that God loves you and desires your salvation.
Our lives are in his hands; we are his people.

Prayer of Confession

O Lord, we confess that too often the ways of the world have been our ways. We have lingered at the altars of fear, greed, impatience, and unkindness. Our actions have not been consistent with our words. We have sought salvation in unholy alliances and have brought division upon your world. Forgive us our sins and feed us with your grace that we might be a people redeemed and whole, dedicated to the way of Jesus with all our strength and all our minds and all our souls. Amen.

Words of Assurance (based on 1 Peter 2:9)

We are a chosen race, a royal priesthood, a holy nation, God's own strange and peculiar people, empowered to proclaim the mighty acts of him who called us out of darkness into his marvelous light and show sanity to an insane world. Celebrate!

Benediction

You are the people of God. Go forth to live in such ways that by your actions and words others will see in you the life of Jesus and want to follow in his way. Amen. (Chris Andrews)

The God of Mystery

First in a Series of Three on the Trinity: A Christian Doctrine

1 Corinthians 13:8b-12

My two-year-old daughter is a true chatterbox who talks about her friends at preschool, the lady at the grocery store, and the imaginary tiger running through the house, among other things. Only when she falls asleep does the chatter stop. It is easy to tire from the constant talk, but I celebrate her vocal nature as a sign of healthy development. She is becoming more articulate every day, constantly adding new words to her vocabulary, which reminds me that I need to be extra careful in the words that leave my mouth because she is bound to repeat what I say.

One afternoon, I heard a little voice from the other side of the house call out, "Mark, where are you?" My wife was not calling me. Those simple words came out of my little girl's mouth, which actually excited me because she made the connection that I am not only "Daddy" but also "Mark." She is learning that I have different names and multiple dimensions.

The Christian faith developed the doctrine of the Trinity as a way of explaining different dimensions of God. A variety of names are used to describe God, including Father, Son, and Spirit, and yet these three separate parts are united as one God. For many faithful believers, the Trinity is a deeply held belief, and yet it is difficult to understand and explain. The Bible bears witness to the mysterious nature of the Lord by speaking of God's presence to us as our Creator, Redeemer, and Sustainer. And yet, the Scriptures do not explicitly teach a doctrine of the Trinity. It is rather inferred from places like Matthew 28:19, which speaks of a trinitarian baptismal formula, and 2 Corinthians 13:13, where Paul offers a similar three-part benediction of Jesus, God, and Holy Spirit.

The doctrine of the Trinity frames the Lord in three separate yet united parts as an attempt to help us wrap our minds around God. Mystery is at the heart of God. How God created the heavens and the earth is a mystery. How Jesus fed five thousand hungry mouths with only a few fish and a few loaves of bread is a mystery. How God's spirit simultaneously works in an infinite number of places is a mystery. Perhaps Paul had this sense of mystery in mind when he wrote, "For now we see in a mirror, dimly" (1 Corinthians 13:12). Our understanding of God is limited, and to say that God is three separate yet united parts is nothing more than our faith affirming that we cannot possibly know everything about God.

Paul's comments in 1 Corinthians come in the context of a church struggling with conflict. Different groups within the church are trying to assert their own agendas and opinions, to which Paul responds by stating we know only in part and we see dimly. In other words, we should not be arrogant with our own agendas and opinions. We will not see clearly or know the full truth until we enter the kingdom of God, and until that day arrives, we are encouraged to be united in the Spirit because there is much we do not understand. We cannot explain how God became a human being. We cannot explain Jesus' miracles. We cannot explain the resurrection. These are mysteries of God.

Rather than trying to solve every mystery, the Lord invites us to embrace the mystery of living in this world. As much as we have learned, there are still many things we cannot explain. I am still amazed and yet baffled at the mystery of birth. It is a modern-day miracle because so many things can go wrong, and yet babies continue to be born. After watching the birth of my own daughter, I was left wondering, "How does she know to start breathing? How did she learn to nurse just minutes after entering the world?" The mystery of birth has not kept me from loving my daughter, nor should a lack of understanding keep us from loving God. We should embrace all of God—the parts we understand and the parts that are mysterious.

We have named God as Father, Son, and Holy Spirit, and we have affirmed God as our Creator, Redeemer, and Sustainer because we have experienced God in these many ways. All of these descriptions and all of our experiences with the Lord help us see a bit less dimly. Our faith is opening our eyes to God, helping us see that God took on human form in order to connect with us. Our faith teaches that God became flesh in Jesus to experience life as we experience it. Our faith promises that we have the Spirit of God, who guides us and gives us strength and hope. We experience God in all these ways and yet, as Paul reminds us, we still see dimly.

In our poor vision and lack of understanding, we are challenged to embrace the mystery of God. Complete understanding of the Trinity is not the goal because we need mystery in our lives. Arrogance fools us into thinking we know it all, but mystery allows us to imagine and dream and get excited. Mystery enables us to live with a sense of discovery. Mystery helps us see each day as an opportunity to experience God in new ways. Isn't it time we embrace God in all of God's mystery? (Mark White)

Worship Aids

Call to Worship
In the chaos of life,
O Lord, we take refuge in you.
You are our rock and our fortress.

In the midst of struggles and troubles,
O Lord, we take refuge in you.
   You are our rock and our fortress.
In the midst of questions and doubts,
O Lord, we take refuge in you.
   You are our rock and our fortress.

Invocation

Eternal God, we open our hearts to you and ask to receive the good gifts you offer. Open our eyes and ears that we might hear your word for us today. We pray in the name of the Father, Son, and Holy Spirit. Amen.

Benediction

May the mystery of God inspire you to journey into new places with the Lord. May a sense of discovery fill your heart. And may experiences with God the Creator, Redeemer, and Sustainer bring you life. Amen. (Mark White)

MAY 29, 2011

❧❧❧

Sixth Sunday of Easter

Readings: Acts 17:22-31; Psalm 66:8-20; 1 Peter 3:13-22;
John 14:15-21

Of Freedom, Love, and Pain
John 14:15-21

Preaching on Memorial Day weekend is difficult for preachers. A good many of those who attend American worship come with the expectation that the service will, in some way, focus upon military veterans. This is a perfectly fine thing for the country to do, but the church, in a spiritual sense, is not national territory. When we gather to worship God as known in the life, teaching, death, and resurrection of Jesus Christ, our focus should be on the biblical God rather than upon nationalism of any sort. We come to Christ's house to honor and praise God, not nations. So, recognizing that this country is remembering its veterans this weekend, for this hour of worship we will also seek truths of God that go deeper than any nationalism.

To learn of the God known in Jesus Christ is to learn of a God who loves us enough to set us free. Unfortunately, because of this freedom, terrible things happen. We live always in the deep puzzle of love, freedom, and pain. God loves us. We are free. Pain is all around. God did not make us puppets, and our freedom is often misused. This holiday reminds us of the sometimes terrible cost we pay for our freedom. Wars and rumors of wars are the long human story. That story can be one of self-sacrifice and heroism, but it is also a story of the death of the young and the maiming of the innocent. For countless centuries, human beings have tried to settle their differences through violence. That is a choice our freedom offers us. God could have created us in ways that prevented us from choosing violence. But to do this, God would have had to make us puppets rather than free. This is a holiday that remembers the cost that comes with our freedom to choose violence.

One of the reasons God gives us the gift of freedom is because the God who loves us will not coerce our love in return, but wants it given back freely. The God who loves us invites, but does not force, our love in return. Yet this is a costly freedom that leaves us at liberty to make war, deal drugs, drive our cars drunk, and countless other horrors. In a world so full of hurts like these, one of the things that we must always learn when we come to worship God is that God is not the author and the source of the violence and the pain of life. God is the one who loves us into freedom—even at great cost.

Our Gospel lesson offers us another truth about God's love. We reciprocate God's love by keeping Christ's commandments. The God who loves us wants us to love back by keeping Christ's commandments. This is a choice our freedom offers. It is important to understand this clearly. God is not primarily interested in a mushy, syrupy love. Rather, God wants our love shown in the actions of our lives, in the ways we love God, self, and others through following Christ's commandments.

To love God is to use our freedom wisely. To love God is to choose the Christlike way. To love God is to imitate the deeds of Jesus. "If you love me, you will keep my commandments" (John 14:15). How easy and cheap it is to claim to love God without accepting the hard tasks of keeping Christ's commandments. Our world and our churches are full of people who want an easy love, love that makes no demands, love of feeling rather than action. Our Gospel lesson makes it clear that a meaningful love of God is shown through a life lived in harmony with the way of Christ.

This understanding of our use of freedom is vastly more robust than simple affection for God. It is infinitely more demanding. It recognizes we have the freedom to reject Christ's commandments. If we are honest, we know that our freedom has largely been misused and abused. Much of the terrible pain of the world is the result of our choice to follow our own way rather than the commandments of Christ.

Finally, our Gospel lesson promises that those who love God by obeying the commandments of Christ will have help. Jesus speaks of sending the "Advocate" (14:16), which is generally understood as being the gift of the Holy Spirit. An advocate supports and defends us. In our culture, *advocate* is another term for an attorney who stands at our side and offers counsel and support.

But Jesus' words suggest another understanding of the work of the advocating Holy Spirit: "If you love me, you will keep my commandments. And I will ask the Father, and he will give you another Advocate, to be with you forever" (14:15-16). The Advocate is sticking up not so much for us, but for Christ's commandments, advocating for our faithfulness to the way of Christ. When we make beginning efforts to keep Christ's commandments, we are rewarded by further encouragement to grow in the keeping of those commandments. The Advocate advocates not for us, but for Jesus. The Holy Spirit reinforces our least desire to follow Christ. Our free choices to love God by obeying Christ are encouraged and empowered by the Spirit's presence, urging the choices for good.

On this weekend when the nation honors those who have paid a terrible price for humanity's choice to follow its own way rather than the way of Christ, we are reminded of the gift of God's love. We are reminded of God's gift of freedom. We are reminded of God's invitation to love God by obeying Christ's commandments. We are promised that each right choice will be empowered and reinforced by the Holy Spirit advocate. Let us love God by choosing the way of Christ. (Carl L. Schenck)

Lectionary Commentary
Acts 17:22-31

The hill of the Areopagus stands between the Acropolis and the forum in Athens. On the Acropolis stood the Parthenon, which was the temple of Athena, the goddess for whom Athens was named. In Paul's day the Parthenon was already more than four hundred years old. On the other side stood the forum, where merchants sold their wares and where the city gathered for marketing, conversation, gossip, and fellowship.

On the hill between these two centers of city life, Paul calls for a truth that cannot be found in either. The God proclaimed by Paul is neither from the pantheon of Greek gods nor from the secular world of commerce. Rather, standing in the center of the great city, Paul challenges the claims of both the false deities and the marketplace. Paul calls upon the people to repent of their reliance on things that do not satisfy and to turn to the truth of God known in Jesus Christ. This choice stands before people of every age and culture.

1 Peter 3:13-22

First Peter is a letter of encouragement and instruction, both rooted in the author's call for Christians to remain true to their identity. In earlier parts of the letter, Christians are reminded they are "chosen and destined by God" (1:2). This is encouragement built on the identity given in

Christ. Our current text continues this combination of encouragement and instruction; encouragement to remain true to the life of holiness and good works that have already been the experience of the reader. Doing good is grounded in a hope that reaches far beyond the immediate. Even suffering in the service of doing good is redeemed by its resemblance to the redemptive suffering of Christ. Therefore, the goodness to which we are to stay true springs, not from our own personal goodness, but from the goodness imparted to us by Christ. By holding firm to this goodness in our daily lives, we hold firmly to Christ himself. (Carl L. Schenck)

Worship Aids

Call to Worship

We gather on a somber holiday.
We remember with sadness those we have loved and lost.
Let us not glorify the conflicts and violence that tear our loved ones from us.
Let us, rather, give glory to God, who calls us to use our freedom peaceably.
Our God is a God of all nations and peoples.
May our worship of God unite rather than divide.

Words of Assurance

The Christ who bore in his own body the sin of the world offers us not judgment, but mercy. In the name of Jesus Christ, we are forgiven.

Benediction

Now may the God of love so equip you with the Holy Spirit's advocacy that you might more and more love God by obeying the commandments of Christ. Go in peace. Amen. (Carl L. Schenck)

The God of Presence

Second in a Series of Three on the Trinity: A Christian Doctrine

John 14:8-14, 25-26

After a long day at church, I enjoy nothing more than relaxing at home. I am usually the first one home, and I use my time alone to kick back on the couch and watch a few minutes of *Sports Center*. The quiet does not last long because the minute my daughter comes home, she is talking and playing with her toys in our family room. She occasionally plays by herself, but most of the time she tries to engage me in her games. If I am paying too much attention to the television, she will crawl into my lap and look me in the eyes so she knows that I am giving her my undivided attention.

We all need and deserve the undivided attention of our loved ones. Whether we are sharing a profound experience from the bottom of our hearts or playing a simple game, we want our friends and families to focus on us. We want them to be totally in the moment, not distracted by anything else. We want their presence. Many people feel a deep desire to connect with God's presence, though the Lord can be mysterious, even distant, which leads some people to believe God does not exist or does not care about our needs. The doctrine of the Trinity teaches that God is present with us in different forms as Father, Son, and Spirit. The Lord comes to us as Creator, Redeemer, and Sustainer, but we go through times when we do not understand or experience God. We desire certainty; we want to know for sure that God is with us.

Philip wants to know beyond a shadow of a doubt that Jesus will reveal God the Father to him. He says, "Lord, show us the Father, and we will be satisfied" (John 14:8). The kind of assurance Philip asks for is not uncommon. Have you ever caught yourself thinking life would have been easier if you had just been able to walk this earth when Jesus did? You could have asked Jesus all your questions and received direct answers. You could have experienced God's presence in the flesh. Philip has walked this earth with Jesus of Nazareth, and he still longs for the same kind of certainty we desire. We are not unlike Philip; we sometimes fail to see God's presence in our midst.

When Philip asks Jesus to show him the Father, Jesus responds, "Have I been with you all this time, Philip, and you still do not know me?" (14:9). We may fool ourselves into thinking that seeing Jesus would quench our thirst for certainty, but as Philip illustrates, seeing God in the flesh is not the real issue. The real issue is recognizing God's presence.

When we think about God's presence, we ought to acknowledge that there are two sides to this coin. One side of this coin deals with God's presence to us. God is present to us, as Jesus says to Philip, through the words of Jesus. God's presence comes to us as we study the scriptures and pray the words of Jesus. Today, many Christians are discovering the practice of praying the questions Jesus asked and meditating on a word or phrase he used. These disciplines of study and prayer help people connect with God's presence.

We especially desire God's presence when we are going through significant life experiences like getting married, making a job choice, celebrating the birth of a child, or dealing with a terminal illness. We depend on the Lord's guidance, and yet even apart from these major life events, more and more people say they want to experience God. There is tremendous interest in books with spiritually themed titles. People want to talk about angels, demons, and God's activity in the world. The bottom line is that people have a deep need to experience God.

The other side of this coin has to do with ways we are God's presence in and for the world. Jesus tells Philip that his works are proof that God the Father is present within his life. When we carry out the works of Jesus, we too experience God's presence. Jesus would later officially commission his followers to continue his work on this earth, which means we are to live like Jesus and do the things he did—teaching, preaching, healing, and caring for the least among us.

We occasionally fulfill this work on short-term mission trips, but it is meant to be a part of everyday life. We are to live like Jesus so we can be God's presence to the world every day. We do the works of Christ when we lead a small group at church, visit a homebound member, tutor a student, or feed the homeless. In all of these ways, we demonstrate a desire to grow in our faith and be more like Jesus, which, in turn, helps us share God's presence with others.

God is present to us through word and works. In our Gospel lesson for today, Jesus wants Philip and the rest of the disciples to understand this truth because he knows one day he will no longer physically be with them. He needs to prepare them for that day, so in addition to his teaching, he assures them (and assures us) that an Advocate, the Holy Spirit, will come and teach them and be present with them. The Spirit of God is active in the world and in our lives, fulfilling God's promises. God has promised to be with us, God has promised us peace, and God has promised to answer us when we ask for help so that the Lord might be glorified. We should not be afraid of this life because God is with us as Father, Son, and Spirit. (Mark White)

Worship Aids

Call to Worship

As we gather to worship you, O Lord,
Let your face shine upon us.
As we turn our concerns and worries over to you, O Lord,

Let your face shine upon us.
As we lift up our voices in praise and adoration, O Lord,
Let your face shine upon us. Amen.

Invocation

God of Presence, may the joys of this day and the concerns of our hearts drive us toward you. May the words we utter, the songs we sing, and the prayers we lift help us see your face. In the name of Christ we pray. Amen.

Benediction

Go forth with the promises of God.
Go forth with God's presence by your side.
Go forth with the peace of Christ.
And now go forth to serve your Lord. Amen. (Mark White)

JUNE 5, 2011

Ascension of the Lord Sunday/Seventh Sunday of Easter

Readings: Acts 1:1-11; Psalm 47; Ephesians 1:15-23; Luke 24:44-53

Ascended into Heaven
Acts 1:1-11

Today is one of those relatively obscure Christian holidays of which many are unaware: Ascension Sunday. This is the day in the church calendar when we celebrate the ascension of Jesus Christ into heaven. In all honesty, the ascension is a rather difficult idea for the modern mind to handle. It's the story of how Jesus went to the Mount of Olives after his resurrection from the dead. There, according to the book of Acts, Jesus literally flew off into heaven. "He was lifted up, and a cloud took him out of their sight" (Acts 1:9).

In the first century, the understanding of the cosmos was very different from ours. People understood heaven to be a place that was literally, geographically, "up" from the earth. They could visualize Jesus leaving them and going "up" into heaven. With our scientific view of the cosmos, we know there is no *up* or *down* in the universe. Even our notion of heaven is not of a geographical location or direction. When contemporary people think of the ascension, it is a little hard to imagine the Lord Jesus Christ flying off like a one-person space shuttle into the skies.

Yet, despite our scientific reservations, the story of the ascension is spiritually important to us. The ascension was the church's way of dealing with a fundamental fact. The earliest disciples had experienced the bodily presence of the risen Lord, the one who was no longer under the claim of death. After a passage of time, this experience of the risen Lord as bodily present with them seemed to pass. He didn't appear again. They accounted for his absence by saying that the risen Lord was now in heaven. They had to go forward without his physical presence. He had ascended into heaven.

Christians today have the same circumstance. We believe in a risen Lord who is no longer physically present. The body of Jesus is not here any longer, except in the church as the body of Christ. So on Ascension Sunday, we do well to think about what Jesus' physical absence means for Christians today.

First, the absence of the physical Jesus calls us to take seriously the church as the body of Christ. This is a concept with which we all are very familiar. We say that the church is the body of Christ without thinking about what that might actually mean. If the church is the body of Christ, then we are called to give to the church the devotion and respect that Christ deserves.

Think about it. How precious to you is the church? How central to your life is the mission of the church? It is easy for us to think that we would respond to the physical presence of Jesus with all the love and devotion we could humanly summon. Yet we often treat the church as just one more volunteer community organization. Now civic clubs do good work; health-related charities appeal to us, especially if we have lost a loved one to the disease the charity seeks to overcome; organizations that support our schools do important work. But none of these organizations are the body of Christ. Only the church is Jesus among us. Its mission is to be consistent with Jesus' mission. The love we have for it is the love we have for Jesus.

The church is the closest we will ever come on earth to having Jesus to care for and to love. On Ascension Sunday, we are called to reassess our devotion to the church as the physical body of Christ still among us. The risen Lord is not here; he has ascended. The body of Christ is very much here, and the way we treat the church is the way we treat the risen Lord.

Second, Ascension Sunday reminds us that we are each, individually, a part of Christ's body. To honor the church as we honor Christ is also to remember that in a powerful way, we are each a part of this body of Christ. When we neglect our part in the mission of the church, we disable the body of Christ. As Paul said, each of us is a physical part of the body of Christ. We are the arms and legs, the eyes and ears; we are limbs and organs of Christ's present body. When we fail to do our part, the body becomes disabled. Christ becomes disabled without the limb or organ that each of us is called and gifted to be. (See 1 Corinthians 12.)

The absence of the physical body of Jesus places a claim upon us to relate to the church as we would relate to Christ. It also reminds us that without our individual faithfulness to our role in the church, the body of Christ is weakened and disabled.

Last, Ascension Sunday reminds us that if Christ's work is to continue, it is up to us to do it. Now that is not to say we receive no godly help. Next Sunday is Pentecost, and we will celebrate our empowerment by the Holy Spirit. But this divine help comes to empower us in doing the work of Christ. Jesus is no longer here to heal the sick. He is no longer here to touch the outcast. He is no longer here to feed the hungry. It is up to us, the body of Christ, to continue this work. If the church fails to be the body of Christ, Jesus is absent. If the church fails to be the body of Christ, Jesus is nowhere to be seen.

Yes, this is an obscure Christian holiday. It celebrates an event that is difficult for the modern scientific mind to take literally. At the same time, this is a critical day in our personal and collective self-understanding. It is significant that the risen Lord ascended into heaven. His ascension invites us to relate to the church as we would to Christ. It reminds each of us of the critical nature of our role in the body of Christ. It calls us to take up Jesus' work on earth. This is a most important obscure day. (Carl L. Schenck)

Lectionary Commentary
Ephesians 1:15-23

Studying Ephesians is like eating pecan pie. It is so rich, one must go slowly or risk being unable to digest the fare. In this passage we find two related themes.

A first theme is of the exalted place of Christ, who is revealed to be seated at the right hand of God (1:20), waiting for the day when "all things [are] under his feet" (1:22). This high Christology challenges the believer to picture Christ, not as the friend at one's side, but as the mighty Lord high and lifted up. This is no "what a friend we have in Jesus" view. Rather, it bows before Christ reigning in glory.

In a second theme of the passage, the author describes his prayers for the reader's growth in faith and for the breadth of understanding of the revelation. In this passage, the growth of the believer is understood to be a gift of God rather than an accomplishment of the Christian. This gift is one that imparts great blessing described as enlightenment, riches, hope, and the glorious inheritance of the saints (1:18). Just as Christ is lifted up to glory in the first theme, so the believer receives a faith that is so much greater than a warm feeling inside. Rich fare, indeed.

Luke 24:44-53

Luke's vision of the world has its hub in Jerusalem. In this text, Jesus declares that the gospel will be proclaimed to all nations, "beginning from Jerusalem" (Luke 24:47). So the disciples are to wait in Jerusalem. Luke differs from the other Gospels, in which the disciples encounter the risen Christ and receive their final instructions in Galilee. In Luke's vision, the disciples do not return to the place of their first association with Jesus, but remain in Jerusalem waiting for the Holy Spirit to come and launch the mission from its hub in Jerusalem. The instruction to wait makes plain that the power for that mission lies not in the disciples themselves, but in God. They must wait for God's Holy Spirit, and only then will they be ready for the world mission.

Luke's Gospel ends where his book of Acts begins: with the ascension. Jesus' ascension removes him from the physical scene. The disciples must look elsewhere for the courage and power they will need. Jesus is risen, but he has also left. They are to wait dependently for God to supply the resources they will need for the mission that lies ahead. (Carl L. Schenck)

Worship Aids

Call to Worship

Welcome, body of Christ.
We come to praise the risen Lord.
In our praise may we be changed
   that we might ourselves become
   the presence of the risen Lord in the world.

Prayer of Confession

O Lord, we confess that we have too often failed to be the body of Christ in the world. We have each gone our own way, and we have neglected to walk the ways of Jesus. We have avoided the sick and been blind to the hungry. Have mercy upon us and make us again the body of Christ. Amen.

Words of Assurance

The Lord has risen and is among us! Look around! We are the body of Christ, alive and empowered to change the world. Rejoice!

Benediction

May Christ so dwell in you that through your lives Christ might continue
to be present and transforming in today's world. Amen. (Carl L.
Schenck)

The God of Power

Third in a Series of Three on the Trinity: A Christian Doctrine

Acts 10:34-48

Many of us are proud weekend warriors, willing to tackle almost any
home improvement job. I am one of them, although there are great limits to what I can do. When my friend Billy asked for my help on a small
electrical project at his parents' home, I told him up front that I knew
nothing about electrical systems. He told me not to worry, assuring me
that our job was simple. We would replace the electrical outlets in each
room of the house. I did not think this job seemed overly complicated,
but I knew I needed instruction. Billy explained how to properly install
an outlet, which I thought was simple enough, until I accidentally crossed
two of the wires. A surge of power rushed up my arm and jolted the screw-
driver out of my hand. I was shocked that Billy had not turned off
the power, but I assumed wrongly and Billy laughed at my hair-raising
experience.

When we hold firmly to certain assumptions about our faith, the power
of our Lord can surprise and shake us up by moving in unexpected directions. The astonishing way God works is seen in no clearer image than
that of the Trinity. God did not have to take on three separate forms, and
yet the surprising work we experience from God as Father, Son, and Spirit
reminds us that the Lord is doing a new thing.

The circumcised believers who accompany Peter to Cornelius's home
are shocked that the Holy Spirit has been poured out on the Gentiles. Up
to this point, those who believed in Jesus had followed Jewish customs
and traditions such as circumcision, but with the advent of the Holy
Spirit, we see God doing something new. Peter learns through his vision
and conversation with the Gentile centurion Cornelius that God is doing
a new thing, which requires believers in Jesus to change their attitude
toward outsiders. It shocks Jewish believers that God has moved in this
direction because the Gentile life is so different and foreign from Jewish
ways of life and thinking.

Peter has his own struggles with what God is doing, but his willingness to follow the Lord leads him to say, "What God has made clean, you must not call profane" (Acts 10:15). God was doing a new thing, and as surprising as it may have been, Peter should have expected a surprise. As a faithful Jew, Peter would have celebrated the surprising ways of God's power, as when the Lord freed Israel from slavery and provided manna when they wandered in the wilderness. As a dedicated disciple, Peter would have witnessed the power of God working through Jesus as he healed the sick and fed the hungry. Peter would have experienced this same power when the Holy Spirit came "like the rush of a violent wind" (Acts 2:2). Peter was no stranger to the power of God and the surprising ways God works in the world.

Although surprised the Lord would work among the Gentiles, Peter responds to the Lord's work by coming to the belief that "God's chosen people" includes all people. We church folk make a similar assumption, and yet, we qualify it. We say, "Anyone can believe in Jesus, but first, they must say this and do that before they really become a Christian." We also put labels on people that imply they do not meet the standards of a good Christian. We label people as conservative, liberal, Democrat, Republican, divorced, homosexual, or felon. Our labels, however, only function as walls that separate people. We separate the clean from the unclean, the circumcised from the uncircumcised, and the Jew from the Gentile.

The God of power breaks down these walls of ours and does the unthinkable. God throws our labels away by including Gentiles among the people of God. What people are we treating as Gentiles in the twenty-first century? Might it be drug addicts, immigrants, nontraditional families, people covered in tattoos, minorities, or the marginalized? The walls of exclusion need to come down. God is doing a new thing by embracing all people as heirs to the gospel of Jesus Christ.

We should therefore expect to be surprised by God because we do not have it all figured out. We have more to learn, and so the gospel continues to open our eyes so we can see God in unexpected places. The gospel continues to open our ears so we might hear the voice of God with more clarity. The gospel continues to open our hearts so we might love in greater ways. Only by the power of God can eyes, ears, and hearts be opened in such dramatic ways.

Peter's faith in the God whom we call the Trinity enables him to see the walls he has built. Then God gives him the power to overcome and embrace those who are different. Like Peter, we need to ask God to help us see and hear something we cannot see or hear on our own. We need God's power to help us identify injustice in the world and to shed light on our personal and corporate sins, but we also have to take responsibility for our lives. Herein lies a great truth about God's power. We proclaim God is all-powerful, and yet our struggles and problems do not disappear. We pray that God would step down from heaven and fight our battles for us, and yet God has restrained God's power so we might grow in faith by taking responsibility for our lives.

God gives Peter a new vision so he might more fully take responsibility for his life. He sees a vision that includes both Jews and Gentiles as God's chosen people, and he responds by putting aside his prejudice of the uncircumcised. Peter embraces the fact that God is doing a new thing. The God we know as Father, Son, and Spirit is working in new places, surprising us with power, and yet reminding us that the gospel is for all people. (Mark White)

Worship Aids

Call to Worship (based on Psalm 98)

Sing to the LORD a new song, for he has done marvelous things.
All the ends of the earth have seen the power of our God.
Make a joyful noise to the LORD, all the earth;
Let us break forth into joyous song and sing praises. Amen.

Invocation

Holy God, we praise you for your majesty. Your wisdom is seen in all your works. Your grace and truth are revealed in Jesus Christ. Your presence and power are given to us through the Holy Spirit. As we now enter into worship, our prayer is that you would abide with us and that we would also abide with you. Amen.

Benediction

Go forth, knowing you are a child of God.
Go forth, for you are loved by Jesus.
Go forth, filled with the power of the Holy Spirit. Amen. (Mark White)

JUNE 12, 2011

❧❧❧

Day of Pentecost

Readings: Acts 2:1-21; Psalm 104:24-34, 35b; 1 Corinthians 12:3b-13; John 7:37-39

Birthday Stories
Acts 2:1-21

The anniversaries of key markers in our lives are important. Birthdays are a good example. Some of us age until we're not crazy about birthdays. They are a sign we're getting older, but even as we age, birthdays are important. Birthdays celebrate the labor of the woman who gave us birth; they celebrate the way in which we were nurtured as children; they celebrate another year given to enjoy. Birthdays are a big deal. So it is with other key anniversaries in life, such as wedding anniversaries or the milestones of our children's lives. This is confirmation time, and some of us are completing high school or college at this time of year. These are marker events remembered and celebrated annually. These anniversaries mark the significant passages of our lives.

They also give us the framework for our stories. This is true not only of happy times, of course, but also of our difficult times. If you've experienced the breakup of a marriage, each year you remember the time when that happened. If you've lost a loved one—a spouse, a parent, or a child—those dates are forever pressed upon your memory. Those anniversaries are not marked by parties, but they are times of remembrance. My father died on Christmas Day. That's a part of my life, and so my Christmas stories will be different from other people's Christmas stories.

This is important, not only for individuals, but also for countries. In the United States, we have Independence Day celebrations with fireworks and outdoor barbecues. The celebration calls to mind the stories of the founding days. Every year, some people remember Pearl Harbor Day or the anniversary of the killings at Kent State or the day that will forever be etched into our memories with digits: 9/11.

Anniversaries remind us of our stories, so it's important today that we observe this church anniversary of Pentecost. This is the day when we tell the stories and celebrate the events that gave birth to the church. In the first weeks after the Resurrection, there was no organized church, just people who had known or followed Jesus, who had experienced his resurrection.

One day they are all together, and then, suddenly, miraculous events begin to happen. A mighty wind blows through the house and shakes the very foundation. Tongues of fire leap from person to person. People begin to speak in the languages of the world. Then, after all this chaotic uprising of the Spirit, the Spirit expresses itself in yet another way as Peter quiets everyone down and preaches. He explains to them the meaning of the events that have just taken place. Peter tells the story.

Just as the stories of our births, our graduations, our marriages, and so on mark our lives and teach us something about our roots, so the story of Pentecost teaches us about our roots as the church. Telling and retelling the story reminds us of the fundamental truths that are deeply embedded in our birth as the body of Christ.

One of those truths is that the church was born of the Holy Spirit, and God is its birth mother. We need that reminder because we live in the mundane "everydayness" of the church. Every one of us can find something to criticize in the church. We all can tell of disappointment, or even of hearts broken by the church. It's important, then, to remember that the church is more than the fallible human beings it comprises. The church is the birth creation of God. To use the words of an old creed, "The church is of God and will be preserved until the end of time," not because we are the church, not because we embody the full measure of what the church should be, but rather because it is not ours, it is God's. For all of its faults and failings, it is through the church that we have been told the stories of the love of God in Jesus Christ. The church, for all its human messiness, is a gift of God. That's part of our birth story.

A second thing I think the Pentecost birthday story of the church teaches us is that the church, from its birth, was multinational, multicultural, and multilingual. We need frequent reminders of this. From the very first, from its first moment, from its birth, the church was multinational, multicultural, and multilingual. Try reading today's text aloud. It's not easy. Reading the Pentecost story aloud requires us to pronounce all the obscure names of those long-dead places. The text is a testimony that at the church's birth we were multinational, multicultural, and multi-lingual. We certainly don't look like it most of the time, do we?

Unfortunately, our congregations are often not reflective of the God-given nature of real church. We have to tell the story to be reminded of our true self. Our true self isn't monolithic; our true self isn't mono-cultural; our true self is multicultural, because that's the way we were at our birth. That's the way God made us on the first day.

There's something else in the birthday story that's worth remembering. After all the chaos and uproar of wind and fire and languages, Peter calls for order and preaches a sermon in which he attempts to interpret what all of this means. In that sermon, Peter tells us the other thing we'll do well to remember. Peter uses as his text some lines from the Old Testament prophet Joel. In those lines, Joel looks forward to a day when "your old men shall dream dreams, and your young men shall see visions" (Joel 2:28).

You see, the church, from its birthday, was meant to be a big dreamer, to dream big dreams for God. The church, from its birth, was to be a visionary change agent, not an agent of conformity. The church, from its very birth, was meant to have visions and to dream dreams. Peter, on the day of Pentecost, the day of the church's birth, tells us so. The church should always be dreaming God's big dream. When our dreams are small or absent, when we are satisfied with the status quo, when we think we've done as much as we can possibly do, we've quit being the church, because the church is a dreamer. The church is visionary; the church is a possi-bility place.

It's important to tell our birthday stories and remember again our beginnings. Happy birthday, Church. (Carl L. Schenck)

Lectionary Commentary
1 Corinthians 12:3b-13

In this familiar passage, Paul touches upon two important spiritual real-ities. First, Paul describes the varieties of gifts of the Spirit. While some interpreters seek to limit the gifts of the Spirit to some precise list, Paul is lifting up examples of the contributions that different individuals are equipped to share. The keys to understanding lie, not in the exact list of gifts, but in three key insights. These capacities are gifts of God, not pos-sessions of the individual. These capacities are of various natures as the community of faith has various needs. Individuals have one or more of these capacities, but no individual possesses them all.

The second important spiritual reality to which Paul points is that these capacities exist for the common good. They are not for the glorification of the individual but for service to the community. These capacities are given for the sake of the whole community, not for the primary benefit of the individual. Only as each person shares his or her spiritual capacities does the whole community come to its full potential.

John 7:37-39

The Gospel lesson for today connects to Pentecost only in that it is a reference to the coming Holy Spirit. For those churches or pastors who do not wish to emphasize Pentecost, it offers an alternative look at the Holy Spirit. It is a great day when Jesus invites the thirsty to come to him and drink. John's addition of the phrase "the great day" (John 7:37) is a reference, of course, to the Jewish Festival of Booths and also a reference forward to Jesus' words. It is a great day when Jesus issues his invitation, and it will be a great day when the thirsty respond. This thought holds considerable preaching possibility. What is our thirst? What is holding us back from quenching that thirst in Jesus?

This short lesson is also a reminder of the source of the believer's blessings that are to be shared. "Out of the believer's heart shall flow rivers" (7:38). John has Jesus quickly clarify that this flow is not from the abundance of the believer, but from the gift of the Holy Spirit. The believer is a channel for the river, not the source of the river.

Finally, the text reminds us of John's understanding of the relationship in time between Jesus' glorification and the gift of the Holy Spirit. (Carl L. Schenck)

Worship Aids

Call to Worship
Inflate the balloons.
Decorate the halls.
Get in the Spirit.
Celebrate a birth.
The day of Pentecost has come!
The church is born.

Invocation

O Lord, send your Holy Spirit as once you did in Jerusalem so long ago. Join us in this place and time and give us the fire that transforms and renews. Burn away all our complacency, and consume the cords that bind us to the ways of a dying world. Give us the life that lives in your praise and service. We pray in Jesus' name. Amen.

Benediction

May the joy of new birth, the transformational power of new possibilities, and the burning love of Christ make all of your days a Pentecost of hope. Now and always. Amen. (Carl L. Schenck)

The Power of Image

First in a Series of Four on the Power of Genesis

Genesis 1:27-28

Our job as Christians is always to "begin from the very beginning," wrote Karl Barth when describing the task of theology (Karl Barth, John McTavish, and Harold Wells, *Karl Barth, Preaching through the Christian Year* [Grand Rapids: Eerdmans, 1978], 11). We are to begin in the beginning with God. "In the beginning God created..." (Genesis 1:1 NIV).

Our series on Genesis begins with God, creating and setting into motion God's creation. It begins with God's promise to bless humanity and to depict a God who covenants to share in creation from beginning to end, forming creation out of nothing (Genesis 1:1–2:4a), and creating a unique people where there is no people (12:1-3). Here we discover a God who does not simply stand aloof but steps into creation. Here we find a God who creates a cosmos in which goodness is depicted throughout: "And God saw that it was good" (1:25). Here is a God who speaks creation into being and says, "Let us make humankind in our image, according to our likeness," and who charges humankind to "have dominion" over all living creatures upon the earth (1:26). This God calls humankind to the responsibility of stewardship and care of the earth. This God's image is stamped into humanity's very being, and this God commands humanity to be fruitful and multiply (1:28).

Therefore, when we speak of God's image in humanity, we speak also of God's identity, or the way God relates to what God creates on the one hand, and of how we are to reflect back to God and to creation the very good purposes of God on the other. What we see in the beginning in Genesis is how the image of God in humans is that part of creation that discloses something about God's reality in the world; for here is a God who is known peculiarly through the Creation: God has brought forth human beings. Therefore, whatever we may say about the power of being created in God's image, we need to speak of what is life-giving and not life-destroying, in terms of what is good and not what is bad. We need to see the power and freedom of being created in God's image!

Being created in God's image is a blessing, but it is a blessing we often use in ways that oppose God's true purposes and intentions. Too often we fail to use our freedom for God and others. We fail to see how our freedom affects the web of relationships in which we live and move and have our being, including our relationship with the earth. We fail to see how our relationships with God and with others are to flow out of deep respect for all of life rather than manipulation of life. In short, we fail to see how our "image" has become less than what God intended in the beginning!

In fact, what we realize throughout Genesis is that our "image problem" is really a reflection of our own failure to see our condition as it really is—a reflection of our own disobedience and sinfulness, an inability to see how we have fallen short of God's glory or how, by God's grace, we can be restored. We fail to see how, through God's Spirit, we can be changed. It is only in admitting such failure that we can ever learn what it means to be renewed in the knowledge that we were created in God's image in the first place, or that we can be reconciled to Christ, who is the firstborn of all creation, the true image of the invisible God.

Again and again, we do whatever we can to cover up or "improve" upon God's image in us, to the point that we lose the blessings of freedom to live in fruitful community with others; we lose our moral dimension when we seek to distort God's purposes for creation. In short, we lose ourselves in distrust as we usurp what rightly belongs to God.

Companies spend millions of dollars running commercials to project the "right" image to potential consumers or investors, in order to make more money to sell more products. Politicians hire consultants to communicate an image of strength and confidence, but only to spin opinion or influence the media. Sports stars use high-powered agents or performance-enhancing drugs to make sure they stay on top, then work just as hard to conceal the truth about themselves. We will do almost anything to enhance our images and keep people from seeing who we really are.

We have often seen, in recent years, how images projected into the world are not always honest. Our efforts to betray God's image often lead to a betrayal of trust in our public, family, community, and national lives. Corporations such as AIG Insurance, Investors Overseas, WorldCom, Enron, HealthSouth, Sunbeam, and Waste Management; and individuals such as Charles Keating, Michael Milken, and Bernard Madoff all projected images of success that only concealed betrayals as old as Adam and Eve.

All of our attempts to enhance our images cover up the truth: we stand in need of restoration and redemption. At the heart of our image problem is the need to recover the calling for which we were first created: to live in true fellowship and freedom with God and one another, and to live in the kind of community of trust that reflects God's gracious intent for creation. We are creatures to whom much is given and from whom Christ expects much in return. It is this image problem for which Christ came and suffered, and it is for the promise of new life and blessing for all that he rose and comes to us today and always. As we clean up our image, and reclaim our inheritance as children of God, we all can sing God's glory: As it was in the beginning, is now, and ever shall be, world without end. Amen! (Andrew D. Kinsey)

Worship Aids

Invocation

Creator God, in whom we live and move and have our being, speak your word of life as we gather in your holy presence. Speak words of promise and blessing as we praise and worship you. Speak in the power of your Holy Spirit as we open our lives to the joy of Christ our Lord and Savior. We place our trust in you and you alone, sharing always in the blessings of truth and grace. We pray in Jesus' name. Amen.

Prayer of Confession

O Lord, you have created all that is, and yet we forget to whom we belong. You have ordered this world according to your purposes, and yet we neglect your ways. You have created us in your image and likeness, and yet we misuse your gifts of freedom and power. Forgive us, O God, for the ways we fail to care for your good earth; forgive us for taking for granted all your blessings of life and truth; forgive us when we fail to see the good in the world. Forgive us, gracious God, for our self-centered pride, and pardon us for our ingratitude and sloth. Restore to us the joy of worshiping and serving you in Christ's name. Amen.

Words of Pardon

Christ's gift of forgiveness is true and everlasting. Receive the good news: We stand forgiven and redeemed! Amen.

Benediction

For the goodness of God's creation, we thank and praise the Lord. For the fellowship we enjoy in Christ, we rejoice. For the power and freedom God grants and bestows, we offer our lives in service to the Spirit's reign and rule. May we all reflect God's image of love and justice in all we say and do, going forth to witness always to the peace and grace of our Lord Jesus Christ. Amen. (Andrew D. Kinsey)

JUNE 19, 2011

❧❧❧❧

Trinity Sunday/First Sunday after Pentecost

Readings: Genesis 1:1–2:4a; Psalm 8; 2 Corinthians 13:11-13; Matthew 28:16-20

God's Property Managers
Genesis 1:1–2:4a

Global warming, acid rain, rain forests, old-growth forest, chemically intensive or organic agriculture, endangered species, Three Mile Island, Chernobyl, urban sprawl, the greenhouse effect, clean coal, biosphere, gene pool, monoculture, bioculture—not long ago, these were not words and phrases in everyday vocabulary. In the last two or three decades, however, we have become increasingly aware of the threat that humankind is to itself and to all living things upon the earth.

Biblical people have been accused of being primary causes of the problem. Some have claimed the most destructive words ever written were the words attributed to God in the book of Genesis: "Have dominion over…every living thing that moves upon the earth" (1:28). Some say we have interpreted this command as license to use and consume and destroy for our own short-term benefit.

The so-called Christian world has often acted that way, but properly understood, the Bible is a document of holy environmentalism. The unknown poet who wrote the first chapter of Genesis was the first environmentalist. The writer was the first to declare that God considered creation good. The later psalmist wrote or sang, "The earth is the LORD's, and the fullness thereof" (Psalm 24:1 KJV). The fundamental biblical understanding is that life and all creation belong, finally and ultimately, to the creator. That makes people temporary custodians. Whether we own a corner lot or a huge farm, we really own nothing. We are simply temporary custodians or, in the language of the Bible, stewards. We are property managers for the creator.

While environmental protection is a task larger than any one of us, there are things we can do to align our daily living with our calling to be God's property managers. Care for the environment is a holy task that must be translated into practical, pragmatic action.

First, we can study. None of us know or understand enough about the consequences of our actions upon our environment. The more we learn, the more we read, and the more we think, the more likely we are to become responsible stewards. What have you read lately on the environment?

This learning project must be both global and local. To be God's property managers, we must expand our understanding of the big picture and understand the local implications of that big picture. If the burning of fossil fuels is contributing to global warming, then what does that mean for the way we generate electricity? What does it mean for the way we propel our cars? We need to understand those big issues in order to be good property managers for God.

We also need to have a local perspective. If we are managing on God's behalf, what kind of car should we drive? How should our community fund public transit? How can our households decrease the amount of electricity we use and the amount of gasoline we consume? To be good property managers, we have to study the issues.

Second, a good property manager is an activist. A good property manager does not wait for the leak to damage the interior of the building before replacing the roof. A good property manager keeps the building painted so it does not suffer damage from the elements. The good property manager is an activist.

Biblical people should be advocates for environmental and energy research. It will be expensive to engineer ways to produce clean electricity. We know that wind and solar can help. We also know that we do not have the technology to produce enough power from these clean sources. Can we use coal to produce electricity in ways that are truly clean? Can we produce significantly greater amounts of energy using sunlight? Can we produce clean energy from cold fusion? All of this research will be expensive.

What a difference it would make if churches and synagogues would become advocates for research into the solutions we need. Good property managers constantly expand their knowledge base. It's time for God's people to become active advocates for funding the research that will create the needed technologies to care for God's fragile planet.

Biblical people also need to become activists for the long term. Our economic system is heavily biased toward the short term. There is little or no profit to be made in the short term for environmental protection. We cannot reasonably expect the marketplace to create the necessary incentives. In this respect, God's property managers are different from a building superintendent. A building superintendent cares for the building to ensure its economic value for today and tomorrow, but has little incentive to look fifty or a hundred or a thousand years into the future.

In contrast, God's property managers have a vision fifty, one hundred, and one thousand years into the future. There may not be economic incentives in the marketplace for this kind of long view, but in the absence of the long view we are likely to be bad managers of God's good creation. When the author of Genesis tells us that God has charged humanity to "have dominion over the fish of the sea and over the birds of the air" (1:28), God's command is not to make short-term economic gains, but to protect these creatures for God.

A third kind of activism that we as God's property managers may demonstrate is to have dominion over our own numbers. Self-restraint and social restraint regarding population are required to preserve this precious creation God has entrusted to our care. A good building superintendent knows that the elevator has a limited load capacity. If that weight is exceeded, the results are disastrous. The same is true of the planet. Responsible dominion is not only over the birds of the air and the fish of the sea, but also over ourselves. This fragile planet has a limited carrying capacity of human beings. The resources of the planet are not infinite and can support only a limited number of passengers. Because we do not know what this carrying capacity is, we must exercise responsible dominion over the world's population. There are no easy ways to do this, but we must become activists for population control the world over if we are to be good property managers for God.

"God saw everything that he had made, and indeed, it was very good" (1:31). It is our holy task to keep it good. (Carl L. Schenck)

Lectionary Commentary
2 Corinthians 13:11-13

In Paul's final salutation to the church at Corinth, we find him still focused on the concerns this church has placed on Paul's heart. The people of this church, who have been so divided by conflict, are admonished to "agree with one another" and to "live in peace" (1 Corinthians 13:11). Paul has spent a good deal of his energies teaching, advising, and even pressuring the fractured saints at Corinth to heal the divisions that have plagued the church almost since its founding. They have been in conflict over power arrangements, divided loyalties, ethical confusion, sacramental inclusion, and theological perspectives. In his last words to them, Paul is still calling for them to become a community that can be seen as the body of Christ. He ends with an allusion to the Trinity and its gifts of grace, love, and communion. One wonders if they will ever learn. One wonders if we will ever learn.

Matthew 28:16-20

In this famous text, we have Jesus issuing final instructions to the disciples. Their months of teaching and close fellowship are over. The horror of the cross and the shock of the resurrection are behind. Now the future beckons and Jesus transmits his mission to the disciples. Often this text has been seen primarily as a call to evangelism. Certainly it is that, but it is much more. The command is to "make disciples" (Matthew 28:19). This is not a multiple-choice mission. It has the single imperative of causing persons to become disciples of Jesus Christ.

But the command has two components. The first is to baptize these new disciples. Through baptism they are incorporated into the company of Christ. The second component of the singular mission of disciple-making is too often neglected. Jesus' words are "teaching them to obey everything that I have commanded you" (28:20). Disciple-making is not just baptism into the faith, it is also instruction to complete obedience to Christ's commands. To make a disciple is not just to call a person to Christ, but just as important it is to teach disciples to love God and to love their neighbors as they love themselves, including their enemies.

The great commission is not a simple command. It does not help people fit into the world more easily. Rather, it is a command to create people who are radically different from the world. The great commission is revolutionary. (Carl L. Schenck)

Worship Aids

Call to Worship
The earth is the Lord's and the fullness thereof.
Praise be to the Lord for this good creation.

Go and have dominion over the earth.
We praise the Lord through our care of God's good creation.

Prayer of Confession

Merciful God, we confess that we have not been good stewards of your creation. We are treating it as our own rather than yours. We have been careless in our use of natural resources and extravagant in our unnecessary comforts. We have not been accountable to you for the way we have cared for your creation. Have mercy on us. Heal us and change us, we pray in Jesus' name. Amen.

Words of Assurance

In the name of Christ, you are forgiven.
In the name of Christ, you are forgiven.
We are renewed and refreshed by God's love and forgiveness. Amen.

Benediction

May the gracious creator re-create us that we might become God's good property managers today, tomorrow, and always. Amen. (Carl L. Schenck)

The Power of Blessing

Second in a Series of Four on the Power of Genesis

Genesis 12:1-3

One evening as I watched television, I saw a man speaking to a large crowd. He was quite successful, and he said the secret of his success was the way God had blessed him. He said that God had been the power behind his profits and achievements. In fact, his level of success was so great, he no longer had to go to work!

Yet, listening to this gentleman, I couldn't help but ask, "Is this why God blesses us, so we can take off work and live in the lap of luxury?" Something doesn't seem right here. In this picture, God has become nothing more than a cosmic bellhop who gives us what we want. Surely there is more to God than the blessing of a business!

For close to two thousand years the church has had to wrestle with the divine-human relationship. Where do God's promises and blessings end and our responses begin? Where does God's will meet our will in the divine-human encounter? It has not always been easy to discern. If we can do it all on our own, or if God is simply at our beck and call, then why bother with God? Why take the time to talk about God's blessings when behind the scenes we plot our own course anyway? It's as old as Genesis itself: Adam and Eve, Cain and Abel, Noah, the tower of Babel—all point to the human desire to sneak around God's promises and do what we want.

And yet, the power of God's call to Abram is the ability to see beyond our needs to God's blessings. That power helps us realize that the only reason we *can* is because God already *has*. We can accomplish what we do because God has already accomplished all things. God said yes to us long before we said yes to God. God has been there all along, giving us strength to do what God has called us to do.

The story of God's blessing and call of Abram reminds us that the focus of God's blessings is not on the one being blessed. Rather, God's blessings focus on how to share with others. Abram is blessed to be a blessing, not for personal gain. That's the vision!

In other words, God did not say, "I will bless you so that your name will be great and everyone will love you" or "I will bless you so that you may live a life of luxury" or "I will bless you so that you won't have responsibilities and concerns anymore." Rather, God says, "I will bless you, and make your name great, so that you will be a blessing" (Genesis 12:2).

The central purpose behind the blessing of Abram and Israel is to bless the world. Abram's primary role is to ensure that all children become blessed. The whole thrust is to foster ways of showering blessings on the least brothers and sisters. In short, Abram's mission is to set into motion God's plan of creation, the blessing of every last creature.

God blesses, and we then bless others. That's the logic of the mission. Why does God give us gifts and talents? Why does God grant us peace and even sometimes prosperity? The answer is not found in keeping things to ourselves. Rather, it is found in the movement from self to God: God does not bless us for our own sake. Instead, God blesses us so that we can be a blessing to others—even those who may hurt or injure us.

In Luke 18:9-14, Jesus tells the parable of the Pharisee and the tax collector. Both men went to the temple to pray. The Pharisee was confident of God's favor upon him, thanking God that he was not like other people (thieves, adulterers, even tax collectors). He boasted of fasting twice a week and tithing. The tax collector, on the other hand, stood far off with his head down. He beat his breast and said, "God, be merciful to me, a sinner!" (Luke 18:13). Jesus told the crowd that the tax collector went home "justified" (18:14). In God's kingdom, Jesus said, all who exalt themselves will be humbled, and all who humble themselves will be exalted.

In God's way of putting the world right, blessings come to us not for gain but to share in Christ's reign of redemption. All of God's creation is good, and God chooses to bless all creatures.

In Genesis, the promise to Abram is to become the father of many nations, not just one. Abram's children will come from many tribes. To all who seek a mission today in a world of violence and war, is there a better mission and call than to be a blessing to others? Abram's call is the first hint of the "Great Commission" to make disciples of all peoples and nations (Matthew 28:16-20). Our mission, as God's people, as Christ's church, as fathers and mothers, is not simply to take care of our own, but to take the promise of blessing and hope beyond ourselves to all of God's children today and in the generations to come. (Andrew D. Kinsey)

Worship Aids

Invocation

God of blessing and God of hope, in your holy presence we pray that you will infuse our spirits with a vision of goodness and truth. We pray that you will strengthen our call and renew our faith in the promises of your covenant love, so that we may truly share with others the blessings of your Son and the light of your Spirit, moving us into the world to worship and serve you as God's holy people, for Christ's sake. Amen.

Prayer of Confession

Holy and living God, teach us to see ourselves as we truly are. Help us to see that we are blessed not because of what we have done but because of who you are. You sent us your only son; help us to see not only the blessings he has given us but also the blessings we might become beyond our own family and tribe, beyond our own nation and race. Forgive us for taking Christ's blessings for granted, and for failing to share them with others. We confess and pray in Jesus' name. Amen.

Words of Assurance

O Lord, grant us new opportunities to serve you today. Grant us strength to share with others the blessings and gifts of your kingdom. Fill us with your Spirit that we might open to receive the mercy only you can bestow and the love only you can give. For this we pray in Christ's power and truth. Amen. (Andrew D. Kinsey)

JUNE 26, 2011

❧❧❧

Second Sunday after Pentecost

Readings: Genesis 22:1-14; Psalm 13; Romans 6:12-23;
Matthew 10:40-42

God Will Provide
Genesis 22:1-14

There are times when we open the Bible and read or hear a text that not only offends us, but cuts to the core of what it means to be human. We have just heard such a reading today. The story from Genesis where God commands the patriarch Abraham to sacrifice his only son, Isaac, is more than offensive; it drives a stake into the very heart of our Christian faith. How could God, the Father of our Lord Jesus Christ, ask, much less command, a father to murder his child as an act of worship? This story does not make sense. Just hearing it assaults every core value we hold as human beings. But there it is and here we are and now that we have heard it, what in God's name do we do with it?

My first inclination is to do with this text what Thomas Jefferson did with so many passages in the Bible. Simply cut it out! If you have been to Jefferson's home in Monticello, Virginia, you have seen his edited copy of the Bible lying open on a table. Our brilliant founding father, the towering intellect who crafted the Declaration of Independence and established the University of Virginia, literally cut out of the Bible any passage he found offensive, illogical, or uncomfortable.

Now before we come down too hard on our third president, let me remind you that we all do the same thing. Our sensitivities probably prohibit us from using scissors to remove difficult Bible verses or stories, but we cut texts out of our Bible every day. We avoid them, ignore them, read around them, or, in some cases, cut them out of our personal and collective memory. If a text challenges some secret sin or takes issue with our pet political view, we read around it. If a pastor or biblical scholar points out a verse that takes issue with one of our prejudices, we turn a deaf ear or, worse, accuse the minister or theologian of being either a liberal or a fundamentalist. That's the way we routinely do business in the Christian church: ignore, label, and malign all texts and teachers of texts that offend our values or question our views.

Believe me. This is a passage I would gladly cut out of my Bible. I do not like it, and I have rarely found anyone of faith who does.

Here is another, equally tempting, option: hear and accept the story, but interpret the passage as metaphor or allegory. In other words, make the text fit our world rather than taking the risk of entering its world and time. This raises a curiously challenging problem for anyone who reads the Bible. There are roughly four thousand years between 1900 B.C.E. and 2011. Time, space, culture, language, values, religious practices, family customs, political arrangements, even dietary choices are but a few of the differences between Abraham and Sarah's world and ours. What we do when faced with these differences is predictable. We walk into an old story as if these people had friends on Facebook and ate pizza on Friday nights. In a word, we think we can overlay our story on the Bible's story. And in so doing, we miss the Bible's power and dismiss the Bible's message.

So what exactly do we do with Genesis 22:1-14? Simply put, I believe we must hear it, accept it on its own terms, voice our discomfort, and then take the bold step of asking what God may be saying to us. Let's give that a try and see where the Spirit leads us.

To begin, we must hear this story in its brutal "that-ness." Abraham and Sarah lived in a world where parents sacrificed their children to mute and lifeless deities. We must accept the fact that this older couple, groping toward a relationship with God Almighty, did not know what we know: that God is One, that God is love, and that God is full of grace. We must accept that Abraham believed God was calling him to sacrifice Isaac. But the story does not stop there and neither can we.

Move through the story to its conclusion. Yes, Abraham takes Isaac to a far mountain, no doubt believed to be sacred by those ancient people. Yes, Abraham builds an altar, stacks dry wood on its crown, binds his son, Isaac, and places him on that wood. Yes, Abraham raises a jagged knife and almost kills his son on that altar. But God stops him, changes the story, and shows Abraham another way. It is that change, that move to the other way, that is good news today.

Although none of us would think of killing one of our children to appease God, we can and often do act in death-dealing ways. Children watch our every move and pick up messages we never intended to send. We can let work drive a knife into the beating heart of a marriage. We can bind our families with cords of anger and addiction that feel like living death. If we are not aware of or sensitive to others, we will kill life's most precious relationships.

The story tells us that God provides a way that leads to life, not death; that sacrifice does not require the death of a child or a spouse. God calls us to worthy dreams and ennobled human values. In the thickets of our often complicated lives, God has resources offering better ways to live. Jesus lived, died, and rose again to show us that giving our lives to others in sacrificial love is God's way of life.

When you think about it, God provides a way that calls us to sacrifice our lives for others rather than sacrificing others for our selfish desires. Listen carefully and look around. God has a better way, another way, shown in the risen life of our Lord Jesus Christ. Amen. (Timothy Owings)

Lectionary Commentary
Romans 6:12-23

These verses are in the middle of a lengthy passage in which Paul challenges his readers' understanding of the grace of God. Apparently some in the Roman church believed that the more they sinned, the more grace they could experience. Just before our focal verses, Paul points to baptism as the outward sign of God's re-creating work in every life. Because we have also "died to sin" (Romans 6:10), God's grace triumphs through our lives. We are "alive to God in Christ Jesus" (v. 11).

In this text, Paul summons the Roman believers to become "slaves of righteousness" (6:18) whose master is the risen Christ. The Christian life is a daily choice to be men and women of transforming grace. The evidence of sin in our lives is behavior that turns up its nose at grace and cripples life. "The wages of sin is death" (v. 23) in no uncertain terms. "But the free gift of God is eternal life in Christ Jesus our Lord" (v. 23). Meaning what? At its core, we are called to live aware of sin's damaging power while being fully alive to God's grace.

Matthew 10:40-42

The power of hospitality is no better illustrated in our Lord's teachings than in these three verses. The key words are *welcomes* and *gives*. The culture of the Middle East is seasoned with generous hospitality. People who visit Jerusalem today always comment on the warm hospitality extended by shopkeepers. To have the honor of showing hospitality is rooted in this culture.

Here, Jesus summons his disciples to be men and women who welcome others as if they were welcoming him. We Christians are called to be people who live with open arms, open minds, and open acceptance. To take this idea further, Jesus identifies giving a cup of cool water "to one of these little ones" (Matthew 10:42) as the ultimate expression of hospitality. Tempted though we are to show deference to the powerful and wealthy, Jesus calls us to express the same level of concern to "little ones"—the marginalized, voiceless, abused, and forgotten. (Timothy Owings)

Worship Aids

Call to Worship (based on Psalm 13)

How long, O LORD! Will you forget me forever?
  How long will you hide your face from me?
How long must I bear pain in my soul,
  and have sorrow in my heart all day long?
How long shall my enemy be exalted over me?
Consider and answer me, O LORD my God!
  My foes rejoice because I am shaken.
But I trusted in your steadfast love;
  my heart shall rejoice in your salvation.
ALL: I will sing to the LORD,
  because he has dealt bountifully with me.
Sing to the LORD a new song! Sing to the LORD!

Invocation

God of unfailing faithfulness, we worship you as the one in whom we live and move and have our being. So awaken our lives to your faithful and generous grace that we will sing of your mercy and rejoice in your love. May our worship lead us from every death-dealing thought and behavior to the place of life and love so that your will may be done on earth even as it is in heaven. Through Jesus Christ our Lord. Amen.

Prayer of Confession

Loving God, we confess that our thoughts are not your thoughts and our ways are not your ways. We often choose what is best for us rather than what is best for others. We weigh our lives in the scale of selfishness and meet an emptiness that robs life of its glory. Forgive us, we pray, and lead us to the place where others matter more and things matter less; where life is valued more than death and you are the one whose life matters most. Living Lord, make us new through the power of the risen one, our Lord Jesus Christ, in whose name we pray. Amen.

Pardon and Assurance

In the name of Christ, you are forgiven.
In the name of Christ, you are forgiven.
Thanks be to God. (Timothy Owings)

The Power of Hope

Third in a Series of Four on the Power of Genesis

Genesis 17:15-22

The story of Abraham and Sarah requires us to cross the threshold of faith in ways we cannot imagine. Do you ever wonder what could have been going through Abraham's and Sarah's minds as they received the news they were going to have a baby? We know that God made a covenant with Abraham and promised to make him the father of many nations. We have journeyed with Abraham and Sarah to this juncture, and now we are left with a question: How will God work out the covenant promises? How will hope be victorious where barrenness rules?

Perhaps it is an understatement to share that in times of uncertainty people begin to look for hope. In fact, politicians run on the theme of hope, proclaiming that they represent a break with the past; indeed, they are the ones who can provide hope! Give hope a chance! In times of uncertainty, it is easy to send out a search party to find hope. Where can we find it? Where is it?

Since September 11, 2001, and Hurricane Katrina, we have been wondering what else there is. What does the future hold? Will we continue to resort to endless violence? Will we continue to expend our every waking moment on endless activities of sports and entertainment? If the future does not seem to hold much promise, why not get lost in the present, why not live for today? Who cares about tomorrow?

When we are young, we want reassurance about the purpose of our lives. We want to find our way in this world. We seek some kind of reaffirmation amid the confusion of the world's competing voices and interests. But we also expend energy on the now, pursuing life without giving much attention to what is to come. It's a paradox, and in the course of our seeking, fear and anxiety can take hold. As we grow older, we seek reassurance about the promises of life, in particular, about eternal life. We want to believe in tomorrow, even when we encounter trouble today. Regardless of age, though, the message is the same: without hope, we fall into despair and lose touch with the promises of the future.

The story of Abraham and Sarah speaks to the power of hope. When we first meet the couple, God has chosen them to bring into existence a great nation with a future full of promise. This covenant brings into focus, not simply the future of a people, but the story of a creator who makes something out of nothing. Where there was nothing there is now a new people—God's people. God blesses Israel to be a blessing, living among the other nations. That's the promise—and the challenge.

But in our story, there is an obstacle to the promise—barrenness; not simply the inability to conceive, but the inability to hope. That's the kind of barrenness Genesis describes. Barrenness is not simply the absence of children but the absence of hope, the absence of a future, the absence of promise. Abraham and Sarah are barren, without hope.

God steps in to remind Abraham that he will become the father of many nations and that his descendants will be as numerous as the stars, that the land he will inhabit will be a "perpetual holding" (Genesis 17:8). God's covenant promise is fertile with hope. But still no children, until God blesses Sarah's womb with life, and she conceives. She bears a son, Isaac, who will carry the covenant into the future. From Isaac's offspring will come forth children to bless and populate the earth. Isaac will be the covenant-bearer. Isaac will take the promises into tomorrow.

All of this sounds unthinkable to the older couple. Sarah laughs so hard she falls on the floor crying: How can God fulfill this kind of promise? Abraham has no reason to hope. He looks at the land of Canaan, and he looks at Sarah, and he sees nothing but barrenness. He looks at his circumstances and thinks, *Nothing can come of this!* But Abraham has every reason to hope; God has made a promise to him. God has called him and given to him the hope of a new future. God will fulfill the promise.

Hope is not fleeting, and hope does not disappoint. In fact, to live in hope means to live with the assurance of God's presence in our lives, knowing that "suffering produces endurance, and endurance produces character, and character produces hope, and hope does not disappoint us, because God's love has been poured into our hearts through the Holy Spirit that has been given to us" (Romans 5:3-5).

One of the most difficult aspects of the Christian life, then, is not so much the call to sacrifice as to hope—to continue to hope through the authentic trials of life—to hope against hope.

By its very texture we realize that hope is a gift of God. It is the gift of God's covenant love with Israel and the church, the gift of God's grace when the Son dies on the cross and when despair seems to have the upper hand. That's the paradox of hope: It is the power God gives of eternal life in the face of sin and death.

Sound unthinkable? Given the evidence, yes, it is unthinkable, even laughable. Who can imagine such hope? But given the one who makes the promise, no, it is not unimaginable. It is the power of God in salvation, the gift that doesn't disappoint—and never will. Thanks be to God! Amen. (Andrew D. Kinsey)

Worship Aids

Invocation

Almighty God, fill us with hope as we come into your presence. Grant us wisdom and courage to follow in the way of your Son, Jesus Christ, as we open our hearts to his will and as we seek the renewal of our minds by his grace. Grant to us the power to worship and serve you in all we do as we promise to serve you in ways pleasing and acceptable in your sight. We invoke your holy name in the Spirit's power. Amen.

Pastoral Prayer

Holy and living God, our help in ages past and our hope for years to come, teach us to live with hope. Amid the challenges of this world, teach us to look up in faith to the promises of your Son. Teach us to share in the covenant of your word and in the power of your Holy Spirit. Help us to know that you are with us and that you call us to new life and to peace. Fill us with the joy of your salvation that we may offer to others the mercy and compassion of Jesus Christ.

Gracious Lord, we pray today for those whose lives and work bring hope where there is no hope. We pray for those who work to bring peace where there is no peace but only violence and conflict, where the seas of indifference clash with the sands of concern and care, and where the voice of justice speaks to power and corruption. May we, O God, as your people who seek to worship in your name, walk in the way that leads to life, and may we as your church serve Jesus in righteousness and truth, as we discover the fullness of your hope and glory. We pray in Christ's Spirit. Amen.

Benediction

May the Father of our Lord Jesus Christ, the God of all hope, the God of all peace and grace, keep and guide you, as you go into this world, sharing the blessings of Christ's eternal covenant, and praising God for the Spirit's call to love and give. Amen. (Andrew D. Kinsey)

JULY 3, 2011

❦❦❦

Third Sunday after Pentecost

Readings: Genesis 24:34-38, 42-49, 58-67; Psalm 45:10-17;
Romans 7:15-25a; Matthew 11:16-19, 25-30

Rest for the Restless
Matthew 11:16-19, 25-30

Someone has rightly called Matthew 11 the chapter for the contemporary church. At first glance, you might not see it that way, but let's look a bit closer. This chapter actually begins a new section of Matthew's Gospel. We learn in the first verses that John the Baptist is in Herod's prison. Hearing of our Lord's teaching and healing ministry, John sends messengers to Jesus asking, "Are you the one who is to come, or are we to wait for another?" (Matthew 11:3).

Jesus answers the Baptist's questions by recounting the work God is doing: "the blind receive their sight, the lame walk, the lepers are cleansed, the deaf hear, the dead are raised, and the poor have good news brought to them" (11:5). Poor John, languishing in a dungeon, hoping with every hope that Jesus is the promised Messiah, but wondering, if he is, why imprisonment, questions, and soon, death?

Then we come to our text. With rhetorical puzzlement, Jesus asks, "To what will I compare this generation? It is like children sitting in the marketplaces and calling to one another, 'We played the flute for you, and you did not dance; we wailed, and you did not mourn'" (11:16-17).

In other words, we are fickle and restless; unfulfilled in laughter and unmoved by sorrow. We act like spoiled children, never satisfied but often complaining.

Do you see now why some see this chapter as a commentary on the contemporary church? When contemporary worship was all the rage, every church, no matter what its history, had to have a contemporary worship service. Several decades ago, the rage was gifts of the Spirit. In

211

other times, books on Revelation, filled with half-baked ideas on the world's end, flew off the shelves. In one season, spirituality is popular; in another, music; in a third, mission endeavors; and in yet another, recreational binges. Perhaps it has always been so, but ours seems like such a restless, moody, unsatisfied generation of Christians.

After some time Jesus, weary from all the restless roamings of his followers, looks up to heaven and prays. The substance of his prayer offers thanksgiving to God that the basic, core meanings of life are really simple, rooted in a childlike faith built on trust. That trust, according to Jesus, is found when we cast our restless lives on God's unchanging, faithful presence.

Hear again the invitation of our Lord: "Come to me, all you that are weary and are carrying heavy burdens, and I will give you rest. Take my yoke upon you, and learn from me; for I am gentle and humble in heart, and you will find rest for your souls. For my yoke is easy, and my burden is light" (11:28-30).

There are no more elegant, winsome, nourishing words in all of scripture. What is God saying to us?

First, nothing—no thing—can hold the place reserved in our lives for Jesus Christ. "Come to me" is still the invitation our Lord extends to each of us. Why do we chase after things that can never satisfy? Choose your worship style. Embrace whatever theological opinion of the day seems important. Read the latest book written by the touted, best Christian mind of the day, and you will still long for a personal, heart-to-heart relationship with Jesus Christ. When our restless lives plop exhausted in the uncomfortable spiritual chair of our own making, we will still long to come to Jesus.

Second, come to Jesus in your exhaustion and weariness. Our Lord recognized this restless tendency in us. Psychologists call the urge to travel "wanderlust." In my judgment, every human being is infected with spiritual wanderlust. We look here and there for meaning and, without fail, find ourselves exhausted in every search that does not include a personal connection with Christ.

Viktor Frankl survived the horrors of Auschwitz and wrote a book that now, years after his death, is still printed and reprinted. *Man's Search for Meaning* is Frankl's story of courage and survival in which human beings came through to the other side of the Nazi madness with meaning. How? Simply put, Frankl believed that the supreme need in every life is not for pleasure, as Freud suggested, or for power, as Adler proposed. But rather, the highest need in every life is for meaning. All of us long for meaning that transcends our work, every success, and life itself.

Our Lord invites us to find in him the energizing, vital meaning that life offers. That discovery begins when we come to him, acknowledging that we are exhausted and empty from spiritual wanderlust that has taken us places rather than to a person.

Third, our Lord promises rest for the restless. We are a generation that longs for answers, solutions, neat formulas for success. Here, our Lord offers rest. "I will give you rest." When life implodes on us, when death robs us of a loved one or disappointment snatches a friendship from our future, when even faith seems hollow and answerless, our Lord offers rest for our souls. Think about it: if you have answers but no rest, what do you have but a string of words? God in Christ offers us a much better gift.

But how? "Take my yoke upon you, and learn from me; for I am gentle and humble in heart, and you will find rest for your souls" (11:29). A wise pastor once said that when we begin to follow Jesus, we enroll in the School of Jesus and never graduate. The Christian journey is one in which we are lifelong learners—disciples—of this one who loved us even unto death. The rest for which we long can finally and supremely be found when the one who loved us all the way to Calvary and beyond becomes the one in whom we learn to trust now and always.

At the end of the day, or the week, or even a life, there will be one who welcomes our wandering, confused, and restless lives. I commend this one to you today as the Lord of life, the Lord of love, the Lord of all, even Jesus Christ. Amen. (Timothy Owings)

Lectionary Commentary
Genesis 24:34-38, 42-49, 58-67

The story of Abraham sending his servant to find a wife for Isaac is one of the great love stories in scripture. To give the story any measure of justice, you must read the entire twenty-fourth chapter of Genesis. Abraham makes his servant swear that he will go to Abraham's clan and there find a wife for Isaac. Armed with ten camels and "all kinds of choice gifts" (Genesis 24:10), the servant travels to the region of Abraham's roots looking for Isaac's wife. The servant prays that God will reveal the chosen woman to him, which God does through the maid Rebekah.

The texts selected as the Old Testament lesson focus on the servant's conversation with Laban, Rebekah's brother, after he meets her at a well.

Probably nowhere in scripture do we see such a detailed account of Middle Eastern culture as in this chapter. Notice the extensive hospitality Laban offers this servant. Savor the speed with which a deal is struck for Rebekah to go with this stranger back to Abraham to marry Isaac, and note that Rebekah is consulted about the arrangements, truly unusual for that ancient culture.

But most of all, relish the narrator's comment in verse 67 that Isaac "took Rebekah, and she became his wife; and he loved her." This is one of the rare places in the Bible where we read of a man's love for his wife. There is no more tender or beautiful love story in God's word.

Romans 7:15-25a

Paul peels back the cover of his ego and here reveals the great struggle of his life. Having argued for the power of God's grace over human sin in chapter 6 and the first part of chapter 7, he tells the Romans that life, by its nature, will always include moral and spiritual struggle. Contrary to what many believe about Paul's pride, he is utterly transparent here, admitting, "I can will what is right, but I cannot do it" (7:18). And again, "For I do not do the good I want, but the evil I do not want is what I do" (v. 19).

Finally, exhausted from this internal struggle with which all believers identify, Paul exclaims, "Wretched man that I am! Who will rescue me from this body of death?" (7:24). In response to his own question, he declares, "Thanks be to God through Jesus Christ our Lord!" (v. 25). Rather than conceding power to sin's reality, Paul names the power of sin while lifting up the ultimate power of God. Paul's transparent, honest confession of his struggle in these verses propels him with integrity toward his discussion of the freedom we have in the Spirit, which will occupy most of Romans 8, which follows. (Timothy Owings)

Worship Aids

Call to Worship (Unison)
God of grace and God of glory, we gather to worship you as the source of all life and the giver of every good and perfect gift. Give us voice today to praise your name, courage to name our sin, boldness to believe your promises, and wisdom to live in the power and strength of your

love; to the end that we will be and become your people of winsome grace and generous love. Let us worship God!

Pastoral Prayer

Loving Lord, hear us as we pray. This past week has found us wandering in the world you made, weighed down with life's cares and wearied by life's demands. Forgive us for turning away from your still, small voice of love. Forgive us for not believing the faith we sing and the grace we have received. Forgive us for taking our own way while ignoring your word.

We especially pray today for all who bear burdens not of their own making. Grant comfort to those who mourn, healing mercy to those who are sick, and sustaining grace to those who are disillusioned. Fill all of us—whether we struggle with life's difficulties or rejoice in life's blessings—with a sense of your presence. Remind us as the scriptures are read and the word proclaimed that you are the ever-living, faithfully loving Lord whose great delight is for us to know your love and joyfully follow you.

God of all comfort, Savior and friend, renew us through the work of your Spirit that we will go from this place of worship to the places where you have called us to serve, quickened by your love and strengthened by your mercy to be your people of hope and promise through Jesus Christ our Lord. Amen.

Benediction

Now may the God who raised Jesus from the dead, who has given to him the name that is above every name, so fill you with hope that you will be and become God's hands and God's feet, God's voice and God's love, to all with whom you live, work, and serve, to the honor of God the Father, God the Son, and God the Holy Spirit. Amen. (Timothy Owings)

The Power of God's Goodness

Fourth in a Series of Four on the Power of Genesis

Genesis 50:15-21

Over the last three Sundays, our journey through Genesis has been revealing. We have heard that God goes to great lengths to covenant with a particular people for the redemption of the world (Genesis 12:1-3). God offers a kind of "scandalous goodness" toward Abraham and

Sarah's offspring as they journey toward becoming a great nation. Despite dysfunction and barrenness, deception and despair, God is faithful to the covenant (17:15-22). God's grace provides freedom, even within the contingencies of Israel's history (2:15-17).

Therefore, it may seem odd on the Sunday before Independence Day to share a sermon on the power of God's goodness! In fact, it may seem odd not to focus on God's grace "shed on thee," or on America as a "shining city on a hill." Never mind that Jesus called the church to assume this position among all the nations of the world. The whole notion of a "royal priesthood" might pale in comparison to the power of the state (1 Peter 2:9). Nevertheless, we ask: How does the power of God's goodness provide a message of hope to a people struggling to remain faithful in a time of uncertainty? Indeed, how may we, as God's chosen, overhear what God is saying to us as both citizens and disciples? Perhaps Joseph and his "band of brothers" supply the necessary clues and answers.

The story of Joseph is fascinating; it occupies the last third of Genesis (37–50). To many of us, the name Joseph may conjure up all kinds of images—the coat of many colors, jealousy among the brothers, the father's favorite son, or the dreamer. As the story opens in chapter 37, Joseph is the youngest of Jacob's eleven sons, firstborn of Rachel. He is seventeen years old and has a very special relationship with his father. He has been blessed with unique gifts and talents and has been the center of attention since birth, so much so that the attention sparks envy among the other ten. In fact, we will learn that the older brothers plot against Joseph and sell him into slavery. I can hear the complaint of Tommy Smothers, of Smothers Brothers fame, in the background: "Mom always liked you best."

To be sure, this is probably not the story to help us brush up on family values. In fact, we wonder why Jacob and Rachel don't handle this better. After all, they surely know how brothers can act. Jacob and Esau began fighting before they were born. Why doesn't Jacob pay more attention to what is happening in his own family? Doesn't he see what is taking place?

The obvious answer is no. Jacob, like his father, Isaac, doesn't see what is unfolding beneath his own nose. His sons sell Joseph into slavery, making arrangements with a band of Ishmaelite traders on their way to Egypt. The deal is sealed, and with Joseph's coat still dripping with goat's blood, Joseph becomes a slave in Egypt.

In Egypt, Joseph matures, becomes a different person, and rises to prominence, becoming the pharaoh's prime minister and one of the most powerful people on earth. Who would have thought Joseph would gain in stature in this way? And who would have thought that he and his brothers would meet again? With famine spreading, Joseph's brothers come to Egypt seeking relief. Because of Joseph's advice, Egypt is one of the few places food can be found.

When the brothers arrive, they don't recognize Joseph. Joseph was merely a boy when they betrayed him. Now he is an adult wearing the clothing of nobility. Joseph recognizes them, but they don't recognize him.

Now comes one of the most dramatic scenes in the Bible. Joseph instructs his brothers to fetch their father, Jacob, who is nearing death. Joseph wants to see his father one last time. He also requires that the youngest son, Benjamin, stay behind while the brothers go back to Canaan. It's a tense situation. In time, though, with all the family gathered, there is a reunion. Then Jacob dies, and the brothers fear that, with Jacob gone, Joseph will take his revenge.

Joseph offers forgiveness instead. Rather than revenge, he offers mercy. In fact, there are tears: Joseph cries, the brothers cry, everyone cries tears of reconciliation. Joseph expresses the grace of the moment: "Do not be afraid! Am I in the place of God? Even though you intended to do harm to me, God intended it for good, in order to preserve a numerous people, as he is doing today" (Genesis 50:19-20).

Even though the brothers intended harm, God intended good! This is certainly not to say that God intended for Joseph to be treated inhumanely, or that God intended for the brothers to plot murder. The glorious point here is that there is nothing beyond God's redemptive power of grace.

Yet this story resists easy notions of God's providence. Joseph's encounter with God is real but elusive; God remains in the shadows and behind the scenes, working toward the best possible end. This story transcends national boundaries. It is grounded, not in party affiliation or denominational heritage or national identity, but in God's goodness toward creation. Ultimately, nothing can prevent God's goodness from being fulfilled. This story reminds us that God isn't finished with us yet.

That's good news! In a world becoming fragmented through racism and war, in a nation becoming fractured by violence and poverty and drugs, and in a church becoming divided by indifference on the one hand and zealotry on the other—the promise of God's goodness remains steadfast. Despite our worst intentions, God redeems. God can take the fragile pieces of our lives and weave them into a new creation, working behind the scenes to shape a whole new future. Amen. (Andrew D. Kinsey)

Worship Aids

Invocation

O God, as we come into your holy temple, may we enjoy your goodness and peace; may we receive the blessings of your Son, as we worship you in spirit and truth, and as we experience the presence of your Holy Spirit in our lives, that we may once again see the fruits of your righteousness and the power of your hope in the world as we declare and proclaim the depths of your love and grace. In Christ's name, we pray. Amen.

Offertory Prayer

May the God of all goodness continue to bless and keep us as we labor in the fields of hope and mercy. Despite the challenges we face and the obstacles we encounter, may we continue to serve and give out of gratitude for what Christ has done for us on the cross. May our gifts truly reflect God's goodness, and may our church continue to grow in faith. For the wonders of your providential care, O Lord, may you now receive these, our gifts; in Christ's name. Amen.

Benediction

May the Lord of life and peace, the God of all goodness and truth, bless and keep you as we depart this place. May the Parent of our Savior, Jesus Christ, provide for and nourish us all as we go forth to serve in this world. May the Spirit of Christ, the very presence of God among us, apply to our own hearts the benefits of the cross as we proclaim anew the wonders of God's love. Amen. (Andrew D. Kinsey)

JULY 10, 2011

❧❧❧

Fourth Sunday after Pentecost

Readings: Genesis 25:19-34; Psalm 119:105-112; Romans 8:1-11; Matthew 13:1-9, 18-23

A Generous Harvest
Matthew 13:1-9, 18-23

When we think of the parables Jesus told, the parable of the prodigal son and the good Samaritan come quickly to mind. My hunch is the parable of the sower would be third on our list. Recorded in both Mark and Matthew, this parable is not only one we remember but also one of the few parables to which our Lord gave an interpretation. In case you are already saying to yourself, "Heard that, know that, thank you very much," I dare you to listen again. You might just hear another twist on this old story.

As Jesus told the parable, a farmer put a heavy seed bag on his shoulder and went out to his field to sow seed. In those days, farmers broadcast seed across a fallow field before plowing. That's right; seed was first sown, and then gently plowed into the ground. You might find it interesting that this methodology is being reclaimed today by farmers wanting to better care for God's earth. "No-till" corn is quite the rage in parts of the Midwest. Using refined technology, a farmer can sow and cultivate a corn crop without deep-plowing the field. "The more things change, the more they stay the same." Imagine that!

Here, as this farmer broadcast his precious seed, some fell on a well-worn path cut by foot traffic through the fallow field. When fields lay fallow, foot travelers would cut walking paths through the fields, taking the shortest distance between two points. Fencing was rarely if ever used in the first century. So some seed landed on the path. And when it did, the birds quickly enjoyed lunch.

219

Other seeds, said Jesus, fell on rocky ground. Because there was little soil there, the seedlings sprang up quickly and then withered under the scorching sun. Thorns choked off other seeds, denying them the light of day and the promise of their bounty. Finally, some seed fell on good ground and brought forth a bumper crop yielding thirty, sixty, even a hundredfold. Jesus ended the story admonishing all to listen; listen carefully, deeply, thoughtfully. Listen!

Some time passes. Probably alone with his disciples, Jesus gave an interpretation to this beloved parable that has endured through the ages. Many believe that our Lord's interpretation of the parable, as representing various kinds of people, is the only legitimate interpretation. What if, as I believe, this parable has, can have, and even must have many meanings to it? As with all our Lord's parables, the key is to listen and let the word take root in our lives.

I have another take on this great story; a twist to the text I invite you to consider. What if the parable could be applied with equal power to every individual life, to everyone who listens? If that is so, all of our lives have worn, rocky, thorny, and yes, good soil in which seed can germinate and grow. What if this parable is about you and me? If so, what is God saying to us?

If your life is like mine, you know how daily living creates well-worn paths. We call them ruts. We drive to and from work using the same route day after day. We shop at the same grocery store, fill our tanks at the same convenience store, thankfully attend the same church, and, more times than not, feed our families predictable menus of foods we know they will eat and enjoy. Routines are often required, but sometimes in our relationship with God, routines can become ruts. We can attend church week after week, hear the scriptures read (like this familiar parable), sing familiar hymns, go through the church routine, and in so doing, give the good seed God sows us to the birds of indifference. Trust me. It happens and may be happening even now.

Truth be told, God's seed also falls on the rocky places of our lives. Life, by definition, can leave us cold, sharp, soilless, and rough. Pain, the cruelty of insensitive friends, and the crude comments of strangers can leave us lifeless and unmoved, rocks void of God's bounty. Thorns pop up in our life's ground as well. None of us intend to succumb to the cutting brutality of thorns, but there they are, choking out God's blessings, robbing us of God's promise.

But thanks be to God, some seed falls on good ground. When it does, the miracle of germination, cultivation, nourishment, sunshine, rain, and care yield a generous harvest no one thought was possible. It happens in all our lives in ways that leave us speechless.

I am thinking today of countless individuals through the years who have started to tell me a story with these words: "You'll never believe what happened to me today." Or, "I had no idea God could take what I did and use it to bless another's life." Tell your story. Look back and see all the times God sowed good seed on the good ground of your soul, and from that small beginning came a generous harvest that still leaves you amazed.

Here is the needed twist in this old, old story. Yes, there will always be people who are worn out, rocky, wasted, and yes, good. But the gospel reminds us there is far more good in all of us in which God's grace can take root than any of us imagine. All manner of ground exists in the fields that are our lives. Why don't we clear out the rocks, cut down the thorns, change up the routines, and give God even more opportunities to grow from our lives the generous, bountiful, giving people God in Christ made us to be? I dare you to believe it today and to discover it as you do the amazing work of God in and through your life. Amen. (Timothy Owings)

Lectionary Commentary
Genesis 25:19-34

The births of Esau and Jacob are the genesis of a great tragedy in the lives of the patriarchs. Isaac, the promised only child of Abraham and Sarah, takes Rebekah, the woman he loves, to be his wife. Barren for years, they finally conceive twins. At their births, *Esau*—meaning "ruddy" or "red"—is born first. Gripping his heel is the second-born son, whom they name *Jacob*, or "heel." The writer of Genesis clearly tells us that Isaac is partial to Esau; Rebekah loves Jacob. From infancy, this sibling rivalry would lead to sorrow, estrangement, and even war.

The story that follows tells of Esau selling his birthright to Jacob for a pot of red, meaty stew. Focused on his bodily cravings for food and hungry for the acceptance Jacob enjoys from his mother, Esau gives up his birthright to satisfy an earthly hunger. The writer ends the story with the sad news that Esau "despised his birthright" (Genesis 25:34). The plot created, this tragic episode will color the rest of Esau and Jacob's relationship to their sorrow and that of the offspring who will come after them.

Romans 8:1-11

Having just lamented the war between the flesh and the Spirit in his life, Paul now transposes his faith into the higher key of rich confidence. In the original language of the Bible, Paul begins Romans 8 with transitional words captured by the NRSV: "There is therefore now no condemnation for those who are in Christ Jesus." To be in Christ is to live in a reality that names the battle between the flesh and the Spirit but celebrates the triumph that is ours through our Lord's victory.

Paul recapitulates this truth in verses 5-8, where he distinguishes life in the Spirit and life in the flesh. But he will not stay there. Verse 9 emphatically tells the Romans—and us—that "you are not in the flesh; you are in the Spirit, since the Spirit of God dwells in you." Here we glimpse the mystery of faith that seasons much of Paul's writing. To use the title of James Stewart's beloved book, *A Man in Christ*, we who live by faith live in Christ, because of Christ, with Christ, following Christ. There is no higher or more profound reality offered human beings than this spiritual, mystical union with the risen Lord. (Timothy Owings)

Worship Aids

Invocation

God of old stories and new beginnings, open our lives today to the *new* that you long to accomplish in our lives. As you called Abraham and Sarah to walk faithfully with you, speak our names today, call us to higher purposes, fill us with your Spirit that we may worthily praise you and magnify your holy name. Through Jesus Christ our Lord, who lives and reigns with you and the Holy Spirit, one God now and forever. Amen.

Prayer of Confession

God of life, Lord of mercy, we confess that, like Esau and Jacob, we selfishly make decisions that do not honor you or others. Believing ourselves wise, we foolishly follow our own way, falling short of your glory. Our pride keeps us from being honest about ourselves, our sin, and our needs. Forgive us, we pray, and grant us the gift of your healing grace. Restore again both the joy of knowing you and the freedom of being known by you. Make us new and lead us in the way of life everlasting. Amen.

Words of Assurance

Our gracious and loving Lord is the essence of generosity and patience. Rest in and rely on God's love and forgiveness. Amen.

Benediction

The time of our gathering has come to an end; the moment of our parting is at hand. God of gatherings and partings, lead us from this place of worship to the many places of service and need that we, gathered and sent by your Spirit, may be your people of grace and truth. May God—Creator, Redeemer, and Sustainer—fit us for every good work to the glory of your name. Amen. (Timothy Owings)

Our Cheating Hearts

First in a Series of Four on Romans

Romans 2:1-16, 25-29

We will spend the next few weeks looking at parts of Paul's letter to the Romans. Romans is considered Paul's most important letter. Chapter 1 starts out in the typical way of Paul's letters, with greetings and praise for the congregation. By verse 18, however, he is fully into the heart of his message and begins talking about the wrath of God. We should not ignore God's wrath, but we should never use it to oppress people. Paul uses it for the appropriate purpose of getting the attention of the Romans. After hammering home his theological conviction that we are all sinners, Paul is ready to address the Romans specifically in chapter 2. *[Read text.]*

It may seem as though we could pop a blood vessel trying to understand Paul's thought. Paul is deep and complex, hard to summarize. All of our attempts to get a handle on Paul run the risk of oversimplifying. One way we might understand this chapter is to look at the word *heart(s)*, repeated three times (2:5, 15, 29). We share with Paul the conviction that *heart* is shorthand for our emotions, our will—the core of who we are. We use *heart* to mean love, courage, dedication. We may not understand everything about Paul's thought, but we all have an interest in what is going on deep in our hearts.

How we respond to what Paul says first about our hearts may tell us something about our spiritual maturity. Paul says first that our hearts are "hard and impenitent" (2:5). We may bristle at Paul's charge. How dare he say that about us? Doesn't Paul know how good we are? Yes, Paul does know that; but he also knows that something deep inside us is not quite right, that we can be stubborn, mean, and selfish.

As I said, how we respond to Paul's words here is a test of our spiritual maturity. The more we try to be good, the more we realize how hard it is to be good. The more spiritually mature we are, the more we realize how mixed our motives are. The harder we try to grow spiritually, the more we realize how difficult spiritual growth is. One part of spiritual maturity is a healthy realization that we are not what we could be. Paul simply calls us to be honest about ourselves.

On the other hand, if we try to pat ourselves on the back, we may live out what Paul says about us. The more we try to defend our goodness, the more we may prove Paul right. Paul's main goal here is to burst the bubble of self-righteousness. A part of self-righteousness is defending our goodness. Self-righteousness is failing to recognize that we harbor dark thoughts in our hearts. Paul especially wants us to see that our hearts are hard toward God. Paul sees the root of all sin as idolatry. We are supposed to love God, but we love everything except God. We love our own pleasure and security.

Paul especially wants us to see how we trick ourselves. If we sin and get away with it, we assume it is okay, that what we did must not have been so wrong. Paul tells us that lack of punishment for sin comes from God's grace and kindness. God's grace and kindness are not approval, but offer an opportunity for us to repent.

Paul wants us to understand just how deep our sin goes. Paul is not trying to browbeat us or make us give up in despair. Paul wants us to see that our relationship with God is broken. He wants us to understand that our sin hurts people. Paul also sees good in us. If we did not have any good in us, we would have no hope. Paul believes that some good exists in all people. He would say that we have at least the capacity for good.

Paul uses the theological term *law* to talk about the goodness in us. In the Bible, the law is God's teaching. The law is a gift. The proper attitude toward the law comes from Psalm 19:7, which says that the law revives the soul. The law is a guide for how to love God and how to love other people. Paul writes that the law can be written on the hearts of all people (Romans 2:15). We know how to give and receive love. We know how to show kindness. We know some things are wrong. We know what courage and caring are. The capacity to know right from wrong is God's gift, written on our hearts. If the law were not written on our hearts, we could not do better than we do. We would have no hope of growing into people who love God and our neighbor fully.

In the last reference to our hearts in this chapter (2:29), Paul gives us hope. If the law is written on our hearts, then we need a way to enable that law, that teaching to grow. Paul writes that true circumcision is a circumcision of the heart. All that we do in church is meant to nourish our hearts. We sometimes think that we cannot worship until we get our hearts right, but the opposite may be true. We worship so that our actions will get through to our hearts.

Paul writes that what we need is for our hearts to be circumcised (2:29). I don't want to be too graphic, but circumcision is a cutting away. God's circumcision cuts away what is hard and impenitent in our hearts. God cuts away the things that hold us back. Sometimes what separates us from God is our rebellion, our stubbornness. God cuts that away, so that we are open to love. Sometimes, what makes our hearts hard is that life has hurt us. Pain and grief keep our hearts from rejoicing, from the joyous love of God. Circumcision cuts away the hurt, the grief, and the pain. We are free to love and to rejoice.

How will we know that we have truly worshiped this day? Our hearts will be different. We have truly worshiped if something inside of us has changed. The deeper the change, the more significant the worship. Our hearts will feel joy, love, and hope. In trust, let us turn our hearts over to God. (Chuck Aaron)

Worship Aids

Invocation

God of grace and mercy, we gather as your church this day. Send your Holy Spirit among us that we might be healed, taught, empowered, convicted, and transformed. We bring here both our deepest needs and our strongest talents. We offer both to you. Give us grace for our needs and direction for our talents. In the name of Jesus the Christ. Amen.

Prayer of Confession

Most Holy God, we confess to you our sin. Our neediness, our fears, and our anxieties lie underneath our sin, but we come not to make excuses.

We come to confess. Our neediness, fear, and anxiety arise because we do not trust in you deeply enough. In your mercy forgive our sin. Strengthen our neediness, allay our fears, and ease our anxiety. Enable us to resist temptation, so that we can more fully bear witness to you. Amen.

Words of Assurance

Open your hearts and rest in the assurance that God strengthens; God allays; God eases. Thanks be to God.

Benediction

Go out now with changed hearts to bear witness to those who have not yet found the law written in their hearts. Go out in joy with God's blessing. (Chuck Aaron)

JULY 17, 2011

✁✁✁✁

Fifth Sunday after Pentecost

Readings: Genesis 28:10-19a; Psalm 139:1-12, 23-24; Romans 8:12-25; Matthew 13:24-30, 36-43

Weed Control
Matthew 13:24-30, 36-43

Jesus understood reality in ways none of us will ever know. He lived in our world as the Son of God and the Son of Man—the incarnation of God in human flesh—fully God and fully human. His awareness of the interrelatedness of all life shines no brighter than in his parables. In our Gospel lesson today, an earthly story with a heavenly meaning, Jesus peels away a simple truth that we too often miss.

The parable describes a farmer who broadcast good seed in his field. As in years past, he set aside the best seed from last year's harvest, rightly believing the health of his farming business was dependent upon sowing the best seed year after year. But this year, something terrible happened. An enemy sowed weeds among the wheat, a sinister act that even the most experienced farmer could not detect until the young plants broke through the ground and began to mature.

As he looked over his field one morning, he noticed that ugly, choking weeds were growing among the prized wheat that gave him his livelihood. His workers, fearing for their jobs, asked the farmer: "You sowed good seed in your field, didn't you?" Can you hear what they were really asking in that question? They were asking for mercy, lest their master believe they had sabotaged the crop. Thinking on their feet, the workers offered to go into the field and pull up the weeds.

The master, however, stuns the workers by telling them to leave the field alone. "In gathering the weeds you would uproot the wheat along with them. Let both of them grow together until the harvest; and at harvest time I will tell the reapers, Collect the weeds first and bind them in bundles to be burned, but gather the wheat into my barn" (Matthew 13:29-30). End of story. Thank you very much!

Or is it? Actually, as with the parable of the sower, our Lord offers an interpretation in verses 36-43, teaching his disciples then and now that weeds are a fact of kingdom life, sown in our world by the enemy but destined for the fire of judgment at the end of time. In a word, there is no escaping the reality of weeds; the enemy sows weeds in our world, they grow among the wheat, but in God's great harvest, the weeds will not prevail.

There is another message here worth hearing that has as much to do with our lives right now as it does with God's harvest at the end of time. Make no mistake about it: God will bring the harvest at the end of the age. When God does that transforming, re-creating work, all the weeds of life will be bundled and burned in the fire of God's consuming life.

What does this parable mean today? Perhaps the key to hearing this parable has to do with weed control. Think of just one of the ugly, hurtful, death-dealing realities in our world today: war, hunger, poverty, disregard for the sacred nature of life, hatred, racism. You get the picture. At times, our world seems to choke from the weeds growing in God's field. What do we do? We rally to weed control. Take almost any destructive issue among us, and you will find faithful people who urge us to organize, march, petition, and marshal all the forces of God's church to root out the weeds.

Jesus offers another option. It's not popular, and some among us will say that our world is so corrupt, Christian people must fight to root out the weeds! Yet that's not what our Lord advises. In fact, Jesus not only suggests but commands that we leave the weeds alone! This one, singular instruction flies in the face of what we would call common decency. I mean, we just can't let the weeds take over, can we?

No, Jesus does not suggest that either. To the contrary, Jesus actually admonishes us to be so focused on sowing, nurturing, encouraging, and growing gospel wheat that the weeds will not survive. Rather than pulling up the weeds, Jesus calls us to grow strong, healthy, bountiful wheat.

This is exactly the same message our Lord gave Peter. Jesus gave Peter the keys of the kingdom, saying to him, "You are Peter, and on this rock I will build my church, and the gates of Hades will not prevail against it" (Matthew 16:18). Meaning what? Meaning that hell's fury will never stop God's church when God's people are committed to grace, living in love, and being God's presence in this world.

Weed control has nothing to do with pulling up the weeds. Rather, weed control has everything to do with being strong, healthy, nourishing wheat. You ask: How does that work? Simply put, Jesus said, "If anyone forces you to go one mile, go also the second mile" (Matthew 5:41). Stun people with how generously you serve. And again, "If anyone strikes you on the right cheek, turn the other also" (5:39). More gospel grows on a turned cheek than a clinched fist.

This is the power of the gospel unleashed in a world that knows neither how nourishing God's love in Christ really is nor how transforming God's grace can be. Weed control has nothing to do with pulling weeds. Weed control has everything to do with being God's people of grace and truth, acceptance and forgiveness, generosity and hospitality in this world. The way of life in Christ is ultimately the way of love.

This week, refuse to get caught up in any cause other than the movement Jesus launched two thousand years ago. His movement is like a field in which a farmer sowed good seed, believing that God would one day gather a bountiful harvest from the choices we make to live the good news of Jesus Christ. Amen. (Timothy Owings)

Lectionary Commentary
Genesis 28:10-19a

Jacob's dream of the heavenly staircase is one of the more familiar narratives from his storied life. The anger sown between the twins when Esau sold his birthright for a pot of stew has come to its tragic conclusion. Jacob has tricked his feeble father, Isaac, into giving him the patriarchal blessing. Jacob now flees for his life, attempting to escape the fury of his brother, Esau. And when he does, he comes to a place where God meets him in a dream.

With a stone for a pillow, Jacob falls into exhausted sleep as angels ascend and descend on a staircase between earth and heaven. It is of interest to note that the angels ascend from earth before they descend from heaven. The text suggests God's angels were traveling with Jacob all along. It is this stunning revelation that brings the trickster twin to his senses. At dawn, he wakes up, builds an altar, and names the place *Bethel,* meaning "house of God." This one episode sets the stage for Jacob's encounter with Laban, a man more devious than himself, who will, after fourteen years, marry off his two daughters to the patriarch and make him a wealthy man.

Romans 8:12-25

This text is the midpoint of a much longer argument in which Paul celebrates the life of the Spirit as the very life of God in human experience.

The beautiful language incorporating the parent-child relationship reveals Paul's conviction that we are "heirs of God and joint heirs with Christ" (Romans 8:17). The intimacy of this tender relationship in the Spirit is no more profoundly expressed than in Paul's instruction that we address God as "Abba! Father!" (v. 15). We are "children of God" (v. 14), and as such, know freedom from the death-dealing ways of "the flesh" (v. 13). That is the essence of being Christian.

Paul goes on in verses 18-25 to apply this intimate relationship with God to the realities of a broken and anguish-ridden world. The very freedom we know in Christ will one day be the universal, cosmic experience of all reality. "Creation itself will be set free from its bondage" (8:21), and, with all God's children, will also know a freedom that is nothing less than the very life of God. But not yet! Now, in this present reality, we taste the "first fruits of the Spirit" (v. 23), breathing the rarified air that Paul calls "hope" (vv. 24-25). Hope in Christ, rather than being thin wishful thinking, is robust energy born of God's life, which draws us into the future of God's coming kingdom. (Timothy Owings)

Worship Aids

Call to Worship

The earth is the Lord's and the fullness thereof;
   the world and all who live in it.
Thanks be to God for God's good and beautiful world!
The earth is the Lord's, broken by sin and marred by injustice.
Thanks be to God for God's gift of salvation,
   liberating the world from its bondage and decay!
The earth is the Lord's, hopeful that God's people will care for God's world.
Thanks be to God for God's call
   to be a people who care for all creation
   by sharing the good news of Jesus Christ!
All: Thanks be to God!

Invocation

Creator God, out of the bounty of your being, you have brought all that is into existence. The earth and the heavens, the moon and the stars, animal and human life, and all the magnificent beauty of created life reflect your power and glory. On this day as we lift our voices to praise your name, so fill us with the gift of gratitude that we will live in and by your Spirit to call all creation to follow our Lord Jesus Christ, who lives and reigns with you and the Holy Spirit, one God, forever and ever. Amen.

Pastoral Prayer

Almighty and all-loving God, creator of life and giver of grace, hear us as we pray. The living of our daily lives is often polluted by decisions that dishonor your name and bring reproach upon your people. Forgive us for failing to remember who we are and in whose power we are called to live. Restore to us not only the joy of our salvation but also the renewing and life-giving power of our faith. Remind us that we are baptized and being made new by the presence and power of your Spirit.

We pray today for all who have lost hope or succumbed to the poison of cynicism. Life has imploded upon their highest values and most cherished dreams. Illness, disappointment, betrayal, and even death have robbed them of joy. Come to them, we pray, as the loving and healing parent whose heart ever seeks those who know pain of heart, body, mind, and spirit. Heal the sick, bring comfort to the grieving, bless all who proclaim your word today, and come among us as Holy Spirit to bind us ever closer to you and one another.

God of nourishing grace, so remake us by and in your love that we will be a people known for the ways we love one another and you, showing by our actions and our words that you are the risen and living one. Through Jesus Christ, our Lord, we pray. Amen. (Timothy Owings)

New Life in the Spirit

Second in a Series of Four on Romans

Romans 7:1-13

Paul really wants us to find joy. I make a point to say that because Paul often receives a bad rap as one who wants to give us a guilt trip. He does not leave us in guilt, but wants us to end in joy. Paul's road map to joy is difficult to follow, however. We talked last week about the complexity of Paul's thoughts. Besides being a deep thinker, Paul had a restless mind. His brain was like a child on a pogo stick. He would leap from topic to topic, metaphor to metaphor, causing us to strain to keep up with him. As an example, Paul starts off chapter 7 talking about marriage. By verse 6, he has already changed the metaphor to slavery. We see in that jump how much trouble Paul had staying focused.

In making his argument about marriage and slavery, Paul seems at first to be dealing with something that no longer matters to us. He is talking about the relationship Jewish people had to the law. When we hear *law*, our defenses come up. We don't like to be told what to do. A more helpful translation might be *teaching*. The law was God's teaching on how the people of Israel could be the people they were called to be. The teaching was God's gift for how to live a life that reflected love of God and love of neighbor. If we want to translate that into our own situations, we might ask about how to decide the way to lead our lives. What should govern our behavior? How can we make good decisions?

The more we wrestle with those questions, the closer we can come to understanding what Paul is trying desperately to say in this chapter. Paul is not entirely logical in what he says, but eventually he helps us understand a kind of trap that we are in. We sometimes think of law as oppressive, joyless, nitpicky, but Paul would disagree. For Paul, God's teaching was inherently good, but sin corrupted the law. Sin turned the good law bad. In the twenty-first century, we know all about that. We see many examples of how sin turns good things evil. Have you ever noticed that every time technology comes up with a good invention, sin warps it, distorts it? Human ingenuity invented the telephone, which sin corrupted into obscene calls. Do I even need to say anything about the Internet? Sin corrupts everything it touches.

Paul wants us to understand how sin corrupts us, turns us into distorted versions of who we should be. In the 1970s, a psychologist conducted an experiment to study the effects of imprisonment on good, stable people. He selected carefully screened volunteers. He assigned some as guards, others as prisoners. The volunteer "prisoners" were kept locked up; the "guards" had authority over them. The experiment was intended to last for two weeks. The researcher had to pull the plug after only a few days. He stopped the experiment, not because the prisoners were suffering too much, but because of the effect on the guards. Average, stable, carefully screened college students became mean and sadistic, abusing the prisoners. These were college students who might have hung out together under different circumstances. The students randomly assigned to be guards were corrupted by the experiment itself. Good people, placed in a bad situation, turned evil (http://www.prisonexp.org/).

Paul wants us to know that such a thing has happened to us. Last week, we talked about Paul's understanding of our hard and impenitent hearts. That is the sin that comes from within us. We are responsible for the sin that arises in us, but we are also in a bad situation. For Paul, all of God's creation has been corrupted by sin. Sin is a kind of power that has trapped God's creation. We are in the midst of that bad situation, which keeps us from being the good people we could be.

We can fully understand Paul here when we try to be good. The more we try to shake off a bad habit, rise above our sins, or become more spiritual, the more we realize what a struggle that is. Paul says that the law, or teaching, is one way God tries to free us from that struggle. God gives us the teaching so that we know how to be good. But Paul also says that the law, or teaching, is not enough by itself. The metaphor Paul uses is that we are married to the law as a couple is married until parted by death. For Paul to be consistent, he would have to say that the law died. What he says is that we died to the law. The law, or teaching, became corrupt, like a computer infected with a virus. It no longer works the way it is supposed to work.

He picks the example of coveting, one of the ten commandments. The way it should work is that we choose not to covet because the law teaches us not to covet. Instead, we are too weak to follow what the law teaches. We yearn for what we do not have. Coveting can drive us crazy and keep us from being thankful. We need not only the law to teach us not to covet but also the strength to live out our choices.

That strength comes from the Holy Spirit. Paul says we have a new life in the Spirit. The Holy Spirit enables us to be grateful for what we have. We may work harder and save smarter to have more, but we do not covet what we do not have. The Spirit enables us to find serenity.

We truly understand Paul if we have ever tried to be good, to really love God and other people. When we find ourselves getting in our own way, we see what Paul meant. Know the law, but rely on the Spirit, who gives us strength and power, so that we find the freedom and joy Paul really wants us to have. (Chuck Aaron)

Worship Aids

Invocation

Eternal God, our creator, we praise you for forming us as the church. In this time of worship may we find the resources to be the church you call us to be. May the Spirit move among us, awakening our sense of your presence, enabling our genuine devotion and creating loving fellowship among us. May our adoration delight you, and may your grace renew us. Amen.

Prayer of Confession

O pure and righteous God, we confess our sin to you and before one another. We admit that we do not notice the trap that corruption of your law has set for us. We confess that we do not make a true effort to escape that trap. We confess that we turn away from the strength and power the Spirit offers us. Forgive us, O God. Enable us to experience the joy of forgiveness and freedom.

Words of Assurance (based on Philippians 4:13)

I can do all things through the Holy Spirit who strengthens me.

Benediction

Go out now in joy to experience the freedom God has offered us in Christ. Go out with the sustaining presence of the Spirit that draws us to God and to one another. (Chuck Aaron)

JULY 24, 2011

෨෨෨෨

Sixth Sunday after Pentecost

Readings: Genesis 29:15-28; Psalm 105:1-11, 45b; Romans 8:26-39;
Matthew 13:31-33, 44-52

Sighs for Help
Romans 8:26-39

It was early on a Thursday morning, long before daybreak, that I found
myself driving north on I-75. My mother had been diagnosed with
esophageal cancer, and I was making the drive to Atlanta to help my sisters care for her. I'm not sure how many weeks I had been making that
weekly pilgrimage to help take Mom to radiation treatments, but it had
been going on long enough that I was weary. As I drove, I realized that I
was weary like I had never been before. I was weary in body, mind, and
spirit. I was feeling overwhelmed and uncertain of the future. I wondered,
*How long will our family have to keep up this schedule? How long will my
mother have to endure this illness? How long can I balance the demands of work
and family?*

I don't remember forming any words as I drove, but I remember sighing a lot. I don't remember that I was intentionally praying, but I do
remember sensing that I was crying out to God in my heart. Many minutes of silence passed, and then, as the sun rose in the distance, these
words came to me: "My grace is sufficient unto the day." It was the answer
to a prayer I didn't even know that I had offered but desperately needed.
I was assured that God was present with me in that moment. I couldn't
know the future, but I could trust that God would give me what I needed
at the exact time that I needed it. It was a promise that I carried with me
in the days, weeks, and months to follow. It was an assurance that I held
on to through my mother's illness and following her death.

The eighth chapter of the book of Romans is perhaps my favorite chapter in all of Scripture. It offers words of comfort and reassurance to those

of us who carry heavy burdens. At times, we are all too aware of the brokenness of our world. We know that our lives are marred by sin, and we experience suffering in our daily lives. We experience physical illness or loss. We endure the pain of broken relationships. We come across stories of violence, economic need, and hopelessness. As we look around us, it is easy to become discouraged, overwhelmed, and uncertain of the future. I believe that Paul addressed these words to people like us. They bear witness to the compassionate heart of a pastor, trying to encourage a community in the midst of some of the most devastating trials that life has to offer.

In the verses previous to today's text, Paul has spoken of the suffering that not only we but also all creation experiences. He writes that "the whole creation has been groaning in labor pains until now" (Romans 8:22). Suffering is a reality that we live with each day, evident not only in our human struggles but also throughout the created order. Although, as people of faith, we know that God's glory will one day be revealed, we find ourselves crying, "How long, O Lord?"

Sometimes, as on that dark Thursday morning, the suffering becomes too much. There are moments in life when we are literally rendered speechless. How do we begin to express the depth of our sorrow as we realize our deep need for God's help? How do we find the words to cry out for our redemption? Sometimes we don't. Sometimes we can't. These are the places where God's grace breaks into our lives most powerfully.

"Likewise the Spirit helps us in our weakness; for we do not know how to pray as we ought, but that very Spirit intercedes with sighs too deep for words" (8:26). What a wonderful gift God has given to us, that even when our words fail, God's Spirit is present in ways beyond our human understanding. As N. T. Wright so insightfully observes, "Those who cannot see that for which they eagerly hope need assistance to peer into the darkness ahead and to pray God's future into the present" (*The New Interpreter's Bible*, vol. 10 [Nashville: Abingdon, 2002], 598).

The wonder and the grace of prayer is that many times we can't offer a prayer in our own strength. Prayer, as the early church fathers and mothers taught us, is often a heartrending struggle. Yet it is in these moments that we can receive what is most needed for the journey. We can be offered that assurance of God's love and grace in a more powerful way because all the words, the human certainty, and the illusion of control are stripped away. We receive what we need the most "because the Spirit intercedes for the saints according to the will of God" (8:27).

The Spirit of God intercedes for us and reminds us of the great love of God our creator. Our lives, the lives of those we love, the life of the world may still be broken, but our concerns are brought into the presence of God, and we are reminded again of the future that God has in store for us. We are reminded that God works for our good in all things.

Paul knew the power of the gifts received through God's Spirit. He knew them because he had experienced them, and when the words returned, it was sheer doxology:

> No, in all these things we are more than conquerors through him who loved us. For I am convinced that neither death, nor life, nor angels, nor rulers, nor things present, nor things to come, nor powers, nor height, nor depth, nor anything else in all creation, will be able to separate us from the love of God in Christ Jesus our Lord. (Romans 8:37-39)

(Wendy Joyner)

Lectionary Commentary
Genesis 29:15-28

This passage recounts the story of Jacob working for Laban in return for the privilege of marrying Laban's daughters. Initially, Jacob is attracted to Laban's younger daughter, Rachel. Laban makes an agreement with Jacob for seven years of labor, after which he will allow Jacob to marry Rachel. Once Jacob's seven years are completed, however, Laban tricks Jacob by substituting Leah, the older daughter, for Rachel. Jacob does marry Leah and then works seven more years in payment for the privilege of becoming Rachel's husband.

These verses are a prelude to later events, including childbearing, which will have far-reaching consequences for God's people. In recounting these complicated human relationships, sibling rivalries, and working arrangements, the writer of Genesis explores the interplay of human decisions and the plans of God. The divine ultimately will not be frustrated, but there is much to be negotiated in human terms.

Matthew 13:31-33, 44-52

These verses offer several kingdom-of-heaven parables: the mustard seed, yeast, hidden treasure, the pearl, and the great catch of fish. Each one of these parables could be explored individually, but when placed in conversation with one another, they expand our understanding of the kingdom of heaven.

The preacher could reflect upon the priceless nature of the kingdom in preaching on the treasures or expound on the underlying work of God in the world and the mystery of God's kingdom. Another option might be to explore the wonder of God's work within the coming kingdom. These parables can offer an important reminder that it is ultimately only God who can discern what is of value in the kingdom and what is not. (Wendy Joyner)

Worship Aids

Call to Worship (based on Psalm 105)

Give thanks to the LORD and call upon God's name.
We will make known God's deeds among the people.
Let us seek the LORD's presence in this place.
We will seek the LORD, and remember all of God's wonderful works.

Invocation

God of all mystery, draw near to us in this hour of worship. Hear us as we cry aloud to you this day. Help us to celebrate your grace, to rejoice in the truth that your power is made perfect even in our weakness. Amen.

Benediction

Go forth in God's peace, feeling the embrace of the Holy Spirit. Know that nothing in all creation can separate you from the love of God in Christ Jesus our Lord. Amen. (Wendy Joyner)

Walking according to the Spirit

Third in a Series of Four on Romans

Romans 8:1-11

Before we truly can hear Paul this morning, we have to have a proper understanding of our guilt. We don't like to talk about this, but we can't grow in our faith unless we reflect on our guilt. We approach our guilt in several ways. We sometimes deny our guilt. We rationalize, defend ourselves, blame others, or make excuses. We become stubborn, lashing out at people who point out our sins. Paul talks of this in the first two chapters of Romans. He tells us that we are all self-righteous sinners, finding idols everywhere. Paul leaves us no place to hide.

The flip side of this first attitude is that guilt can be like Velcro, sticking to us so that we can't shake it off. This feeling can be so miserable, it is no wonder we deny our guilt. We may look back at something we have done, and we just cannot let the guilt go. In chapter 7, Paul addresses this feeling of excessive guilt. He describes the agony of wanting to do better and be better but not being able to get there: "I do not do the good I want, but the evil I do not want is what I do" (7:19). Then Paul speaks on behalf of everyone who has ever felt guilt as a weight: "Wretched man that I am! Who will rescue me from this body of death?" (v. 24).

That sentence reflects Paul's own anguish, as well as the anguish he knows that we feel. He knows the struggle we have with guilt. When people try to say that Paul gives us a guilt trip, they haven't read enough of him. It's true that he doesn't want us to be self-righteous, ignoring our guilt. He doesn't want us to be self-satisfied and smug about our relationships with God and other people. But he doesn't want us to wallow in guilt either. Once we realize what our guilt is, he wants us to be rescued, living in peace.

Paul proclaims that Christ offers us that peace. By working in Christ, God has broken the power of sin in our lives. In chapter 7, Paul has talked about how sin corrupts everything it touches. God gave the law as a gift, but sin corrupted the law. The law became a burden rather than a gift. Paul uses the example of coveting to show the law has become corrupted. Coveting drives us crazy. We become jealous and then frustrated when we look at what we don't have. The law, as gift, tells us not to covet. Sin corrupts the law so that we not only covet because we lack strength to obey, but we also feel guilty about coveting because it is against God's law. Trying to fulfill the law on our own leaves us with both frustration and guilt.

Christ has broken the power of guilt. Christ has disarmed guilt so that it does not have to weigh us down. There is no condemnation for those who are in Christ Jesus. That frees us from the trap of guilt added to frustration.

We still face our weakness, however. Christ frees us from condemnation, but we still cannot obey the law, rising above our weaknesses by our own strength. So Paul offers us the Holy Spirit. The Holy Spirit strengthens us from within. Paul says that our choice is to set our minds on the flesh or on the Spirit. To set our minds on the flesh is death. When Paul uses the word *flesh* he does not mean just sensual sins. We are bombarded with powerful sensual temptations that affect our behavior. We have made sensuality into an idol. Nevertheless, Paul means more than sensuality when he talks about setting the mind on the flesh. The flesh includes the many manifestations of our sinful side. Greed and the desire for revenge are as much a part of the flesh as anything else.

The alternative is to set our minds on the Spirit. To set our minds on the Spirit is to let the Spirit work within us, letting God's strength take over when we are too weak. Setting our minds on the Spirit does not mean that we will never sin or face frustration again. Setting our minds on the Spirit means that God is nurturing within us the grace to become loving, strong, joyful. Setting our minds on the Spirit leads to life and peace.

Paul knows that we are still weak and that we live in a fallen world. Paul's understanding of our sin is complicated. Paul believes on the one hand that we are responsible for our sins. We choose idolatry, rebellion, and submission to temptation. On the other hand, Paul says that we are not responsible for our sins. The whole creation is not what God wants it to be because it is held captive to the powers and principalities. The sin of the whole creation spills over onto us.

We have three choices. We can deny our guilt, we can wallow in our guilt, or we can recognize our guilt. In this third approach, we acknowledge that we are sinners who live in a sinful world, and we open ourselves to forgiveness. We face no condemnation. The Spirit enables us to resist temptation and grow in grace.

In chapter 7, Paul uses the example of coveting. We covet because we see others with more than we have. We feel jealous and insecure, making ourselves miserable. The law tells us not to covet, so we know that coveting is wrong, and then we feel guilty about it. Christ has broken that cycle, taking our guilt for coveting. The Holy Spirit enables us to learn to live abundantly with what we have. We don't define ourselves by what we own. We know that we are not more important because we have more money or a bigger car. We are content.

With the economy as unstable as it is, we cannot say to those who really are in desperate straits, "Be content with what you have." We have an obligation to help others. If our needs are met, the Holy Spirit enables us to look at what we have and be at peace so that we have the strength and the will to reach out to those in need. (Chuck Aaron)

Worship Aids

Invocation

Most gracious God, we have been called together by the restless, unpredictable Holy Spirit. As we worship, may we become more attentive to the influence of the Spirit, open to the places the Spirit would lead us. May we surrender more of ourselves to the Spirit, drawing, not on our own resources, but on the power available to us. May our worship this day be enlivened by the Spirit, so that our praise is true and heartfelt. Amen.

Prayer of Confession

Demanding but merciful God, you have put before us the choice of setting our minds on the flesh or on the Spirit. We confess that we give in too often to the flesh, to our base impulses. We give in to our greed and selfishness, to the desire to gratify our senses. Forgive us for our sins of weakness and our sins of rebellion. Enable us to set our minds on the Spirit that leads to life and peace. Draw us forward with the promise of the glory about to be revealed to us. Amen.

Words of Assurance

Set your minds on the Spirit and find life and peace waiting there to set you free. Amen.

Benediction

Let us go out now in the strength of the Spirit. Let us celebrate our freedom from condemnation, blessed by a God who has promised us a glorious future. (Chuck Aaron)

JULY 31, 2011

❧❧❧

Seventh Sunday after Pentecost

Readings: Genesis 32:22-31; Psalm 17:1-7, 15; Romans 9:1-5;
Matthew 14:13-21

You Give Them Something to Eat
Matthew 14:13-21

One of the most wonderful things about having four Gospels is the great variety of ways that they tell the stories of Jesus. The variety and the unique perspective of each Gospel writer is most evident when you take the opportunity to compare all versions of the same event in the life of Jesus. When we look at stories like this morning's account of the feeding of the five thousand, it is important to pay attention to the wonderful slant that Matthew gives his account. True to Matthew's emphasis on the life of the church, his account of the feeding miracle encourages us to look not only at the ministry of Jesus but also at the ministry that we share as the body of Christ.

Following the death of John the Baptist, Jesus continues to minister to the great crowds that come seeking his help. We are reminded that "he had compassion for them and cured their sick" (Matthew 14:14). It has apparently been a long and exhausting day, and when night begins to fall, Jesus' disciples come to him and suggest, "Send the crowds away so that they may go into the villages and buy food for themselves" (v. 15). The disciples are being very practical here. The people need to eat, and they are all in the middle of nowhere. Yet, here is where the story begins to get interesting.

Jesus says to his disciples, "They need not go away; you give them something to eat" (14:16). I can almost see the looks of confusion and consternation on the faces of his friends. The people are hungry, but there is no way the disciples can feed such a large crowd. They barely have enough food for themselves! They protest, "We have nothing here

242

but five loaves and two fish" (v. 17). Jesus tells them to bring him what food they have, and he encourages the crowds to sit down.

The rest of the story is familiar. Jesus takes the five loaves and two fish, blesses and breaks them, and provides abundance. Matthew tells us that following the miracle, Jesus "gave them to the disciples, and the disciples gave them to the crowds" (14:19). All in the crowd were fed, and there was a huge amount left over, even after more than five thousand people had eaten! Jesus had once again provided for the people in their time of great need.

First, the most striking thing to me about this story is the role of the disciples. We tend to focus on this story solely as a miracle of Jesus, but I think it has many things to say about the role of the disciples and the call of the church. First of all, notice that Jesus initially tries to get the disciples to take part in meeting the needs of the people. The first reaction of the disciples is to send them away, but Jesus tells them in no uncertain terms that it is their job to help feed those who are hungry. As Jesus has compassion on those who have gathered, so also he calls his followers to have compassion on the people that they encounter in a time of need.

The disciples' attitude is one that we sometimes reflect in the life of the church. We are tired and overwhelmed, and sometimes we want to pass the buck to someone else. Surely there is a government program to assist the hungry. Maybe if people asked their families for help, then they could get fed. Yet Jesus says to the church, "It's not someone else's problem to fix." The body of Christ is called to help those who are hungry. Jesus says to us, "Don't send them away."

Second, this story demonstrates a common fallacy in our thinking about ministry. The main point of the disciples' resistance is that they don't have the physical resources to feed the crowd. They weren't necessarily being coldhearted in their refusal to feed the crowds, but they just didn't see how it was possible. Jesus reminds the disciples to bring all that they have to him. It is only when the disciples bring their loaves and fish to Jesus that the miracle takes place.

How many times in the life of the church do we look around, and all we see is scarcity? We look at our meager resources and think, *We don't even have enough here for ourselves, much less anyone else.* It is tempting to hold our hands shut. It is easy to fall into the trap of thinking that all we have to offer is dependent upon what we ourselves can produce. Jesus says to us, no matter how meager our resources, "Bring them to me." It is only when we offer all we have to the Master that he can break it and bless it.

What we have might not be sufficient, but Jesus takes what we offer and produces a bountiful meal.

Finally, this story reminds us that Jesus wants us to help do God's work in the world. Did you notice at the end of the story, after Jesus had broken the bread and blessed it, he gave it back to the disciples? Jesus didn't distribute the food. The disciples were his hands and feet. The disciples were an integral part of this miraculous feeding. They trusted Jesus to provide for the crowd, and they shared the blessings that Jesus provided with all who were seated in the grass that day.

The church is still called to be the hands and feet of Christ. This story is an important reminder that we have received grace upon grace from the hands of the Master. May we respond to need with compassionate hearts, offering all we have to Jesus, that he might bless it for us to share. (Wendy Joyner)

Lectionary Commentary
Genesis 32:22-31

This passage recounts the story of Jacob wrestling at Peniel. The passage begins with Jacob in isolation, having sent his family ahead of him for their own safety. Jacob is preparing to meet his brother, Esau, and he is uncertain how this reunion will turn out. He has deceived his brother, and he knows that there is no guarantee he will be able to make amends for the wrongs he has committed.

In the dark of night, when Jacob is most alone, a visitor confronts him. Scholars are divided in their opinions as to whether this visitor was a bandit, an angel, or perhaps God. It is clear, however, that Jacob wrestles intensely with the visitor, and that he is permanently changed by the encounter. Jacob has wrestled with the demons of his past, and he emerges from the time of struggle with a blessing. His encounter with the divine during the hours of struggle has prepared him for the meeting with Esau.

Romans 9:1-5

In these verses, the apostle Paul very openly expresses his sorrow and grief over the failure of the Israelites to accept Christ. He recounts all the advantages that the chosen people of God possess by heritage, but expresses wonder that they cannot receive this part of the promise. Paul actively mourns their disbelief. Paul says that the Messiah comes from this very people, the chosen race. He yearns for them to see the truth about the work of God throughout history, especially its culmination in the death and resurrection of Jesus. (Wendy Joyner)

Worship Aids

Call to Worship (based on Psalm 17)

Attend to our cry, O God, and give ear to our prayer.
We call upon you, O LORD, for you will answer.
You are the Savior of those who seek refuge.
Show us your face, O God, and we shall be satisfied.

Invocation

Creator God, we give you thanks for this holy day. We give you thanks for the opportunity to gather in your house and worship in this family of faith. Be present with us and among us that we may hear your voice and be strengthened for service in your name. Amen.

Benediction

Go forth in peace and in joy to serve the Lord. Know that the Lord our God will provide abundantly more than we could ask or imagine, as we seek to minister to all the world in Christ's name. Amen. (Wendy Joyner)

Getting Our Hate Right

Fourth in a Series of Four on Romans

Romans 12:9-13

If we read and study scripture slowly, we catch little nuances, small phrases that we might miss if we go quickly. This little four-word phrase in Romans 12 is one of those: "Hate what is evil" (v. 9). This phrase comes in an important part of the letter to the Romans. The first verse of chapter 12 contains an important theological term for Paul, *therefore.* When Paul says, "therefore," he is turning a corner. If we look at what comes before the "therefore" in 12:1, we see how Paul first helps us understand our sin and guilt. We have both good and bad within us. God circumcises our hearts, cutting away the bad. We are trapped in our own sin and in the sinfulness of all creation.

The whole creation is held hostage to the power of sin. It pervades all of life. In his death and resurrection, Christ set us free from this trap. We no longer face condemnation for our sins. We are absolved of our guilt. The Holy Spirit empowers us to live into the grace God offers us. The Holy Spirit works within us, enabling us to love God, love ourselves, and love one another.

God's love, grace, and power are all cause for joy. Paul pronounces one of the most reassuring phrases in scripture in Romans 8:18: "I consider that the sufferings of this present time are not worth comparing with the glory about to be revealed to us." That hope pulls us forward.

That's what comes on the front side of the "therefore" in 12:1. We are set free and empowered. We have hope in Christ. "Therefore," this is how we should live our lives. This is how we should respond to the freedom, grace, joy, and hope God gives us. On the other side of "therefore" is our response. We can set our minds on the flesh or on the Spirit. The flesh is our sin and weakness. The Spirit gives life.

Paul uses a peculiar term in 12:1; he teaches us that we should present our bodies as a "living sacrifice." That's a funny thing to say. A sacrifice is burned up. To be a living sacrifice doesn't make sense, but that's what Paul calls us to be. We are still alive, but we sacrifice our comfort, our prestige, our security, our wants for Christ. We sacrifice our money, our time, our talents for the ministry of the church. The rest of the chapter teaches us how to be a living sacrifice.

All of that is the context of the phrase "hate what is evil." We hate evil because of what God has done for us. We hate evil as part of being a living sacrifice. We are probably more attracted to some of Paul's other phrases. Paul tells us to let love be genuine, to love one another with mutual affection. Those sound good. They are not as easy as they sound, but we like hearing such teaching.

When Paul tells us to hate, we may want to turn away. We don't like the thought of hating. Hate is bitter and sour, a kind of poison. Hate seems destructive. We think of hate as irrational. Two people from rival groups who don't even know each other will hate each other just out of custom. Why would Paul even use such a word, one that in Greek is never used elsewhere in the New Testament?

In trying to understand this word *hate*, we can think of how we experience hate and what hating evil might mean to us. Certainly, when Paul tells us to hate what is evil, he is teaching us that our response to God is more than just avoiding things. Our response is active. Hate is at least passionate. We have all heard the old expression that the opposite of love is not hate, but indifference. If we hate, we still care; something still matters to us. Too often, our attitude toward evil is resignation. If we hate what is evil, at least our passion will keep us engaged.

The real reason we hate what is evil is that we love others. If we truly love people, we will hate what destroys people. If we truly love, we will hate the poverty that robs people of hope. If we truly love, we will hate the violence that damages people in body, soul, and spirit. If we truly love, we will hate the bullying that plays on vulnerability and exploits weaknesses. If we truly love, we cannot be apathetic when people suffer.

Nicholas Kristof is a courageous journalist. One of his recurring themes is the slavery of girls and young women in Asia. What Kristof found in Cambodia is enough to make us cry. Girls at very young ages are taken into slavery and degraded beyond imagination. In the basement of the businesses where they work are torture chambers, to force the girls to comply. A typical method of torture is electric shock, because it doesn't leave visible damage. If we have experienced God's love, we will hate what is happening to these girls.

Kristof gives us an important insight. He says that when he comes away from Cambodia he is not depressed, despite what he has seen. He is inspired by those who are trying to help. Many of those who are helping these young women are former slaves themselves. They have opened shelters and rescued as many girls as they can ("If This Isn't Slavery, What Is?" *New York Times* Online, 01/04/09).

We do not have to go to Cambodia. We can find suffering here. We can hate the evil that is right next door. We do not give up in despair. If we hate evil, we will cling to the hope that Paul offers us in the new creation.

We hate what is evil. Hate gives us passion, keeps us from apathy and resignation. Our hate springs from love and ends in love. Even in the midst of hate, we respond in love. We practice our hate by healing, by transforming, by overcoming evil with good. We shine the light of God's grace into the darkness. Because God loves us, has set us free and given us hope, let us offer ourselves up as living sacrifices. Let us go out and practice a holy hate of what is evil. Let us transform what is evil by our love. (Chuck Aaron)

Worship Aids

Invocation

Most glorious God, we gather here to worship you, to offer you our songs, our praise, our gifts, and our attention. As we worship this day, may we experience your love so that we can love one another and you more fully. May we exchange our weakness for the strength only you can provide. May we accept the grace you offer so that we will feel renewed and empowered to live triumphantly in a world trapped by the power of sin. Amen.

Prayer of Confession

O God who grieves for our sin but loves us still, we confess to you that we do not sacrifice much in response to your love. We hold on to what we have. We clutch our money, our time, and our talents. We love not genuinely, but halfheartedly. We let our grief and hurt control us rather than embrace the grace you offer us. We embrace evil rather than fight it. We give up the fight against evil too easily. Our passion for good fades away. Forgive us and teach us how to present our bodies as a living sacrifice. Amen.

Words of Assurance

God waits; God empowers; God strengthens us to overcome evil with love. Thanks be to God.

Benediction

Let us go out now in God's blessing to a selfish world, offering ourselves as living sacrifices, so that the world can see true faith and trust. (Chuck Aaron)

AUGUST 7, 2011

᭞᭞᭞᭞

Eighth Sunday after Pentecost

Readings: Genesis 37:1-4, 12-28; Psalm 105:1-6, 16-22, 45b;
Romans 10:5-15; Matthew 14:22-33

Dangerous Dreamers
Genesis 37:1-4, 12-28

The story of Jacob's family would make a wonderful television mini-series. As we read the tale of the twelve sons of Jacob, we can see so many elements of the story that ring true to not only ancient times but our modern times as well. At the beginning of today's text, we see clear signs of sibling rivalry and family dysfunction. We are told outright that Joseph is Jacob's favorite son. Jacob "loved Joseph more than any other of his children, because he was the son of his old age; and he had made him a long robe with sleeves" (Genesis 37:3). Jacob demonstrates his favoritism, and it causes resentment among the brothers. Then, to make matters worse, Joseph is a tattletale. We are told that he was a helper to his brothers in their work and that he "brought a bad report of them to their father" (v. 2). All of these factors create animosity between the brothers, and "they hated [Joseph], and could not speak peaceably to him" (v. 4).

Yet I think the straw that broke the camel's back and caused true division among the brothers was not simply the favoritism or the tattling, but Joseph's dreams. Today's text does not include verses 5-11, but these verses are crucial to understanding the rest of the story of Jacob's children. Joseph dreams of sheaves bowing down to his sheaf, and the sun, moon, and stars bowing down to him. It is in the sharing of these dreams that "they hated him even more because of his dreams and his words" (37:8). Joseph's dreams place him in a position of honor and authority, and neither his brothers nor his father respond well to this vision of the future. Yet, we know that these dreams are from God, and speak to the future of not only Joseph but also his family for generations to come.

My reflections on this passage have caused me to wonder about the hatred that Joseph's brothers felt for him. Things come to a head rather quickly in the story after Joseph goes to find his brothers as they shepherd the flocks. "They saw him from a distance, and before he came near to them, they conspired to kill him. They said to one another, 'Here comes this dreamer. Come now, let us kill him'" (37:18-20). The dreams that Joseph articulates most threaten the brothers. When they hear Joseph share the vision of the future that God has given to him, they respond in violence and hatred. History proves that it is sometimes the dreamers in our world that we find most threatening.

I think about Martin Luther King, Jr., articulating a dream of unity. We remember his sermon on the Washington Mall, where he spoke of a day when people would be judged by their character and not the color of their skin. This was a dream from God about a future of hope and inclusiveness. The dreamer was a threat to the status quo, and, ultimately, those who resisted his words and his dream silenced him.

I think of Archbishop Oscar Romero, archbishop of the Roman Catholic Church in San Salvador. Archbishop Romero was a pioneer in liberation theology, and he worked with the poor and oppressed. He spoke with a strong, clear voice about the need for basic human rights to be observed. He lived his life among those who had the least in terms of material possessions. Romero was a dreamer, and he was assassinated as he presided over worship.

I think of Dietrich Bonhoeffer, a German Lutheran pastor who fought against Nazism in World War II. He was a leader in the Confessing Church and became involved in the anti-Hitler resistance movement. He was arrested, charged, and found guilty of sedition in a plot to assassinate Hitler. He was hanged for his resistance to Nazism, but he continues to speak to us through his writings, as he encourages the church to live out its prophetic calling within community. Bonhoeffer was a dreamer who bravely lived out what his conscience dictated, even when it meant going against the powerful structure of Nazism and public sentiment.

These three individuals are just a few examples of those who have been spoken to by God, and who showed great courage in living out their convictions. They had a dream of what a just world would look like, and they spoke the truth of God to all who would listen. They were not embraced, however, and each paid the price with his life. Dreamers like Joseph sometimes end up in the bottom of a dark, deep pit.

The church today continues to need those who are open to the movement of God in their lives, and who will dream divine dreams of what the world might become through the power and grace of God. Yet we must realize that to be a dreamer can often be dangerous. Those around us are not always willing to hear words of challenge or confrontation. The community of faith is sometimes resistant to the very changes that are most needed. The world will not understand the way of Jesus Christ. Those around us may not embrace the ways of God.

Dreamers sound naive at best and crazy at worst. Dreamers proclaim that the meek are blessed. Dreamers demand that the outcasts be welcomed. Dreamers beat plowshares into pruning hooks. The world is in need of dreamers. Are we willing to risk our lives in proclaiming the truth? Are we willing to risk our lives to embrace the dreams of God? (Wendy Joyner)

Lectionary Commentary
Matthew 14:22-33

These verses recount the story of Jesus walking on the water. The disciples are in the boat alone, and a terrible storm comes upon them. They are frightened, far from the land, and there is little hope that the situation will improve. Early in the morning, they see a figure walking on the water and cry out in fear. They think that Jesus might be a ghost, but Jesus offers reassurance. Jesus speaks words of peace and reminds them that he is with them.

Peter, who often voices the doubts of those earliest followers of Jesus, challenges the Lord. He wants to know for certain that it is Jesus, and he asks Jesus to command him to come across the water. Jesus invites Peter to come, but when Peter sees the storm continue to rage, he becomes frightened. Peter begins to sink, and Jesus reaches out his hand in rescue. Jesus rebukes Peter for his little faith, yet ultimately calms the storm and delivers them all.

This passage presents many opportunities to reflect upon the nature of faith, doubt, and negotiating the storms of life with Jesus' presence.

Romans 10:5-15

This passage is pivotal in the book of Romans. Here Paul expounds upon the central truth that God's salvation is for all people. He boldly proclaims that salvation is not based upon righteous behavior or ethnic heritage, but rather received through belief in the Lord Jesus. Paul writes eloquently about the inclusiveness of God's grace and the generosity of God to all who call upon him for salvation. (Wendy Joyner)

Worship Aids

Invocation

God of grace and glory, be present with us in this hour of worship. Allow us to dream dreams, and to see anew a vision of the people you have called us to be. Draw near to us, that we might worship you in Spirit and in truth. Amen.

Words of Assurance (Romans 10:12b-13)

Hear the good news: The Lord hears us when we confess our sins, and when we cry aloud to be forgiven. "The Lord is generous to all who call on the Lord. Everyone who calls upon the name of the Lord shall be saved."

Benediction

Now with the blessing of God our creator, Jesus our redeemer, and the Holy Spirit our sustainer, go forth to dream the dreams of the kingdom. May God grant us courage, that we might bear witness to the truth, this day and forever. Amen. (Wendy Joyner)

The Spirit Comes as an Odd Sort of Dove

First in a Series of Four on the Manifestation of the Holy Spirit

Mark 1:9-13

Ever concerned to cut to the heart of the matter, the Gospel of Mark begins its account of the "good news of Jesus Christ, the son of God" (1:1) with the inauguration of Jesus' ministry at his baptism. The author introduces us to John, dressed like Elijah and preaching a thundering message of repentance in the wilderness. John offers a baptism in water in anticipation of another baptism, a baptism in the Spirit performed by the one who is to come. Then something unusual happens. The "one who was to come" does come; Jesus goes out to John and requests baptism as well. When Jesus comes up from the water, the heavens are torn open, the voice of God speaks a blessing, and the Spirit descends on him like a dove—and we encounter the Father, Son, and Holy Spirit, Trinity in unity.

After this stunning self-revelation of God, something equally shocking follows. We are told, "And the Spirit immediately drove him out into the wilderness. He was in the wilderness forty days, tempted by Satan" (1:12-13). This Spirit—the one with whom Jesus would baptize, the one who descended upon him like a dove—is now driving him toward an encounter with Satan in the desert.

Something seems amiss, doesn't it? After all, we know that a dove is a symbol of peace and tranquillity. We release them at weddings and the opening ceremonies of the Olympics as an expression of joy and celebration. The dove carries an olive branch, for goodness' sake! But here this very odd dove leads Jesus into the wilderness for a tête-à-tête with Satan. What kind of dove is this, anyway? Perhaps that is the very question this passage hopes to provoke.

At Jesus' baptism we encounter a powerful moment of divine self-revelation. God momentarily pulls back the curtain—or in this case, rends the heavens—and says, "This is who I am." In this moment we discover that God is far more than we could have ever imagined. Although the ancient confession was "Hear, O Israel: The LORD is our God, the LORD alone" (Deuteronomy 6:4), we now discover that the "LORD alone" is Father, Son, and Holy Spirit. While Jesus teaches us that God is a Father who reveals self through the Son, the Spirit remains a mystery over which even the earliest generations of Christians puzzled.

This manifestation of the Holy Spirit at Jesus' baptism suggests that the Spirit is like a dove, the same bird that gave hope to Noah as the waters receded by suggesting that new life on earth was beginning to flourish. The dove suggests that God is the Lord and the giver of life.

The symbol of the dove contains a grave temptation, however. One might mistake its gentle coo for weakness and imagine that the bird of peace is the kind of bird that can be domesticated. One might even presume to cage it or train it to sing on cue. How mistaken we would be, were we to assume that the dove comes in peace—if by *peace* we mean that it comes for our comfort.

The dove came in the midst of great distress to Noah, who had been tossed by waves and surrounded by destruction for far too long. The dove didn't come to rescue Noah; it came as a sign of hope. In the same way, the Spirit does not preserve Jesus from discomfort. In fact, the message of the Gospel of Mark is that the Spirit leads Christ into the desert, empowering him for what he would face. The Spirit does not promise us freedom from all affliction, but instead promises comfort and the fruits of the Spirit's presence—love, joy, peace, patience, kindness, goodness, gentleness, faithfulness, and self-control—in the midst of great trials. This is the message of Exodus, Psalms, and the Gospels. God doesn't simply alleviate pain; God joins us in our place of suffering and walks with us, enabling us to make the journey.

It has been said that Celtic Christianity was fond of another symbol for the Holy Spirit: the wild goose. Perhaps they were onto something. Although the work of the Spirit is oftentimes subtle, softly present like the dove, sometimes the wild goose shows up and demands undivided attention.

Geese are funny that way. A neighboring town is known for its ponds and the many geese that have made that place home. There is no mistaking the fact that they feel at home: even if it is rush hour, when they decide it is time to cross the road, they set out strutting and honking at the cars, demanding that they screech to a halt in both directions. Without a care, they lead their goslings across the road as if it is their own. The Celts felt that the wild goose captured the Spirit in all its messy glory.

They rightly recognized that there is nothing placid about the workings of God. When God shows up, water turns to wine, a box lunch feeds a multitude, a dead child is raised to life, a blind man sees, a leper is healed and restored to the community, a shameful past is named and transformed, a persecutor of the church is converted into its greatest missionary, and a baptism reveals the very nature of God.

Within the breast of that meek and holy dove beats the heart of a wild goose, and we ought not be surprised if we hear it honking. (Cameron Jorgenson)

Worship Aids

Invocation
Come, Holy Spirit, fill the hearts of your faithful and kindle in them the fire of your love. Settle on this body of Christ as you did on Christ at his baptism. Fill us; enliven us; surprise us. Lead us to worship. Amen.

Pastoral Prayer
Our God, we celebrate that you graciously invite us to participate in your good work in the world. Although fulfilling that call may take us to

lonely places, we are comforted that you go with us. This day may we hear your call and trust in your presence. Amen.

Benediction

May the untamed dove, the wild goose who led our Lord, lead you also as you leave this place. Go now in the love of God, in the peace of Christ, and in the power of the Spirit. Amen. (Cameron Jorgenson)

AUGUST 14, 2011

❦❦❦

Ninth Sunday after Pentecost

Readings: Genesis 45:1-15; Psalm 133; Romans 11:1-2a, 29-32; Matthew 15:(10-20), 21-28

Opening Our Eyes to See God's Hand at Work
Genesis 45:1-15

This week, the story of Joseph and his brothers continues, and we have the account of their reunion in the royal courts of Egypt. Last week, we heard the story of sibling rivalry in the extreme. Joseph's brothers were jealous of his favored status in the eyes of their father, and they were enraged by his dreams of power and success. Joseph came to find them while they tended the sheep, and they made a drastic decision. They decided to get rid of him forever, and so they threw him into a pit and left him for dead. Only the intervention of one of his brothers caused them to rethink their plan. They eventually decided to spare Joseph's life by selling him into slavery.

I wonder what the many years without Joseph were like for his brothers. Were they relieved that they no longer had to put up with their nagging younger sibling? Were they guilt-ridden as they watched their father grieve the loss of his beloved son? Were they curious as to what happened to Joseph once he began his service as a slave? Did they think that Joseph's dreams never did come true because of their actions? Did they wish for an opportunity to make amends for their horrible deed?

The reader knows the details of the intervening years, but the brothers do not. All they know is that a famine has devastated the land, and they have been sent by their father to get some grain. Their journey is literally a matter of life and death, and all they can do is beg for the mercy of the pharaoh. When they arrive in Pharaoh's court, things go from bad to worse. They begin to think they are being punished for their treatment of

Joseph. They have no idea that it is Joseph who is standing before them, holding their fate in his very hands.

Joseph remains silent as long as he can, hiding his identity from those who had mistreated him. Finally, he can hide the truth no longer and reveals himself to his adversaries. It would have been easy for Joseph to embarrass his brothers. It would have been easy for him to deny their request for assistance. It would have been easy for him to hold a grudge and to recount all that he had suffered and lost because of their actions. Yet Joseph does none of these things. Joseph instead does one of the most amazing and grace-filled things he could possibly have done—he not only forgives his brothers, but he helps them to begin to forgive themselves.

Joseph reminds them: "God sent me before you to preserve for you a remnant on earth, and to keep alive for you many survivors" (Genesis 45:7). He confidently asserts that God has been at work in the midst of all the conflict. Joseph helps his brothers to open their eyes and see God's hand at work.

Terence E. Fretheim writes that "wherever there are signs of life rather than death, signs of reconciliation rather than estrangement, God has been at work in, with, and under human affairs" (*The New Interpreter's Bible*, vol. 1 [Nashville: Abingdon, 1994], 647). This knowledge was the gift that Joseph gave to his brothers. It is a gift that each of us is challenged to embrace. It requires a completely radical stance of faith, as it enables us to look at whatever life sets before us as an opportunity for grace to break into our lives. As Joseph relates, "So it was not you who sent me here, but God" (45:8).

It is part of the divine mystery of life that God is active in human affairs. Joseph's brothers held hatred in their hearts, and their actions were born out of that hatred, but their hatred and sin did not have the last word. That is the miracle of how God works in each one of our lives. In fact, at the very end of this family's story, Joseph affirms, "Even though you intended to do harm to me, God intended it for good, in order to preserve a numerous people, as he is doing today" (Genesis 50:20).

Many times, if we will open our eyes and look back over our lives, we can see the fingerprints of God. We can embrace the truth that God brought life where there was death and peace where there was strife.

Fretheim perhaps summarizes Joseph's gift to his brothers best when he writes, "He invites them to view the past from the perspective of the present" (644). What a powerful way to live into our faith and to see the hand of God at work! For some of us, viewing the past from the perspective of the present will mean that we have to let go of regrets that continue to haunt us. We will be challenged to look at the people we have become through the grace of God. We will have to daily refuse to dwell in guilt and shame.

For others of us, viewing the past from the perspective of the present means that we, like Joseph, will forgive those who have harmed us. It might mean that we embrace the possibilities of our lives now, even though they might not be what we anticipated or imagined. It might mean looking for the ways that God is opening new doors for us. Who is to say that these new doors might not be more wonderful than those that were closed to us? Perhaps the wounds of our past will enable us to be a blessing in this time and place. After all, our God raised Jesus from the dead. His power is made perfect in weakness, and an instrument of shame became the way to our salvation. (Wendy Joyner)

Lectionary Commentary
Matthew 15:(10-20), 21-28

This passage tackles one of the most difficult issues the early church faced, and it allows Jesus to address the inclusion of the Gentiles within his own ministry. First, the optional verses in the lection (10-20) speak of the things that defile. Jesus teaches that outward purity is not as important as inward purity. Jesus speaks the truth that maintaining religious and ritual purity is not what is pleasing to God, but rather a heart that is pure.

Immediately following this teaching about inward purity, Jesus encounters a Gentile woman. The disciples have ignored her cries for help, and even Jesus seems reluctant to engage with this Canaanite woman. When Jesus does speak to her, he seems to be telling her that his ministry is focused upon the Israelites and not the Gentiles. The woman is a model of persistence, however, and she challenges Jesus by reminding him that not only the Israelites but also the Gentiles have need of his healing touch. Jesus relents, commends the woman for her great faith, and heals the woman's daughter.

By honoring this woman's request and extending grace to her, Jesus embodies the truth that he spoke about earlier. He demonstrates that external markers and human distinctions are being radically abolished in God's new work.

Romans 11:1-2a, 29-32

Paul here again writes about the people of Israel and God's plans for them. Paul offers assurance that God has not rejected the original heirs to the promise in favor of the Gentiles. God's gifts are true and sure, and God's attitude toward us is always one of mercy. All of humanity has been held in bondage to disobedience, but God's love for us is stronger than our sin. The gifts and calling of God cannot be rescinded. (Wendy Joyner)

Worship Aids

Call to Worship (based on Psalm 133; John 15:12)

How very good and pleasant it is when kindred live together in unity! How pleasing to God we are when we follow Jesus' command to love one another as he loves us. May our worship be pleasing to God as we join our hearts and voices this day.

Prayer of Confession

Our Savior God, forgive us this day for our lack of faith. We confess that we have lived our lives in fear of the future. We have trusted in what our eyes can see rather than trusting in the truth of your love. We do believe; help our unbelief. Amen.

Words of Assurance

God loves us as we were, as we are, and as we will be. Believe and be free.

Benediction (Genesis 50:20-21; Romans 8:28)

As you go forth, have no fear. Even in the things that might be intended to harm us, God intends to bring about good. Know that in all things God works together for good for those who love God, for those who are called according to God's purpose. Amen. (Wendy Joyner)

The Spirit Comes as a Unifying Fire

Second in a Series of Four on the Manifestation of the Holy Spirit

Genesis 11:1-9; Acts 2:1-12

At Pentecost, we celebrated the birth of the church and the fulfillment of Jesus' promise: the gift of the Holy Spirit. On the day of fulfillment the manifestation of the Holy Spirit was dramatic. A mighty wind roared into the upper room where the believers were gathered, and something that looked like tongues of fire fell on each. The believers were empowered and emboldened. Before they knew it, they were speaking in languages they did not know, and the people from the numerous nations that were assembled in Jerusalem for the Festival of Weeks heard the gospel proclaimed in their own languages. As one might expect, this miraculous sign drew a mixture of holy awe and dismissive ridicule. But Peter, prompted by the Spirit, preached the first sermon of the new church, and three thousand people with ears to hear joined the church that day.

That is the story we celebrate at Pentecost. But we would miss one of the most important ways in which the Holy Spirit is made manifest in this event if we see it only as the birthday of the church or as some "new thing" that God is doing in the world. In fact, what one sees in this event is the resolution of one of the oldest stories in Scripture; it sets right one of the oldest human wrongs.

Genesis tells the story of God's loving act of creation, culminating in the formation of humankind made in the image of God. Before long the story goes awry, however, and humankind misuses its gift of freedom, choosing the way of pride and self-assertion rather than fellowship with God and one another. Sin slithers into the garden and the consequences are dire; a cycle of violence and murder stains the human family and a tragic course is set.

As sin spirals ever downward, Genesis tells of God's grief over what was becoming of the creation. Like a radical amputation to save the life of the patient, God sends a flood to wipe out life on earth, starting over with one righteous person, Noah, and his family. Yet the story that follows suggests the depth of the problem of sin. Before long we see humankind gathered in one place, speaking a common language, plotting to build a great city with a tower that reaches into the heavens so that they can make a name for themselves and resist spreading throughout the earth according to the divine command. Once again, humanity chooses the path of pride and self-assertion.

This time God, having promised never to destroy the earth again in a flood, punishes in another way that vividly illustrates the nature of sin. God confuses their languages, scattering the human family into tribes and nations. Sin's effects are clearly demonstrated, tearing the garment of humanity to tatters and scattering the discordant pieces throughout the earth. Sin divides. Sin conquers. Humanity is broken and defeated.

When the Holy Spirit shows up as wind and flame on the day of Pentecost, more is happening than the birth of a new religious community—what we see at Pentecost is the reversal of Babel's curse. Consider the details: rather than the nations' being scattered throughout the earth, "there were devout Jews from every nation under heaven" (Acts 2:5) in Jerusalem during the festival. Rather than a tower that reaches into the heavens, the disciples gather in a humble upper room to pray and wait on God's promise of the Spirit. When the Spirit comes in power, the disciples begin to speak in other languages as the Spirit enables them; this time the many languages are intended to communicate, not to confuse.

Although some misunderstand this sign, the international visitors do marvel that these Galileans are suddenly prophesying in their own languages. The unpredictable spirit of God acts in ways no one could have predicted, upending the discord and fragmentation of Babel and reassembling the broken pieces of humanity into a new whole: the body of Christ.

Peter's sermon makes clear the Spirit's intention. When the crowd misunderstands the sign of tongues, Peter reminds the crowd of Joel's prophecy: "In the last days it will be, God declares, that I will pour out my Spirit upon all flesh" (2:17). Peter boldly asserts that the inauguration of a new era is taking place, a time when young and old, sons and daughters, will join in the work of the Spirit of God. The Spirit came to give new life and to reassemble what sin had torn apart. That unity can be the work of only the Spirit.

In our own days of international strife—a time when the title "United Nations" seems as oxymoronic as "jumbo shrimp"—we long for Babel's reversal to be completed. We long for the day when nation will no longer rise against nation, but instead the nations will constitute the "great multitude that no one could count...from all tribes and peoples and languages" (Revelation 7:9), offering praise to God at the end of all things. This aspect of the kingdom of God, like so many others, is an "already, but not yet" reality. A new thing was begun at Pentecost; it continues to unfold and will be complete only at the culmination of all things.

The sobering reality is that we learn in Acts that this reversal of Babel is work that takes place in and through the church. The body of Christ itself is the sign of a new and unified humanity. So when we lament the brokenness of humanity, our first task as the church is to recognize our own brokenness, our own inner Babel, and to pray that the wind of the Spirit will blow again, making us one.

The great miracle of Pentecost is not the wind, or the fire, or even the miracle of tongues—the miracle is the inaugurated healing of the human family, begun in a humble upper room and extending out to all humanity. (Cameron Jorgenson)

Worship Aids

Invocation

Come, Holy Spirit, fill the hearts of your faithful and kindle in them the fire of your love. May your presence blow like a mighty wind in this place. Fill us; unite our hearts; enable us to speak the word of God boldly. Lead us to worship. Amen.

Pastoral Prayer

Merciful God, we thank you that your gift of salvation goes far deeper than healing individual wounds; you come to redeem our broken relationships, hurting families, and a world at war. Change our hearts, O God, and make us one by the power of your Spirit. Amen.

Benediction

May the refreshing wind of the Holy Spirit blow through your life, fanning into flame God's gifts that are in you and filling your hearts with love. Go now in the love of God, in the peace of Christ, and in the power of the Spirit. Amen. (Cameron Jorgenson)

AUGUST 21, 2011

᭑᭙᭑᭙᭑᭙

Tenth Sunday after Pentecost

Readings: Exodus 1:8–2:10; Psalm 124; Romans 12:1-8; Matthew 16:13-20

The Heart of the Matter
Matthew 16:13-20

"Who do you say that I am?" (Matthew 16:15). Jesus puts the question directly to his disciples. After asking what the crowds say about him—the onlookers and "hangers-on"—Jesus directs the light on those closest to him. "Who do you say that I am?" It is a probing question that forces us to ask where we stand with this Jesus and how far we are willing to travel with him. It is a question that gets to the heart of the matter. Who do we believe this Jesus to be? How we answer this question makes all the difference in the world. It does not change the reality of who Jesus is; rather, it shapes and defines who we will be. For our confession regarding Jesus shapes the way we live as church—as a community of disciples.

If we believe Jesus to be a wise teacher, then we may believe that discipleship or Christianity is merely a matter of our assent to a list of principles or propositions. If we believe Jesus to be a great moral example, then we will understand Christianity to be primarily about our adherence to a set of ethics or ideals. But what if we really live and believe that Jesus, our companion and friend, is the Messiah, the Son of the living God?

The words we find in 16:17-19 are unique to the Gospel of Matthew. Only Matthew links Peter's confession of Jesus as the Messiah, the Son of the living God, with the church. In fact, this is one of only two occurrences of the word *church* in the Gospels. So for Matthew, the church, the community of Jesus' followers, is somehow related to the confession that Jesus is the Messiah, the Son of the living God. Jesus puts the question to his disciples—the church, the *ecclesia*, the gathered community—asking them where they stand, who they are, and how they will live. In reporting their response in this way, Matthew is suggesting that the church is a body of believers that is grounded upon and lives out Peter's confession. Church is the community of the Messiah, the fellowship of the Son of the living God. It is not a social club, a religious institution, a moral society, or a building. Church is a people whose life together is defined by the reign of God manifest in Jesus the Messiah and Son.

But affirming this about Jesus does not mean that we fully understand the implications of such a confession. Saying the right things does not always equate to living them out. We can say the right words about Jesus and still not know their full implication for our lives. The disciples certainly did not appreciate fully what such a confession might mean. Peter himself would discover that saying the words, uttering the confession, as important a first step as that might be, is not the same thing as living the words or embodying them in the life of the kingdom. Following Jesus is a holy adventure, and it often left the disciples dazed and confused as the hard road of discipleship opened before them. It is a way of life that demands active faith, not just belief. As Peter would discover, discipleship means that one day we might be led to places we'd rather not go.

Faith is not the absence of doubt. Faith is our daily, prayerful struggle with God in which we learn the full implications of being the church, of being a people whose life together is shaped by the confession, "You are the Messiah, the Son of the living God" (16:16). This can be a difficult journey. Being friends with Jesus is not easy; the way this confession leads is costly and demanding. But it is also a great gift; the way of Jesus leads to full and abundant life.

In asking "Who do you say that I am?" Jesus invites the disciples, the church, into relationship, to walk with him the often hard and demanding road of discipleship. Through this question, Jesus invites us to let go of our attachment to all the other "lords" that demand our allegiance—ideas, ambitions, and relationships—and to become friends with him.

In making this confession we are saying that we want our lives, our witness, and our ministry to be defined by Christ's life, witness, and ministry. We are often guilty of projecting our own ideas about the nature of discipleship onto Jesus, shaping our confession rather than letting it shape and give content to our life as church. That is because Jesus says things we don't want to hear about the nature of his messiahship and the character of those who would be his friends: "Go sell your possessions"; "Hate your mother and father"; "Take up your cross"; "Deny yourself."

As we come to understand who this Jesus is, we may believe that embodying Peter's confession is frankly impossible. And it is, unless we also acknowledge that we are never alone. Christ walks the way before us and alongside us. Christ is our constant companion. Just as he did with Peter, Christ continues to come to us, to dwell with the church, pulling, prodding, guiding, nudging, calling, and being with us.

"Who do you say that I am?" This is the heart of the matter for us as the church. How we answer this question, with our lips and with our lives, defines the shape of our life together. We make this confession, not by heroic acts of will, but by grace, by a transforming relationship with the God who has come to us in the flesh, who walked the way before us, and who joins us on the road even now. This confession is not our possession; it is not the result of our cleverness or the fruit of our brilliant deduction. It is a blessing to be able to say, and even more to live, "You are the Messiah, the Son of the living God." It is a gracious and costly gift. It will determine everything about us; it demands all our heart, mind, body, and soul. It leads to the cross and to giving ourselves sacrificially for God and for neighbor. But it is also the way that leads to life. (David C. Hockett)

Lectionary Commentary
Exodus 1:8–2:10

The book of Exodus begins with an affirmation and celebration of Israel's well-being: "the Israelites were fruitful and prolific; they multiplied and grew exceedingly strong, so that the land was filled with them" (1:7). But the hope of these initial verses quickly turns to uncertainty as "a new king arose over Egypt, who did not know Joseph" (v. 8). Once again the promise made to Abraham and his descendants is threatened. The children of Israel find themselves enslaved in Egypt, living as captives, and we wonder if God will be faithful to the covenant God has made.

That question lingers behind the narrative, and we watch as God's response unfolds. God has not forgotten the promises made to Abraham, Isaac, and Jacob. As we will discover, though Israel's future appears bleak, God is at work within the context of Israel's history to bring about the fulfillment of the covenant. Israel will have a future, and will worship and serve the Lord, because ultimately God is Lord and Pharaoh is not. Israel and Pharaoh are part of a much larger narrative than the one that appears on the surface; the God who made covenant with Israel is also the Lord of creation who will bring order out of chaos.

Finally, we are introduced to Moses. The baby boy is born, hidden, found, and cared for by the daughter of the enemy, secretly nursed by his own mother, and then raised by Pharaoh's daughter. It is a miraculous story. But it is a story about God before it is a story about Pharaoh, Israel, or even Moses. Throughout the Exodus narrative, Moses is important but not central. It is the God of Abraham, Isaac, and Jacob whose action is central to the story. The Moses narrative is about the often hidden and subtle workings of God in and through ordinary people to bring about God's good purposes. God will have a family, a people. Pharaoh cannot thwart the purposes of God, and Moses will play his role, but God is the primary actor.

Moses is no Wild West, larger-than-life American hero. He is the imperfect servant of God, caught up in a story much larger than the orbit of his own life. We can relate to Moses and the people of Israel because we too have passed through the water, and in Christ our lives are part of the larger plan of God's gracious redeeming work.

Romans 12:1-8

Having carefully and clearly defined how the redemption of God's wayward and rebellious creation is a gift of unmerited grace, Paul now calls the people to respond to that gift by the offering of their lives as living sacrifices to God. This offering should not be construed as a way of earning our salvation; rather it is our response to God's gracious work of salvation in and through Jesus Christ. Paul is clear: we are saved by grace through faith. But while grace saves, grace also makes possible a new way of life. This is not a new attempt to impose the law but an invitation to be faithful because God has been faithful. (David C. Hockett)

Worship Aids

Call to Worship

We come this day to offer ourselves as a living sacrifice to God.
O God, accept this, our sacrifice of praise.
We come as the body of Christ, gifted by the one Spirit for the work of ministry.
Use us, O Lord; make us instruments of your grace.

Opening Prayer

Liberating God, you drew Moses from the water and so provided a liberator for your people Israel. By your mighty hand, Moses led them through the water to freedom and the land that you promised. When we were slaves to sin, you sent Jesus, nurtured in the water of Mary's womb, to be our liberator, our redeemer, our friend. By water and the Spirit we are heirs of Moses, your sons and daughters, and brothers and sisters of Christ. Set us free from all that binds us and holds us captive that we may love and serve you in new life. Amen.

Benediction

You are sons and daughters of God, drawn from the waters of baptism. You are the body of Christ, a living sacrifice to God. Go in peace to live and proclaim the good news—Jesus is the Messiah, the Son of the living God. Amen. (David C. Hockett)

The Spirit Comes as a Refining Fire

Third in a Series of Four on the Manifestation of the Holy Spirit

Acts 5:1-11

The mysterious Spirit who revealed God to humankind came in the Gospel of Mark as an odd sort of dove, giving Jesus peace, power, and a mission, but also sending him into the first great trial of his ministry, an encounter with Satan in the wilderness. Although it is a harbinger of peace, the Spirit of God is anything but tame and predictable. Later, in the book of Acts, the Spirit manifests itself in wind and flame, resulting in a conflagration hot enough to weld together the pieces of humanity shattered by sin into a new reality: the body of Christ. But we find something unsettling about that image; a fire burning that hot and bright is fundamentally unsafe. The basic ingredients are a dangerous combination: wind mixed with flame is the recipe for a wildfire. As the young church discovers through a shocking turn of events, a wildfire can be a dangerous thing.

Immediately after Pentecost, life in the fledgling church is wonderful. "They devoted themselves to the apostles' teaching and fellowship, to the breaking of bread and the prayers" (Acts 2:42). People are in awe as the powerful presence of the Spirit continues to make itself known. Miracles continue to take place, not the least of which is the outpouring of generosity among the believers. They share everything they have with one another, those who have plenty giving generously to those who are in need. The Spirit is present in the young church as they meet daily in the temple courts, "praising God and having the goodwill of all the people. And day by day the Lord added to their number those who were being saved" (v. 47).

There is even a very public healing of a man born crippled. This healing results in the apostles' first taste of persecution as the religious establishment attempts to silence them. As the believers pray for the strength to endure, "the place in which they were gathered together was shaken; and they were all filled with the Holy Spirit and spoke the word of God with boldness" (4:31). The fire of God's presence glows in the hearth of the church, and people gladly gather around to enjoy its warmth.

Despite this beautiful beginning, so reminiscent of the Garden of Eden, something sinister enters the scene. After an individual whom the apostles call Barnabas, or "Son of Encouragement," sells a piece of land and gives it to the church to care for those in need, another person has an idea. Ananias decides to sell one of his properties, keep some of the proceeds, and give the rest to the church with a philanthropic flourish. Perhaps he hopes to ingratiate himself with the apostles as had Barnabas; or perhaps he simply wants to be known as a generous fellow. Whatever his motivation, Ananias plans to deceive the church, and his wife, Sapphira, goes along with him.

When Ananias presents his gift to the apostles, Peter has a rather different response than Ananias expected. He rebukes Ananias for his duplicity and says, "What made you think of doing such a thing? You have not lied to men, but to God." Ananias drops dead! Three hours later the scene repeats when Sapphira arrives and Peter interrogates her, asking if the money is indeed the full price they received for the land. She declares that it is, Peter rebukes her for testing the Spirit of the Lord, and she falls dead as well. As one might expect, "great fear seized the whole church and all who heard of these things" (5:11).

It is an embarrassing story, really. This episode with Ananias and Sapphira is bizarre, even offensive. We may even be tempted to skip over it as we read the book of Acts. But it is an unavoidable part of the story that, as the new church basks in the warmth of the Spirit's presence, God strikes a married couple dead in church. The warm glow turns to a cold shiver. Surely some think, *Even if Ananias and Sapphira had understated the price of the land, it was still a generous contribution to the benevolence fund.*

But now they are dead? The untamable wildfire moves in an unanticipated way, leaving the early church, and us, in slack-jawed disbelief.

We may want to avoid this story and its frightening strangeness, but we ought not miss the message it contains: The Spirit of God conveys peace and comfort, but God is still the holy other. When Moses came to God at Sinai, the people were warned that touching the holy mountain was certain death; the same was true for those who touched the ark of the covenant, symbolic of God's presence. Although it is shocking even to contemplate, it seems that the message of Acts includes a sober warning: the church is like Sinai, the meeting place of God and humanity. It is no longer a box of gold but a holy collection of people; the church is the new ark of God's presence in the world. To taint Christian charity with pride and self-aggrandizement is to touch the sacred things and undermine the very Spirit at work in that place. Lying to the Holy Spirit, deceiving the church, and angling for power and prestige within the community founded on the principle that the first shall be last and the last shall be first constitutes grave corruption that the Spirit will not abide.

As the rest of Acts—and our own experience—makes clear, the Spirit is not in the habit of striking down those who lie to the church or sully the purity of Christian charity with baser motives. Otherwise, there would be a much longer list of names who had met that end. But perhaps the retelling of this shocking story can accomplish the same thing for us that it did for the early church; it can remind us that there is no such thing as a safe wildfire or a tame dove. (Cameron Jorgenson)

Worship Aids

Invocation

Come, Holy Spirit, fill the hearts of your faithful and kindle in them the fire of your love. May your love be the crucible of our hearts, burning off everything unworthy of your presence. Fill us; transform us; purify our hearts. Lead us to worship. Amen.

Pastoral Prayer

Holy God, we are humbled by your invitation to live as your people. Help us to work out our salvation with fear and trembling, for it is you at work in us, enabling us both to will and to work for your good pleasure. Amen.

Benediction

May the refining fire of the Spirit make you ever more like Christ: bold, compassionate, and single-hearted in devotion. Go now in the love of God, in the peace of Christ, and in the power of the Spirit. Amen. (Cameron Jorgenson)

AUGUST 28, 2011

Eleventh Sunday after Pentecost

Readings: Exodus 3:1-15; Psalm 105:1-6, 23-26, 45c; Romans 12:9-21; Matthew 16:21-28

Called to Follow Jesus
Matthew 16:21-28

Peter has boldly professed his faith, claiming that Jesus is the Messiah, the Son of the living God. Jesus responds by telling the disciples that the church will be built upon the solid foundation, the rock of Peter and Peter's faithful confession. But things can change rather quickly, can they not? Making the confession that Jesus is the Messiah, the Son of the living God, uttering the words does not mean that Peter (or we) fully understands the implications of that confession. Oh, we believe it has something to do with where we'll spend eternity, but what about here and now? What might it mean to not only utter this confession with our lips but also truly live it?

We as individuals and as the church often become a stumbling block to those who would hear and respond to the gospel call because what we say is not borne out in the way we live. How often do we shield ourselves and others from the fullness of the gospel? We want to faithfully follow, but...just how far? The challenge unfolds before us in today's Gospel reading; mere moments after Peter's bold confession, Jesus tells the disciples that the way he must go involves suffering and even death. The way of the Messiah, and thus the way of discipleship, is the way of the cross. Peter pulls Jesus aside and says bluntly, "God forbid it, Lord! This must never happen to you" (Matthew 16:22). Jesus immediately rebukes Peter: "Get behind me, Satan! You are a stumbling block to me; for you are setting your mind not on divine things but on human things" (v. 23). Wow! What happened to "On this rock I will build my church"?

We shouldn't be too hard on Peter and the disciples at this point. We too are guilty of opting for cheap grace, for Easter without Good Friday, for resurrection without the cross, for salvation devoid of discipleship, for pursuing new life while clinging desperately to the old. Too often we make discipleship and the way of Jesus an interesting idea that we discuss over coffee with friends instead of a journey that demands transformation, obedience, the death of the old self, and the sometimes painful birth of the new. We too are at times a stumbling block.

We are also guilty of ordering the life of the church in similar fashion. We make the church a purveyor of religious products for discriminating consumers, offering to meet every need and whim while asking very little in return. Grace becomes a cheap commodity freely dispensed to meet a plethora of unchecked needs. But as Peter and the other disciples would discover, the gospel, if it is the gospel of Jesus Christ, is cross-shaped. It is both a demand and a gift. The gospel offers, not a capitulation to the felt needs of our narcissistic culture, but the truth our world so desperately needs to hear, "We preach Christ crucified." The way of Jesus is the way of suffering and the cross. This is not suffering for suffering's sake, but suffering that comes as a result of our willingness to risk loving God and neighbor no matter the cost. That way and only that way leads to resurrection and new life.

The good news the world needs is that life is offered. But this is not life as we often understand it, which is little more than slavery to our own small needs and desires. It is true and abundant life that is found in being yoked to Christ. Jesus calls us to a life of single-minded obedience, to deny ourselves, to take up the cross and follow him. Jesus calls us to be different, to be holy, to grow in likeness with him. But with that demanding call to obedience comes a gift—the gift of abundant life in Christ—if we lose our life in service to Christ and his kingdom, we will find a life beyond our imagining. Moreover, Christ promises the gift of his Spirit to enable and empower our response, to make it possible for us to do the impossible and live as Christ lived. On our own, by our own will, this is not possible, but with God all things are possible. With God we can say yes when Christ bids us to follow, to come and die to self and be made alive to God. With God our lives can become the incarnation of the church's confession—"You are the Messiah, the Son of the living God." By the power of the Holy Spirit the church can avoid becoming a stumbling block on the way to the kingdom, a dispenser of cheap but powerless grace, and can become itself a foretaste and a glimpse of the very kingdom it lives and proclaims.

Matthew is quite clear. Jesus comes offering good news—not self-help advice, not easy answers, not a quick fix—but truly good news. Peter and the disciples didn't want a cross. Perhaps none of us would have chosen this way of redeeming the world. We'd rather take the easy road, meet the needs of the few who come our way, secure a future for ourselves, build a powerful, successful ministry, make the church into something respectable, something we can all be proud of, a helpful institution. But Jesus demands and offers much more. He calls us to find life in being his friends who sometimes endure the suffering that comes as a result of risky, sacrificial, cross-shaped love.

A stumbling block or a rock—sometimes we are both. The call to follow the way of Jesus, the invitation to embody the faith we confess, is both a great demand and a remarkable gift. Jesus offers us the gift of new and abundant life—to let go of all those false gods to which we so passionately cling and to take hold of the cross. Jesus invites us to follow him and find, in the sometimes difficult road of discipleship, a highway straight to the very heart of God. (David C. Hockett)

Lectionary Commentary
Exodus 3:1-15

Moses is engaged in his new vocation, tending the flocks of his father-in-law, Jethro. He has made his way, leading Jethro's flocks beyond the wilderness to Horeb (Sinai). There he experiences a theophany, an appearance of God, and a call to a new vocation, a theological vocation as liberator of the people of Israel. We are told that a bush is burning but is not consumed by the fire. This burning bush attracts Moses' attention, and when God sees that Moses is listening, God speaks.

God addresses Moses directly, calling him by name and revealing to Moses that the one who speaks is none other than the God of Moses' ancestors—the God of Abraham, Isaac, and Jacob. Moses' call is now placed within the context of the larger narrative of God's relationship with and call upon Israel. Moses is being caught up in the story of covenant and promise as his own life becomes a part of the larger purposes of the Holy One of Israel. Moses, the one drawn from the water, now becomes the one who will lead Israel through the water of the sea to the land that God has promised.

Moses responds to this call as we might expect. First, like Isaiah, Moses is overwhelmed by the holiness of God and protests that he is unqualified and undeserving. But unlike Isaiah, Moses does not volunteer. So God persists, assuring Moses of God's constant and abiding presence with him as he fulfills his vocation. We should not be surprised by God's response; after all, it has been God's constant and abiding presence that has sustained the covenant made with Israel. God has been and will continue to be the principal actor in the narrative. Though the people may wander and become disobedient and forget their holy vocation, God remembers and is faithful; God will not be deterred. So God reassures Moses and responds, "I will be with you . . ." (Exodus 3:12).

Romans 12:9-21

Here Paul outlines the Christian's response to grace and the call to live in unity and peace with fellow Christians and those beyond the fellowship of Christ. He begins by defining how the faithful response to grace looks within the context of the Christian community but then broadens his argument to include our conduct with those outside the community of faith.

Paul is careful not to offer a new law through which we can earn God's grace. Rather, as was the case with the law given to Israel, Paul defines behavior that is an appropriate and faithful response to the gracious gift of salvation. Our ethical conduct is not a way to earn God's favor; it is a response made possible by the very grace we have received. In a similar way, obedience to the law was not a means by which Israel earned God's favor, but was a gift that helped Israel define what its life should look like in response to the gift of its liberation from Egypt.

The offering of grace precedes the keeping of the law. The offering of grace precedes the way of Christian discipleship, and even more, it is grace that both initiates and makes possible our response. (David C. Hockett)

Worship Aids

Call to Worship

O give thanks to the Lord, call on God's name, make known God's deeds among the peoples. Sing to the Lord, sing praises to God. Tell all people

God's wonderful works. Glorify God's holy name and let your hearts rejoice. Praise the Lord!

Opening Prayer

God of Abraham, Isaac, and Jacob, we find ourselves in this moment and place on holy ground, for you are in our midst. Grant that we might turn away from all that distracts us and center our attention on you. Enable us once more to hear your call above the noisiness of our lives. We come this day to worship and are overwhelmed by the beauty of your presence. Be who you will be for us, that we might once again become your holy people through Jesus Christ our Lord, who lives and reigns with you in glory everlasting. Amen.

Prayer of Confession

Gracious and merciful God, we confess that our love has not been genuine and our affection for one another is lacking. We have neglected to pray and have been more concerned with our own advancement than with meeting the needs of others. We are quick to curse those who we believe have done us wrong, we are envious of those who rejoice, and we have no time for those who weep. We consider ourselves worthy and deserving of your love while we withhold that same love from those we judge as beneath us or worthy only of your condemnation. Have mercy upon us, forgive us all our sins, and grant us grace that we might not be overcome by evil, but overcome evil with good, in the name of Christ our Lord. Amen.

Words of Assurance

In the name of the Christ
  who calls us to discipleship, you are forgiven.
In the name of Christ, you are forgiven.
Thanks be to God. (David C. Hockett)

The Spirit Comes as an Unexpected Gift

Fourth in a Series of Four on the Manifestation of the Holy Spirit

Acts 10:44-48

As we have seen in the manifestations of the Spirit at the baptism of Christ, Pentecost, and the incident with Ananias and Sapphira, the

Spirit has revealed self as an unpredictable dove, and as the powerful yet dangerous combination of wind and flame, equally capable of healing humanity or rendering judgment. By this point it should come as no great surprise that the Spirit may shock us yet again, but when God gives Peter a bizarre vision while waiting on a rooftop terrace for his lunch to cook, he and all the church are stunned by the work the Spirit has in mind.

Pentecost, despite its international thrust, was a Jewish phenomenon. The Jewish diaspora had taken Judaism around the known world; it was this eclectic group who had returned to the Holy City for the festival and heard the gospel preached in their own languages. To this point, the good news of Jesus the Messiah had been received only among Jews. But there are hints that the wind is shifting.

At the beginning of Acts, when Jesus promises the coming of the Holy Spirit, he says, "But you will receive power when the Holy Spirit has come upon you; and you will be my witnesses in Jerusalem, in all Judea and Samaria, and to the ends of the earth" (1:8). From the earliest days, the church proclaimed the gospel in Jerusalem, but it is not until persecution and martyrdom come to the church that the believers scatter from Jerusalem into Judea and Samaria. Despite the tragic circumstances, the hopeful aspect of the scattering is that as the believers go, so does the gospel.

Philip preaches in Samaria to great effect; there people receive the message with joy. Because of the historic ethnic tension between Jews and Samaritans, other apostles investigate the matter for themselves, but it becomes clear to all that the power of the Spirit to change lives is at work among the Samaritans. Philip also encounters another seeker beyond the church's comfort zone: a eunuch who is a high-ranking official in the Ethiopian royal court. Philip shares the gospel with this man, who is so captivated that he immediately requests baptism. This conversion may raise some eyebrows among the Jerusalem church, but Ethiopia does have a connection to Israel extending back to the days of King Solomon and the queen of Sheba, so the baptism is accepted without incident. One wonders, however, if a conversation is sparked among the apostles: "What if? What if a Gentile were to believe? What then?"

Only in retrospect will the earliest Christians detect the direction that the wind of the Spirit is beginning to blow. Steadily they are being nudged toward fulfilling the promise to Abraham, the promise that his seed will be a blessing to all nations. They are being prompted to see that the Jewish Messiah is indeed the Savior of the world. But that is a truth they cannot quite see yet. A dramatic gale-force wind of the Spirit is needed for the church to set a new course; toward that end, Hurricane Cornelius looms on the horizon.

Peter prays on a rooftop terrace, his lunch cooking in the house below, when he falls into a visionary trance. He sees a tablecloth lowered from heaven loaded with animals considered unclean in Jewish dietary laws. "Get up, Peter; kill and eat" (10:13), says the voice from heaven. When Peter protests that he has never put anything unclean to his lips, the voice replies that Peter is not to call anything unclean that God has made clean. To make the unusual vision unforgettable, if not understandable, the vision repeats twice more. Peter does not have to puzzle long over its meaning, because at the end of the vision God tells Peter that there are people at the gate who have been sent by God. Peter immediately goes down to meet the soldiers, who explain that they have come to take Peter to their master, a God-fearing Roman centurion named Cornelius.

Having understood the vision to mean that he is to judge no one whom God accepts, Peter goes with the men to meet Cornelius. The centurion has assembled his friends and family for the occasion and asks that Peter share what God has given him to say. Peter shares the gospel, beginning with his new insight that God does not show favoritism, but accepts all who fear God and do what is right. Peter then shares the essential message of Christ's life, death, and resurrection, that "everyone who believes in him receives forgiveness of sins through his name" (10:43). While he is still speaking, the Holy Spirit comes upon those assembled in as dramatic a fashion as at Pentecost itself. Despite his point about God not showing favoritism, Peter is astounded that the Gentiles have been given the gift of the Spirit. Knowing just what to do, he exclaims that since they have received the Holy Spirit, they ought also to receive baptism.

As might be expected, Peter comes under intense questioning by the Jerusalem church; after all, he admitted people to the church through baptism without first converting to Judaism. This act of inclusion provokes a significant question about the nature of salvation and the relationship between the church's Jewish identity and the universal scope of its message of salvation.

Through this early theological crisis, the Spirit reveals the nature of God once again. The message is plain: God's unpredictable Spirit is working to redeem and transform broken humanity. (Cameron Jorgenson)

Worship Aids

Invocation

Come, Holy Spirit, fill the hearts of your faithful and kindle in them the fire of your love. Let us participate in your redemptive initiatives in the world as you redeem the creation that you love. Fill us; draw us to yourself; send us on your mission. Lead us to worship.

Pastoral Prayer

Redeeming God, we thank you that you continually reach out in love; you break down boundaries to your grace; you include us in your work. Draw us all into your liberating embrace and teach us to love others as you have loved us. Amen.

Benediction

May the Lord catch you up into the unfolding drama of salvation, as both an ambassador and an object of divine love. Go now in the love of God, in the peace of Christ, and in the power of the Spirit. Amen. (Cameron Jorgenson)

SEPTEMBER 4, 2011

❦❦❦❦

Twelfth Sunday after Pentecost

Readings: Exodus 12:1-14; Psalm 149; Romans 13:8-14;
Matthew 18:15-20

Remembrance Is the Secret of Redemption
Exodus 12:1-14

Do you like to eat? My spouse and I enjoy finding wonderful places to eat when we travel. We often will spend less money on a room so that we have more left for dining adventures. A good meal is an experience: the food; the flavors, aromas, and textures; all carefully chosen by the chef to tell a story for the eyes, nose, and mouth. But there is more than the food in any good meal. There is ritual and story, and intimacy often not found in other social settings. Meals are important parts of life. Meals have a place of importance beyond the nourishment they provide.

Anyone who has been around the church knows that eating together is an important part of the Christian community's life. In part this is true because meals were important to Jesus. He ate with sinners, he shared table fellowship with his disciples, and he established a meal as one of the central and defining acts of what it means to be counted among his friends. Likewise at the heart of the lives of Jesus' ancestors was a meal. For centuries before him and continuing today, Jesus' own people were shaped and defined by a meal. The passover seder is still a central and defining practice in the Jewish community. Perhaps that is partly why meals were so important to Jesus, so central to the life of the early church; he was shaped by a very important meal.

God called Moses to lead the people to freedom from slavery in Egypt into the promised land. There they would worship and serve the Lord their God. The people were to hurriedly prepare and eat a holy meal prior to their liberation. This meal would become the most central and important festival within the life of Israel—passover. From that day forward the

279

people were to gather to eat and drink in celebration and remembrance of what God had done for them. Even more, in remembering what God had done, they were reminded of who they were called to be, and of what it meant to live as the people of God.

Yet this was no ordinary meal: roasted lamb, bitter herbs, and unleavened bread, all of it eaten hurriedly, sandals on and ready to bolt out the door at any given moment. This was no ordinary meal, eaten in homes with blood smeared on doorposts in the darkness of the night, anticipating what God might do. This was a symbolic, redemptive meal. It would define and shape God's people and serve as a reminder of their enslavement, of all God had done on their behalf, and of the life they were called to as the people of promise. This was no ordinary meal—this was worship, ritual.

In observing Israel at the passover table, we learn that worship, ritual, and table fellowship have the power to shape us, to define us, to tell us who we are and how we should live and be. Worship helps us remember and become again the people God intended us to be.

It was likely the passover meal that Jesus shared with his disciples the night before his crucifixion and death. He gathered them around the table, they ate the roasted lamb and bitter herbs, drank from the cup of blessing, and remembered together the story of God's redeeming, liberating work of love. They remembered how death passed over the houses of their ancestors, how they were led to freedom through the sea, how they were set free to serve and worship the Lord their God. Jesus offered them bread and wine, but even more, Jesus offered himself, the Lamb of God, given that all people might share in the exodus, in being set free from the oppressive power of sin and death. At table, sharing a meal with Jesus, we become a passover people.

Like the Jews, Christians are a people of the table, of a meal. In the breaking of bread we remember what God has done in Christ to liberate us from sin and death. Our fellowship at the Lord's table is a sacrament, a means of grace, a point of encounter with the living God, and an invitation to share in God's ongoing work of salvation. In the breaking of the bread and the sharing of the cup, we share in Christ's life and are reminded that we too are a community of the exodus, set free to worship and serve the Lord our God.

Like Israel at passover, our remembering and our eating are more than just memorials; they are ways of experiencing now the saving power of that past event. In the bread and the cup and the fellowship we share at the table, Jesus is truly present and offers again his body and his blood, food for the journey. "Take and eat," he says. "Remember what God has done for you, is doing for you now, will do for you in the future. Remember who you are; remember and don't forget so that you may serve the Lord your God with glad and generous hearts."

"Remember me," Jesus said. "When you eat this bread and drink this cup, remember me and don't forget." Remember that you once were slaves to sin and death, living in exile. But by the grace of God you have been bought with a price, marked by the sacrificial blood of the Lamb of God who takes away the sin of the world. Remember what God has done for you; remember who you are liberated to be.

And of course this remembering takes us beyond the eucharistic table. As it is with Israel at passover, the table is only the beginning. How different might our lives look if we were a people defined by our fellowship at the table where we truly remember? What might it mean for our lives if each moment our hearts and minds resonated with the realization that all we do and say is in remembrance of our passover lamb?

My brothers and sisters, the good news is God has never forgotten you, not once. How good it is to know that we are remembered. When we eat together, may God grant us the grace of a good memory so that we might never forget what God has done for us, so that we might never forget who we are and who we are called to be. The table has been set and a meal prepared; let's eat. (David C. Hockett)

Lectionary Commentary
Matthew 18:15-20

It can be argued that Matthew is more explicitly concerned with the life of the church than any other Gospel. We see that concern depicted here as Matthew addresses the reality of division and sin among members of the body of Christ. Matthew's vision of the church is both sober and painfully realistic. Even in the community of faith, among those who are called brother and sisters in Christ, exist division, quarreling, angry words, dishonesty, sin, broken trust, and shattered relationships. The issue is what to do not *if* division occurs but *when* such division occurs.

Jesus instructs his disciples on how to handle the painful times when the community of faith falls short of the unity, peace, and love to which we have been called. Jesus' instruction focuses on reconciliation and restoration, not judgment and punishment. We are to treat one another with the same mercy and compassion that God has shown to us. In humility and with a spirit of grace and forgiveness, we are to work diligently to restore the one who has violated the covenant of Christian fellowship for the sake of the witness of the church. This is not an individual ethic for personal behavior; we do this in community with the guidance and support of our fellow brothers and sisters because unity is critical to our mission.

But what happens when our best, most prayerful efforts at reconciliation fail? Matthew says if we do everything in our power to restore the offending member and that person will continue to undermine the fellowship of the church, then we are to follow Jesus' example and treat that individual like "a Gentile and a tax collector" (Matthew 18:17). Of course here we recall that Jesus ate with Gentiles and tax collectors. While we try to limit and ration forgiveness, with God mercy and grace abound.

All are unworthy of the mercy and forgiveness God offers in Christ Jesus—Gentiles, tax collectors, sinners of all sorts, including Jesus' closest friends. And yet it is offered because God is merciful and gracious. As followers of Christ we are called to do likewise, to do all in our power to work toward reconciliation for the witness of the gospel.

Romans 13:8-14

Paul here answers the question "How do we treat our neighbors?" Paul's answer is grounded in and grows out of the larger theological and ecclesiological framework he established earlier in the letter. For the disciple of Christ, the relationship with one's neighbor is based upon more than what the laws of the state require. It is not enough for the follower of Christ to say, "I have acted legally toward my neighbor." The relationship between Christian and neighbor is defined by love. Jesus is the incarnation of God's love. He acted out of love; his life defines the shape and character of love. Love, Paul argues, is the fulfillment of the law given to Israel. In Christ we discover what the law looks like, we discover the end or purpose of the law, and that end or purpose is the love of God, out of which grows the perfect love of neighbor.

But what is love? Is love primarily an emotion or feeling? If so, how are we to muster up positive, warm, happy feelings about those we do not like, much less our enemies and those who would seek to do us harm? Paul argues here and elsewhere that love properly understood is the active pursuit of the good of the other, including our enemy. Love is sacrificial serv-ice extended toward all made possible because of the sacrificial love of God manifest in the cross of Christ. As followers of Christ, our relation-ships are to bear witness to that kind of love. In that way Christ is pro-claimed and we begin to anticipate the future reign of God here and now.

Paul ends this section with just that sort of reasoning. We are to love God and neighbor sacrificially and without reserve, not only because of what God has done in the past, but also because of what God will do in the future. The kingdom of God implies that salvation is nearer to us now than ever before and indeed is coming. Therefore, live in anticipation of the consummation of God's kingdom of love now. (David C. Hockett)

Worship Aids

Call to Worship
The light is far gone, the day is near.
Let us put aside the works of darkness
   and put on the armor of light.
Come, worship the Lamb of God
   who takes away the sins of the world.
Praise be to you, Lord Jesus Christ.

Opening Prayer
Loving Lord, you promise that when we gather in your name you are here in our midst. We come, called and gathered by your Spirit, to hear once again the story of our salvation and to feast at your table. Speak to us once more the good news of our liberation from sin and death. Feed us with the Lamb who takes away the sins of the world. Grant us grace that we might be as merciful with our neighbors as you have been with us. Amen.

Will Our Children Have Joy?

First in a Series of Four on Back to Church/Back to School

Psalm 98

When I was of school age, the month I hated the most was August. That's because August signaled the beginning of school. Somewhere toward the end of that month I would have to give up my carefree sum-mer life and accept the rigors of another school year. Summer was fun! It meant family vacations, camps, playing sports and games, hanging out with friends, staying up late (really late!), and lots of other fun things. I didn't like giving up these things for school.

But as I eased into the new school year, an interesting thing happened. It happened every fall, but I forgot it every summer. Joy hadn't been snatched from me. New pleasures quickly replaced the ones I had enjoyed in the summer. There was always a class to which I warmed up quickly or a new teacher who became a friend. Life was more structured, but that wasn't so bad. A whole schedule of interesting activities began to draw my attention. Here and there a deep satisfaction washed over me—the realization that I was growing. I was growing not only intellectually but also spiritually, since my attendance at Sunday school and worship was more constant in the fall and winter.

Life has a rhythm. We feel that rhythm at this time of year when we enter a new school year. It's a big shift we make, and we all make it together. Today and for the next three Sundays we want to explore some of the meanings of life that become evident to us at this time of year.

We humans are the only creatures who are born with virtually no instincts. We have to learn everything! We spend all of our lives in both formal and informal education. It takes family and school and church working together to mold us into the mature, well-adjusted people that God intends us to be. This process of learning and growth is long and tedious, and it never really ends.

We want this process of learning and growth to go well. We desperately need for it to go well. It must go well if we are to become healthy people. In these sermons I'll put the focus on our children and how we can best nurture them toward maturity as Christians, but the principles apply to all of us at all times.

Let's go back to the matter of finding enjoyment in every season of life. The rhythm of your life may be different from mine, or you may experience that rhythm differently, but there is a rhythm that we can all talk about.

One of the things that really gets us through the ups and downs of life is enjoyment—a capacity to have fun. When we can find enjoyment in our jobs and in our educations and in even mundane tasks, everything just naturally flows better. We are much happier and healthier than we would otherwise be, and we help others to be happier as well.

Psychiatrist William Glasser says that we humans have five basic needs, and one of these is having fun (the others are survival, love and belonging, power, and freedom; www.wglasser.com). The ability to have fun is essential to good health. Without it our lives are not satisfying or productive, and they go off track. Life is to be enjoyed.

The Bible is in complete agreement with this view of life. The words *joy* and *enjoy* and forms of them, as well as several synonyms, are liberally sprinkled throughout the Bible. The devotional and liturgical literature of the Bible is especially rich in this language. The high point of Jesus' great prayer in John 17 is that his followers "may have my joy made complete in themselves" (v. 13).

Christians have found many ways to talk about this. The familiar Westminster Catechism says that the chief end of mortals is "to glorify God and enjoy him forever." This is joy in its fullness, and it's what the life and teachings of the church pull us toward.

Little enjoyments are the building blocks by which we arrive at life's greater joys. We learn such joys in the family, at school, and in the church by the way we nurture one another. Something as simple as taking delight in the beauties of nature and fostering that delight in our children is no little thing. Turning a family chore day into an enjoyable group activity is the best of all ways to get things done.

Family vacations are an important part of growing up. They don't have to be expensive or elaborate. When I was a boy, vacation usually meant visiting relatives in a neighboring state. Nothing was more fun to me than exploring the woods on my uncle's farm and fishing in his pond. Playing sports and board games with my cousins was pure delight. As I grew up and turned my attention to my own children, I was amazed at how little it took to make them happy. We refer to one of our most memorable times together as the "Fishing Vacation," a week in which I, a not so gifted angler, took my wife and sons on a fishing trip that included several misadventures in which the laugh was usually on me. Chevy Chase had nothing on us.

Our text, Psalm 98, points us to the joy that flows through all of God's creation. The psalmist imagines that the seas and the hills join us humans in rejoicing in God's steadfast love. We and our children have every reason to be joyful, for God's faithfulness and goodness never fade. They go with us into every season of life—even into those seasons that we prefer least.

As the seasons change and we go back to church and school, may we and our children draw ever closer to God, the giver of every joy, the wellspring of all gladness. (Sandy Wylie)

Worship Aids

Call to Worship (based on Psalm 98:4, 7-9)

Make a joyful noise to the LORD, all the earth.
Break forth into joyous song and sing praises.
Let the sea roar, and all that fills it.
The world and those who live in it.
All: Let the hills sing together for joy
   at the presence of the LORD.

Prayer of Confession

O loving God, we confess that we have let the stealers of joy oppress us.
We have given in to doubt, worry, discouragement, and so many other
things that rob us of joy. We know we must turn back to you, for only you
can restore our joy. Help us, we pray. Amen.

Words of Assurance (based on John 10:10)

Jesus came that we might have life and have it abundantly. Hallelujah!

Benediction

Go forth as those who walk with God and share in the joy that flows
through all of God's creation. May God's faithfulness and goodness glad-
den your hearts in this and every season of life. Amen. (Sandy Wylie)

SEPTEMBER 11, 2011

❦❦❦

Thirteenth Sunday after Pentecost

Readings: Exodus 14:19-31; 15:1b-11, 20-21; Romans 14:1-12; Matthew 18:21-35

The Practice of Forgiveness
Matthew 18:21-35

I once heard a conversation in which two individuals, one who had been assaulted and raped and the other who had been wrongly accused and convicted of the crime, discussed the power of forgiveness in their lives. Both spoke of the horrible circumstances that brought them together and that had almost destroyed their lives. Both spoke of sleepless nights, anger, fear, depression, and shame; but each also spoke of the beauty and goodness they had found in being able to forgive. They talked about what it meant to not be defined by their pasts, to be set free from a burden they had not chosen, and how life-giving the practice of forgiveness had been.

Today's text from Matthew moves us to consider one of the most difficult practices of Christian discipleship—forgiveness. Forgiveness is a hard road to walk, but it is the way to life and life abundant. Forgiveness is the way of Jesus, the way of the cross. While at first glance revenge may seem much easier and more desirable, in fact it leads to bondage and death. From the place of death, vengeance, and coercive violence—from the cross—Jesus spoke words of forgiveness, pointing to the way that leads to life. At the heart of discipleship lies the painful and challenging practice of forgiveness.

Matthew tells us that Peter came and said to Jesus, "Lord, if another member of the church sins against me, how often should I forgive?" (Matthew 18:21). Jesus said to him, "Not seven times, but, I tell you, seventy-seven times" (v. 22). I cherish this answer. Jesus gives clear instructions about the importance of forgiveness as a way of life in the kingdom.

Perhaps sensing that Peter hasn't quite gotten the point, he tells a story. In the parable Jesus deftly describes our propensity to seek vengeance, to demand a righting of the scales of justice in a manner that we believe balances our accounts with others. A man experiences undeserved mercy and compassion from one to whom he owes a significant debt. Instead of shaping and defining his dealings with others by the mercy he has undeservedly received, he immediately turns to one who owes him a much smaller debt and demands the account to be paid and the debt settled.

Upon hearing what he has done, his master, who had extended him mercy, now calls him to account and hands him over for punishment. The man is in bondage to his own greed, his misguided sense of justice. He, who had been set free for life, chose the way that leads to bondage and torture. He chose not to forgive. Sadly, so many of us do the same.

In relating this story Jesus holds up a mirror for us to see our tendency to withhold the very mercy and forgiveness we have received. The only righteous judge, Jesus, says from the cross, "Forgive them." We, from our positions of self-righteousness, cry out, "Pay me what you owe." What a tragedy that we forfeit the gift of freedom because we are unable to allow the spirit of love to form us into a people who practice the abundant economy of forgiveness rather than the bankrupt market of vengeance, getting even, and settling the score. I know forgiveness is a hard road. It may take months, years, countless tears, and endless prayer to say, "I forgive you." But Jesus was clear: grace is costly and forgiveness involves the way of the cross. True life is found only on the other side of Golgotha.

Let's be very clear about what we are talking about. Forgiveness is a practice, a discipline made possible by the grace of God, not some heroic act of the will. It is something that we practice again and again, on a daily basis, until it becomes a part of who we are.

Forgiveness is not forgetting. One cannot forgive that which is forgotten. Forgiveness involves telling each other the painful truth, not to hold something over the other person but to find a way forward that breaks the cycle of eye-for-an-eye violence in which we so often find ourselves trapped. Forgiveness is not about becoming a doormat and relishing the role of victim. Forgiveness is about being victorious, freed from the horrible things others might have done to us. Likewise, forgiveness is not a strategy for turning our enemies into our friends; it is instead a grateful response to what God has done for us. We forgive others as a way of saying "thank you" to God, who in Christ has graciously forgiven us.

Finally, practicing forgiveness does not deny the possibility or the necessity of justice. Rather, it redefines justice, and ensures that it is God's peculiar brand of justice we are practicing and not the retribution and retaliation that often masquerade as justice. In calling us to forgive, Jesus offers us a different kind of justice that holds open the possibility of a new future, a way through the hurt and pain that can lead to resurrection and new life. Forgiveness is about having our lives defined by the justice of God's kingdom rather than the justice of the kingdoms of this world.

Today is the anniversary of 9/11—a day when horrible atrocities were committed in the name of God. The events of that day led to a violent response from our own nation as it pursued "justice," also in the name of God. Thousands of men, women, and children on all sides have lost their lives. Whatever we think or feel about the events of the past several years, it might be good for us to ask, "How does one follow Jesus and practice forgiveness in such a time?"

I have to be perfectly honest and say that I'm not entirely certain how to answer that question except to say that maybe Jesus knew there would be times such as these. One day on a hill by a lake, he gathered his disciples and told them to pray like this: "Forgive us our sins, as we forgive those who have sinned against us. . . ." Perhaps that is where we begin. With all the hurt, pain, shame, guilt, anger, and betrayal, perhaps that is where we should begin today. Let us pray. "Our Father . . ." (David C. Hockett)

Lectionary Commentary
Exodus 14:19-31

Earlier in the chapter Moses had exhorted the people of Israel, saying, "The LORD will fight for you, and you have only to keep still" (Exodus 14:14). Here we see the fulfillment of Moses' promise to the people. God does indeed "fight" for the people, protecting them with an angel and a cloud, providing safe passage across the sea, and destroying their pursuers—the Egyptian army. We see God's providential care for the people.

But it's important to remember that God's care for Israel is less about Israel and more about God's desires and purposes. The reader might wonder, with the Egyptians at their backs and the sea before them, how will the promise made to Abraham and Sarah be fulfilled, how will the covenant made with Moses stand? The answer—"Thus the LORD saved Israel that day" (v. 30). Once again God makes a way out of no way. Order and goodness are brought forth from chaos as the Spirit of the Lord, calling to mind the creation narrative, divides the waters and creates the possibility of a future for God's people and for all of creation.

At the sight of what God has done, even the Egyptians are moved to confess, "The LORD is fighting for them against Egypt" (14:25). In some strange way Egypt comes to recognize what Israel in slavery perhaps had forgotten—salvation belongs to God. Israel's true vocation is on the other side of the sea, where they can worship and serve the Lord their God.

Exodus 15:1b-11, 20-21

In response to the mighty acts of God, Moses and the people offer a doxology, a song of praise to God for all that God has done. "The Song of Moses," as it is often called, speaks of the radical nature of Israel's liberation. It is the Lord of all creation who is due glory and praise, not Pharaoh or any other earthly ruler. The song is also a reminder to Israel and to us that our salvation and our life together as God's people are not achieved by our cleverness or hard work, but by the gracious hand of God. Moses was an obedient servant, but it was by the right hand of God that Israel's liberation was won.

This text reminds us that our worship and our preaching should be first about God, the one God, and that our lives are to be doxological—acts of praise that point to the one in whom we live and move and have our being. Our passage ends with a question to which the answer is obvious: "Who is like you, O LORD, among the gods?" (15:11).

Romans 14:1-12

What may seem on the surface to be petty squabbling over insignificant details is in fact a serious matter to Paul. He addresses eating and abstaining, observing holy days and the like, over which fellow Christians may at times differ. The issue at stake, however, is not so much the behaviors themselves as it is the undermining of the unity of the body caused by members of the body who stand in self-righteous judgment over their brothers and sisters. One group must not uphold its particular understanding of the faith as the only standard by which faithfulness to the gospel is measured. There are obviously some behaviors that cannot be a part of the life of discipleship. There are others that Paul suggests are not essential matters in the witness of the gospel. It is important that we not allow our own personal feelings about such practices and behaviors to tempt us to judge others and thereby undermine the unity of the body.

Paul is clear God is the only judge, that each of us is accountable to God for our behavior and for how we treat others. Our lives must be defined by humility and honest acknowledgment that whether "weak" in the faith or "strong," we all are dependent upon and stand in need of the gracious mercy of a loving God. (David C. Hockett)

Worship Aids

Call to Worship

The Lord is our strength and our might and has become our salvation. Come, let us sing to the Lord, for God has triumphed gloriously. Who is like you, O Lord, among the gods? In your steadfast love you have redeemed us, and so we come to worship you.

Opening Prayer

Loving God, yours is a kingdom of love, justice, and peace. Your justice is mercy and your mercy abounds. We come to this place of worship, called by your Spirit. We come empty-handed, unable to repay the debt we owe. But you, O Lord, are merciful, and where we would demand satisfaction, you offer forgiveness. Where we would demand debts to be settled, you offer mercy. In our worship this day, may we be caught up in your life and become as merciful with one another as you have been with us, so that your reign of justice and peace may come upon the earth through Christ our Lord. Amen.

Words of Assurance

In and through our self-centered disobedience, we have amassed a debt that cannot be repaid. Were payment to be demanded of us, we would find that we are incapable of settling our accounts. But God is merciful and God's forgiveness is perfect. In Christ we are no longer debtors, but children and heirs of the immeasurable riches of God's grace. As we have been forgiven, so now let us forgive one another to the glory of God. Amen. (David C. Hockett)

Will Our Children Have Power?

Second in a Series of Four on Back to Church/Back to School

Joshua 14:6-14

Whenever I walk into a school, I'm immediately taken back in time to when I was a schoolboy. As I walk down the halls, look at the walls and

291

into the rooms, and inhale the smells, I'm overwhelmed with a flood of memories and feelings that are hard to describe. My guess is that most of us are affected in ways such as these as we move into a new school year. It's exciting and scary and lots of other things to be back in school.

One of the most exciting things about being back in school is that we learn lots of new things and discover new interests and abilities. That's how it was for twelve-year-old Harriett Beecher as she attended Litchfield Academy in Connecticut. At that stage in her life, she was beginning to get caught up in a great love for writing. She and the other students were required to turn in an essay at the end of the term. Harriett put her whole heart into that essay. She wanted it to be good.

Much to Harriett's delight, the judges awarded first prize to her essay. Moreover, the headmaster would read her essay at the graduation ceremony! Harriett waited anxiously. The day finally came, and it was a day that set the course of Harriett's life. Two things happened that she would never forget. First, when the headmaster finished reading her paper, the audience broke into applause. The second event had even greater impact on her. She turned and saw the proud smile on the face of her father, Lyman, who was pastor of the local church. She cherished her father's radiant smile the rest of her life. It lifted her up and gave her the power to meet the many challenges that lay ahead of her (see Noel B. Gerson, *Harriett Beecher Stowe* [New York: Praeger Publishers, Inc., 1976], 10).

Harriett kept writing. Eventually she married a man named Stowe, and under the name Harriett Beecher Stowe she wrote a novel called *Uncle Tom's Cabin*, one of the most influential books in American literature. Harriett Beecher's impact on our nation's history is undeniable. She had the same characteristics that almost all successful people have. She was strong, self-confident, and loving. She developed her character through contact with other strong, caring people in her family, school, and church.

Psychiatrist William Glasser says that one of our five basic human needs is our need for power and recognition (the others are survival, love and belonging, freedom, and fun; www.wglasser.com). Like our need for fun or joy, mentioned last week, this need for power and recognition is essential to good health. Without it our lives are not satisfying or productive, and they go off track.

One of my favorite biblical characters is Caleb, whose story is told in the books of Numbers and Joshua. He was one of the twelve spies Moses sent into Canaan. When the spy mission was over, only Caleb and Joshua came back believing that they and their people were strong enough to conquer the land. The majority gave in to timidity and thus wandered in the wilderness for forty more years.

Today's text takes us forty-five years down the road. Caleb comes before Joshua at Gilgal. He's now eighty-five years old but declares, "I am still as strong today as I was on the day that Moses sent me" (Joshua 14:11). In the next chapter Caleb goes up against the cities of Hebron and Debir and wins a battle that he was hindered from fighting forty-five years earlier!

Caleb always knew where his power came from. It came from God, and it had a divine purpose. All of us know, or should know, that the power that surges up from deep within us is the presence of God working in our lives. The goal of any Christian education program is much more than giving students the facts. It's giving them strength and self-worth.

Mary Ann Bird wrote a short story entitled "The Whisper Test." It's a true story from her life. She grew up with the painful knowledge that she was different. She was born with a cleft palate and other deformities; and when she started to school, her classmates made it clear that she looked and sounded different. When someone asked, "What happened to your lip?" she would say, "I fell on a piece of glass." She was convinced that no one outside her family could ever love her.

Mary Ann had a teacher in the second grade named Mrs. Leonard who was adored by all the students. Every year Mrs. Leonard gave the students a hearing test. Mary dreaded that test because she was virtually deaf in one ear. But she discovered that if she didn't press her hand tightly upon her ears as she was supposed to do, she could pass the test.

The test was simple. The students would stand by the door and cover one ear, and the teacher, sitting at her desk, would whisper something that the students would have to repeat back. One day Mary Ann was standing by that door, straining to hear Mrs. Leonard's voice. What she heard were seven words that she later believed God must have put in her teacher's mouth. Those words changed her life. Mrs. Leonard said, in her whisper, "I wish you were my little girl" (as told by Hal Brady in the sermon "Children Aren't Child's Play," FUMC, Dallas, TX, May 14, 1995).

The most powerful language spoken in any classroom or family or church is the language of affirmation. Wherever words of love and approval are uttered, children become strong. They connect with their inner selves and with others in powerful ways. They walk with the confidence of those who know who they are and what they can become. As they have been blessed by God, they go forth to be a blessing to others. (Sandy Wylie)

Worship Aids

Call to Worship (based on Psalm 46:1-7)

God is our refuge and strength,
    a very present help in trouble.
Therefore we will not fear,
    though the earth should change and tremble.
God is in the midst of the city;
    it shall not be moved.
The LORD of hosts is with us;
    the God of Jacob is our refuge.

Invocation

O God of all power and might, the world is full of your wonders and your grace. Draw near to us, we pray, and grant us the clearness of mind to worship you and the strength of body and spirit to serve you, both now and in the days ahead. Amen.

Benediction

As you have been blessed by God, go forth to be a blessing to others. May the one who has strengthened you grant you the power to do all that love requires. Go in peace. Amen. (Sandy Wylie)

SEPTEMBER 18, 2011

❧❧❧

Fourteenth Sunday after Pentecost

Readings: Exodus 16:2-15; Psalm 105:1-6, 37-45; Philippians 1:21-30; Matthew 20:1-16

Dying to Live: A Life Worth the Living
Philippians 1:21-30

The only letter of Paul not written to instruct or discipline is his letter to the church at Philippi. This church in ancient Macedonia was the first European congregation founded by Paul, the first major penetration of the gospel into Gentile territory. Traveling with Silas, Timothy, and Luke in Asia Minor on his second missionary journey, Paul receives a powerful invitation in a vision as a man standing before him urges, "Come over to Macedonia and help us" (Acts 16:9).

Paul's first converts in Philippi are Lydia, a seller of purple, and her whole household, who become the nucleus of the new church (Acts 16:15). Imprisoned when an earthquake shakes the cell, Paul brings a jailer into the faith through many amazing experiences (vv. 25-34). Paul has an intimate relationship with this church.

The Philippian congregation becomes a source of ongoing support for Paul's ministry, an example to the Corinthian church when Paul is soliciting funds to help support the Jerusalem congregation following a devastating famine. Paul's letter to the church at Philippi is really a thank-you note in return for the loving generosity of the congregation, who sent a "care package" to Paul while he was imprisoned.

Throughout this wonderful loving letter, Paul continues to point his disciples back to the true source of all that they have received, the one who sustains him in good and difficult days. Paul uses powerful language in his opening lines, "living is Christ and dying is gain" (1:21), and again in his closing comments, "I can do all things through him who strengthens me" (4:13).

Those powerful words come to mind when I think about the fastest-growing religious group in America, the "undecided denomination." People who honestly doubt the existence of a creator God continue to grow as the influence of Christianity in America declines. A conversation with one young man who said, "I don't have a reason to believe," led me to wonder what one needs to really have faith. People today seem to struggle with a reason to believe. Perhaps what we need is something worth giving our lives for. Maybe we need to believe in something for which we're willing to die.

In his best-selling book *A Purpose Driven Life*, Rick Warren reminds us that life is not about us; we are the result of a loving creator who has created us with both plan and purpose. For Paul, the bottom line begins and ends with the Creator, who out of love for the creation pursued us through God's Son, Jesus Christ. If we could ask Paul about the purpose of his life, the answer would be a resounding "Jesus Christ, and him crucified" (1 Corinthians 2:2).

What makes life worth living? Some years ago a group of scholars began studying the lives of individuals who had suffered "near-death experiences." Person after person noted that their lives were never the same following the event. We all know individuals deeply altered by experiences of cancer or heart attacks or terminal conditions. Coming face-to-face with death changes life. My mother, in the early days of a twelve-year bout with Parkinson's disease, would say to us, "You must live until you die." The problem is that many people have died long before they take their final breath.

Paul wants to encourage the congregation at Philippi with faith and optimism. He looks without fear at the adversaries they all face now and will face in the future. Paul knows he has already won, and he encourages the church to celebrate their victory as well. To live is to serve the ones he loves, continue preaching the gospel, and follow Christ. To die is to realize the fulfillment of the resurrection promise.

One reason the young man I spoke with had no reason to believe was that he had seen no one worth following. You have heard the phrases "walk the walk" and "walk the talk." Years ago, the Fellowship of Christian Athletes helped to bring that phrase into common use among high school and college athletes. In their huddles, the meaning was clear: "Practice what you preach," or more important, "Practice what you believe."

Paul reminds the church at Philippi and us to do more than merely declare allegiance to Christ; we are called to live our faith. As Saint

Francis of Assisi is reported to have said, "Preach the gospel at all times and when necessary use words."

Our parsonage sat on a large lot. During the warm-weather months, I spent hours mowing that large, beautiful lawn. Time and time again as I set out to mow that lawn I looked behind me to see our then four-year-old son pushing his toy lawn mower directly behind me. Those were "Hallmark card" moments in my life, realizing that he followed me because in his childish way he idolized his father. Those moments reminded me of the incredible responsibility I had to "walk the walk" before my three sons.

A young officer being considered for promotion stopped to purchase a newspaper. A passerby dropped some coins in the machine, took out a paper, and held the door open for the officer. "Go ahead and take one; no one will know," he offered. For a moment the officer held the door as the purchaser went his way. Finally, he closed the door, inserted his coins, and took his paper.

Later that morning, in the interview supporting his promotion, the attending general retold the newspaper story. "I watched to see what you would do. Had you taken the paper without paying, I was determined to pass you over for the promotion. You see, I am looking for men of character who live their principles even when no one is around."

The very future of the gospel is in our hands, and we never know who may be watching. Don't just talk the talk; walk the walk. (Guy Ames)

Lectionary Commentary
Exodus 16:2-15

About a month out of Egypt on their wilderness journey, the Israelites begin to complain and long for some of the amenities of even their days of slavery! They recall, not enslavement, but meat. How very quickly they have forgotten their deliverer, and instead accuse Moses and Aaron of conspiring against them. Much like those who have been rescued from a flood but blame their rescuers for not arriving sooner, these Israelites complain, "We should have died in Egypt."

The Lord tells Moses to deliver a message to the people of Israel. They shall be given bread in the morning, a dew-like substance called manna. In the evening quail will arrive. They shall be given just enough bread for each day, with twice as much on the sixth day and none on the seventh, so they must then collect enough for two days. God provides for Israel so that they shall know that God has provided. Israel will once again see God's "glory" in saving acts.

Matthew 20:1-16

The parable of the vineyard and the laborers is an extension of Jesus' earlier conversation with his disciples and the rich young man. Jesus concludes that conversation with, "But many who are first will be last, and the last will be first" (Matthew 19:30). Now Jesus sets a familiar scene for his next parable, a scene that would be enacted daily in first-century Palestine. Landowners regularly sought out workers to tend to their vineyards. A typical workday was twelve hours, so the first hires worked the full twelve hours, while the last worked about an hour. One would naturally expect wages that took into consideration the time spent in the field, but that was not the thinking of the vineyard owner in Jesus' parable. He chooses to pay all the workers the same amount.

The vineyard owner represents God, whose generous grace does not consider how long one has labored in the kingdom fields. Grace is abundant and freely given to all, even the Gentiles, the "sinners," the unclean, and the unrighteous who were commonly excluded by law-abiding Hebrews. The parable gives attention to the giver of grace rather than the recipients. God rewards according to grace, not accomplishments. Those who complain about God's generosity really do not understand the economy of the kingdom of God. (Guy Ames)

Worship Aids

Call to Worship (based on Psalm 105:1-3)

O give thanks to the LORD, call on God's name,
Make known God's deeds among all people.
Sing to the LORD, sing praises;
　tell of all God's wonderful works.
Glory in God's holy name;
　let the hearts of those who seek the LORD rejoice.

Invocation

Almighty and most merciful Lord, who has given us grace time and time again; you have called us to worship once more. Help us draw near to you in faith and lay aside the many things that keep us from truly centering on your presence. As we gather in this time of worship, we pray that you might set the inward eyes of our hearts and minds on Jesus, the pioneer and perfecter of our faith, the one who has opened the door for faith. Stir up the gifts within us and increase our faith so that the longer we are on this earth, the better we may serve you. May our obedience be more willing, our daily living more consistent, and our devotion more complete. Let us declare with the apostle Paul, "Living is Christ and dying is gain." We pray in the name of Jesus Christ, the Lord. Amen.

Benediction (based on Philippians 4:13; Hebrews 12:1-3)

Since we are surrounded by a great cloud of witnesses, let us lay aside every weight and sin that hinders us, and let us run with perseverance the race that is set before us, looking to Jesus, the pioneer and perfecter of our faith, who for the joy that God set before him endured the cross. So keep your eyes on Jesus so that you may not grow weary or lose heart, knowing that we can do all things through him who strengthens us! Amen! (Guy Ames)

Will Our Children Have Freedom?

Third in a Series of Four on Back to Church/Back to School

Luke 15:11-32

"There was a man who had two sons" (Luke 15:11). Any story that begins this way piques our interest. We know that it will likely deal with the differences between the boys. We parents know how our children spring into this world with minds of their own. No two children have the same interests and temperaments. The kind of discipline that works with one may not work with the other.

In Jesus' story, the younger son comes to his father and says something like, "Dad, I've got a big favor to ask. I want to have my inheritance now. I've got a lot of living to do, and I just can't wait any longer!" Sadly, his deeper message is that he wishes his father were dead. The father has committed the offense of living a little too long.

The son's request is outrageous in every way. In this ancient culture, land confers identity and status on a family. The boy is calling for a premature division of the land—a move that will diminish the standing and welfare of the whole family. So it's a blow directed, not just at his father, but at his older brother and the rest of the family. The family suffers disgrace. The boy will become a pariah because of his disrespect. The father will be ridiculed for letting this happen. Everyone loses.

The next frame of the story is just as shocking. Without batting an eye, the father gives his son what he wants.

Now we know how the boy's going to wind up in the "distant country" (15:13). He squanders everything "in dissolute living" (v. 13). On top of this, there's an economic recession that makes things even harder. The boy has to get a job, and the only one he can find is a job feeding pigs. By Jewish teaching the boy is now under a double curse: he's feeding pigs and working for a Gentile.

Stories like this often don't end well, but this one does. When the boy is at the end of his tolerance, a glimmer of light shines through. As Jesus puts it, he "came to himself" (15:17).

He gets to thinking about his father: "My father's hired hands are better off than I am! You know what I could do? I could just go home. Yes, a little room out back or even a corner in the barn—that would really be all right." So he departs for home and rehearses a speech about his unworthiness along the way. There is no guarantee that he will even be allowed on the land, much less given a corner in the barn.

Nothing could have prepared the son for what happens next. As he nears his father's house, muttering his speech to himself, he gets the jolt of his life. He sees his father . . . running! The older man has hiked up his robe, and he's racing toward his son at top speed. So much for dignity.

When the father reaches his son, he flings his arms around him and kisses him passionately. The son starts in on his speech, but the father interrupts and starts barking orders: "Get him an Armani suit. Give him Ferragamo loafers and a dozen shirts from Neiman Marcus. Take my own signet ring and put it on his finger. Kill our fatted calf. We'll party tonight!"

Have we got this straight? There are no lectures on morality, no "I told you so," no probationary period. There's hardly a proper repentance. The father fully reinstates his son on the spot. There's nothing but pure joy!

What is Jesus' story about? It's a story about freedom. It follows a classic plot line: Boy has freedom; boy loses freedom; boy regains freedom. Psychiatrist William Glasser says that freedom is one of our five basic human needs (the others are survival, love and belonging, power, and fun; www.wglasser.com). It's important to us to feel that we have freedom of choice in all areas of our lives, including: where to live, what to work at, whom to marry and associate with, and what to believe. In the first two sermons in this series we discussed our needs for joy and power. Alongside these we now place our need for freedom.

Nothing creates a stronger reaction in our children than the heavy hand of control. A family laughed as one of their children said to her mother defiantly, "You're not the boss of me!" Training a child in the ways of freedom is an art. We have to guide and protect, but at the same time we have to give enough slack to let the child develop independence.

The boy in Jesus' story learns one of the first lessons we have to learn about freedom: our freedom isn't just for ourselves; it's not for self-indulgence. If we decide that the point of life is to serve our bodily appetites, we're going to have a very severe taskmaster. For a time we may feel that we have freedom and happiness, but we will soon realize that we have neither.

The Bible teaches that we find true freedom in service to God and others. We find it in the building of relationships. By denying some of our wants in order to help others, we actually gain far more than we give up.

We know how much children imitate adults. They do what they see us do. If they see us acting respectfully, they will act respectfully. If they see bravery and honesty in us, they will imitate these things. That's good news, isn't it? As the seasons change and we go back to school and back to church, we have new opportunities to shape our children and thus to shape the future for all of us.

When we model service to God and others for our children, we set an enduring example. Their feet will naturally follow ours. They will learn the path that leads to joy and peace and freedom. No matter how far they may stray, they will always know the road home. (Sandy Wylie)

Worship Aids

Call to Worship (based on Galatians 5:13-14)
You were called to freedom, brothers and sisters,
   only do not use your freedom for self-indulgence.
But through love become slaves to one another.
For the whole law is summed up in a single commandment:
You shall love your neighbor as yourself.

Pastoral Prayer
Gracious God, much of your creation is in bondage. Indifference and evil are on every side of us and in us. We long for the freedom that you bring

in Jesus Christ—the freedom to serve our neighbors and be loosed from selfish desires. Grant us this freedom as we grow in your service. Amen.

Benediction

Go forth as servants of the living Savior, who frees you and sets your feet on solid ground. Serve him in gladness and sing forth his praise. Amen. (Sandy Wylie)

SEPTEMBER 25, 2011

❧❧❧

Fifteenth Sunday after Pentecost

Readings:: Exodus 17:1-7; Psalm 78:1-4, 12-16; Philippians 2:1-13; Matthew 21:23-32

Dying to Live: A Life Worth Dying For
Philippians 2:1-13

During the second century C.E., Irenaeus, the feisty bishop of Lyon, spoke out loudly against the rising tide of alternative views of the apostolic faith. The growth of gnosticism (now made famous by Dan Brown's writing and Tom Hanks's portrayal of the *Da Vinci Code* stories) threatened the life of the still-infant church.

Irenaeus argued against the ascetic approach to spirituality. Some gnostics taught that true faith demanded denying oneself the joys and pleasures of such things as sexual intimacy, laughter, fun, and food. This created a dilemma for Christian leaders, many of whom fasted from both food and sex. Irenaeus saw in the life of Jesus one who embraced the totality of life, and he declared in his classic work *Against Heresies*, "The glory of God is man fully alive!"

A few years ago, a youth group reread the Christian classic *In His Steps* by Charles Sheldon. It's a fictional account of what might happen if a group of Christians lived life by asking first the question "What would Jesus do?" These youth created an acronym, WWJD. The idea caught on and some advertisers made serious money on the concept. Bumper stickers, Bible covers, apparel, jewelry, books, and studies came out of that simple idea. Ad campaigns included: What car would Jesus drive? What food would Jesus eat? and so on ad nauseam. Sadly, the real message got lost in the marketing frenzy: How would Jesus live? This is what Paul shares with the Philippian congregation. "Let the same mind be in you that was in Christ Jesus" (Philippians 2:5).

I was a PK (preacher's kid), the son of a preacher who was also the son of a preacher. Not once did our father tell us to behave because we were preacher's kids. Nonetheless, each time I left the house for a significant outing, my father unabashedly reminded me, "Don't forget who you are." By that he said so very much. He reminded me to remember that I represented our family and the integrity of our name. Many times our parents said, "I don't care what other families may be doing, we are not those families; this is the way we do things." Dad reminded me that our home had standards: trust, and consequences for failing to maintain those standards. As I grew older and took on the personal calling of a Christ-follower, Dad also reminded me that I bore the responsibility of being a witness for Christ.

On one occasion I announced that I was going to see a particular movie that was quite controversial. Dad merely said to me, "You can see that if you like, but I don't really believe that the material is in keeping with your faith and your convictions." I did not go.

A young father pulled his children out of a local Christian after-school program. When asked why, he replied, "I don't want them to be overly influenced by a religious group. I want them to be free of biases about faith so that when they are adults they can choose freely for themselves." As he walked away from that conversation, he passed drug dealers on the street corners, prostitutes plying their trade, gangs organizing in the alleys, and a passed-out drug addict on the stairs outside his apartment. How naive it was for him to assume that his children were not under the influence of groups and events outside the Christian program.

The Philippian congregation delivered a care package to their pastor, most likely with words of concern for both his health and the future of the church. How does Paul say thank you? He asks them to remember who they are. Although he knows the fiery storm is yet to come, Paul is filled with gratitude.

Paul's challenge to the larger question, "How then shall we live?" is, "Who do you want to follow?" Don't you love that attitude? It's the kind of life I want for myself, but the truth is that most of us, me included, rush first to complain, criticize, blame, or whine when we face difficulties.

I'm convinced that the reason Paul could live a life so abandoned to Christ was that he had come face-to-face with the profound and humbling power of the cross. Too often, we miss the meaning of the cross. I believe this little thank-you note to Philippi reminds us of that meaning and tells us who Paul really is: jealous, not for himself, but for the gospel;

single-minded, not for a religious organization, but for the disciples whom he has taught; and harsh toward those who arrogantly believe they are a cut above others but tenderhearted toward those who humbly serve.

For Paul, the heart of the incarnation is not the manger or the resurrection; the centerpiece of the incarnation is found in the cross. The one who was blameless took on death as the ultimate expression of God's love for us. Jesus experienced complete abandonment to God, the total loss of self. I think that's why Paul describes Jesus' ultimate incarnational act as the humiliation of the cross. Real meaning—authentic humanity—is achieved through a life worth dying for. (Guy Ames)

Lectionary Commentary
Exodus 17:1-7

In the wilderness of Sin, the Israelites experience water shortages and, once again, begin to quarrel with Moses. In fact, they threaten to stone Moses if they don't receive water. As in the earlier "food fights," they accuse Moses of deliberately putting them in harm's way. With the people demanding some action, Moses takes their complaints to the Lord.

God directs Moses to go to a rock, or "the rock at Horeb" (Exodus 17:6), and strike the rock with his staff. God promises to deliver water. One can almost picture an artesian outpouring from the rock as the people once again watch the incredible provision of their deliverer. Moses then gives the desert watering hole two new names: *Meribah*, which means "argument" or "strife"; and *Massah*, which means "testing." In this context, it is the Israelites testing whether or not God is truly with them.

Matthew 21:23-32

Jesus, in the last week before the crucifixion, converses with the rising tide of criticism from the religious rulers. They raise questions about his authority. Jesus pushes back and asks them to make a stand on John the Baptist's authority. Naturally the chief priests and elders are afraid to answer this question. If they answer that John's authority was divine, then they face the political fallout of suggesting that King Herod and his illegitimate wife killed God's messenger. If they answer that his authority was not divine, then they face the wrath of the popular public who have lionized John as a martyr to the faith, one who stood faithfully for the highest principles of the law. Either answer places them in political jeopardy. Consequently, they take the politically expedient approach of refusing to answer at all. Jesus, knowing the predicament and their lack of principled leadership, then refuses to answer their question.

But his parable that follows goes straight to the heart of the issue. The son who refuses the father but then acts faithfully is, in fact, a faithful son. The son who says, "Why of course, Dad, I'll mow the lawn," and then doesn't lift a finger to do the work is unfaithful. This is exactly what the religious elite, the Pharisees, scribes, and Sanhedrin, have done. They have taken advantage of their prized positions, giving lip service to the faith without lifting the load and doing the work. (Guy Ames)

Worship Aids

Call to Worship

Rejoice in the Lord always.
  I will say it again: Rejoice!
Let your gentleness be evident to all.
  The Lord is near.
Do not be anxious about anything, but in everything,
  by prayer and petition, with thanksgiving,
  present your requests to God.
And the peace of God, which transcends all understanding,
  will guard your hearts and your minds in Christ Jesus.

Litany (based on Philippians)

I thank my God every time I remember you. In all my prayers for all of you, I always pray with joy because of your partnership in the gospel, being confident of this, that he who began a good work in you will carry it on to completion until the day of Christ Jesus.
To live is Christ and to die is gain.
If you have any encouragement from being united with Christ, any comfort from his love, any fellowship with the Spirit, any tenderness and compassion, then make my joy complete by being like-minded, having the same love, being one in spirit and purpose.
We can do everything through him who gives us strength.
Do nothing out of selfish ambition or vain conceit, but in humility consider others better than yourselves. Each of you should look not only to your own interests, but also to the interests of others.
Have the same attitude as that of Christ Jesus:

Who, being in very nature God, did not consider equality with God
something to be grasped,
**but made himself nothing, taking the very nature of a servant, being
made in human likeness.**
And being found in appearance as a man, he humbled himself and
became obedient to death—even death on a cross!
**Therefore God exalted him to the highest place and gave him the name
that is above every name, that at the name of Jesus every knee should
bow, in heaven and on earth and under the earth, and every tongue
should confess that Jesus Christ is Lord, to the glory of God. Amen.**
(Guy Ames)

Will Our Children Have Faith?

Fourth in a Series of Four on Back to Church/Back to School

1 Samuel 3:1-10

A Hebrew woman named Hannah was barren. Hebrew theology
believed that there were three parties to any conception: the mother, the
father, and God. If a couple couldn't have children, it was a sign of divine
disapproval—reflected on the woman, not the man. Of course, times
have changed. Through the eyes of modern medicine we see things very
differently now. But this story occurred long ago.

So we see Hannah weeping in the temple and pleading with God for a
child. Any child that she has, she will give back to God to be in God's
service. Lo and behold, Hannah conceives and bears a son! She waits
until Samuel is weaned, then takes him to Shiloh and gives him to the
older priest.

Today's text takes us several years down the road when Samuel is older.
It begins with the announcement that "the word of the LORD was rare in
those days; visions were not widespread" (1 Samuel 3:1). This is evidently
a very low time in the religious life of the Hebrew people. The priest Eli
is a descendant of the priestly family at Shiloh. We are not told much
about Eli except that he is quite old.

However, we are told plenty about Eli's sons, Hophni and Phinehas.
The kindest word that the writer of 1 Samuel applies to them is
"scoundrels" (2:12). God is thoroughly fed up with these boys. Evil things
are going on in the temple, and there is no relief in sight. So God's first
commandment to Samuel is for him to tell the sons of Eli that they are
all washed up. But that is only the beginning. Samuel becomes the most

powerful man in all Israel. Kings are powerful, but Samuel is the king-maker. No individual becomes king without Samuel's blessing.

We can't read the Scriptures without being struck by the importance of children. Children are always a central part of God's plan. They become the agents of new beginnings: the baby Moses hidden in the bul-rushes, the boy Samuel, the boy Jeremiah, the manger of Bethlehem . . . so many chapters in biblical history begin with the birth of a child. God has this startling way of entering human history through our children, who become the sign of hope and renewal.

Some theologians have been telling us for a long time that we now live in a secular age. They point out that God speaks in the marketplace and in political events and in unexpected places. But God speaks in another place too—in the sanctuary among the people of God. Although God raises up a lot of unlikely prophets, God also raises up those such as Samuel and Isaiah, who are brought up in the sanctuary—those who from their birth are given to God.

It's disheartening that many decades-old congregations can't name a single person who has entered ministry from their ranks. It isn't an acci-dent that some churches produce more full-time Christian workers than others do. In such churches we usually find members who have excep-tional vision and commitment and who have a "green thumb" with children.

In 1976 John Westerhoff wrote a book called *Will Our Children Have Faith?* (from which I've borrowed the sermon title). Notice that the title is not "Will Our Children Have Knowledge?" Westerhoff says that the end of the church's work with children isn't so much knowledge as it is faith. Faith is essential to Christian life.

This is the last of four sermons in which we have been discussing the things that are vital to our children and to all of us. Up to now we've dealt with the basic human needs that William Glasser identifies in his "Choice Theory" (survival, love and belonging, power, freedom, and fun; www.wglasser.com). Unfortunately, Glasser doesn't include a specifically religious component in his theory, but we Christians might substitute "faith" for his items of "survival" and "love and belonging." Faith is the vital element that makes these others possible. So we must add faith to the list!

Now some might think that acquiring knowledge will help us with these other vital elements. Knowledge is good, and it's necessary. But in itself it guarantees nothing. People have all kinds of knowledge that they never apply or that they ignore. Knowledge has no power to direct our will or make us well. What we need is faith! Faith is the engine that powers Christian people.

We express the difference between knowledge and faith by saying that knowledge is taught, while faith is caught. People get faith primarily in two ways: by hearing it proclaimed and by being around faith-filled people. The family and the church are the natural workshops in which we and our children put together our faith. We need both.

Paul says that "faith comes from what is heard" (Romans 10:17). If we spend any time around children, we know that they pick up an amazing assortment of information, and they assemble it in fascinating ways. They are often better listeners than adults are. Though we prepare Sunday school lessons, worship, and sermons with great care, we can't quite predict what children are going to take away. We can be sure, however, that when we earnestly speak the language of faith, hope, and love in our churches and in our families, the effect will not be lost on even the youngest.

Jesus was always looking for faith. We see this in the healing stories when he asks again and again: "Do you have faith?" Faith is what gets people well. It's what gives them a future. Jesus' concern about faith even extended to the boundaries of history. One day he said to his disciples, "When the Son of Man comes, will he find faith on earth?" (Luke 18:8). That's a haunting question for us as we move into this new season of growth and possibility. (Sandy Wylie)

Worship Aids

Invocation

O God of all joy, power, and freedom, be for us the source and strengthener of our faith. Come to us in the quiet spaces of this hour and tune our hearts to your will for us. Remind us, we pray, of who we are and what we need to be about. Amen.

Prayer of Confession

O gracious God, you call us to faith and obedience; but too often we give in to doubt, fear, and timidity. We have taken the road of low expectations and light risk. Forgive us, we pray. Turn us toward your sufficiency and strengthen us in faith and witness. Amen.

Words of Assurance (based on 2 Corinthians 12:9)

Hear these words of assurance and be at peace: "My grace is sufficient for you, for power is made perfect in weakness." Amen.

Benediction

Go forth as believers of the gospel. May our gracious God strengthen your faith and lift your spirit. May God's blessings rest upon you and those whom you love and serve. Amen. (Sandy Wylie)

OCTOBER 2, 2011

❧❧❧

Sixteenth Sunday after Pentecost

Readings: Exodus 20:1-4, 7-9, 12-20; Psalm 19; Philippians 3:4b-14;
Matthew 21:33-46

Dying to Live: Losing in Order to Win
Philippians 3:4b-14

Mildred always dressed like a rainbow. Not a particularly attractive woman, she wore designer clothes, pounds of makeup, and offered her faith to everyone she met. She had come to call on the new preacher's family. In the course of the visit, she told story after story of answered prayer. She capped it off by telling us she had heard of Dad through a parishioner from my father's previous appointment, and she prayed that God would send us there. As she left I asked incredulously, "That wasn't true, was it, Dad?"

During our four years at that church, I watched this outlandish Christian woman model abandonment to God in ways I had never before witnessed. Each Sunday evening when it was time for words of witness, Mildred would jump to her feet with words of thanksgiving for God's great grace. "I'm not what I ought to be," she would always say, "but thank God, I'm not what I used to be."

After prayers and a devotional message at our last Holy Thursday Communion service at the church, the invitation was given: "Ye that do truly and earnestly repent of your sins and are in love with your neighbor and intend to lead a new life, draw near with faith and take this holy sacrament unto yourself." As I knelt at the railing, Mildred knelt beside me. As the bread was placed in her hands she began to weep, the deep tears of remorse and forgiveness. Her weeping became, for me, a holy song of gratitude and sheer love for the one who had delivered her from a life of human indignity. I never really knew her past, but somehow I knew that Mildred had seen the worst of the human condition, and somewhere along her journey Jesus Christ rescued her.

From time to time I meet people who declare that they have no regrets. I have come to suspect that these individuals either live in perpetual denial or have conveniently chosen to forget the indiscretions of their past. Paul never forgot his path. Conversion for Paul never could erase his sense of shame and indignity at having demeaned Christ and having injured the young church through torture and execution. If God could forgive the persecutor of the early church, then indeed God's grace was large enough for the gravest of sinners. Paul had been humbled by the cross.

For Paul, the greatest danger was not the threat of death but the ever-present "false teachers," who lay in wait until Paul had moved on to another town. These well-meaning teachers wanted folks to be good Hebrews before they could become Christians. Paul contended that salvation is available to all because of Christ's work, and that no amount of work on our part can bring peace with God. If anyone qualified for salvation based upon heritage, Saul of Tarsus had the bloodline. But he refers to those Hebrew accolades as "loss" and garbage in comparison to the "surpassing value" of knowing Jesus Christ (Philippians 3:8).

Paul could live a life abandoned to Christ because he had come face-to-face with the profound power of the risen Christ. He calls us to the simplicity of surrender to Christ. Similar to the opening lines of a 12-step program, Paul "came to believe that he was powerless over (you name the addiction)." This is the abandonment of one who could not do for himself, but who called on the one alone who could put his life right.

Somewhere between his conversion on the road to Damascus and his prison letter to the Philippian church, Paul faced his failures. Perhaps it was in those dark days after his ride to Damascus, or alone as an outcast from the infant church in the Syrian Desert. Paul came to grips with his failings and inadequacies and discovered true meaning and authentic humanity.

I know something of that struggle. I reached a point when everything seemed lost. Day by day our home, instead of being a haven of blessing and peace, was a battlefield. Months had passed without one day in which mental illness had not reigned supreme behind the walls of the preacher's home. No doctor seemed to offer any hope. I had no idea how to help my wife or my children. Desperate, I found myself in a meeting of men who had gone through similar family circumstances. I can't tell you how uncomfortable I was because of my need to go to a meeting like that. . . . I really should have been lecturing those men, shouldn't I? Then I began to weep unashamedly; the years of stress, the months of brutal living, came up through every pore of my being. I realized that I could not do for myself what was needed, and there was something powerfully freeing about being among others who would hold me up when I couldn't stand.

Christian martyr Dietrich Bonhoeffer chastised the church in his book *The Cost of Discipleship*. His argument that the church had become the dispenser of cheap grace still rings loud. Cheap grace demands nothing in return for God's costliest gift. Jesus simply said, "Those who find their life will lose it, and those who lose their life for my sake will find it" (Matthew 10:39).

The twenty-first-century church in the United States needs a conversion. We need conversion from believing that we can put things right, and that we are in control. We need fresh abandonment to God, who can work in us all possibilities. God can set us free from having to know where the Spirit is leading the church, and give us renewed conviction that God's abundant love holds us. May God make us willing to be lost even for the sake of Christ. The future is completely uncertain—we don't have a written rule book for successful churches or living in this day. No, all we have is the risen Christ. (Guy Ames)

Lectionary Commentary
Exodus 20:1-4, 7-9, 12-20

On Mount Sinai, Moses receives commandments from God. Accompanying the delivery of these commandments is a grand display of light and sound that naturally frightens the people. A commentary regarding the second and fourth commandments is found in Exodus 20:5-6, 10-11. The giving of these ten "words" (for each commandment is a single Hebrew word) is the climax of the exodus salvation event. The challenges before Pharaoh, the ten plagues, the passover, the Red Sea crossing and deliverance, and God's provision in the wilderness all lead to this climactic giving of the law. This is the moment that Israel moves from purely a nomadic people to the beginnings of a nation.

These ten laws form the foundation of the Judeo covenant and of what we know as the Judeo-Christian understanding of relationships with God and one another. Jesus notes that the law can be summarized into two parts: "'Love the LORD your God' . . . and '[love] your neighbor as yourself'" (Luke 10:27). The Ten Commandments can easily be divided into these two parts; the first four relate to our worship of God, and the last six refer to human relationships.

Matthew 21:33-46

The parable of the landowner and the wicked tenants continues the theme of Jesus' conversation with the rich young man. "The last will be first, and the first will be last" (Matthew 20:16) is a notion that challenged the general religious economy of Jesus' era and continues to challenge that of our own time. The parable points a finger at the religious elite of Jerusalem. As the story unfolds, the Pharisees know that Jesus is speaking about the unfaithful history of Israel, who refused the witness of prophets, killed God's messengers, and now deny the witness of Jesus, whom some have called the Messiah.

The heart of the parable is the wicked and violent way that stewards of the law and the temple have failed through the centuries to acknowledge God's clear message of justice and righteousness. Now the Son has come to give a clear message, and the attitude is still the same. These men of power will not stand much longer for this kind of teaching. (Guy Ames)

Worship Aids

Call to Worship (based on Psalm 19)

The law of the LORD is perfect, it renews the soul;
The decrees of the LORD are sure, making wise the simple;
God's precepts are right, rejoicing our hearts;
The commandments of the LORD are clear, enlightening our eyes;
The ordinances of the LORD are true and righteous altogether.
All: As we gather in worship and praise,
   let the words of our mouths
   and the meditations of our hearts
   be acceptable to you, O LORD, our Rock and our redeemer.

Prayer of Confession

Almighty God, our gracious redeemer and friend, we raise up prayers of confession in the tradition of the church throughout the ages. Truthfully, though, O God, we are embarrassed to admit our true sins and thoughts before you. We come to church with our best "Sunday go to meeting" faces, knowing that our faith and our lives don't really measure up to the standard that we profess. The truth is, God, we have not kept the faith the way you intended. Instead of trusting you, we worry. Instead of thanking you in all circumstances, we complain and even cast blame on others for our discomfort. There are days when we don't want anyone to know that we are Christians because of the ways we have acted and the things we have said.

Forgive us, O God, and free us from the denial that keeps us from honestly confessing our weaknesses. Forgive us for the way in which we have made your grace seem cheap by our lack of commitment and gratitude. We take comfort, Lord, in knowing that you have walked where we walk; we know you understand our lives, and we ask you to strengthen our resolve that we might live as those who have given up self to follow Jesus Christ. We pray together in the name of Christ, who died for our sins. Amen.

Words of Assurance (Unison, based on Philippians 3:12-14)

We have not already obtained perfection or reached the goal, but we press on to make it our own because Christ Jesus has made us his own. Forgetting what lies behind and straining forward to what lies ahead, we press on toward the goal for the prize of the heavenly call of God in Christ Jesus. Amen. (Guy Ames)

Something to Sing About

First in a Series of Four on Singing the Apocalypse: Hymns in Revelation

Revelation 4

The book of Revelation is without a doubt the strangest book in the New Testament. The apocalyptic form of writing does not lend itself to literal and straightforward interpretation, which tends to lead people accustomed to taking what is written at face value either to reject the book out of hand, or simply to ignore its existence. Others, whose religious understandings of reality tend to focus primarily on "end times," use the strange and obscure passages of Revelation as a basis for timetables to predict when and how existence as we know it will play out. Some simply use this book as supporting evidence for their private religious eccentricities.

The great Reformation leader Martin Luther did not think this book should even be in the New Testament. He placed it at the end of the New Testament, where it remains today. Ulrich Zwingli was equally doubtful that the book belonged in the New Testament.

Most Christians, including learned scholars of the Bible, find the book of Revelation to be generally difficult and in places absolutely puzzling. But in spite of the inherent difficulties with this New Testament apocalypse, many thoughtful Christians find it to be meaningful scripture when studied in the light of the historical setting in which it was written. They understand it as a classic piece of literature, written in a form that was commonly understood and accepted by our Jewish forebears.

Apocalyptic literature, such as the book of Daniel, was a most useful tool of bringing hope to the dispossessed and desperate people of God in the Old Testament. Revelation served the same purpose for early Christians in the darkest and most desperate time of their faith. When all seemed to be lost and there was no hope on the horizon, this form of writing saved people from ultimate despair.

When the reign of David ended, the fortunes of the Jews, God's chosen people, fell dramatically. When all the great promises God made to the Jewish people seemed beyond fulfillment in this world, the apocalyptic writings refocused their expectations. Their hope for justice was in a cataclysmic end to the present world and in the arrival of the Messiah, who would reestablish the world in keeping with God's ancient promises. The divided kingdom would be reunited. The people of God would become one. The Jews who were scattered over the world would return to Jerusalem. The Jews divided history into two parts: the present age and the age to come.

The book of Revelation appropriates an Old Testament concept of reality as an instrument of hope for the early Christians whose situation was very much like the dispossessed and desperate post-Davidic Jews. The Jews looked for the coming of the Messiah. The early Christians looked for the return of the Messiah. In both cases, the arrival of the Messiah would mark the end of the present age of persecution, injustice, and wickedness and introduce a whole new age in which fortunes would be reversed. The wicked would be punished, losing not only their power and wealth but also their lives.

The first readers of the book of Revelation found reason to be faithful unto death because unspeakable joy and happiness awaited them in the world to come. The adversity of this brief and transitory life was a small price to pay for eternal life in the presence of God. The promise of rich rewards in heaven also runs like a golden thread through the letters of Paul.

During his imprisonment he wrote to the Philippians: "For to me, living is Christ and dying is gain. If I am to live in the flesh, that means fruitful labor for me; and I do not know which I prefer. I am hard pressed between the two: my desire is to depart and be with Christ, for that is far better; but to remain in the flesh is more necessary for you" (Philippians 1:21-24).

The book of Revelation takes this thought and expands it in classic apocalyptic form. The Christians may not have had much to sing about in the travail of this present age, but when the writer of Revelation wrote of looking up at heaven and seeing an open door, and hearing a voice like a trumpet saying, "Come up here, and I will show you what must take place after this" (4:1), it was something to sing about.

Those of us who face little or no adversity, and who have no personal acquaintance with martyrdom, may find it difficult to get excited by the fourth chapter of Revelation. But if we were facing persecution and death every day for our Christian convictions, getting a peek through that open door would put hope in our hearts and a song on our lips.

Jesus is coming, and that is something to sing about. A few years ago, my smart-aleck daughter put a large-lettered plaque on my office door that reads: "Jesus is coming, look busy." "Busy" is okay, but to the early Christians, the message of Revelation was: "Jesus is coming, take courage and hang on." (Thomas Lane Butts)

Worship Aids

Invocation

Dear God, here we are again, needing a fill-up for our spiritual tanks. Faith, hope, and courage are all running low. May the Scripture, sermon, songs, prayers, and the touch of friends become fuel for the journey ahead. In the good name of Jesus. Amen.

Words of Assurance

The Lord Jesus, who calmed the storm on the Sea of Galilee, can calm the storms in your life too. Take courage and place your trust in him.

Benediction

Remember the words you have heard today and repeat them. Remember the songs you have heard today and sing them. Forget the fears you have left behind and take courage. Forget the sins you have confessed and be forgiven. Go in peace. Amen. (Thomas Lane Butts)

OCTOBER 9, 2011

❦❦❦❦

Seventeenth Sunday after Pentecost

Readings: Exodus 32:1-14; Psalm 106:1-6, 19-23; Philippians 4:1-9;
Matthew 22:1-14

Think of These
Philippians 4:1-9

Everyone needs encouragement, if only because the occasions of *dis-couragement* (loss of heart, loss of confidence, loss of conviction) are endless. It seems that anything we undertake for Christ and his kingdom is frontally assaulted or gradually falls prey to the inertia that overtakes those who lose heart for a project dear to them but less dear to others. We no longer have the resources to make the effort to maintain ardor amid setbacks and betrayals. For instance, those among us concerned with environmental pollution begin to feel that what is hugely important to them, other people find insignificant. Only fresh heart, encouragement, can keep our zeal aflame, our spirits from bitterness, and our patience resilient as we continue to pursue what we know God has given us to do.

Paul encourages his readers in Philippi on many fronts; not least, he encourages them to resist mind-pollution, and therefore to resist heart-pollution. "Whatever is true," he says, "whatever is honorable...just...pure...pleasing...commendable...think about these things" (Philippians 4:8). When Paul writes "Think about these things," he doesn't mean ponder them now and then; reflect on them once in a while; mull them over when nothing else is occupying your mind.

"Think about these things" means hold them up; hold them up in your mind; soak your imagination in them. "Whatever is true...honorable...just...pure...lovely...gracious" (4:8 RSV); steep yourselves in all this until it's fixed in your mind and heart and bloodstream. Whatever is fixed in our minds and hearts and bloodstreams will effervesce through us for the rest of our lives. When we wake up, when we fall asleep, when our minds are relaxed and unguarded, when we "let down" at the end of the day or haven't yet "geared up" at the start of the day, when we are all alone, even when we lie in bed week after week as we wait to die; what's going to flood into our minds and soak our hearts? Precisely what we've held up in our minds for years.

Everyone agrees that reason is part of the definition of humanity. In other words, reason is essential to being human. Where we are frequently one-sided, however, is our restricting reason to *reasoning*. We assume that reasoning is thinking deductively or inductively. One instance of deductive thinking is: "All humans are mortal; Socrates is human; therefore, Socrates is mortal." Inductive thinking is what we do when we experiment scientifically. Having performed many experiments and made many observations, we conclude that water consists of two parts hydrogen and one part oxygen.

The mistake we make is assuming that deductive and inductive thinking are all there is to reason. We forget that there's yet another kind of thinking: pictorial thinking, imagistic thinking, everything that fills up our imaginations. At the level of scientific thinking, a child opens an encyclopedia and reads, "Horse: an herbivorous quadruped that runs on one toe." Perfectly true. But at the level of the imagination (where children live) the child thinks *black stallion*. Then there swims into the child's mind a wonderful assortment of images around the black stallion: adventure, danger, affection, strength, loyalty.

Years later, the child, now an adult, hears at one level of reason such expressions as "immigrant," "New American," "refugee." At another level of reason, this time the level of imagination, he or she is flooded with negative images that foster contempt and hatred; these images are purely destructive.

Let's be honest: we adults live in our imaginations far more than we live in purely deductive or inductive reasoning. So, what are the images that swim through our heads night and day? What are the images that we foster in one another and nourish in ourselves? Paul knows that we live chiefly in our imaginations. For this reason he urges us to hold up that which is true (always a good place to start), just, honorable, pure, kind, gracious, lovely, and commendable. Soak your imagination in things with these qualities because these images are going to effervesce night and day, bubbling up from your unconscious mind to your conscious and then back down to your unconscious where they shape you when you aren't even aware of it. The apostle is profound here: abstract reasoning doesn't govern our minds; concrete images—pictures—govern our minds.

When we hear the word *true*, I wonder what concrete images come instantly to mind? When I hear the word *godly*, the image that comes to me automatically is sitting with a certain man in his living room. The fellow I speak of was a former professor of New Testament at a major North American seminary. He was the most transparently godly, unaffectedly godly, compellingly godly person I have ever met. I think of the man every day. In his natural, credible, transparent, uncontrived manner, he said to me (among many other things), "Victor, if we genuinely fear God, we shall never have to be afraid of him." (Think about that; think about that every day.)

"Whatever is just, whatever is fair—think about it," writes the apostle. Fair? One day when I was in my last year of undergraduate studies I was discussing World War II with my father. I began to speak disdainfully of German history, German people, and German military personnel. My father didn't rebuke me or argue with me. Instead he told me a story about Winston Churchill. When General Erwin Rommel's forces were hammering the British Eighth Army in North Africa, hammering the Brits so badly that the Brits were on the point of going under, a British member of Parliament rose in the House of Commons and spoke contemptuously of the German general.

Churchill took it for as long as he could, then he leaped to his feet and shouted, "I will not permit you to speak such villainies about so fine a soldier." That's all my father said. He had hung up in my mind, in my imagination, a picture I shall never be without—"whatever is fair."

Whatever is just, whatever is pure, whatever is commendable, Paul says, "Think on it." He means "Catch the vision of it." Corrie ten Boom, the Dutch woman who survived Ravensbruck, the forced labor camp (and death camp), years afterward told a story about her sister, Betsie, who didn't survive. One day the two sisters were unloading boxcars when a guard, angry at Betsie's low productivity (she was very ill), cut her with his whip. Corrie was enraged at seeing her sister struck and bleeding, but Betsie put her hand over the wound and cried, "Don't look at it, Corrie; don't look at it. Look at Jesus."

"Whatever is..." You fill it in. Think about it. Catch the vision of it. Fill your imagination with it. Because as it is with our imaginations, so it is with us. (Victor Shepherd)

Lectionary Commentary
Exodus 32:1-14

While Moses is on Sinai receiving, on behalf of his people, the "Ten Words" that the world will never again be without, the people are fast forgetting the God who rescued them from bondage, misery, and hopelessness in Egypt and who gave them a land, a future, and a nation; above all, who gave them nothing less than the divine self. The treachery of the human heart finds the same people ungrateful, unperceptive, and disobedient. Disdaining the true and living God who can be heard (a characteristic of the Holy One of Israel is that he speaks) for an idol that can only be seen, the people exchange truth for a lie, reality for illusion, and obedience for rebellion. They jettison the God whom they are supposed to serve for a deity they believe they can control. They want to throw off God, in whose image they have been made, for an idol they can make in their own image. Submitting to the Lord strikes them as demeaning, while fashioning a deity seems to be a sign of creativity and freedom.

Moses recognizes that God is rightfully angry, even as he knows that God's anger, unrelieved, will end in the destruction of the people. For this reason Moses pleads with God to "remember" (Exodus 32:13) God's promises to Abraham and Isaac and Israel (Jacob), where *remember* has the Hebrew force of making an event in the past the operative reality in the present. In other words, as God remembers those covenant promises, God will spare a recalcitrant people, not because they deserve it, but because God's covenant mercy unfailingly brings to God's people a boon beyond their merit.

Matthew 22:1-14

Under no circumstances should this passage be regarded as counseling ecclesiastical coercion. In its history, the church, impatient with God's schedule for bringing people to faith in Jesus Christ through the church's mission, has craved seeing something happen more quickly (if not more dramatically) and has attempted to take out of God's hand what in truth is invariably God's alone: the work of the Holy Spirit. When the church, thinking *it* has to convert people, attempts to do what *God alone* can do (since only the Spirit can turn the human heart to God), it commits two sins at once.

First, it announces that in the name of God it doesn't believe in God—since it now assumes that God can't do the work God has pledged to do; and second, it persecutes all who don't agree. The persecution may be physical, institutional, social, or psychological, but it is persecution nonetheless. Witness and evangelism are the church's work; conversion is God's work.

The parable brings before the reader a crisis that cannot be avoided; namely, when an invitation to the kingdom is issued, all other earthly concerns—entirely legitimate in themselves—are radically relativized. While it is easy to recognize the bad as the enemy of the good, only the kingdom-sighted can recognize that the good (*good* because God-ordained—e.g., marriage or proper burial accorded the dead) is qualitatively distinct from the kingdom. For this reason there is no excuse for not hearing, heeding, and happily acknowledging the invitation to the kingdom that is also and always nothing less than a summons to the kingdom.

The "robe" that rightly admits one to the wedding banquet is said elsewhere in scripture to be the righteousness of Christ; in "putting on our Lord," we clothe ourselves with his righteousness and therein clothe ourselves with a "new self" in "righteousness and holiness" (Ephesians 4:24). Therein we are qualified, or made fit, for the messianic banquet to which we have been invited. (Victor Shepherd)

Worship Aids

Call to Worship

The apostle Paul writes, "You know the generous act of our Lord Jesus Christ, that though he was rich, yet for your sakes he became poor, so that by his poverty you might become rich" (2 Corinthians 8:9). Our Lord has humbled himself in order that he might exalt us. In this hour of worship let us humble ourselves before our humiliated and exalted Lord, only to find ourselves exalted with him and cherished by him forever and ever. Amen.

Prayer of Approach

Eternal God, in this time of worship, acquaint us once again with the riches of your gospel in all its splendor and profundity and power. Acquaint us once again with our fellow believers, whose suffering is as little known to us as ours is to them, and with our own unutterable need, for in admitting it without dissembling we shall find in this moment and in this fellowship all that your compassion has appointed to meet our need, relieve us of our distress, and cause our hearts to sing in gratitude. Amen. (Victor Shepherd)

Perpetual Doxology

Second in a Series of Four on Singing the Apocalypse: Hymns in Revelation

Revelation 4:6b-11

According to the prophet of Patmos, there is a lot of singing going on in heaven. In no other book in the Bible, other than Psalms, is there so much music. If you do not love music, heaven is no place to be. It is not a matter of an anthem here and there; it is perpetual. The only exception to the singing without ceasing is the occasion of the opening of the seventh seal. "When the Lamb opened the seventh seal, there was silence in heaven for about half an hour" (Revelation 8:1). Other than that occasion, there is nonstop singing in heaven. It is not music that is piped in, like elevator music; it is live!

John does not offer a wordy description of how he was transported through the open door that he was called upon to enter. He simply writes: "At once I was in the Spirit" (Revelation 4:2a). He was suddenly in the throne room of the Great God Almighty. The one who is seated on the throne is not named, but the identity is obvious. The spectacular throne room scene is composed of symbolism and creatures from the Old Testament, primarily from Ezekiel and Isaiah. The scene is breathtaking and mysterious. A review of the literature interpreting the identity and meaning of the creatures and the physical arrangement of the throne room shows that the interpretations are far from universally consistent. Identifying and interpreting each item and aspect of the room is not nearly as important as feeling the overpowering impression of the scene. It is important to see that God is at the center. God is being given the highest and most elaborate praise and adulation that John can possibly find words to describe. He borrows from past apocalyptic visions and adds his impressions. This scene does not beg to be described so much as to be felt.

The four living creatures sing an unending doxology of praise. They sing without ceasing, day and night. They are joined by the twenty-four elders who fall before the one on the throne, casting their crowns before the throne and giving voice to their own doxology. What a marvelous sight and sound to see and hear! One of the great hymns of praise, which is found in most every Christian hymnal, is "Holy, Holy, Holy! Lord God Almighty" (Reginald Heber). Each stanza begins with "Holy, holy, holy!" The lyrics are the words and thoughts from these two doxologies in Revelation 4:8-11.

The holiness of God is praised. God is not like humans. God is of a different order. Isaiah wrote:

> For my thoughts are not your thoughts,
>   nor are your ways my ways, says the LORD.
> For as the heavens are higher than the earth,
>   so are my ways higher than your ways
>   and my thoughts than your thoughts. (Isaiah 55:8-9)

God is inexplicably different. We are moved to awe by the mysterious difference of God. The above-cited hymn has a line that captures that thought: "Though the darkness hide thee, / though the eye of sinful man thy glory may not see." Thus we sing with the four living creatures who repeat this doxology night and day, without ceasing. The twenty-four elders clad in white express their awe and praise by falling before the one who sits on the throne and casting their crowns before God.

Several years ago, I was guest preacher in a church on Communion Sunday. The usual manner in which United Methodist Christians receive this holy sacrament is to kneel (if they are able). I was momentarily thrown off my routine of administering the sacrament when a woman prostrated herself full-length before the altar and reached her hand up to receive the elements. Although this was shockingly unusual to me at the moment, upon reflection, I reasoned that she was more properly reverent before the altar than those of us who kneeled or stood. I think that if she had been wearing a hat she would have cast it before the altar. Complete surrender of the self before God is proper, in whatever way we are able to offer it.

The four living creatures praise God for God's omnipotent power. What a comfort it must have been to the persecuted and powerless Christians who first read this document to know that the final chapter of history would be written, not by the Romans, but by almighty God.

The perpetual singers praise God for being everlasting. What a beautiful way of expressing this attribute: "Who was and is and is to come" (4:8). This undergirds the theological thought that God sees the past, present, and future in one panoramic view. I do not understand that, but it is a great comfort to know that such is the nature of the God we worship. That is something to sing about—day and night and forever. (Thomas Lane Butts)

Worship Aids

Call to Worship

This is the day the Lord has made, let us rejoice and be glad in it. Let us cast aside any and all elements of pride that may obstruct us from making ourselves completely humble before the Lord our God.

Offertory Prayer

We acknowledge, O Lord, that you are the source of all the material blessings we have received. We acknowledge that there is nothing we can give that would enrich you, and nothing we could withhold that would impoverish you. But we are enriched by our giving and impoverished as we withhold our gifts. Amen.

Prayer of Confession

We confess, O God, that there are so many ways in which we could better spend our time and energy. We have committed the sin of taking the easy way of dealing with relationships and other human realities. We have done "good" when we could have done better. Forgive us for our failure to distinguish between what is good and what is best. We pray not only to be forgiven for those sins that come to our awareness at this moment, but also to be forgiven for those sins that have become so much a part of our routine of living that we do not notice them anymore. In the name of Jesus, we pray. Amen. (Thomas Lane Butts)

Words of Assurance (Revelation 4:11)

You are worthy, our Lord and God,
    to receive glory and honor and power,
for you created all things,
    and by your will they existed and were created.

OCTOBER 16, 2011

❧❧❧

Eighteenth Sunday after Pentecost

Readings: Exodus 33:12-23; Psalm 99; 1 Thessalonians 1:1-10;
Matthew 22:15-22

Power, the Holy Spirit, and Full Conviction
1 Thessalonians 1:1-10

As the apostle Paul reflects on the congregations he has established, visited, or is about to see for the first time, he never hesitates to declare his assessment of the state of any one Christian community. The congregation in Galatia, for instance, has compromised the gospel with a cramping legalism, confusing faith in Jesus Christ with moral achievement and ritual observance. Paul tells them bluntly they have denatured the gospel, turning wine into water. At the other extreme, Christians in Corinth have come to think that faith in Christ entails no moral commitment whatsoever. He tells them sadly they are a disgrace.

The Christians in Thessalonica, however, Paul has found exemplary; he can hold them up as a model for all of Asia Minor. While he has a few suggestions to make, Paul has no major criticism. In fact he glows over them, telling them that they are his "glory and joy" (1 Thessalonians 2:20). Why are they a model of Christian faith and practice?

First, Paul reminds them that when the gospel took hold of them it came not in word only (it must always come at least in human speech) but also in power and in the Holy Spirit and with full conviction. While no one disputed that a Christian herald had spoken, everyone was startled as the weight of God's truth fell upon the people, crumbled their unbelief, and stamped itself upon them indelibly. The messenger of the gospel was eclipsed by the substance of the gospel as Jesus Christ forged himself within them. The power Jesus uniquely bears and bestows—the Holy Spirit—sealed them thereafter as his people, possessed and protected by him exclusively. They were left with as much assurance as they would ever need concerning the truth of the gospel, the reality of him whose gospel it is, and their inclusion in the life of the risen Lord himself.

We must note that the full conviction born of the Holy Spirit's inherent power overcomes unbelief in those who have not yet come to faith; it relentlessly dispels the doubts that nibble at those possessed of faith; and it renders all gimmickry ("Come out tonight and hear Brother Billy and his musical saw") as superfluous at best and tawdry at worst.

Following Paul's visit, the church in Thessalonica continued to exemplify something too readily overlooked in the church today: the mark of pastoral effectiveness isn't so much what happens while the pastor is in the congregation, but rather what continues to happen once the pastor has left it. The "full conviction" (1:5) that the Spirit's power quickens in believers is no flash in the pan, but is rather the abiding attestation that as surely as the church brings the gospel in words, the Spirit brings conviction and commitment, with the result that the community thereafter suffers no "power failure." The life of the risen Christ enlivens it.

Second, the Thessalonians are Paul's glory and joy in that they turned from idols to serve the living and true God. To modern folk the word *idols* suggests semicivilized people dancing around and bowing to a wooden carving or a metal artifact. We are wrong to think this as a characterization of idolatry, and wrong again to think idolatry unique to primitive persons. Luther was more profound; idolatry, he never tired of saying, is that to which we give ourselves, that to which we look for our greatest good.

Of course the subtlest idolatry isn't the adulation of what is manifestly bad; it's the unwarranted confidence in what is undeniably good, even in what is God-ordained. It is good, for instance, to be economically self-sufficient, a financial encumbrance to no one. Yet an all-engrossing concern for financial gain renders self-sufficiency idolatrous, and like all idolatry, totalitarian in its grip on us because no degree of wealth for the financially preoccupied is ever sufficient. Education is good, even God-ordained, since God insists that we love God with our minds. Unnecessary ignorance, therefore, is sheer disobedience. But education rendered idolatrous announces itself as the only good, or at least as the singular saving good; and of course it renders its victims insufferable snobs and contemptuously cruel.

More to the point, everywhere in scripture idolatry spawns moral collapse. The Israelites, who preferred the golden calf to the God who had delivered them at the Red Sea, came to prefer paganism's indulgent immorality to Sinai's claim upon their obedience. The collapse doesn't happen overnight. To be sure, it begins in one generation, casting a shadow on the believer's demeanor and testimony. In the next, the accelerating downward spiral effects a compromise evident to everyone except the one who is now preoccupied with rationalizing it. By the third generation, there is no compromise or hypocrisy because no one is making a Christian profession anymore. The Thessalonians had turned away from this situation; every day they thanked God for that "turn" that scripture everywhere calls repentance.

Finally, Paul glories in the Christians in Thessalonica because "in spite of persecution" they "received the word with joy inspired by the Holy Spirit" (1:6). The Thessalonians quickly see that the light now enlightening them simultaneously provokes resentment among those who prefer to cloak themselves and their work with darkness. He who is the light of the world is just that: the world's only hope. Yet, just as Jesus Christ had found throughout his earthly ministry—from the day his birth announcement provoked the slaughter of the infants to the day his trial found the crowds preferring the release of Barabbas—so the Thessalonian Christians rejoiced at their intimacy with their Lord even as they knew their proximity to him would bring upon them what the world had visited upon him: trouble. Like him, however, they remained unyielding in their confidence in God, undiminished in their joy, and undeviating in the kingdom work to which they now knew themselves appointed.

Paul insisted that his one and only sermon announced Jesus Christ crucified. In the wake of his Damascus-road encounter, he never doubted the resurrection of Jesus. How could he, in light of the fact that he remained the beneficiary of that resurrection? He insisted thereafter that the resurrection of Jesus vivified the preaching of the cross. Yet his stock sermon highlighted the cross. Plainly Paul knew, with his Lord before him, that the gospel advances as someone takes up a cross and trusts God to vivify such cross-bearing anywhere in life. The persecution discipleship precipitates is one such cross. It must be borne and borne cheerfully (or it is not borne at all but merely resented). The Thessalonians received the gospel with joy—and continued to exude joy—in the midst of the hostility that love for their Lord attracted.

What happened in Thessalonica will unfailingly happen elsewhere when the gospel is brought in word and the Holy Spirit supplies power and unalterable conviction, even as Jesus Christ continues to flood his people with his joy amid their hardship. (Victor Shepherd)

Lectionary Commentary
Exodus 33:12-23

Moses, like Jacob before him and countless women and men after him, is unafraid to wrestle with God, unafraid to contend with God until blessing appears. Such "wrestling" is not wheedling or cajoling or even pestering; it is, rather, confirmation of our commitment to the freedom-bringing God who has already committed to us; it intensifies our awareness that God is not merely our ultimate good but the one and only good from whom all creaturely goods come and by whom they are made ours.

God declares that he knows Moses "by name" (Exodus 33:12), that is, God has encountered Moses in the profoundest intimacy. Aware of this, Moses now wants to encounter God in similar intimacy, intimacy that can be only splendid. He cries, "Show me your glory" (v. 18), where God's glory is God's innermost splendor turned outward and visited upon us. Customarily, however, God gives his people better than they ask; Moses is given to apprehend not God's glory but rather God's goodness (that which characterizes God), even as God proclaims his name, "The LORD" (v. 19).

The Hebrew word for *name* means "presence," "power," "purpose," "identity," and "deserved reputation." Moses is not allowed to see God's face, for such would imply that Moses had mastered God. Instead Moses is propped up in a cleft in the rock, for to apprehend anything of God will prove to be an overwhelming experience. As Moses is allowed to "see" the "back" (v. 23) of God, he discerns God's goodness and name to be *mercy*. Such mercy Israel must not subsequently trade on, but such mercy Israel will always be able to count on.

Matthew 22:15-22

Jesus' enemies relentlessly attempt to trap him. They try to expose him as disobedient concerning the Torah of Israel (see the sabbath-keeping controversies) or concerning the laws of Rome. Here Jesus' enemies begin by flattering him: "We know that you are sincere . . . and show deference to no one" (Matthew 22:16). Immediately they put a question to him that they think will condemn him regardless of the answer he gives. If he says that taxes should not be paid, he will appear to violate Roman law and render himself indictable. If he says that taxes should be paid, he will appear to be recognizing an emperor (and the government vested in that emperor) whose claim to merit worship violates the law of Israel.

As Jesus does everywhere else in the written Gospels, he refuses to answer the question he is asked. Instead he asks for a coin and queries his would-be accusers, "Whose head is this, and whose title?" (v. 20). When they answer, "The emperor's" (v. 21), Jesus tersely informs the Pharisees that what rightly belongs to the government (the state, the New Testament maintains, is God-ordained for our protection and preservation) should be accorded the government, while what belongs to God (alone) should be rendered to God (alone).

In the course of turning the tables on his detractors, Jesus instructs his followers in how they may and must honor the God-ordained state even as they discern the limits of the state's claim upon them, thereby recognizing and resisting the encroachment of state-fostered idolatry. (Victor Shepherd)

Worship Aids

Call to Worship (based on Psalm 45:1)

The psalmist writes, "My heart overflows with a goodly theme." Let us worship, that God might receive our praise, and our hearts might continue to overflow as we extol God for divine mercy, thank God for enduring patience, and love God for the love with which God has loved the only beloved Son to death and loved God's people to life.

Invocation

O saving God, you have placed in our hearts that longing for you that you alone can fulfill, even as everything else crowds upon us claiming to render you superfluous. Help us this day to hear with Elijah of old that still, small voice that orients us to you, that keeps us from surrendering ourselves to what is evil as well as what is merely good, but not yet you, our great God and Savior. Amen.

Assurance of Pardon

Throughout his earthly ministry Jesus announced, "Your faith has saved you; go in peace." All who have confessed their sins must now be assured that to bow at his feet in penitent faith is to be exalted in honor, for now he sends us forth in the shalom, peace, of relationships restored and righteousness made new. (Victor Shepherd)

Worthy Is the Lamb

Third in a Series of Four on Singing the Apocalypse: Hymns in Revelation

Revelation 5

The prophet from Patmos finds himself in a setting that is unlike anything he has ever seen. John is in the presence of God, in a throne room that is beyond description. Strange creatures are singing. Twenty-four elders, persons of unexplained importance, are prostrating themselves before the one who sits on the throne. They abdicate their power and authority by casting their crowns before the throne. Then they sing. The nature of their praise of the one who sits upon the throne is beyond mere words. Only the magic of music will empower their words to the intensity appropriate to the situation at hand. The scene is such that John can hardly take it all in.

Then John sees in the right hand of the one seated upon the throne a scroll with writing on the front and back. The scroll is sealed with seven seals. This scene John is describing, like so many other scenes in Revelation, is taken almost in whole cloth from his favorite Old Testament apocalyptic source, Ezekiel. "And when I looked, behold a hand was stretched out to me, and, lo, a written scroll was in it; and he spread it before me; and it had writing on the front and on the back" (Ezekiel 2:9-10 RSV).

This seven-sealed scroll contains God's plan for the final destiny of this sinful world. The contents of the scroll are so secret that only God knows what is in it. This is consistent with what Jesus said about the time at which heaven and earth would pass away. "But of that day or that hour no one knows, not even the angels in heaven, nor the Son, but only the Father" (Mark 13:32 RSV). People in every age have longed to know. A few, here and there, have claimed to know; dates have been set, but have passed without the end coming. Some have had the audacity to keep revising their timetables, and beyond rational understanding, a larger-than-expected group of sincere Christians gives credence to this tomfoolery. One might expect that even if the continual passing of the dates set by these false prophets did not deter the naive, at least they might remember what Jesus said about the matter.

Well, the time has come for the veil to be lifted and the secret to be revealed. John sees "a mighty angel proclaiming with a loud voice: 'Who is worthy to open the scroll and break its seals?'" (Revelation 5:2). No one in heaven or on earth steps forward. Here John gets involved in the scene he is reporting. It is a momentous time. The answer is so near, and no one is able to take the final step. John begins to weep because no one is worthy to open the scroll or look into it. We can hardly blame John for his emotional involvement. I think I would have wept!

One of the twenty-four elders comes to the rescue. He dries John's tears with these words: "Do not weep. See, the Lion of the tribe of Judah, the Root of David, has conquered, so that he can open the scroll and its seven seals" (5:5). Here is the moment of revelation and truth toward which John's story has been moving. Here comes Jesus! He is in strange form to the Western mind, but he is here as the "Lamb that was slaughtered" (5:12). Before the throne of God, among the elders, he takes the scroll from the right hand of the one seated on the throne.

Every creature and person present and even those a world away realize at once that everything is going to be all right. How many times on earth did Jesus dry tears, calm the storms, and ease the worried minds of people? Now in heaven, he is doing the same thing. Here is where the singing begins! The four living creatures and the twenty-four elders strike up the music and lead the singing. They break out their harps and golden bowls of incense containing the prayers of the saints, and they begin to sing a new song. The joy spreads. The words and music of praise are taken up by a choir of angels that number "myriads of myriads and thousands of thousands" (5:11). (I know about thousands of thousands, but I had to look up myriads of myriads. *Myriad* is an indefinitely large number, countless, innumerable.) What a choir! They are singing with full voice.

But hold on, John; there is more to come. John hears "every creature in heaven and on earth and under the earth and in the sea, and all that is in them, singing" (5:13). What a wonderful sight and sound! No voice is left out. Even the dead (under the earth) are singing. To what end is all of this singing? It is a universal hymn of praise and thanksgiving to and for the Lamb who is "worthy" (v. 12). It is an act of worship that is beyond words. Only the magic of music can give the words the intensity and depth that is adequate to the situation at hand.

Jesus, the only begotten Son of God, who is one with the Father, who is the Lamb that was slain for the sins of the world, is being affirmed and recognized and justified in the presence of all creation. When no one else, in heaven or on earth, is worthy to open the scroll and break the seven seals to reveal the secret of the future disposition of the world, the Lamb that was slain arrives on the scene. John does not say this, but in my mind

I can hear the voice of God repeating the affirmation given at Jesus' baptism: "This is my beloved Son with whom I am well pleased." Can you hear that too? When that hymn is finished, the four living creatures say, "Amen!" (5:14), and the elders once again fall down and worship.

The theological implications of this pivotal chapter in Revelation are "myriad." Volumes have been written on this chapter. It is the central point to which the first four chapters move, and in it is the authority upon which the remaining seventeen chapters are based.

When the seven seals are broken by the one who is worthy, there is a lot of violence, judgment, and divine retribution turned loose upon the world. The Lord is about to set things right, and it is not going to be a pretty sight. Not to worry. There is still lots of singing going on. (Thomas Lane Butts)

Worship Aids

Call to Worship

My friends, the world is too much with us. We have lost some of the divine spark with which we came into the world, and there is a blank spot in our lives from which that spark has gone. Do you feel it? God can fill it once again. It is to that end that we have come here today.

Prayer of Intercession

Dear God, Father and Mother of us all, we are not here just to pray for ourselves, although we feel the pain of need for it. We pray for the people who feel lost and undone, from whose lives joy has gone, and who do not know where to turn or what to do. We all know some of them, one or two here and there, at home, next door, or where we work. Grant us both the concern and the courage to reach out to them in helpful ways. Save us from the error of giving out too much advice, and help us to depend on the influence of living out our faith in their presence. We trust that will be enough for us mere humans. We trust you can do the rest. In the name of Jesus. Amen.

Benediction

It is my prayer that, at the church door, you can leave a little bit of what you don't need and appropriate a little bit of what you need but don't have to keep you strong in the hard spots of your life this week. Go in peace. Amen. (Thomas Lane Butts)

OCTOBER 23, 2011

Nineteenth Sunday after Pentecost

Readings: Deuteronomy 34:1-12; Psalm 90:1-6, 13-17;
1 Thessalonians 2:1-8; Matthew 22:34-46

What a View!
Deuteronomy 34:1-12

Wow! What a view! Have you ever said those words? I wonder if Moses said them when he climbed Mount Pisgah and looked out at the promised land. Most of us have taken in beautiful vistas from on high. I remember a winter ski trip to Colorado I took with my family. Besides the exciting skiing and the beautiful white snow, there were absolutely gorgeous views of the snow-covered Rocky Mountains. Another trip my wife and I took was to the wilds of Alaska. Again we had opportunities to see beautiful landscapes and wondrous mountains. Maybe you have been at the top of a skyscraper and looked out over a city. Perhaps you have been flying and looked out the window at the amazing view below.

Still, I wonder if Moses was filled with awe by what he saw. Did Moses see the green and fertile land around the flowing river Jordan? Did he see the Dead Sea and the hills that surround it? Did he see the towns and villages of the people the children of Israel were about to displace? Were there roads and pathways connecting one village to another? Did he see the smoke from distant fires?

Besides wondering what Moses saw when he climbed that mountain, what was he feeling? The Scriptures are void of Moses' personal emotions and feelings. I wonder if Moses felt sad and disappointed when he climbed Mount Pisgah and looked out over the promised land. He had been through so much with these people: wandering around in the wilderness for forty years, listening to their complaining and bickering, defending them before God. Moses had seen the mighty hand of God work miracles in their midst. He had experienced God's anger when they were disobedient and went astray. Now, having come all this way, Moses would be allowed only to view the promised land from the top of this mountain, but he would not be allowed to enter it.

It seems so unfair. Moses hadn't asked for this job and actually did all in his power to say no to God's call to go to Egypt and bring God's people out. Yet we see God's tender mercies in the fact that God was on the mountain with Moses when he viewed the promised land and when he died. We are told that God buried him in a place no one has ever known. He allowed Moses to live for 120 years, and "his sight was unimpaired and his vigor had not abated" (Deuteronomy 34:7).

I wonder if Moses was angry as he looked out over the land. We know that there was definitely an angry streak in his personality; he had, after all, committed murder. Perhaps as Moses looked out over the land, he was angry with the children of Israel for their lack of faith and disobedience. When the spies returned from visiting the promised land, why didn't they listen to the good report of Caleb and Joshua? These two men encouraged the people to have faith in the power of God to conquer the people of this land. But the people listened to the report of the ten spies who feared they could not penetrate the well-fortified cities or defeat the "giants" (Numbers 13:33 KJV) they saw.

The children of Israel rebelled against God and were punished. They were made to roam in the wilderness for forty years, one year for each day the spies spent in the promised land. If only they had been faithful, they could have been enjoying the fruits of the land by now. Perhaps Moses was also angry with God for not allowing him to enter the land. Hadn't he done all God had asked of him? Hadn't he been patient and loving to these people who wanted to replace him and who questioned his authority?

Then again, maybe Moses felt a sense of relief. It had been a long forty years wandering about the desert. The children of Israel were a difficult bunch. The Bible tells us that they were stubborn and stiff-necked. Perhaps Moses was not looking forward to a prolonged fight to conquer the people of the promised land. He could imagine how they would complain when they lost a battle or when things weren't going their way. Maybe Moses was happy to have the younger Joshua lead this people into battle.

As I thought about Moses and the promised land, I recognized that we all have our own promised land that we are trying to enter. We all have goals and dreams that we pursue. Perhaps our goals are academic, to attain certain degrees or achieve academic status. Maybe our goals are to have a great marriage and a wonderful family. Perhaps our goal is to be healthy or to get in great shape or to attain our perfect weight. Maybe our dream is that perfect job or that perfect house. Like Moses, we might find ourselves seeing these dreams and goals from afar but we may not be able to attain them. There are times when we have to give up our dreams or lower our goals. How does this make us feel? Do we become sad and disappointed? Do we get angry with God, ourselves, or others? Are we relieved that we don't have to carry that burden of achievement anymore? Wherever you may be and whatever you may be facing, know this: God is with you, just as God was with Moses. (Neil Epler)

Lectionary Commentary
Matthew 22:34-46

In this passage we find two crucial questions that touch the heart of our faith. The first question is addressed to Jesus by a lawyer, an expert in the law. He asks Jesus about the greatest commandment. If we could condense all of the Scriptures into one or two statements about how we should live and act, what would they be? The answer is both simple and profound: love God with all your being and love your neighbor as yourself. These statements sound so simple and indeed they are, for even a small child can understand them. The great difficulty comes in living them out each and every day.

The second question was addressed to the Pharisees, but we also need to answer it: "What do you think of the Messiah? Whose son is he?" (Matthew 22:42). We must each come to grips with who Jesus is and what he has done for us. Is he just a great teacher and miracle worker or is he something more? Do we believe he is who he says he is? Do we believe what the Scriptures tell us about him? Knowing the commandments is critical, but knowing what we think about the Messiah is the key to living them out each day.

1 Thessalonians 2:1-8

What keeps us from sharing our faith? For most of us it is simply the fear of rejection or the fact that people might make fun of us. Paul mentions that his visit to the Thessalonians was not in vain. Even when we feel the message we have shared may have been rejected, we never know the difference it could make later in the person's life. Paul reminds the

Thessalonians of his imprisonment in Philippi just before his visit to them. He did not allow fear to prevent him from sharing the gospel. Neither should we let fear of being mocked prevent us from sharing our faith. God will give us the strength and courage we need.

Sharing our faith is not only about speaking the right words but also (and more critically) about sharing ourselves. When we offer ourselves to others through time, talent, and service, we are God's love in their lives. We do not do this seeking praise, but in gratitude for what God has given to us and to help others know of the God who loves them and gave all for them. (Neil Epler)

Worship Aids

Call to Worship
O Lord, as we gather in this place to worship, remind us that you have called us to the promised land. You gave the children of Israel a land flowing with milk and honey. You give to your children today the promise of abundant and eternal life, a life in which we experience your forgiveness and grace. Help us to worship you as we continue our journey. Amen.

Litany of Promise
When I feel discouraged
Show me the promised land.
When I am weary and burdened by this world
Show me the promised land.
When I am angry with myself and with others
Show me the promised land.
When I am confused and I don't know which way to turn
Show me the promised land.
When the day is done
Give me your rest.

Benediction
Now may the God who called Moses to deliver the Hebrew children from captivity, who gave him the law on Mount Sinai, who walked with him through the wilderness, and who laid him to rest in the land of Moab, bless and keep you this day and forevermore. Amen. (Neil Epler)

The Victors' Songs

Fourth in a Series of Four on Singing the Apocalypse: Hymns in Revelation

Revelation 15

Chapter 15 is the prelude to the final and terrible judgment of God being poured out upon the wicked. The prophet of Patmos has shown us the opening of the seven seals and the sounding of seven trumpets, each of which has brought severe judgment upon the wicked by destructive acts that are not fit reading for the fainthearted. It appears, however, that the worst is yet to come as the seven angels with seven plagues prepare to pour out seven bowls of the wrath of God. John shows us this scene in heaven as the angels cue up and the spectators assemble. There are situations that have to be dealt with before justice is properly and finally administered. Only then can we come to the blessedness of a new heaven and a new earth, where "death will be no more; mourning and crying and pain will be no more" (Revelation 21:4).

Revelation is not only a source of hope for the faithful, it also brings a clear warning to the unfaithful—the wicked—that there are consequences to choices and acts in this world. Even as John brings his vision of the future to an end, he brandishes a two-edged sword for all to see. Three times in the closing chapter, the heavenly Christ says, "See, I am coming soon." This is not only a happy promise to the righteous but also a stern warning to the wicked: "See, I am coming soon; my reward is with me, to repay according to everyone's work" (Revelation 22:12). That is music to the ears of the faithful, but not a very happy sign for the wicked.

The prophet of Patmos sets the scene as an artist would paint a picture. Spectators are present for the event, and there is going to be some significant singing. This appears to be taking place in the throne room, but the throne is not there. There is the sea that looks like glass, which we have seen earlier in Revelation 4:6, but with an added feature; the glass seems now to be mixed with fire (15:2). Standing beside this sea are the martyrs. They are the victors who conquered the beast.

History describes the terrible acts of persecution of the martyrs by the Roman emperors. The most notably cruel of them all was Domitian, who was most likely the person Revelation had in mind as the beast. Domitian took seriously the idea of the emperor being a god. His acts of cruelty to those who dared not worship him were unspeakable. But the martyrs marched into the arena by the thousands with a spirit of joy. They were about to go to be with Jesus. Many even volunteered to be martyred. The persecutors watched them die and thought they had defeated them. Not so. Like Jesus their Lord, they laid down their lives to gain life eternal. When Jesus was dying on the cross, even his executioners soon began to wonder who had won, him or them. These who died in his name, the martyrs, are the spectators for the event that is about to unfold.

They arrive at the scene with the harps of God in hand. The singing is about to begin. As they sing, the avenging angels arrive and prepare to depart with bowls from which they will pour out the wrath of God on those who thought they had won when they killed the martyrs.

The choir of 144,000 sings two songs. First they sing the song of Moses for which John has set an appropriate scene: the sea that looks like glass is now mixed with fire, which gives it the appearance of the Red Sea; the martyrs' safe crossing of the sea by death is reminiscent of the Israelite slaves' escape from Egypt by crossing the Red Sea. The song of Moses in Exodus 15:1-18 gives a detailed description of the destruction of the Egyptian army. It rings with great satisfaction in this song as the Israelites praise God, not only for God's holiness, but for God's terrible deeds. They sing on, not only celebrating the annihilation of the Egyptians, but anticipating a similar fate for the occupants of the land they plan to occupy. It is appropriate for the martyrs to sing that song from Exodus because their erstwhile enemies will soon suffer a similar or worse fate. The seven angels with seven bowls of divine wrath are poised in readiness. The Egyptians were probably lucky compared to what is about to happen here.

But the martyrs then sing their own song, the song of the Lamb. It is a song that no one else could learn except the 144,000 who have been redeemed from the earth. But here it is in John's apocalypse for all to see (15:3-4). We need not belabor this seeming inconsistency. The Bible always needs breathing room. We may read the words, hum the tune, and identify the source of the words and phrases, but we cannot learn it. We would have to have been with them in the arena, under the altar in heaven, and standing by the fiery crystal sea—harp in hand. It is uniquely their song! They sing it with feeling born of the martyrs' experience.

Like so much of Revelation, the song is laced with quotations and thoughts from the Old Testament. However, this song is considerably more temperate than the song of Moses. The blessed martyrs do not allude to their suffering in the song. It is a song of pure praise to God. It is also inclusive: "All nations will come and worship before you" (15:4). The Jewish national and religious exclusiveness is gone. Sing on, victors!

May we live and die in such manner that we may someday stand there with you and sing our hearts out too. (Thomas Lane Butts)

Worship Aids

Opening Prayer

We come into this place today with the smell of life on us. We come from a world divided over things we cannot fix. We pray to be lifted a little higher here than we were before we walked in. Lift us above petty bickering about things that are not as we think they should be. Help us to see not only things as they are but ourselves as we are—if we can stand it. Help us, Lord. Amen.

Pastoral Prayer

Dear God, we have drawn aside from the ordinary to this place where we pray to catch some glimpse of the divine. We have seen your signature on so much of our experience this week. We saw you at the supermarket standing in the checkout line, counting coins and shuffling food stamps. We saw you at the Salvation Army thrift store picking through used clothes and trying on an old pair of shoes. We saw you in the emergency room at the hospital cradling a sick child in your arms. When we walked into the room where someone had just died, we thought we heard the rustle of angel wings. We know you are out there, Lord. We know you have been out there all along. Forgive us for not seeing you, for closing our eyes, for walking away, for making fun of you and for walking by on the other side. We know you are out there, but we pray today that we may find you in here; though you may feel uneasy with our soft cushions and polished altarware, our expensive clothes and gold jewelry and the sound of our coins in the offering plate. We pray that you will be in here with us until we can get a little more comfortable with bumping into you out there.

Forgive our unbelief, and help us to see the truth about life here and hereafter. Touch us with grace as we seek the special and unique blessings that we need. Bless any who are experiencing paralyzing fear and apprehension. Bless those who are waiting for test results, and bless those who are concerned with their physical or mental health. Help us to be more acutely sensitive to our spiritual needs. Help us to learn how to get as upset over our spiritual ills as we are about our high blood pressure, irregular heartbeats, or arthritis.

Be near to those here today who have needs about which we do not know, or to which we have not been sensitive. We pray that something good may come of our being together today. Amen.

Benediction

May this time of worship so strengthen and encourage you that you will leave this place dancing as if no one is watching, singing as if no one is listening, loving as if you have never been hurt by love, working as if you don't need the money, and living as if God's kingdom really has come. Amen. (Thomas Lane Butts)

OCTOBER 30, 2011

❧❧❧

Twentieth Sunday after Pentecost

Readings: Joshua 3:7-17; Psalm 107:1-7, 33-37; 1 Thessalonians 2:9-13; Matthew 23:1-12

Practice What You Preach
Matthew 23:1-12

"Why don't you practice what you preach?" Have you ever said those words? Maybe someone has said them to you. Hypocrites are people who pretend to be something they are not. They may say one thing and then do the opposite. They may act one way in a certain setting and then act another way in a different setting. It is very important that as Christians, we follow the example of Jesus Christ. It doesn't matter where we are or who we are with. The words we speak and the things we do should always reflect our faith. Sometimes we are good at telling other people what they should do and how they should live, but we fail to follow our own instructions. We need to, as the saying goes, "walk the walk, not just talk the talk."

Some time ago, I saw a *Peanuts* comic strip that had Snoopy on top of his doghouse with a flock of baby birds. The time had come for the baby birds to learn how to fly, and Snoopy was their teacher. Snoopy flapped his ears and walked to the end of the roof of the doghouse. He leaped into the air and continued to flap his ears. Unfortunately he landed right on his head. He got back up onto the roof and shared this lesson: "Do as I say to do and not what I do."

In today's scripture, Jesus tells the crowds and his disciples to do what the Pharisees and the scribes *teach* them to do, "but do not do as they do, for they do not practice what they teach" (Matthew 23:3). In other words, the leaders talk the talk, but they don't walk the walk.

Why is it important to practice what we preach? The most basic reason is the integrity of our faith; we are the body of Christ for the world.

In Matthew 5:14, Jesus tells us, "You are the light of the world. A city built on a hill cannot be hid." People should be attracted by the light of the way we live and the words we speak. Whether we like it or not, people are watching us and seeing how we respond to the ups and downs of everyday life. Children watch adults and then imitate what they see and repeat what they hear. Are our words and actions something we want repeated by our children? Our friends, neighbors, coworkers, family members, and classmates are watching us. What evidence do we offer of our profession of faith? Are our responses any different from those of persons who don't profess to know Christ? Not only are nonbelievers watching us, but so are other Christians. Persons who are new to the faith often look to more-mature Christians. Do our words and actions encourage and build up other Christians?

Our church's young men's softball team was in a hard-fought battle with another church's team. The two teams had been rivals for several years. The games were always exciting and well played. One of our players was up at bat. He hit a hard line drive to center field and quickly ran to first base, then turned the corner toward second. The outfielder made a good play on the ball and threw perfectly to the second baseman. The play was very close, but the runner was called out. Our player protested the call and began yelling at the umpire. We encouraged him to get off the field, but his anger escalated. His language became coarse and abusive. When we finally got him off the field, we admonished him to remember who he was and what he represented. We reminded him that young people and perhaps people who did not know Christ were watching him. Was this what he wanted them to see? It was an important lesson for him.

How do we practice what we preach? One way is to be careful about the words we speak. You can tell a lot about a person by the words they use. You can tell even more by the words they use when they are distressed, angry, or threatened. James tells us the tongue is very dangerous. It can set a great forest ablaze. We can tame all kinds of animals, but we cannot tame the tongue (James 3:3-6). People are listening to the words we speak. Do our words build people up or cut them down? Do our words bring peace and calm to a situation or do they add fuel to the fire? The words we speak should match the person we claim to be. If we profess that we are followers of Christ, then our words should be a reflection of that relationship.

We practice what we preach when we live our lives as reflections of the life of Christ. The way we act at work should be the same way we act at home, at church, around other Christians, in the supermarket, or waiting for a bus. My wife and I have always said, "What you see is what you get." We try to act the same wherever we are. When people see us, they should see a reflection of Christ. Do we live our lives in ways that reflect him? (Neil Epler)

Lectionary Commentary
Joshua 3:7-17

Joshua is now in command of the armies of Israel. God seeks to encourage Joshua and the children of Israel; God guides Joshua to take actions that have a wonderful connection to the long history of the Israelites. First, Joshua is to select twelve men, one from each of the twelve tribes, just as Joshua was selected as one of twelve men, one from each tribe, sent into the promised land by Moses to spy out the land. That first mission failed when the people did not listen to the truth that Joshua and Caleb shared. Now Joshua selects twelve men who will carry stones as a monument to remind them of how God brought them into the land.

God also causes the waters of the Jordan River to part under Joshua's direction, as had the waters of the Red Sea under the direction of Moses. When the priests who bear the ark of the covenant dip their feet into the edge of the river, the waters stop flowing and stand in a heap. The children of Israel cross over on dry land. When we are facing new challenges in our lives, it is important to remember how God has been faithful and delivered us in the past.

1 Thessalonians 2:9-13

God's word is truly amazing. We are told that "the word of God is living and active, sharper than any two-edged sword" (Hebrews 4:12). The Bible "is inspired by God and is useful for teaching, for reproof, for correction, and for training in righteousness" (2 Timothy 3:16). Paul gives God thanks that the people of Thessalonica recognized that the words they spoke were not human words, but they were truly the words of God. Do we recognize this when we hear the word read or a sermon preached?

God has given us an awesome responsibility. We are called to share the divine word with others. We need to recognize that these are God's words and they have a great deal of power. It is important for us to grow in God's word so that we can share it. We do this through daily reading, memorization, and study of the Bible. (Neil Epler)

Worship Aids

Prayer of Confession

Lord, we confess that we have not always practiced what we have preached. We are often guilty of talking the talk but not walking the walk. Forgive us, we pray. Help us to be sure that our words and actions are reflections of our faith. Help us to be consistent in the way we live so that others might see Christ in us. Amen.

Words of Assurance

Know this: the Lord is good and God's loving-kindness is forever. God will never fail us or forsake us. Even when our actions do not match our teaching, God is ready to forgive us. The Lord will give us the strength we need to do the things we are called to do. God will fill us with the Holy Spirit.

Offertory

Remind us, O God, how important it is that we not only speak about being faithful stewards, but that we are faithful in our giving and our service. You have called us to rely on you and to bring our tithes and offerings to your house. Help us to not just talk about our giving but to give in response to the abundance you have bestowed upon us. Amen. (Neil Epler)

A Picture of Sacrificial Service

First in a Series of Three on Celebrating Communion

Matthew 26:26-28

On this Sunday before All Saints' Day, it is fitting that we once again celebrate the grace of God in our lives. When Luther nailed his theses on the door of the Wittenberg Church in October 1517, he reemphasized the grace of God for all Christendom. Celebrating Communion today reminds us again of this amazing grace of God.

As we think about Communion and the original institution of the Lord's Supper, several thoughtful considerations cast added light on the significance of the occasion. First, this took place toward the end of a three-year association on the part of Jesus and these disciples. These individuals did not just meet on the streets of Jerusalem and decide to have supper together. These disciples had walked and talked with Jesus, had heard his amazing teachings, had witnessed his miraculous power, and had seen his awareness of God. Though not fully understood at the moment, this act on the part of Jesus created a sense of expectancy.

Second, the ideas flowing though the Lord's Supper had roots deep in the tradition of the Jewish people. The passover meal was not new; rather, it was history in the finest sense of the word, handed down from their forebears and observed every year. Every facet of the observance had significance, and the new application was a rich blossoming-forth of a great religious heritage as well as a picture of the coming sacrificial death of our Lord.

Third, remember that this dramatic and constantly used observance was not instituted in the temple, not even in the synagogue, but in a home, just as passover had been observed down through the years. This ought to remind us of the importance of the home as religious teaching opportunities in the mind of God.

Fourth, Jesus chose a common meal, an inevitable, daily event, as the backdrop for his eternal message. The Lord took the bread and wine at the table as the basic tenets of his symbolic message. Jesus chose them to indicate that the basic elements of this memorial supper might be easily available whenever, wherever, and with whomever its observance would be desired. Jesus often used the simple things to indicate deep spiritual truth.

Fifth, observe that Jesus gave thanks and blessed the bread and the wine as he gave it to each of the disciples. In this intentional act of prayer, Jesus recognized God as the source of all life's mercies. Beyond any arguments of the "real presence" during the Communion service, by this prayer the bread and the wine were set apart, dedicated to the sacred and mystical presence of God during the act itself.

Finally, Jesus identified the bread and wine as "my body...my blood of the covenant, which is poured out" (Matthew 26:26, 28) for the sins of humankind. We must never forget that this giving of self was a willing act of expiation, atonement, and reconciliation. Further, Jesus told us to share this meal in remembrance of him. If you want to know what the Lord wished those disciples, and us, to remember, here it is—his sacrificial death, burial, and bodily resurrection.

For the Protestant tradition, this observance is symbolic and memorial—an outward sign of inward grace. From the Catholic tradition, this

Communion is sacerdotal, a tangible channel of saving grace. For those of us in the Protestant heritage, the service is a symbol, a memorial, and a visible reminder of Christ's death and of our obligation to live a cross-centered life. Indeed, this is what he said: "If any want to become my followers, let them deny themselves and take up their cross and follow me" (Matthew 16:24). Just as this observance is meant to convey a mystical presence of the living Lord, our lives are meant to be vehicles of his presence, the medium through which we commune with him and serve him. We are God's witness in this world.

Think of it! A dozen disciples—fishermen, tradesmen, even tax collectors—gathered in an upper room celebrating passover, not realizing they were about to begin a journey that would change the world. A simple assemblage was lifted by Jesus' act to a level of uncommon glory.

A testimony remaining to us from that upper room is that the simple stuff of everyday life can be transformed into channels of God's grace. Through these God can break through upon our human scene with the divine living presence. We may approach any Communion service seeking to leave the encounter with God a little more possessed with reverence for life, a lot more aware that all of life is holy, and fully dedicated to living life in a sacrificial manner. Anything less brings to mind the stern warning of the apostle Paul:

> Whoever, therefore, eats the bread or drinks the cup of the Lord in an unworthy manner will be answerable for the body and blood of the Lord. Examine yourselves, and only then eat of the bread and drink of the cup. For all who eat and drink without discerning the body, eat and drink judgment against themselves. (1 Corinthians 11:27-29)

As we partake of the bread and the wine in every Communion service, let us be clear about its meaning and its application. Let us prepare spiritually for the observance itself. Above all, let us reexamine ourselves and rededicate ourselves to live out Jesus' lifestyle in our daily lives. (Drew J. Gunnells Jr.)

Worship Aids

Invocation
Dear God, abide with us today as we take this journey back in time, seeking to understand more about your last passover observance with your disciples. In so doing may we, your disciples in the present, grasp anew the

transcendent meaning of that event. Remind us of the cost of our salvation as well as the responsibility this grace brings to each of us. Give us the passion and daring to be your people in our day and time. We pray this in the name of Christ, our Lord and Savior. Amen.

Benediction

Lord, with the disciples on the night you instituted this supper, we yet mull over its full meaning. There are those about us who seem to have all the answers. Grant us, O God, freedom from the arrogance that claims to have all truth, as well as the cowardice that shrinks from new truth. May the mystery of your presence in this Communion service be both inspiration and motivation. In Jesus' name. Amen. (Drew J. Gunnells Jr.)

NOVEMBER 6, 2011

❧❧❧

All Saints' Sunday/Twenty-first Sunday after Pentecost

Readings: Revelation 7:9-17; Psalm 34:1-10, 22; 1 John 3:1-3; Matthew 5:1-12

For All the Saints
1 John 3:1-3

Today we celebrate All Saints' Day. This is the day we remember all those who have passed on from this life to the life eternal. On this day we are especially reminded that we are surrounded by a great cloud of witnesses. When someone mentions the word *saint*, what image comes to your mind? Perhaps you think about the saints you have read about in books. These are persons who have done great things for God and perhaps even performed some type of miracle. Maybe you think about statues you have seen of saints, especially in Roman Catholic churches or in cemeteries. Maybe you think about necklaces and medallions made of the saints. I can remember a special gift I was given when I was growing up. It was a silver necklace with a Saint Christopher's medal. I was told that it would keep me safe and protect me as long as I wore it. I'm not sure I really believed that, but the necklace became part of my everyday attire. I continued to wear it until it started to tarnish so badly that it turned my neck green.

A saint can be defined as a holy person, a person who has been redeemed, or someone who has been declared righteous by God. By this definition, anyone who has received Jesus as their Lord and Savior is a saint. The book of Acts (9:32-41) tells of Peter going down to the saints, the followers of Jesus, who lived in Lydda and to a disciple named Tabitha (or Dorcas), whom Peter restored to life. The Bible also tells us the importance of meeting the needs of the saints. In Romans 12:13, we read, "Contribute to the needs of the saints"; in 2 Corinthians 9:11-12, we find, "You will be enriched in every way for your great generosity, which will produce thanksgiving to God through us; for the rendering of this ministry not only supplies the needs of the saints but also overflows with many thanksgivings to God." The words *saint* and *Christian*, or follower of Jesus, are used interchangeably.

Today's passage from the First Letter of John reminds us that when we accept God's love through Jesus Christ, we are called "children of God"— saints. A person becomes a saint through the love of God. Saints can be called children of God because of the great love God has poured out for us. As God's children, we have worth beyond this world, but being a child of God is not some distant or future state; we are God's children here and now. As God's children we live differently, following the example of Jesus. It is as if the world does not even know us. We live abundantly, filled with love, joy, hope, and peace. "The fruit of the Spirit is love, joy, peace, patience, kindness, generosity, faithfulness, gentleness, and self-control" (Galatians 5:22-23). These are the characteristics of a saint and a child of God. Are these fruits evident in our lives? What are we doing to cultivate them?

The passage also tells us that being a saint is a work in progress: "what we will be has not yet been revealed" (1 John 3:2). I love the children's song that states, "He's still working on me, to make me what I ought to be" ("He's Still Working on Me," by Joel Hemphill). In this life, we strive to become more and more like Christ. We are becoming reflections of God.

This process of becoming a perfect reflection of Christ will take us all of our days on this earth until one day when we see God face-to-face. If this is our hope and our destiny, then we will do all in our power to make ourselves ready: "All who have this hope in him purify themselves" (3:3). Paul talks about his own process of becoming all that God wants him to be:

> Not that I have already obtained this or have already reached the goal; but I press on to make it my own, because Christ Jesus has made me his own. Beloved, I do not consider that I have made it my own; but this one thing I do: forgetting what lies behind and straining forward to what lies ahead, I press on toward the goal for the prize of the heavenly call of God in Christ Jesus. (Philippians 3:12-14)

Paul would later refer to this process as a race (2 Timothy 4:7). All Saints' Sunday reminds us of the saints along that racecourse who encourage us and cheer us on. We are truly surrounded by a great cloud of witnesses.

On this day I invite you to remember those who have entered "the Church Triumphant." Perhaps they died during this past year or some time ago. Remember that they are still with us. They surround us each and every day. As you travel this road of life, striving to become what God wants you to be, know that you are not alone. Standing along that path is a great cloud of witnesses, and they are cheering you on. May we all persevere until the day when we see Jesus and our loved ones face-to-face. (Neil Epler)

Lectionary Commentary
Matthew 5:1-12

On this All Saints' Day we wonder, "Who are the saints?" Many of us think about people who have been especially holy. A look at the beatitudes reminds us of some of the characteristics of a saint. The first beatitude talks about the poor in spirit; saints are humble and many have lived in poverty. The next beatitude mentions those who mourn; saints often cry for the lost and the hurting of this world. The next beatitude speaks about the meek; saints turn praise for their own actions aside and believe they do just what any Christian should. Hungering and thirsting for righteousness is another beatitude and characteristic of a saint. Saints diligently study God's word and seek ways to apply it in their lives and in their ministry. Saints show mercy to others, keep their hearts and lives pure, and strive for peace in this world.

Perhaps we think about the persecution saints often suffer for their faith. Many have been charged with heresy. Many have paid for their faith with their very lives. These saints are blessed because they are persecuted for the sake of the gospel. The truth is often difficult to take, and the beatitudes are a model for all of us—all believers in Christ are saints.

Revelation 7:9-17

"Oh, Lord, I want to be in that number, when the saints go marching in." What a fantastic scene! People from every nation and race, too numerous to count, surround the throne of God. The Lamb of God is present, as are all the angels, the elders, and the four living creatures. This is like the grand finale of an epic movie. The victory has been won. Heroes are being recognized. People are rejoicing and celebrating. We can only imagine what it will be like to stand with that amazing congregation before the throne of God and praise and sing to God's holy name. I want to be in that number.

How do we get to be part of this crowd? How can we be sure we are a part of this great celebration? We are told that the ones gathered here "have washed their robes and made them white in the blood of the Lamb" (Revelation 7:14). This is a reminder of Isaiah 1:18: "Though your sins are like scarlet, they shall be like snow; though they are red like crimson, they shall become like wool." The blood of Christ cleanses us of our sins and makes us righteous in God's sight. When we accept Christ as Lord we become one of God's children, one of God's saints. May we all "be in that number, when the saints go marching in"! (Neil Epler)

Worship Aids

Call to Worship

O God of all the saints, bless us as we gather in this place to worship you. Help us to remember all of those who have gone before us. Help us to join with the saints in praise and adoration. Remind us of the cloud of witnesses who gather with us this day and every day. May we be numbered among the saints and join our voices with theirs before your heavenly throne. Amen.

Litany of Witness

May we run the race that is set before us,
Since we are surrounded by so great a cloud of witnesses.
May we never be afraid, even if the path becomes dark and narrow,
Since we are surrounded by so great a cloud of witnesses.
May we overcome every obstacle that stands in our way,
Since we are surrounded by so great a cloud of witnesses.
And may we persevere until we reach the goal that is set before us,
Since we are surrounded by so great a cloud of witnesses.

Benediction

May the God of all saints fill your heart with joy and peace. May God strengthen you with the hope of joining in that great congregation before God's holy throne. May God make you aware of the divine presence and the cloud of witnesses that surrounds you. May God grant you peace and anoint you with the Spirit. Amen. (Neil Epler)

November 6, 2011

Three Dimensions of Communion

Second in a Series of Three on Celebrating Communion

1 Corinthians 11:23-26

The service of symbols should never be underestimated. I believe it was Goethe who reminded us that the highest cannot be spoken. There are truths in life too profound to be put into music or literature. They must be expressed symbolically. A handshake or a hug, offered in joy or sorrow, conveys more than language can. The very sight of our national flag can bring tears to the eyes or fire in the blood without a word being uttered. A beautiful wedding ring is a silent and eloquent token that the wearer has entered into one of the most sacred relationships on this earth that nothing should ever sever. The church takes bread and wine, available in the simplest of homes, and remembers a body that was broken and blood that was shed for each of us. The symbol works in any culture, in any language, in any nationality.

"Do this," the Lord said, "in remembrance of me" (1 Corinthians 11:24). Jesus knows our nature better than we do, and our memories are short. The heart of our faith in symbol appeals to our senses—sight, touch, and taste. Every time we do this, we recall the sacrificial love of our Savior; and our faith is nourished, our hope is kindled, and our strength is renewed.

In a very real sense these symbols of Communion look to the past, the present, and the future. The past lets us once again look at the cross, at a broken body and a sacrificed life. We celebrate the birth of most great people, but the Lord asks us to remember his death. As important and miraculous as are his birth, baptism, ministry, and even the transfiguration, Jesus asks to be remembered by his death.

He transformed the cup of suffering into a cup of grace. The Lord could have escaped all this: "No one takes it [my life] from me, but I lay it down of my own accord. I have power to lay it down, and I have power to take it up again. I have received this command from my Father" (John 10:18).

John's Gospel reminds us that it was God's love that sent Jesus to the cross. This death that Communion recognizes is not the death of a patriot or a martyr, but the death of the redeemer of all people of every tongue, race, and nation.

This symbolism also has a present reality. As we partake of this supper, we realize once again our unworthiness, we feel afresh the burden of guilt, and we receive anew the assurance of forgiveness. This service is often referred to as the *Eucharist,* which is the Greek word for "thanksgiving." You cannot spiritually enter into a service of Communion without offering to God your thanksgiving. This implies surrender of all pride and self-sufficiency and recognition of our grateful dependence upon our God. In addition, we sense again the fellowship that binds our hearts together. In many Baptist churches the Communion service closes with the singing of "Blest Be the Tie That Binds," which includes the lyrics "The fellowship of kindred minds is like to that above" (John Fawcett, *UMH,* 557).

Luke tells us in Acts 4:32 that the church was "of one heart and soul." It is comparatively easy to get modern Christians together, but to get them to be "of one heart and soul" is almost a miracle. Yet there is something about Communion that minimizes our differences and magnifies our commonalties; making the words of the hymn true: "In Christ There Is No East or West."

There is yet another dimension, one of hope, which points to the future. The Lord said, "I tell you, I will never again drink of this fruit of the vine until that day when I drink it new with you in my Father's kingdom" (Matthew 26:29). Thinking of those words against the picture of the death, burial, and resurrection of our Lord brings hope to each of us. When we think of the future, fear seems to creep into our minds; fear of physical disease, of monetary loss, of failure, of death itself. Yet Jesus stood on the eve of his own death and talked calmly and confidently about the future. This is a test only the strongest can endure. What an inspiration for us!

The opposite of all fear is hope, glorious faith, and inner peace. The message of the Communion Table is eternal. We know the forces of righteousness will overcome the powers of evil, that justice and truth are eternal. If Christ could go to the cross with this hope and speak of drinking this cup anew with each of us in the future, then I can hope too. I will! Will you? (Drew J. Gunnells Jr.)

Worship Aids

Call to Worship (based on Psalm 103)

Bless the LORD, O my soul, and all that is within me.
Bless the LORD, O my soul,
 and do not forget all God's benefits.
Who forgives all your iniquity, who heals all your diseases?

Who redeems your life from the pit;
  who crowns you with steadfast love and mercy?
Who satisfies you with good as long as you live
  so that your youth is renewed like the eagle's?
The LORD is merciful and gracious,
  slow to anger and abounding in steadfast love.
Bless the LORD, O my soul!

Pastoral Prayer

Heavenly Lord, teach us the importance of thanksgiving. Forgive our tunnel vision that focuses on our problems instead of our blessings. Give us a widening dimension of understanding that shows us your grace in a new light. Once again in this Communion service, remind us of your sacrificial life and your command to take up our cross daily. Help us to see that this lifestyle is not for cowards but for the courageous. Thank you again for the hope that wells up within us when we share in Communion fellowship. In Jesus' name we pray. Amen.

Benediction

Send us away, dear Lord, conscious anew of the great sacrifice you made on our behalf and determined to show our gratitude by a lifestyle worthy of your name. We pray this in the name of Jesus. Amen. (Drew J. Gunnells Jr.)

NOVEMBER 13, 2011

❦❦❦

Twenty-second Sunday after Pentecost

Readings: Judges 4:1-7; Psalm 123; 1 Thessalonians 5:1-11; Matthew 25:14-30

Christians Got Talent
Matthew 25:14-30

Based on the success of the American television program *American Idol*, Great Britain started its own version, *Britain's Got Talent*. It became an instant hit thanks to a woman named Susan Boyle. She was in her forties and very plain and old-fashioned. Everyone was amazed when she began to sing; she had a voice like an angel. I got to thinking about a Christian talent contest; perhaps it could be called *Christians Got Talent*. As I considered the possibility, I wondered what prize could be offered. Since all Christians receive the gift of eternal life, what better prize could there be?

Today's Scripture text is the familiar parable of the talents. Three servants are given money ("talents") to manage while their master is away on a trip. Each one receives an amount equal to his ability. One is given five talents, another is given two talents, and a third is given one talent. When the master comes home, the two servants who invested their talents present the master with a 100 percent increase. The third servant, the one given the least amount, buried his talent in the ground and returns to his master the same amount he was given. This servant is severely reprimanded and called wicked and lazy. What little he has is taken away and given to another servant.

Often when people tell this story, they focus on the third servant. They talk about not burying our "talent" (money or other gifts) and about the consequences if we do. I prefer to focus on the fact that all of us have talents, and we need to use them to help others and to serve God. The church is always in need of persons who will humbly serve and minister.

We hold ministry fairs and ask people to volunteer for all kinds of programs and ministries, but there always seems to be a shortage of needed talent. Some people claim that they do not have any talent and so they don't volunteer.

Everyone has talents, gifts, and abilities. Even in the parable, the number of talents may be different, but each servant has at least one. God has endowed each of us with talent. Some of us are gifted in the arts. These people paint beautiful pictures or make glorious music with their voices or instruments. Some people can make wondrous things with their hands. Others cook delicious meals or have excellent mechanical skills. Still others can build things and grow things. The list of talents is as endless as our imaginations. It doesn't take a great deal of creativity to find a way to use these talents in the church and in ministry with and for others. I have known people who offered to change lightbulbs or write notes of encouragement for the elderly and shut-ins.

There are emotional talents as well. Some people are excellent listeners. People often feel a sense of relief just knowing they have been listened to. Some people are gifted advisers and counselors who can look at a situation and offer wisdom that is godly and beneficial. Other people are good at giving hugs, or offering words of encouragement or empathy. All of these talents can be used for the glory of God.

Most people have an occupation or a career where they receive training or gain insight through experience. Many of these skills can be used in ministry. I have known accountants who help the elderly fill out their tax returns, financial advisers who have led classes on money management, and schoolteachers who help with tutoring or teaching English as a second language. With a little creativity, almost any skill can be used to help others and further God's ministry through the church.

Finally, when we receive Christ, we also receive the Holy Spirit and the gifts of the Spirit. Read Romans 12; 1 Corinthians 12; and Ephesians 4. Everyone has at least one spiritual gift, and many people have more than one. These gifts cannot be earned or learned, but we can certainly pray for spiritual gifts and open ourselves to their power. I know that I am always praying for the gift of discernment. Spiritual gifts are to be used for the building up of the body of Christ. It is important that we discover and cultivate them together.

Some people are jealous of others' talents or gifts, but notice in the parable that none of the servants complain about the talents given to the others. The parable tells us that each one is gifted according to ability.

We would be wise to recognize that we each are unique and have differing types and levels of talents and gifts to offer for the work of Christ. We can always find someone who can do something better than we can; we can also always find someone who cannot do it as well. Be thankful for the talents you have, and seek to develop them with God's help.

We cannot use the excuse that we have no talent for serving God. Each of us has talents, gifts, and abilities that can be used to minister to God and others. (Neil Epler)

Lectionary Commentary
Judges 4:1-7

Who is hurt when we sin? Sin often harms us, and it can certainly harm others, but all sin is against God. When we sin we break God's laws and commands. When we sin we disregard God's authority over us. Judges 4:1 states, "The Israelites again did what was evil in the sight of the LORD." As a consequence of their sin, God punished them and sent a foreign army to oppress them. Sometimes God's discipline is a means of turning our attention back toward God.

The Israelites cried out to the Lord for help after they had been cruelly oppressed for twenty years. Why did it take them twenty years to cry to God for help? The Israelites followed their own path and it got them into a mess. This is often true of our own lives. We try to solve our problems ourselves and cry out to God only as a last resort. Still, God is patient with us and hears our cries. In this passage, God lures out the opposing king and his army and delivers them into the hands of the Israelites. The Lord can also help us and deliver us from our distress if only we will turn to God.

1 Thessalonians 5:1-11

In this passage we hear about two different kinds of sleep. The first deals with our not being alert and ready for the coming of the Lord. "Let us not fall asleep as others do, but let us keep awake and be sober" (1 Thessalonians 5:6). We need to be about the Lord's business and be sure that we are well prepared for God's arrival. Will God find us awake and watching or asleep and unprepared?

The second kind of sleep is the sleep of death. Many in the Thessalonian church were concerned about their loved ones who had died. Where were they now? Where would they spend eternity? Many of us worry about the eternal destiny of our loved ones too. Paul reminds the

Thessalonians that God came to bring us all salvation and not wrath. Jesus Christ "died for us, so that whether we are awake or asleep we may live with him" (5:10). We should be encouraged by these words. We can find comfort in the knowledge that our loved ones who know Christ live with him forever. (Neil Epler)

Worship Aids

Prayer of Confession

O God, we confess that we love to make excuses. We make excuses for why we cannot forgive others and why we do not have enough time for you. We make excuses for why we cannot serve your church and why we cannot minister to others. We complain that we do not have any talents or gifts to share. Yet we know you have blessed us abundantly with your forgiveness and love, and you have instilled in us gifts and talents enough to share and time to share them. Forgive us, we pray, and free us to serve you and our neighbors. Amen.

Words of Assurance (Hebrews 4:15-16)

The Lord knows us and our many weaknesses. God loves us just the way we are. "For we do not have a high priest who is unable to sympathize with our weaknesses, but we have one who in every respect has been tested as we are, yet without sin. Let us therefore approach the throne of grace with boldness, so that we may receive mercy and find grace to help in time of need."

Offertory Prayer

God, you have poured down blessings upon us from your bounty. You have given us food to eat, homes to live in, clothing to wear, and family and friends with which to share. You have also bestowed upon us talents and gifts to be used for your glory. Receive our tithes and offerings so that your work may be done on earth. Amen. (Neil Epler)

How Do You See the Man?

Third in a Series of Three on Celebrating Communion

John 19:1-16

Through the symbolism of Communion, we inevitably think of the trial and the crucifixion. Think with me about one particular aspect of these events, the role of Pilate. Jesus is standing before Pilate in the early morning hours of what we refer to as "Good Friday." Jesus has been brought before the Roman ruler by Jewish leaders who claim he is a threat to the Roman government as well as a blasphemer who claims to be king of the Jews. In a brief examination, however, Pilate finds nothing dangerous about Jesus.

Pilate's offer to release Jesus meets with opposition from the Jewish leaders who want blood and from the people who follow them. Pilate has Jesus flogged, hoping this will satisfy the sadistic desires of the people. Then he brings Jesus back out to the people. Jesus' clothing is disheveled, his back is a swollen pulp of bleeding welts, and his hair is matted with sweat and blood. The Lord looks like anything but a king. Pilate says, "Here is the man!" (John 19:5). What did those words mean to Pilate? What did they mean to the religious leadership or to the people gathered in the courtyard? What did they mean to John, the writer of this Gospel? For that matter, what do they mean to each of us?

No doubt Pilate saw Jesus as just another wandering rabbi—maybe popular, but harmless. Pilate says, "Look at him! This person is no threat to anyone, much less the Roman government. This miserable creature could not lead an insurrection against anything or anyone."

When the Pharisees, Sadducees, and scribes looked at Jesus, they saw a dangerous man, a threat to their power. Jesus ran roughshod over their legalistic pettiness; he hung their prejudices out for all to see, and he stood for ideas that, unleashed on the world, would destroy them. Jesus' love for all humankind was a threat to sectarian exclusiveness. They hated Jesus, not because he was weak, but because he was strong. They wanted him dead.

The mob didn't see much at all; they smelled blood. Like most mobs they were driven more by heat than light. The accounts in Matthew and Mark make it very clear that the mob made no decision for itself. The people were little more than pawns on a chessboard. When Pilate offered them Jesus as the one to be released, the priests and elders persuaded the people to ask for Barabbas.

Many modern people, like Pilate, see Jesus merely as a harmless idealist. They regard him as a great teacher with lofty ideals, a man whose teachings have influenced the world, but not as the Savior of humankind. They acknowledge that people are helped by his teachings just as they are helped by the teachings of other great thinkers. They even accept the fact that belief in Jesus, if you can accept it, has a soothing, therapeutic effect on some people. However, they do not accept the truth that he was the divine Son of God—one of a kind.

Like John, the writer of our text, those of us who sit in this congregation today gladly rejoice that Jesus was who he said he was, God's Son. Maybe John was even on the outskirts of that crowd in the courtyard, watching. John was familiar with what the prophets had said about the Messiah being not a conqueror but "a man of suffering and acquainted with infirmity" (Isaiah 53:3). Maybe more of Isaiah's words came to him: "he was wounded for our transgressions, crushed for our iniquities; upon him was the punishment that made us whole, and by his bruises we are healed" (v. 5). John might then have thought, *Here is the incarnate one, the longed for Messiah, the hope of all humankind.*

We may speculate about others' responses, but we must each consider what we see when we look at Jesus. While Pilate might have seen Jesus as a harmless idealist, the religious leaders saw a threat to their power and the mob saw blood. What do we see? We see the incarnate one, Jesus the Christ, the long-awaited Messiah who brought hope to humankind. When we behold Jesus, we see the hope of the world—past, present, and future.

When we partake of Communion, we recall the past—his earthly life, his agonizing death on the cross, and his miraculous resurrection. The bread and the wine also remind us of Jesus' continuing presence among us. But Communion does more; it points to the future. Luke tells us that on the night Jesus instituted the Lord's Supper he said, "I tell you that from now on I will not drink of the fruit of the vine until the kingdom of God comes" (Luke 22:18). Paul also pointed out our future hope, "For as often as you eat this bread and drink the cup, you proclaim the Lord's death until he comes" (1 Corinthians 11:26). (Drew J. Gunnells Jr.)

Worship Aids

Invocation

As we partake of this Communion, dear Lord, make us aware of the centrality of its message. It teaches us the importance of the cross and the resurrection. It reminds us of your continuing presence among us in the person of your Spirit. It gives us renewed hope that the future belongs to you and your people. Let us never take these moments lightly or disrespectfully but reverently and devotedly. We pray this in the name of the one who was, and is, and is to come, our Lord Jesus. Amen.

Responsive Reading (Philippians 2:5-11)

Let the same mind be in you that was in Christ Jesus,
who, though he was in the form of God,
   did not regard equality with God
   as something to be exploited,
but emptied himself,
   taking the form of a slave,
   being born in human likeness,
And being found in human form,
   he humbled himself
   and became obedient to the point of death—
   even death on a cross.
Therefore God also highly exalted him
   and gave him the name
   that is above every name,
so that at the name of Jesus
   every knee should bend,
   in heaven and on earth and under the earth,
and every tongue should confess
   that Jesus Christ is Lord,
   to the glory of God the Father.

Benediction

Send us away, dear Lord, with a renewed consciousness of your sacrificial life and death. May we, as an expression of thanksgiving, promise to walk in your steps this day and always. In Jesus' name. Amen. (Drew J. Gunnells Jr.)

NOVEMBER 20, 2011

❦❦❦

Christ the King/Reign of Christ Sunday

Readings: Ezekiel 34:11-16, 20-24; Psalm 100; Ephesians 1:15-23; Matthew 25:31-46

Scattered . . . Like Sheep
Ezekiel 34:11-16, 20-24

Scattered. Dispersed. People, like boats, can be cast loose from their moorings and drift away. Sheep, preoccupied with grazing, can move from one patch of grass to another until they look up and find they are nowhere near where they began. The same is sometimes true for people. They may drift away of their own accord or be forced off course by calamity.

Calamity! Imagine being one of the Israelites of the Babylonian exile: You see your home overrun. You watch your place of worship collapse in flames. Invaders chase you from your own country into a foreign land, where you have to learn a new language and acclimate to different foods, and people stare at you and whisper behind their hands as you walk by. When you think about your history and what your people have been through, you wonder if God even cares.

If you had lived in Ezekiel's time, you would have wondered what would become of your people. As an exile, a stranger in a strange land, you would live day to day, finding food, working, telling your children the stories of your ancestors, but your mind would have focused on the home you left behind. Like modern-day refugees from Rwanda, Palestine, Afghanistan; like sheep who had been scattered far and wide, you would have felt lost. Leaderless, without a king, you might have wondered who would save your people.

Modern U.S. Christians tend to think of "lostness" as a spiritual issue; the lost sheep is the sinner whom Jesus seeks to bring back into the fold of a loving and forgiving community. For Ezekiel, the lost sheep are the

363

scattered and oppressed of Israel, those dispersed people called "the Diaspora." Ezekiel remembers that they were scattered "on a day of clouds and thick darkness" (34:12). Plenty of people in our world have been scattered, torn from their families by war or by addiction or by violence. Some have had to leave their homes in order to find work. Others, like sheep, have simply wandered away, moving from one experience to another, becoming socially isolated. It is easy to become disconnected and drift apart.

Sociologist Robert Putnam describes our society as one in which people have become disconnected from friends, from families, and from social structures that help give our lives meaning. The title of his popular book, *Bowling Alone*, tells of a people cut off from one another. People hunger for social connection but don't know how to find it. They try to make up for the emptiness by buying things or entertaining themselves, but such pursuits lead to pervasive boredom and a sense of meaninglessness.

Imagine looking down through rooftops at people cloistered in cells, staring at thousands of flickering screens and vicariously living through the communities of television or the Internet—not knowing their own neighbors. We understand what it means to be dispersed and scattered, like sheep who have gone astray.

God has a different vision. "I myself will search for my sheep," says God (34:11). Ezekiel goes on to describe how God will round up the scattered flock and bring them to good grazing land. It might seem unlikely or impossible to gather up all the disconnected lives. We don't know what to do about our isolation. But God makes it clear that God will accomplish it. "I will seek...I will rescue...I will bring them...I will feed them...I will bind up the injured...I will strengthen the weak" (34:11-16). "I will," God says. God will take those scattered by war, by circumstance, by oppression, by their own folly, and make them one flock. "I myself will be the shepherd of my sheep" (v. 15). God plans to make a new community from these scattered ones. God will gather the dispersed people and create a new flock.

It isn't all sweet songs and holding hands. God has some harsh words for those sheep responsible for the scattering. Some of these sheep have had a hand not only in scattering the others but also in fouling the environment and spoiling otherwise good pasture. In what may be one of the most pointed scriptures on environmentalism in the Bible, God addresses those who took more than their fair share: "Is it not enough for you to feed on the good pasture, but you must tread down with your feet the rest of your pasture? When you drink of clear water, must you foul the rest with your feet?" (v. 18). God goes on to talk about judging between the fat sheep and the lean sheep. Once again, God takes the side of the oppressed and the lost. God saves and God judges.

But there is an important feature of Ezekiel's message that we often overlook. God repeatedly says, "I will," and emphasizes that this is God's action by saying, "I myself." The sheep do not judge or save or create a new community. God does. Jesus recognized this when he appropriated the story for his own parable of the sheep and the goats in Matthew 25:31-36. Neither sheep nor goats recognize Jesus: they simply do what they do, and then are surprised when Jesus reveals that he identifies with the poor and oppressed. Likewise it is God who judges between fat and thin sheep, who comes down on the side of the poor and oppressed.

Scattering seems to be a fact of life. We become scattered, either by drifting apart or through some calamity. Yet our God has determined to be a shepherd to this scattered and scatterbrained flock. God has in mind a community where the injured find healing, where the hungry find food, and where the good pasture can be shared by all. God and God alone is savior, judge, and king. (Dave Barnhart)

Lectionary Commentary
Matthew 25:31-46

It's rather difficult for us Western Christians to wrap our heads around the idea of concepts like *king* and *sovereign*. Our leaders are elected, and power is given to them through a social contract with everyday citizens. Not so with Jesus. This leader has been chosen by God, picked right out of the tomb and placed on the throne. Yet his rule is not tyrannical and top-down. According to Matthew's parable of the sheep and the goats, this king is present in "the least of these" (25:40). Anyone who is sick or poor or imprisoned or in debt or hungry is the king. So although his authority comes from above, Jesus' identity and credibility come from below.

Ephesians 1:15-23

The writer of Ephesians describes God's actions in Jesus. God "put [God's] power to work in Christ" (Ephesians 1:20) through the resurrection and Jesus' glorification. Christ is seated at the right hand of God, "far above all rule and authority and power and dominion" (v. 21). In other words, Jesus is in charge. For an early church that sometimes suffered persecution from without and conflict within, the idea that they had friends in high places must have been comforting. "All things"—all authorities, including presidents, emperors, debt collectors, generals, and talk show pundits—are put "under his feet" (v. 22). This is both hopeful and revolutionary talk. (Dave Barnhart)

Worship Aids

Call to Worship (based on Psalm 100)
Listen up, Earth!
When you come into God's presence, be happy!
The I Am is God!
God is our shepherd, the one who made us.
Shout your praises to God!
We sing to God and bless God's name.
All: God's steadfast love endures forever.

Invocation
Lord Jesus, our king, you come to us judging and saving. We pray every day for your reign on earth to come. Be present here among us. Let this place of worship become a little slice of your kingdom. Set us free to be your people, and rule our hearts, our communities, and our world.

Benediction
The king is among us, disguised as the least of us. Carry his message to all who need to hear it, and treat the people you meet as if they are Jesus. When you do, you will find that his reign has come and is already with us. Go now as citizens of Christ's kingdom. (Dave Barnhart)

Genesis on Stewardship: Fig Leaves and Other Precious Gifts

First in a Series of Three on Rethinking Christian Stewardship

(Note: This three-part sermon series looks at Christian stewardship holistically, not merely from the perspective of financial support of the church. It is grounded in texts that may not typically be associated with stewardship sermons that are geared solely toward monetary giving. Although financial giving is addressed,

the preacher may find this series useful whether or not it is associated with a pledge campaign.)

Genesis 1:26-31a

When we think of a sermon about stewardship, we typically think of Gospel passages about rendering to God what is God's, widow's mites, or how our hearts and our treasure are connected. Genesis is not likely the first passage that comes to mind, so when we see it referenced as a stewardship text, we may be left pondering what the preacher has in mind. Is there a stewardship message in Genesis about Adam and Eve being good stewards of fig leaves? Is there some stewardship jewel about not wasting garden fruit (don't think of apples—the text never mentions them).

Although some may not see Christian stewardship as the explicit message of this text, the sacredness of creation and our human role as stewards of all with which we have been entrusted make this a stewardship epic for Christians. The creation story is our story as Christians.

Stewardship and Genesis are both about beginnings and starting anew. They both offer opportunities to examine our outlook on life—who we are, why we are here, and what life is about. When life is seen as something to be treasured, it changes our perspective, focus, objectives, and behavior. Genesis was not only written to answer questions; Genesis compels us to ask questions of ourselves. What value and priority do we give relationships versus material things of life? Where do we focus our energy to concentrate our efforts? What are our objectives and purpose; in essence, for what are we striving? How do we seek fulfillment? What do we consider to be our greatest source of happiness, success, contentment, and wealth? Genesis raises many questions that are worthy of consideration and significant pondering.

I look at Christian stewardship using the metaphor of an altar table. The table of worship stands on four legs that give it solid support. The four legs represent love, self-reflection, gratitude, and generosity. The altar represents the worship of God, which is the root of Christian stewardship because giving is always an act of worship. I proclaim this truth from the pulpit, teach this in the classroom, and explain this to new converts who seek to understand Christ's church and the Christian faith. For Christians, giving is always an act of worship. When the Christian community grasps this basic truth, we need not worry about financial support for mission and ministry. There will always be enough because there is

367

already enough when we are willing to offer what we have in Christ's service.

Love is the beginning of stewardship. God loved life so much that creation is born; we are included in the package, and the entire package becomes God's gift of love to us. Ultimately, God offers Jesus as a divine love-gift to reconnect us to our source, bring redemption to our present, and give us hope for our future. Stewards grasp God's precious loving gift and respond with love that is passed on to others and to the creatures of God's creation. For Christians, God's love is the beginning of stewardship.

Self-reflection is another leg of the altar and occurs when we hold up a mirror to take a look at who we are. The questions above are a good beginning to understand what drives us and where we are headed. It is uncanny that some can be so good at strategic planning for business but do not look ahead to see where their own lives are headed. We can plan ahead for vacations or consider several moves ahead in a chess game, but we are often clueless about how our present choices are connected to future outcomes. I keep a note stuck on my bathroom mirror to look at each day. It is a simple reminder of how my today influences my tomorrow. It says, "When you get to the end of your journey and look back, what will you see?"

Gratitude means to say thank you to the giver of the gift. We are justified by faith—through God's grace (unconditional love)—and we are sanctified by the Holy Spirit working through our lives and all that we do. Gratitude is responding to the giver and the gift with grateful and appreciative hearts. When we are grateful, our spirits are changed. We are not the same. As a pastoral counselor, one of the ways I help people who struggle with depression is to encourage them to find something to be grateful for each day. Gratitude transforms us.

Generosity, the fourth leg of the table, is the result of love, self-reflection, and gratitude coming together. Love yields genuine care for others and is one meaning of the word *charity*, which we use to describe giving to the poor or for missions. Generosity is the outpouring of love toward others and God's creation. Generosity is opening our hearts and hands to others. People filled with God's love are generous in spirit, word, and deed.

Stewards are not only caretakers, they are celebrants, relishing and rejoicing in life and all of the goodness that life embraces. Ms. Angel is ninety-five years old. Her minister was shocked to receive an e-mail from her, so instead of replying, the astonished pastor picked up the phone. "Ms. Angel," the pastor inquired, "when did you start using e-mail?"

The nonagenarian replied, "I told my son to get me a computer and teach me how to use it so that I could keep up with everyone and save postage!" I assume that her son picked up the tab for the computer.

I want to be the sort of steward who celebrates—an active participant in creation and life's amazing journey. (Gary G. Kindley)

Worship Aids

Call to Worship

We gather to worship God,
> the source of all that we have and all that we are,
> as we humbly confess what is true:

Giving is an act of worship!
We gather as a people of glad and generous hearts, declaring:
Giving is an act of worship!
We gather as disciples,
> divinely loved by Jesus Christ.

In our living, serving, praying, and giving,
> we testify to what Christ taught and lived:

Giving is an act of worship!

Offertory Prayer

Remind us, O God, that what we do today in this place is an act of worship—showing up, standing up, and giving up a part of what we have in response to your love for us. As we sing your praises, read your Scriptures, and proclaim the gospel message, may we do so as stewards of your creation and salvation. In the name of our Redeemer, we offer this our prayer. Amen.

Benediction

Go forth as a people of glad and generous hearts, proclaiming God's love in all that you do by sharing God's love extravagantly! (Gary G. Kindley)

NOVEMBER 24, 2011

❧❧❧

Thanksgiving Day

Readings: Deuteronomy 8:7-18; Psalm 65; 2 Corinthians 9:6-15; Luke 17:11-19

Thanksgiving Is More Than a Feeling
Deuteronomy 8:7-18

Does it annoy God when we give thanks? When I ask this question, most people look incredulous. After all, we gather on Thanksgiving and tell one another that we ought to thank God for our blessings. One of the problems with the world and with today's society, we tell ourselves, is that people aren't thankful for what they have. Yet Jesus doesn't say much about any moral obligation to give thanks. There's the reliable story about the ten lepers (Luke 17:11-19), but even this story is not about giving thanks so much as it is about the old rivalry between the people of Judea and Samaria. Look through the Gospels and you will certainly read about Jesus giving thanks when he breaks bread with others, but there are no commandments about our obligation to feel thankful.

The only other significant story about giving thanks from the Gospels is the story of the Pharisee and the tax collector (Luke 18:9-14). The tax collector, extortionist and traitor that he is, weeps and grovels, calling out, "God, have mercy on me, a sinner!" Meanwhile, the religious pillar of the community stands apart and piously prays to God, "Lord, thank you that I am not like other people, especially like this tax collector over here."

Ouch! Do our thanksgivings sound as pompous as these in God's ears? I sit through ecumenical Thanksgiving services, where we gather to congratulate ourselves on being religious. "The world," we will say, "isn't thankful enough. We ought to be thankful. We should thank God." We will go on to talk about *oughts* and *shoulds* and how the world can be divided into two kinds of people: the grateful and the ungrateful. Then we thank God for the blessings of prosperity, for living in a free country, for God's favor—and for not being like others who are less prosperous, enslaved, or ill-favored. Thankfulness can become the most insidious kind of pride. How does this kind of thanks-giving sound to God?

Look at the language Deuteronomy 8:7-14 uses to describe the promised land: a land with springs and underground waters bursting forth from valleys and hills, wholesome wheat and barley, juicy grapes, sweet figs and tart pomegranates, olives and honey. There are material resources too: iron and copper, raw materials for industry and trade. God describes fertile herds producing wool, meat, and milk, and anticipates that people will build "fine houses" (v. 12) and not be hungry. The scripture overflows with good stuff, piling on one blessing after another.

But gratitude comes from being aware not only of blessings but also of the alternative. It didn't have to be this way. Deuteronomy 8:15 describes the opposite: a "great and terrible wilderness, an arid wasteland with poisonous snakes and scorpions," and a life of slavery. Blessings are temporal. There is a past in which we struggled for survival. There may be a future in which we struggle again. There are many who struggle even now in real or virtual wastelands, where real or metaphorical poisonous snakes and scorpions prey on them and where they dream of the tastes of grapes, figs, and pomegranates.

That's the sticky point of giving thanks, isn't it? It forces us to recognize disparity. We thank God for the food we eat because we know it doesn't have to be on our plate at all. We thank God for wealth because we know there are people out there without wealth. Later in Deuteronomy God will order the chosen people to "open [their] hand to the poor and needy neighbor" (15:11). The sheer abundance of the land the author describes means that this wealth is to be shared, not hoarded.

"Take care that you do not forget the LORD your God," says the author, "by failing to keep his commandments" (8:11). "Do not say to yourself, 'My power and the might of my own hand have gained me this wealth'" (v. 17). While entrepreneurial people with a strong work-ethic and persistence can turn their wealth into greater wealth, nobody on earth is self-made. I knew one proud farmer who started his life with little more than a mule and a stretch of ground. He plowed the fields, endured drought and floods, and arrived at the sunset of his life sipping lemonade on the covered porch he had built with his own hands. There is little that can describe the pleasure of resting and appreciating something you have made. Yet his hard work alone did not earn his prosperity. Farmers in Bolivia work just as hard yet do not have the roads to transport their produce to market. Public roads and schools, adequate medical care, and opportunities for success allow some people to thrive. Yet this farmer I knew felt that people who were poor simply hadn't worked hard enough.

We all, to some extent, feel the same. We become possessive of these "blessings" God has given us. We come to feel that what we have is ours by right. We give thanks to God as a way of laying claim to things that are "ours." At Thanksgiving we become Pharisees, thanking God for our property, our prosperity, and our freedom. But in reality, we are tax collectors: what we own and enjoy did not come from our own hands, and we will not take it with us.

True thanks-giving is not a warm and fuzzy feeling of appreciation for our houses and cars and prosperity. True thanks-giving is the feeling of a narrowly missed accident, a sin forgiven. It is the "Whew!" blown out of a throat that has been cooled by a long drink of water on a hot day. True thanks-giving is letting our eyes linger on the wasteland a little while longer, so that we don't forget it, those of us who struggle through it, or the God who brings us safely through. (Dave Barnhart)

Lectionary Commentary
Luke 17:11-19

We read the "ten lepers" story nearly every Thanksgiving because it is one of the few things Jesus said explicitly about giving thanks. Not only that, but it is an annual lectionary text. That people "ought" to be thankful would have been taken for granted by Judeans of Jesus' day. The psalms are full of thanksgivings to God and praise for God's works. The thing that makes the ten lepers story distinctive is its inclusion of the Samaritan. The other lepers did exactly what Jesus ordered them to do: they went to the priests and then, presumably, they hurried home to their friends and family. Perhaps they did not recognize Jesus as the source of their healing. What is certain is that Luke points out yet again that it is the outsider who recognizes Jesus' significance. The Samaritan prostrates himself at Jesus' feet in an attitude of worship. The word used here for "thanked" is *euchariston,* or "good gift," which is where we get the word *eucharist* for the Lord's Supper.

2 Corinthians 9:6-15

This passage describes our response to feelings of gratitude: we give. Those who give sparingly, Paul says, will reap sparingly, and those who give generously will receive generously. This is not the same prosperity gospel that many Christians have come to believe. The harvest Paul describes is not money, but a harvest of God's glory. Those in Jerusalem who receive the charity of the Corinthian church will pray for the Corinthians. Paul obviously thinks that prayer, gratitude, and glorifying God are compensation enough, because he calls the result of this charitable giving an "indescribable gift" (2 Corinthians 9:15). Giving, it seems, is its own reward. (Dave Barnhart)

Worship Aids

Call to Worship

Provider God, we bring you an offering of thanks for the breath in our lungs, the friends and family by our sides, and the earth under our feet. Even when anxiety and scarcity threaten us, your abundance continues. Give us more days and hours and minutes to give you praise. Amen.

Responsive Reading (based on Psalm 65)

God, we owe our praise to you.
You answer prayer and save us.
We see your love in the blessings of nature
In the rain that waters the earth
In the grain that grows from the ground
In the livestock that grazes in pastures
All: In the abundance of life around us.

Pastoral Prayer

God, in the midst of thanksgiving, many of us are still in want. We want healing. We want justice. We want food for those of us who are hungry, and solace for those who grieve. Your children depend on you. Hear the desperate cries of your people, and deliver us, so that we may give glory to your name. Amen. (Dave Barnhart)

Faith in a Jar

Second in a Series of Three on Rethinking Christian Stewardship

1 Kings 17

Trust is one of the most essential and yet most difficult aspects of belief. To have faith—to truly trust in God or an individual, such as the trust one places in a spouse—is a spiritual gift that we can choose to develop. It is a choice, for God does not force belief upon us. We choose whether or not to place our trust in God's goodness and the gift of salvation. Jesus taught, led, and inspired but did not force people into faith. Even when Jesus warned or admonished those who strayed from God's plan (typically the Pharisees, Sadducees, or the arrogant wealthy), he did not coerce people into conviction but gave everyone whom he encountered the opportunity to believe. When people did place their trust in him it was their faith, Jesus explained, that had made them whole.

Christian stewards are followers of Christ who place their faith in God, knowing that God will provide for and equip them as their journey requires. Stewards do not wait for proof, they respond with committed action and obedience. They give, trusting that there will be enough. They serve, knowing that God will never ask of them more than they can produce. They worship out of gratitude and love. They pray to stay connected to the one who is their strength. They witness to their faith by sharing their experience of faith. Christian stewards make real the faith they profess.

Elijah is a faithful prophet who has placed his belief in the Lord God. Elijah's prophetic voice confronts King Ahab, who "did evil in the sight of the LORD more than all who were before him" (1 Kings 16:30). Ahab marries Jezebel, the daughter of King Ethbaal of the Sidonians—a people who worshiped Baal, not the one true God. Elijah follows the word of God and announces to Ahab that there will be a dreadful drought. Elijah proclaims that the drought will not end until he, in the name of the God of Israel, commands that it will. The drought lasts three years.

Elijah is hiding from Ahab, Jezebel, and their court, and God sends him to the home of a widow in Zarephath of Sidon, the same region from which Queen Jezebel had come. Fidelity to God and God's prophets can be found in the least likely of places, for God's Spirit is not limited by race, nationality, or geography. This widow hears and obeys the instructions of Elijah, providing him some flatbread from the last remnants of meal and oil that she has. Elijah then announces that she need not fear, for the jar will not be empty nor will the jug run dry of oil until God once again releases the rain from the heavens. To her amazement, it is so.

The story goes further, and its lesson presses us to inquire: How far are we willing to take our faith? The woman's son dies. It appears that this is her only child and the last connection to her husband, who has already died. In frantic despair, she questions Elijah, blaming him for the death and asking why he has done this. Elijah immediately takes her son and, calling boldly upon the power of God, revives him.

Christian stewards—those who accept the responsibility that comes with taking up the yoke of Christian discipleship—are called to make decisions based on faith. Stewards place their trust in the Lord and know that God will never abandon them or deny them access to the power of the Holy Spirit. By God's Spirit, stewards are empowered to live out their discipleship through spiritual disciplines. Extravagant giving, dedicated service, devotional prayer (interceding for others and listening to God), faithful participation in Christian community, scriptural study, and witnessing to their faith; these all are marks of Christian stewardship. These disciplines can be summed up in five words: prayers, presence, gifts, service, and witness.

The sacred fabric of the biblical drama is woven with faithful stewards of life and with their unique gifts. Esther risks losing her life and her crown for the sake of her people, the Jews, when they are persecuted by Haman. Solomon, son of King David, compelled by his devotion to God, uses his gifts of leadership to build the Jerusalem temple. It is a holy place so breathtakingly constructed that—according to an ancient story not found in scripture—the queen of Sheba, upon entering the temple, lifted her skirt off the glistening marble floor, mistakenly assuming that it was wet! Job remains faithful in abundance and in abject poverty. The apostles leave their lives behind to follow the Christ.

We miss the mark when we limit our idea of stewardship to funding the annual budget of the church. For Christians, stewardship is a transformational way of looking at life. Stewards view success differently. Mature stewards have less anxiety and greater trust. They cultivate a deeper prayer life, use worship as an opportunity to give and to receive, and realize that Christian community is measured not merely by what we get out of it but by how we participate in it.

How great is your faith? Can you bridge the chasm between spiritual trust and daily practice? Like the widow of Zarephath and Elijah, do you have enough trust in God to have faith in a jar? You will be amazed at how transformed your church can become when people begin to grasp the nature of discipleship that is defined by Christian stewardship. (Gary G. Kindley)

Worship Aids

Call to Worship
Trust in the Lord with all your heart!
Proclaim God's faithfulness each day!
Put into practice what you believe by the Spirit.

Draw close to God and have your cup filled.
All: Let us worship with faith, hope, and love.
In this hour, let us be the church together!

Offertory Prayer

Wondrous God, who fills empty bellies and empties sealed tombs, release us from the fear and worry that keep us from wholly trusting you. Open our eyes to a better way of living—a life of faith, hope, and love. We offer these gifts as an act of devotion and a sign of our trust in you. Thank you for placing your trust in us. May we be worthy of our sacred calling. Amen.

Benediction

May the God who provides in times of drought and times of plenty, the God who draws near when we seek God and when we run away, the God who holds us close when we suffer and sheds divine tears when we weep, sustain you through your journey now and forever! (Gary G. Kindley)

NOVEMBER 27, 2011

❧❧❧

First Sunday of Advent

Readings: Isaiah 64:1-9; Psalm 80:1-7, 17-19; 1 Corinthians 1:3-9; Mark 13:24-37

The End . . . or the Beginning?
Mark 13:24-37

We love the end of the world. We love telling stories about how it all ends. Just go to the movies during the summer blockbuster season, and you can watch the world end any number of ways: floods from rising sea levels, asteroids from outer space, nuclear annihilation, pandemics, zombie infestations, and alien invasions. We have a sense that things cannot keep on going this way. Something has to give. Will it be with a bang or a whimper?

We know that we are mortal and will not last forever, and we know that this world we love will end as well. For people of Jesus' time it was the day when God, weary of humanity's sin and stupidity, would invade the world and impose God's own rule on the planet. They called it the "Day of the Lord," the coming of the Son of Man. The dead would rise and be reconstituted and stand before God to be judged according to their deeds. While this may sound like a hellfire-and-brimstone sermon, the fact is that all humanity—religious or not—is conscious of sin and actually longs for judgment. Why else would we keep watching the world destroyed or nearly destroyed again and again? With a mix of fear and eager anticipation, we long for judgment.

Isaiah cries out, "O that you would tear open the heavens and come down, so that the mountains would quake at your presence" (64:1). We want the bad guys to get their comeuppance and the righteous to be vindicated. This is why we love the end of the world and tell stories about how it happens.

You can see the signs, Jesus says. Hopeful signs, in fact. He compares it to the budding leaves of a fig tree. One day you look closely and the first tiny, yellow-green leaves unwrap themselves and spread toward the sky. Then you know the seasons are changing. Soon there will be juicy figs ripening in the sun. When he uses this metaphor, Jesus' followers likely remember all the times that prophets described Israel as a fig tree that kept failing to produce fruit, and the threat that God would soon cut it down. For Jesus to use this symbol of fruitfulness and growing life, then, is a bit unusual. Since he's describing the end of the world, we might expect him to use a metaphor of winter or to talk about the ax at the root of the tree. Instead Jesus views the coming of the Son of Man as a good thing.

The kingdom of God grows imperceptibly, and we stand on the edge of a new age. One season is ending, and another beginning. The coming of the Son of Man isn't so much the end of our world as the promise of another one beginning. You can see the hopeful signs of it blossoming all around you.

"But you don't know when it's coming," Jesus says. Despite the scenarios about the end of the world that one group or another have predicted, the world seems to plow stubbornly along. Sure, there's no question that we can't keep living this way: building bigger bombs, fouling the oceans and air, baking our planet, and dumping pharmaceuticals into our drinking water. We live in an age where the end of the world seems tangible. Yet we don't know when the turning point will take place. Although we are certain there must be a reckoning soon, it isn't a date we can put on our calendars. It isn't like we will see the end coming and say, "Well, I'll only be able to mark four things off my to-do list on that day."

In fact, when the Day of Judgment comes, we will still have things on our to-do lists. There will be clothes in the washing machine and a full in-box on your desk. Whether that Day of Judgment is the end of your own life, or the end of the world, or the glorious return of Christ, you still have a life to live. Jesus admonishes us to "keep awake" (Mark 13:37). Don't let the day of the Lord sneak up on you. Live as though the kingdom is coming now. Leave the speculation about when or how or who will be saved and who will be "left behind" to others.

It is as if your boss left the employees in charge of the family business, says Jesus, and it does not matter if the boss returns "in the evening, or at midnight, or at cockcrow, or at dawn" (13:35). It does not matter if it is seven days or seven millennia from now. When the boss returns, there will be only one question: Have you been faithful to the work you've been given? You'll still have stuff on your to-do list. Is it the right stuff?

What an odd scripture to kick off Advent! When we talk about preparing for Christmas, we don't usually begin by talking about disaster movies. But preparing for Christmas means getting ready for the coming of our king. The world is changing, and there is something new and exciting growing just beyond the edge of our perception, just under the surface of things. We anticipate the end of our corrupted world and the beginning of a new, exciting, peaceful, and just one. God's rule is growing around us, little by little. You can see it grow in unlikely friendships between rich and poor, when people of different backgrounds and from different neighborhoods sing together in the same pew. You can see it wherever the hungry receive food and the sick find healing. In the midst of winter, there are already buds on the trees where new life is preparing to spring out. (Dave Barnhart)

Lectionary Commentary
Isaiah 64:1-9

Isaiah gives voice to the tension most of us feel when we talk about judgment day. On the one hand, we want to see God. On the other, we fear God's judgment. Some Christians I talk with would like very much to see the kind of stories described in the Hebrew Bible, to see God "tear open the heavens" (Isaiah 64:1) and appear in fire and smoke as God appeared to the Hebrews on Sinai. We long to see miracles and God's glory the way concertgoers long to see lasers and pyrotechnics, so that our faith in a faithful God can be confirmed.

Yet God seems hidden and distant. We wonder if God has left us because of our sin. Isaiah's cry to God begs the Lord to remember God's people and return, to vindicate a people who have been exiled.

1 Corinthians 1:3-9

Paul opens his letter to the Corinthian church by buttering them up. He praises their wisdom and their spirituality, even though it is pride in their religiosity and spirituality that seems to be causing some of their conflicts. He begins planting seeds for arguments he will make later, for them to love one another and be unified. He reminds them again and again of the thing they all have in common: "Jesus Christ" is repeated six times in just seven verses. He also reminds them that Jesus will return. (Dave Barnhart)

Worship Aids

Invocation (based on Isaiah 64)

LORD, tear open the skies and come down!
Shake the mountains and boil the seas!
Scare us into obedience! Save us from ourselves!
Save us from our sin and the consequences of our actions!
Lord, you are our Parent,
We are your children.
You are our potter,
We are your clay.
All: Raise us and shape us to serve you this day.

Pastoral Prayer

God, the season of Advent is upon us. The Christmas frenzy begins again. Slow us down to anticipate the coming kingdom together. To those for whom this season is a painful reminder of loneliness or grief, be an incarnate presence through your body, the church. Prepare in us and among us a place for you to be born. Amen.

Benediction

Go into the world with the knowledge that this age is passing away. A new age is dawning. You can see it blossoming around us if you have eyes to see it. Stay awake, keep your eyes open, and look for it, thanking God wherever you see the kingdom happening. (Dave Barnhart)

The Blessing of Addiction

Third in a Series of Three on Rethinking Christian Stewardship

Luke 17:11-19

Thus far in this three-part series, we have looked at Genesis in a fresh way through the lens of Christian stewardship. We have also considered how God has used disparate persons throughout the biblical text to uplift the task, value, impact, and demands of faithful stewardship. Perhaps the title of this sermon seems the least expected of all: "The Blessing of

Addiction." How can addiction be a blessing and what lesson of steward-ship can we possibly learn from it?

I once heard a man who was in a 12-step program declare, "My addic-tion has been a true blessing for me!" From my viewpoint as a Christian counselor, his words do not surprise me. As Christian stewards, they need not surprise us either. We have the power to choose how we respond to what happens to us on life's journey, and we can determine if what we experience is tragedy or turning point—a burden or a blessing. Blessings and burdens are what we make of them. This addict saw the blessing in his struggles, while many would see only the burden of his struggles.

Luke's Gospel reports an encounter that Jesus has with ten individuals as he travels along the border of Samaria—home of what the Jews would call "pagan Samaritans," and the beautiful region of Galilee. The text explains that the ten are suffering from leprosy. Although the Greek word for *leprosy* that is used in the New Testament can represent many various skin diseases, the specific condition of leprosy is assumed for the story. All ten cry out to Jesus, keeping their distance from him and others as the law demands. Jesus commands them to go and present themselves before the priest—a requirement of levitical law. The law of Torah stated that one must be declared "clean" by a priest in order to be acceptable for worship as well as to avoid contaminating those who were already ceremonially clean according to religious law.

Verse 14b reports: "And as they went, they were made clean." This is a miracle story of healing. A dread disease of the first century, for which no efficacious treatment would be discovered for centuries to come, was healed by the words of Jesus. But the story does not conclude with the healing; there are yet more lessons to be learned here.

One of the ten returns to Jesus in ecstatic joy. Praising God at the top of his lungs, he throws himself at the feet of Jesus with overwhelming gratitude for what Christ has done for him. His gratitude is a key lesson of the story. Jesus names it when he observes that ten were healed but only one has returned. Luke has pointed out that the returning person is a Samaritan. Samaritans were a people loathed by the Jews, perhaps more than Gentiles or other foreigners. They were despised for their impure religious practices and their role in Jewish history—left behind while countless Jews were carried off into Babylonian exile.

Jesus identifies the man aloud as a foreigner, the only one who returns from a group that—given the setting—we assume is made up of at least some, if not a majority of, Jews. Once again, as in other healing narratives, Jesus pronounces that the man's faith has made him well.

This is a stewardship story as well as a healing story. It is the account of people healed miraculously, an outsider who alone grasps the nature of the gift that has been given, and a testimony to gratitude as an act of worship for a sign of God through God's incarnate Son.

Disease, be it of sickness of body or brokenness of mind, comes in many ways. In a culture of excesses, addiction is a disease that is easily fueled, whether we understand the origin of addiction to be behavioral, genetic, or a bit of both. When an addict can declare, "It is the best thing that ever happened to me," there is a sense of gratitude, serenity, and understanding that testifies to a deep and enduring faith.

This particular addict went on to explain that he has refocused his life and can now think with greater clarity. He lives in the present moment, a true gift that escapes many of us, instead of rehearsing former successes or sorrows of yesterday's memories or obsessing with irrational fear of possible future failings.

A Christian steward can, like the witness of this recovering addict, not allow life to overwhelm but choose to live centered in the one who is the source of strength and serenity in abundance. Stewardship is not only what we do with our money and our time but also how we cultivate a sense of gratitude for the journey of life with its triumphs and troubling turns.

When Reinhold Niebuhr penned the words of the Serenity Prayer, he began with: "God, give us grace to accept with serenity the things that cannot be changed." Acceptance is a step toward gratitude. Wherever you find yourself, whatever brokenness you face, you are not alone. Every day, people facing all sorts of burdens, obstacles, or addictions can receive help and move from shame to grace.

Gratitude begins with acceptance and ultimately moves toward response. The leper who returned to Jesus did so in a response of overwhelming gratitude. Whether we respond with sharing what we have "off the top" (Christian financial stewardship), by sacrificially giving of our time (Christian service), by spiritually connecting with God and others (prayer and meditation), or through a change of attitude about our life's circumstances (acceptance, gratitude, and serenity), the response is always up to us. You have received a priceless gift. How will you respond? (Gary G. Kindley)

Worship Aids

Invocation (Unison)

Holy God, we are in need of your saving power, for we are a broken people. At times, behind the forced smiles that we wear, we cannot completely hide the hurt. We catch glimpses of joyful living when we read the Gospels, but actually living in joy eludes us. Today, we come to draw close to you, the source of joy and true life. In doing so, may we surrender our burdens and free our minds to allow the balm of your love to wash over us. In the name of our saving Lord, Jesus the Christ. Amen.

Pastoral Prayer

God of blessing and mercy, pour upon us the healing waters of your Holy Spirit, for we are parched and in need of the water that satisfies. We have tried so many things to fill our aching void, but nothing can completely satisfy the emptiness of our lives that only your love was designed to fill. Fill us to overflowing so that we might share with others the testimony of transformation. Free us from the oppressive bondage of excess, addiction, desperation, condemnation, arrogance, self-righteousness, and all sin that separates us from you and one another. Come, Holy Spirit, and transform us this day, we implore you. In your healing name we plead. Amen.

Benediction

People of transformation, allow the power of the transforming God to renew your spirits and make you whole again. Go and testify to God's changing power! (Gary G. Kindley)

DECEMBER 4, 2011

❦❦❦

Second Sunday of Advent

Readings: Isaiah 40:1-11; Psalm 85:1-2, 8-13; 2 Peter 3:8-15a;
Mark 1:1-8

Counting on God's Blessings
Isaiah 40:1-11

A voice cries out. You hear it but don't see the speaker. Isaiah doesn't tell us whose voice it is, although we can probably guess. It says, "Comfort my people.... Speak tenderly to Jerusalem, and cry to her" (40:1-2). Cry, shout, holler these things. Be my herald. Oh, sure, in our electronic age, we have far more efficient ways of communicating: billboards, television, text messaging, Internet. Yet God persists in using human voices. There's just something about the sound of air moving past the moist tissue of vocal cords that affects how we listen.

So God uses this inefficient, faltering mode of communication to carry God's messages. God speaks to those willing to hear the voice, and some who hear have the audacity to speak for God. You can probably rattle off some of their names: Moses, the law-giver; Elijah, the prophet; Jesus, the Savior; Deborah, the judge; Miriam and David, the musicians. Then there are the modern spokespersons for God: authors, preachers, evangelists, prophets such as Martin Luther King, Jr., Billy Graham, Bono, Bishop Tutu... You. Yes, you too, if you hear the voice. Sometimes it's the gut feeling, the startling intuition, a nudge from the Holy Spirit. Sometimes it's an uncomfortable presence, the recognition of truth leaping from the written word of the Bible or even the newspaper. Sometimes you hear it like the breath of God sighing just by your ear. But one way or another, the Spirit prophesies to and through those with ears to hear it. "A voice cries out" (40:3).

We expect to hear damnation. Hellfire and brimstone. We know what the prophets say. They talk about the judgment of God falling upon us sinners for the things we've done. Most Christian theology tells us we all deserve infinite punishment for our finite sins. Jonathan Edwards preached a famous sermon called "Sinners in the Hands of an Angry God," and he crafted a terrifying image of our souls poised on the brink of hell. God looks at us, he said, with a mixture of contempt and disgust. We are like spiders clinging to a rock, which God holds over the fire, and it's only God's mercy that keeps all the terrors of the world and the underworld from collapsing upon us.

People fainted in fear when they heard Edwards preach. He borrowed his language straight from the prophets, even from Isaiah and Jeremiah. They described God's wrath falling upon a wicked planet. Whole countrysides, including Jerusalem, would be turned into wastelands of burning tar pits. We've heard such sermons before. Televangelists tell us when national calamity or natural disaster falls upon us that it is because of our sins. So when Isaiah says he hears a voice crying out, we know what to expect. Hellfire and brimstone. Judgment and damnation.

Comfort! Tenderness! What strange words to shout at the top of our lungs. Peace! Isaiah says something surprising for a prophet: God has declared, "Enough." What would it be like if the church shouted this message at the top of its lungs? Enough, already! Listen! God is not angry with you anymore. The terrible things that happen to you in this world are not the judgments of an angry God. In fact, Isaiah says, Jerusalem has received twice the penalty it deserved. It is time for healing wounds, for comforting the afflicted. Philip Yancey argues in his book *What's So Amazing About Grace?* that the church is the only institution in the world that has been entrusted with the message of grace. Our mandate from God is to declare *good* news to the world. Our job is to shout from the rooftops, "Comfort! Tenderness! Peace!"

God is coming! Not with swords and chariots, tanks and fighter jets. God is coming with a parade. In fact, part of the jubilant message is to build a processional highway, a path for the festival parade. This parade will dwarf the Christmas and Thanksgiving parades. God will lead the parade of God's people. The nations, "all people," religious or not, will line the sides of the parade route to see "the glory of the LORD" (40:5) and throw confetti and ticker tape. The exiled and the lost will gather, and God will set the pace and lead them across a level ground and up Mount Zion to the temple, where everyone—and that means *everyone*—will worship God. Floats and ticker tape, brass bands, majorettes, and clowns. In the midst of the throng, there is God, carrying babies in each arm, their beaming parents trailing behind them like mother sheep.

If this scene sounds familiar, it's because it's the one shown in the movies *The Ten Commandments* and *The Prince of Egypt,* where the people of Israel leave the slavery of Egypt with children singing, celebrating on their way to the promised land. Isaiah invites us to imagine such a scene in our own world: a parade down Main Street. Families who were barely making it month to month, single parents who worried about their children's futures, walk along behind God, who carries their hope in his arms. Folks who would never darken the door of a church cheer the processional. The faithful bang drums and sing at the top of their lungs, while others run ahead and announce the coming parade. The whole way they all shout, "Comfort! Tenderness! Peace!"

God's voice has spoken. Sure, it may sound unlikely, even impossible. If it were only a human voice that we'd heard, we'd have reason to doubt. The billboards, the hollow promises of advertisers and politicians, are as frail and temporary as human life. After all, "all people are grass," and "the grass withers, the flower fades" (40:6-7). But you've heard a message of good news straight from God, whose word "will stand forever" (v. 8). So you can count on it. (Dave Barnhart)

Lectionary Commentary
Mark 1:1-8

Mark begins his Gospel with John "appearing" in the wilderness as abruptly as Isaiah's disembodied voice calls out for comfort for Jerusalem. Isaiah promised the Babylonian exiles that they would soon leave their captivity and return to their homes, that God would establish a new kingdom. Yet five hundred years later, in John's day, the promise is only partially fulfilled. They have their temple, but they still have no kingdom of their own. When John appears, "all the people of Jerusalem" (Mark 1:5) go out to hear his hopeful message. Isaiah's words of comfort to Jerusalem were finally coming true. A faithful shepherd, Jesus himself, would soon show up at the scene, and eventually lead the people in a processional to the temple on Palm Sunday. John fits the role of prophet. John dresses funny, eats a strict diet, calls on people to repent, and predicts the coming of one even more powerful than he.

2 Peter 3:8-15a

In 2 Peter, the author lets his audience know that even though Christ has not returned yet, he will soon. But how you define *soon* depends on what time scale God is using. Still, the author admonishes his listeners to be faithful and uses apocalyptic imagery of loud noises and fire to remind them that the world and all that is in it has a finite amount of time left. The writer of 2 Peter advises patience, which, in this season of Advent, can be difficult. We use the expression "slow as Christmas" to describe someone who is taking forever, but we also say that "Christmas is just around the corner." The same is true of Christ's return. It's always almost here but not quite yet. (Dave Barnhart)

Worship Aids

Offertory Prayer

God of John the Baptist, we have no processional highways to your temple. But we bring our gifts to you just the same. We labor to build those roads of righteousness with our tithes, our offerings, and the work of our hands. Bless our gifts for the upbuilding of your kingdom and for preparing our world to receive you. Amen.

Prayer for Inspiration (based on Psalm 85)

Lord, righteousness makes a path for you into our lives. Let us hear your words to us this day. In your words, passionate love and consistent faithfulness come together. Right living for individuals and peace among communities join hands. Surround us with your grace on all sides, from above and below. Amen.

Benediction

Now may the leader of our parade, the builder of highways, the shepherd of God's people lead you from this place and out among the nations, so that you may become heralds of good news. The Lord is coming! Comfort! Tenderness! Peace! (Dave Barnhart)

Hard Chairs

First in a Series of Four on Advent/Christmas

Genesis 3:1-13, 16-19

At the hospital nearest to my church, the surgical waiting room is a windowless square room fit neatly halfway between the birthing wing and the cafeteria. Most of one wall is missing, providing a wide doorway to the hall, while the other three sides of the room are lined with chairs. On the right wall, the chairs are interrupted by a single, small table bearing coffeepot, cups, and various coffee condiments (sweeteners, creamer, stirrers, and the like). Mounted high up in the front left corner, a TV that blares the latest developments on select news channels oversees the fluorescent-lit room crowded with chairs. On the far wall, next to a door leading back toward the operating rooms, a phone is affixed to the wall and rings at various interludes.

Since this is a waiting room, the chairs are the main focus of the room. In addition to those lining the walls, more chairs are shored up against one another, forming mini-islands toward the center of the room. Somewhat like a few parsonages I have been around, the waiting room seems to receive the chairs that board rooms and administrative offices no longer need. "Gently used" would probably describe the waiting room furniture well. After all, the people who will occupy these chairs won't be here forever. Those who enter the waiting room seem to greet the room with an understanding that they won't be there forever. However, at some point during their waiting, the transitory nature of being in the waiting room becomes elusive. Those who are waiting begin to wonder if they will ever leave. So despite the open invitation of the unoccupied, gently used, multitude of chairs, the one who enters the waiting room is not attracted to the sitting, the waiting, or the emerging hardness of the seat.

At this point, I have a confession to make. I don't like waiting rooms. I am a "doer," a list maker, a get-things-done kind of person. I like productivity—measurable, tangible results. The waiting room holds none of these possibilities for me. Not only do I have to wait, but I must do so while someone else is doing all the work. I must do so precisely because someone else, presumably a doctor, nurse, or surgical technician, is getting results. I must do all this waiting in a room full of chairs, hard chairs.

During the season of Advent, I am reminded of my strong dislike of waiting rooms. The weeks preceding Christmas become a countdown to Christmas Day. Each candle in the Advent wreath is one additional hard chair that must be occupied before the church can get to the real business, the final product of Christianity. I am ready for the baby! I am ready for the Christ to come into our world! I am ready to open the gift! I am ready to receive the healing and be made whole! I am ready now. But the sign on the front door of the sanctuary says, "Take a seat." To be very honest with you, that pew looks a lot like a hard chair in the local wait-ing room.

In the text for this week, we get a close look at the hard chairs of our existence. In response to Adam and Eve's disobedience, God announces the outcome of their actions. Indeed, human beings shall know—have knowledge of—both good and evil. We, the fruit of their union, will all know pain brought forth when we birth children, grand ideas, or hopeful visions of the future. We will all experience the angst that accompanies our most intimate and fulfilling relationships. The life of good work to which we have committed ourselves will produce both enduring satisfac-tion and overwhelming trials and stress. With finality, all of humanity will experience the fullness and precious nature of life always in the shadow of our deaths. Talk about hard chairs.

The story of Adam's and Eve's disobedience fascinates me because the desire to be like God doesn't seem to be deeply opposed to what God desires for human beings. Earlier in Genesis, God's intention is to make humanity "in our image, according to our likeness" (1:26). The fruit that Eve sees, and of which she eats, "was to be desired to make one wise" (3:6). Indeed, Eve and Adam do become wise and aware of their "situa-tion," their nakedness. Adam and Eve assume qualities that make them even more like God.

Are we then to understand that God never desired for humanity to have such qualities? Or did the embrace and consumption of the forbid-den fruit simply preempt God's already stated intentions? In other words, is the crime simply a crime of impatience, an unwillingness to wait?

One can hardly stand in judgment over two people who have within their grasp the opportunity to share a common experience with their maker and creator. How can we judge a pair who find they are unable to wait, no matter how many other trees are in the garden? The fact of the matter is that none of us like to wait for the revelation of God, the work of God to be accomplished. Even more, we find it fairly distasteful that no matter how capable and competent we are, at the moment, our job is to take a seat in a hard chair and wait for God to be God.

At my church, I am privileged to be in ministry with an extraordinary worship committee member. She is always one step ahead of how and where and when banners need to be hung and paraments changed and flowers or candles replaced. Her gifts are even more accentuated during the church's preparation for Advent. By the first Sunday of Advent, the Christmas tree parades its beauty; the banners glisten in purple and gold;

the evergreens and white and gold ribbons drape each open surface. The first Sunday of Advent, the people of the congregation gather in wide-eyed expectation, animated in their expressions of delight and approval of that year's Advent decorations.

However, before the worship service begins that first Sunday of Advent, everyone takes a seat in a hard chair, only to wait for twenty-one more days. (Amy Persons Parkes)

Worship Aids

Prayer of Confession

Lord God, we know the familiar sound of your footsteps. The sound convicts us. Like Eve and Adam, we have hastily grasped for that which you have forbidden. Now we are exposed for our greed and pride and impatience. Forgive us. Cover us. Through Christ. Amen.

Words of Assurance

The God for whom we wait is already waiting for us. Rest. Wait. Amen.

Prayer

God, you probably don't mind sitting in hard chairs. We prefer recliners, but that is not our lot in this life. Give us the grace to accept our lives as they are—broken and messy. Grant us your peace and the ability to wait in hard chairs. For Jesus' sake. Amen.

Benediction

To the waiting we have been called. For the waiting we have been equipped. In the waiting we will be blessed. Go in peace. Amen. (Amy Persons Parkes)

DECEMBER 11, 2011

Third Sunday of Advent

Readings: Isaiah 61:1-4, 8-11; Psalm 126; 1 Thessalonians 5:16-24; John 1:6-8, 19-28

A Cure for the Messiah Complex
John 1:6-8, 19-28

John the Baptist is a prominent figure in Advent, showing up each year in at least a couple of the Gospel readings and reappearing in January when we remember the Baptism of the Lord and renew our own baptisms. In listening closely to John the Baptist, one senses deep humility. "I am not the Messiah. I am not Elijah (the greatest of the prophets). I am not the main attraction. The main attraction is coming, and I am not worthy to shine his shoes."

This humility was not only John's perception of himself; it is also recorded in the Gospel writer's description of him: John the Baptist was not the light, but he came to bear witness to the light. It is important that we claim John as a model for our lives, as human beings and as Christians. You are not the Messiah. I am not the Messiah. A messiah is someone who saves, rules, and fixes people. Many in Israel were waiting for a messiah in the first century. Life was difficult, harsh, and oppressive.

John's entrance into the drama of Advent each year might not seem relevant at first glance, but in fact his is a needed voice. Humility is a misunderstood concept, and it may be helpful to say what it is and what it is not. It is not low self-esteem. We are created in the image of God, and that is good. Humility is not false modesty. We have been endowed with gifts, and they are to be used for the glory of God and the common good. One preacher put it this way: Humility is not thinking less of ourselves. Humility is thinking of ourselves less. Do you catch the difference?

This can be liberating. The congregation that I serve includes lots of folks I would describe as overachievers. I see their names in the newspaper, I hear them being interviewed on television and radio, I write letters of recommendation for them when they are getting ready to go to college. A week does not go by that someone in our congregation is not recognized in his or her profession.

When congratulated they will say, "Oh, it's nothing," or, "It's not as special as it seems," or, "Yes, oh, but you should see what my brother or sister or neighbor or colleague is doing." I am talking about other people, but if I am honest, myself as well. One of my seminary professors poked fun at the "I love me" walls that preachers love to have in their offices—degrees, ordination certificates—and I do wonder about how all of this helps us to preach better sermons about humility!

It is all mixed together with the drive to succeed and with ambition, performance, and goals. If we don't have these hopes for ourselves, we surely have them for our children. There is something constructive about all of this. Objectives are accomplished. Goals are met. Good is done. But there is also a dark side that can be a heavy burden. We begin to think that we are, in fact, the source of light. Sometimes, though, the bulb begins to dim. We might not use the precise language, but we begin to think that we are, in fact, the Messiah. We see other people as problems to be solved; we see daily lives as a series of messes to be cleaned up, dilemmas to be sorted through, damages to be repaired. If you and I don't take care of it, who will? The symptoms of this dark side are burnout, cynicism, frustration with other people, and paradoxically, self-rejection.

But remember, you and I are not the Messiah. We have limitations and boundaries. Advent comes along each year to give us this dose of humility, when once again we meet John, who helps us to get clear perspective.

Make no mistake. John the Baptist was a person of strength. He attracted people to his project. "Among those born of women," Jesus says, "no one has arisen greater than John the Baptist" (Matthew 11:11). John was not weak. "What did you go out into the wilderness to look at?" Jesus asks the disciples who had gone in search of John (Matthew 11:7). "A reed shaken by the wind?" (v.7). The literal meaning was a weather vane that bends with the currents of the wind. John was not weak; he was strong—he could withstand the forces of the winds and the storms—but he was humble. His humility is found precisely in his understanding of who he is and who he is not.

Humility is not weakness, but the awareness of the source of our strength. John reminds us that we are human. I came across the insight that there is a connection between the words *humanity, humility,* and *humor*. Each word has a common origin, in our word *humus*. My grand-parents had a humus pile that included soil and leaves and kitchen garbage and probably some things I would not want to mention. It was a mixture of the most organic matter, the compost pile, and it was a rich, fertile place. That says something about us: in our humanity we are always a mixture of many things and out of all of it come life and growth.

Humility and humor are connected in our ability to laugh at our-selves—and sometimes we do have to laugh at ourselves. This is related to our humanity. We have limitations, boundaries; we are finite. Humanity is a reminder of our need to be grounded—again the connec-tion with the earth. It is not accidental that the most fundamental pos-ture of humility is kneeling. This self-awareness prepares the way for something more, something greater: Behold the Lamb of God who takes away the sin of the world. (Kenneth H. Carter Jr.)

Lectionary Commentary
Isaiah 61:1-4, 8-11

This prophecy of Isaiah calls God's people to "build up the ancient ruins" (61:4). This text was proclaimed by Jesus as he preached for the first time in the synagogue in Capernaum (Luke 4:16-30). The words speak of the deliverance of those who are marginalized, and this mission is accomplished through the power and purpose of God in history. The messianic promise is the fulfillment of human hopes, which have resided in the hearts and lives of people across centuries, and remain even until this day.

1 Thessalonians 5:16-24

In one of the earliest letters of the New Testament, Paul writes to the believers about the importance of remaining faithful in the midst of suf-fering. The letter ends with a note of encouragement: "Rejoice always, pray without ceasing, give thanks in all circumstances" (1 Thessalonians 5:16-18). At Advent, this encouragement helps us to remain hopeful in the midst of external circumstances that move us to despair. The "day of the Lord" (5:2) is coming, and followers of Jesus are called to make their preparations, chiefly in behaviors that exhibit love of God and neighbor. (Kenneth H. Carter Jr.)

Worship Aids

Call to Worship

To you we lift up our eyes, O Lord.
To you we lift up our hearts.
We trust in your power and providence.
You are the light that is coming into the world.

Prayer of Confession

We confess, O God, our lack of humility. We have preferred our wills to your own. Where we are inflated with pride, ground us in the goodness that is your plan and purpose for us. You are the source of our strength. We place our hope in you. Amen. (Kenneth H. Carter Jr.)

Words of Assurance

God is the source of all hope and strength and will. Trust and wait. Jesus is coming.

Benediction

May those who go out weeping return with shouts of joy. May those who endure the night of mourning awaken to the joy of the morning. May those who rejoice in the Lord find their strength renewed. Amen. (Kenneth H. Carter Jr.)

Strong Coffee

Second in a Series of Four on Advent/Christmas

Mark 13:32-37

No waiting room is complete without the coffee. Some waiting rooms have vending machines. Some waiting rooms have two, maybe even three TVs. Still others may be equipped with Wi-Fi. But all waiting rooms have coffee, free coffee. In my younger days, I made the vow never to drink coffee, mainly because while I was growing up my parents would not come alive until the coffee had been brewed and at least one cup drained. My intuition told me that if they didn't have coffee, nothing would be right in the world. So in rebellion against my parents' seeming dependence upon the drink, I vehemently denied any consumption of its dark elixir.

Having now survived the early years of two preschool children and a demanding job in ministry, I have lost the fervor of my denunciation of coffee. I do admit that I still find myself at least three days a week working diligently to make it through the morning without coffee, just to prove that I can, in fact, engage a new day with determination and attentiveness without the aid of coffee. Nonetheless, I fully embrace the fact that there was never a better place for strong coffee than a hospital waiting room.

Most of the people I have ever accompanied to the hospital waiting room arrive there at least forty-five minutes ahead of me. As a pastor, I believe this is one of the greatest challenges of ministry—getting to the hospital before a parishioner is taken to surgery. At least 75 percent of the people I have prayed for and with before surgery must be ready to put on the gown and receive IV fluids before 8:00 a.m. If any significant driving is involved in order to get someone to the hospital, this means one must arise no later than 5:30 a.m. Who doesn't need coffee if the day starts before the sun comes up? Given that scenario, who doesn't need coffee to stay awake after the sun rises, especially in the cavelike atmosphere of our local windowless hospital waiting room?

Strong coffee in a hospital waiting room is, therefore, a necessity. At the same time the one who waits desires to fall asleep and regain some of the lost rest from the night before, she dare not for fear that she will miss some update on what is happening with the loved one who has disappeared into one of those sterile, tiled operating rooms. Wrestling down the desire to close her or his eyes for just a moment more, the one who waits shuffles over to the ever-ready, piping hot coffee stand for a cup of near-instant attentiveness.

Throughout Advent, our waiting is characterized not by resignation but by watchfulness, attentiveness. No matter what the hour, no matter how long the absence, no matter how far the distance to be traveled, the Christian waits as one who expects the appearance of the master of the house, who knows the Messiah who shall come again—unannounced and almighty. Last week we remembered how we got to this earthly waiting room in the first place. We recalled the story of humanity's impatience and the hard chairs of our experience. This week, the text warns us, "Drink the coffee!" Although we might be tempted to succumb to the white noise of the TV or the womblike darkness of the waiting room, Mark cries out, "Keep awake" (13:37).

The call of Mark to keep awake does not simply mean keep your eyes open. "Keep awake" has an element of engagement that goes beyond the literal action of eyes that see what is before them. "Keep awake" is the action of one who embraces the gravity of the situation. The mere fact that humanity finds itself in this ephemeral waiting room signifies that something greater and more profound is at hand. "What we will be has not yet been revealed" (1 John 3:2b).

Several years ago, my clergy spouse and I found ourselves overwhelmed with the responsibilities of leading two different churches and being new and faithful parents to our firstborn child. In the midst of trying to maintain integrity in both our professional and personal lives, we finally arrived at the conclusion that one of us must leave ministry for a time, to care for our child. Because of various factors, we agreed that it would be best for me to request family leave until another solution was available to us.

During those first few months of family leave, I regularly confronted the demons of pride when I found myself thinking of all the more-important things that I could be doing besides washing dishes or playing blocks with our son or planning meals for the week. I had left a position where I preached to 250 people on a regular basis. I had made significant contributions to the revitalization of both the youth's and children's programs in my church and was knee-deep in mission and ministry programs that were engaging parishioners in significant ministry. I was smart and competent and excelled in many areas of ministry. What was I doing just washing dishes?

As I gazed out the kitchen window one raw winter day, I remembered the gift of my visit to a Trappist monastery in South Carolina. On silent retreat for four days, the only time I spoke outside of worship was when my two companions and I gathered for a few moments of reflection after each meal. At the monastery, I became aware, alert, and attentive to the food I chewed, the dirt I tread upon, and the sheets between which I slept. In a moment of clarity, I really saw the dishes I was washing and the suds that amassed between my fingers. In that moment, I realized that the waiting I was doing—the waiting for our situation to change, the waiting for my child to grow up—that waiting was lacking. I was just passing time. I was sound asleep with my eyes wide open. (Amy Persons Parkes)

Worship Aids

Call to Worship
For the salvation of the Lord, we watch and wait.
Even when we are sleepy.

For the salvation of the Lord, we watch and wait.
Even when we are distracted and stressed.
For the salvation of the Lord, we watch and wait.
We watch and wait for the master who comes.

Prayer

God, you don't need coffee or diet cola to stay awake. Often we do. Sometimes we miss the very thing, the very person, the very moment, you want us to see. Empower us to wait, not by counting down the minutes, but by intently seeking your gift of grace in the wait. Through Jesus Christ our Lord. Amen.

Benediction

Go forth from this place with eyes that truly see and ears tuned to listen. We know not the day or the hour when Christ shall appear to us. Amen. (Amy Persons Parkes)

DECEMBER 18, 2011

Fourth Sunday of Advent

Readings: 2 Samuel 7:1-11, 16; Psalm 89:1-4, 19-26;
Romans 16:25-27; Luke 1:26-38

The Impossibility of Love
Luke 1:26-38

It is no accident that Mary takes center stage this time of year. Mary, so venerated by some Christians, so ignored by some Christians, so misunderstood by some Christians. At times Catholics have transformed the peasant Jewish teenage girl into an otherworldly queen. At times Protestants and Evangelicals have pretended that she never existed, or they have missed the truth that she is the first disciple, that she displays radical faith and trust in God.

Mary hears the call of God and she responds. She models faith, obedience, servanthood, discipleship, and hospitality. The Annunciation is the word of God, through the messenger, to Mary. "You have found favor with God. The power of the Holy Spirit will come upon you. You will give birth to the Savior."

"How can this be?" Mary asks. "Nothing will be impossible with God," the angel/messenger says to her. The call of God is to an ordinary woman, and yet the call is to do something extraordinary. God chose an ordinary human being—Mary—to be the vessel through which the Son of God would be born. What is impossible for us is possible with God. Paul, writing later to the church at Corinth, would reflect on this truth that is common and profound: "We have this treasure in clay jars, so that it may be made clear that this extraordinary power belongs to God and does not come from us" (2 Corinthians 4:7).

In a busy season of the year it is good to get clarity about what is happening. God calls ordinary people, people like you and me. This has always been the way of the Lord; again, Paul writing to the

Corinthians: "Consider your own call, brothers and sisters: not many of you were wise by human standards, not many were powerful, not many were of noble birth. But . . . God chose what is low and despised in the world, things that are not, to reduce to nothing things that are" (1 Corinthians 1:26-28).

Or we can go farther back into the tradition and rehearse the call of Moses, who suggested that he was not eloquent of speech and that his brother might be a better candidate for God's mission (Exodus 3).

The call of God comes to ordinary human beings, like Mary. Yet through ordinary people the extraordinary happens. The call of God, found in the Annunciation, finds its response in a later text, the Magnificat (Luke 1:46-56). Mary senses it: "I am an ordinary person. I am not perfect." Preachers grasp this: we are imperfect people, and we preach to gatherings of imperfect people.

The good news of the gospel is that when God begins to search for us, God is not seeking perfection. God chooses the ordinary. God loves the unlovable. In fact, God reverses just about every expectation we might have of how the Lord would enter into this world and save it.

Does God flatter the proud? No, God scatters the proud. Does God seek an invitation from the throne? No, God brings those from thrones down, and lifts up the lowly. Does God hang out at the finest restaurants? No, God throws a banquet for the poor. Does God choose a queen or a princess to be the mother of Jesus? No, God chooses Mary. Does God choose the wise, the noble, and the powerful in this world to accomplish the divine will? No, God chooses you and me. Does God love those who are lovable? Yes, and God loves the unlovable; God forgives the imperfect; God reaches out to the lost.

Christmas is really all about this attribute of God, who loves us, who reaches out, down to us, who stoops to our weakness. "Mild he lays his glory by," Charles Wesley wrote in the carol "Hark! The Herald Angels Sing" (*UMH*, 240). God comes in the unspectacular and the humble.

That is what Christmas is about. As a child growing up, our large family party was always on Christmas Eve. We all gathered—my great-grandmother, my grandparents, their three children, and the eight great-grandchildren. Maybe we do tend to see the past through rose-colored glasses, but I remember those times as among my happiest moments on earth. We were euphoric, ecstatic.

Years later, my grandparents and great-grandmother moved into the city to be near medical care. After my great-grandmother and grandfather died, my grandmother decided that she wanted to move back home. So the house was refurbished. We painted it and cleaned it out. I was in college by then, and walking back into the house, I could not believe how small it was. How did the thirteen of us fit in that room? Then I looked at pictures of those gatherings, and I saw the cinderblock walls—it really was a very simple house—and I looked at the Christmas tree—a Georgia pine tree, not like the large ones we put up now. What was happening in those gatherings?

It all becomes clear again. What made such a setting—simple, nothing grand or extravagant about it—one of the very places on earth that is most holy to me now? The clue is in the call of God to Mary and her response. God chooses the simple to confound the wise. God chooses the humble to shame the strong. God always chooses the ordinary to do something extraordinary. What is impossible for us is possible for God.

In a stable, probably more like a cave, on a hillside in the country, out of the way, a baby was born to two scared young people. They had nothing to offer, only the circumstance of their lives. They heard the call of God, each in their own way. They responded in faith. Christmas, for us, twenty centuries later, is no different. What is the call and what is our response? What is God saying to you this Christmas? What are you saying to God? (Kenneth H. Carter Jr.)

Lectionary Commentary
2 Samuel 7:1-11, 16

David receives a message from Nathan (who will figure prominently at another time in David's life, in the aftermath of his relationship with Bathsheba). The subject is the establishment of the Davidic kingdom, which is physically defined as the building of a house. David's reign, which will later be traced through Jesus of Nazareth (Matthew 1) is a part of God's providence and is revealed to the prophet Nathan.

Romans 16:25-27

The Epistle lesson for this Sunday takes the form of a doxology, a prayer offered to God. The words connect with the Advent season in their communication of the mystery that has been hidden through the ages but is now revealed, the incarnation of God anticipated by the prophets. The purpose of this knowledge is to bring about obedience, and again we find a strong connection with Mary's act of faith. (Kenneth H. Carter Jr.)

Worship Aids

Call to Worship

Let us enter into the house of the Lord.
God has prepared a place for us!
Let us listen for the voice of the Lord.
God has revealed a word to us!
Let us worship in spirit and in truth.
God is with us!

Invocation

Almighty God, who calls not the proud but the lowly: stoop to our weakness, descend upon us in the power of your Holy Spirit, and give us the wisdom to know the truth and the courage to follow in the way of Jesus Christ, our coming Lord and Savior. Amen.

Benediction

Now unto the one who is able to strengthen you according to the good news of the coming Messiah, the one anticipated by the prophets whose message has been hidden across the ages but is now fully revealed—to God alone be glory forever. In the name of the Father, the Son, and the Holy Spirit. Amen. (Kenneth H. Carter Jr.)

Three Calls

Third in a Series of Four on Advent/Christmas

Isaiah 11:1-9

While church buildings can become a burden for a congregation to bear, my affection for those churches built somewhere near the turn of the twentieth century grows and grows in a day and age when church sanctuaries are constructed more frequently for utilitarian rather than aesthetic purposes. Generally, I agree that the cost of one great stained-glass window seems ridiculous when a congregation can add an additional ten rows of chairs to the worship space or install a high-powered projection system. But my assumptions are challenged when I remember one of the two prominent stained-glass windows at the First United Methodist Church of Union Springs, Alabama.

Characterized by a shallow seating area, as the pulpit forms a center to the semicircular room, the sanctuary rests in the bosom of ebony-wooded ceiling joists and planks, an ebony chancel rail and choir loft, and ebony curved pews. The dark wood lends coolness to the room even on stifling summer days. The tomblike nature of the sanctuary is broken by two massive stained-glass windows on the east and west walls. The one that so often captures my imagination and fans my hope is the west window, depicting the stump of Jesse.

In multitoned browns, the window illustrates two complementary wooded columns that have been snapped off near the base of the trunk. Seeing these images reminds me of the tall, strong pine tree that was left with only a jagged base after a tornado ripped through the pine forest. The tree was too soon and brutally harvested. But the stump of Jesse in the west window foreshadows the life that will come forth from the protected and buried roots of the tree. Winding thin and tender in its green, a shoot emerges from the tree trunk; a branch grows from the roots of Jesse's stump. When I see that shoot in my mind's eye, I hear the sharp, shrill sound of a phone ringing.

When the prophet Isaiah is raised up to speak for the Lord, the great King David's legacy has devolved into a people "who make iniquitous decrees, who write oppressive statutes, to turn aside the needy from justice and to rob the poor" (Isaiah 10:1-2). In response to their idolatry, disobedience, and injustice, the prophet tells us that God allows and sends Israel's enemies into its midst.

In our scripture for today, the prophet Isaiah speaks to a people who have known the destruction of all their hope, a people who are broken and hurting. These people have witnessed the looting of their land, homes, and traditions. They have lost all sense of God's presence in their midst and fear that never again will they be a sovereign nation. As Isaiah preaches to them, he reminds them that the wait has an end: "On that day the remnant of Israel and the survivors of the house of Jacob will no more lean on the one who struck them, but will lean on the LORD, the holy one of Israel, in truth. A remnant will return, the remnant of Jacob, to the mighty God" (10:20-21). This remnant will experience a peaceable kingdom when God sends the root of Jesse.

The long wait will be over; the stump will produce new growth; the one who has been cut down will be restored. The spirit of wisdom, understanding, counsel, and might, as well as the knowledge and fear of the Lord will rest upon this great leader. In the kingdom that is coming, righteousness and equity will be the plumb line and level. In a world governed by the root of Jesse, all of creation will live in harmony. Natural enemies will no longer conquer one another; they will rest together. None will hurt and destroy on God's holy mountain. The wait for the kingdom to come is not over, but the long and arduous task of waiting for a new day, a new hope, and an end to come, that waiting is punctuated by the call of hope.

If you have ever waited for someone who is having surgery, then you know just how important the calls are. I sometimes wonder what it would be like in a phone-less waiting room. What would it be like to bid a caring good-bye to your loved one who is guided toward the exclusive back halls of the surgical area while you make your way to the waiting area, without any means of communication? If the surgery is long and the repairs are extensive, the three calls give sustenance to the one who waits. Fortunately, the telephone is available and the waiting is punctuated by calls of progress and hope. The first call informs those waiting that the surgery has begun. The second call gives some affirmation to the progress being made. The third call is a white flag signifying that the ordeal, for the moment, is almost over.

By the fourth Sunday of Advent, we need a call. In fact, in some ways, don't most Sundays of the Christian year seem like the last Sunday of Advent? We have been waiting so long. We have been hoping with all of our might. We have endured the hard chairs, and we are on the fourth or fifth cup of strong coffee. Will someone, please, just call? As the church waits one more year for the Christ to come, for the Messiah to be born in our midst, couldn't someone be so kind and compassionate as to offer an update on the progress being made in the halls and rooms to which we have no access, to which we have not been given clearance?

This fourth Sunday of Advent, the phone is ringing. Isaiah, assistant to the great physician, is on the line. This call is for the church family. Here is the message: "A shoot shall come out from the stump of Jesse, and a branch shall grow out of his roots. The spirit of the LORD shall rest on him, the spirit of wisdom and understanding, the spirit of counsel and might, the spirit of knowledge and the fear of the LORD" (Isaiah 11:1-2). (Amy Persons Parkes)

Worship Aids

Call to Worship

In the dead of winter, we know spring is coming. Bare branches fill the sky, but living roots finger the earth. Be still and know. Be still and know God.

Prayer

Gracious and loving God, may your Spirit rest upon us. May we seek wisdom and understanding rather than power and might. Grant that we may hold fast to righteousness and equity for your sake. Sustain in us a vision of your holy mountain where none will hurt or destroy. Through Jesus Christ our Lord. Amen.

Benediction

The tender shoot of God's mercy is winding its way into this world. Go forth into the world bearing witness to the promise of God's kingdom. Amen. (Amy Persons Parkes)

DECEMBER 25, 2011

❧❧❧❧

Christmas Day

Readings: Isaiah 52:7-10; Psalm 98; Hebrews 1:1-4 (5-12); John 1:1-14

The Light Shines in the Darkness
John 1:1-14

We gather on Christmas Day (or at midnight on Christmas Eve) to bear witness once again to a simple truth: the light shines in the darkness, and the darkness has not overcome it. When God's people have tried to get their minds wrapped around what the glory and greatness of God is like, they have been drawn again and again to the image of light.

In the creation, God separated light from darkness, creating the greater light (sun) and the lesser light (moon). God stopped Moses in his tracks in the form of a burning bush. Jesus was the light coming into the world. The future vision at the end of the story is of a city that is so bright that there is no moon or sun to shine upon it, for the glory of God will be its light and its lamp will be the Lamb.

When we bear witness to the truth about ourselves, about our world, we try to describe what it means to live honestly and not falsely, hopefully and not in despair, faithfully and not superficially, and we could do much worse than this simple phrase of John the evangelist in chapter 1, verse 5: "The light shines in the darkness, and the darkness did not overcome it."

In this one verse, a universe of meaning is contained. First, there is darkness. Christians acknowledge that there is darkness. One of our best novelists, William Styron, wrote the novels *Confessions of Nat Turner*, which chronicled the darkness of the racial struggle in America; and *Sophie's Choice*, which narrated the horror of the Holocaust and the decision that a person should never have to make. Meryl Streep won an Academy Award for her portrayal of the tortured Sophie. Later in his life,

Styron wrote a memoir, *Darkness Visible*, which turned out to be about his own struggle with depression.

In Styron's life and art we see the truth that there is darkness, and the darkness is both out there and in here. Sometimes we project the darkness onto others—that group, that race, that political party, that nation—but the darkness is within us, and that is why we make the connection. Sometimes we deny the darkness within us. The power of William Styron's art, across his lifetime, was his willingness to see the darkness not only in the world but also within himself.

Christians live in a world of darkness. The Bible deals with darkness: "Why do you hide your face?" the psalmist asks God (Psalm 44:24). Elijah in the cave and Jesus in the garden ask where God is. "Why have you forsaken me?" Then Jesus is three days in the tomb, descending into hell, for our sakes. Paul is struck blind on the road to Damascus.

More than one person has noted that our culture wants to live, not only in the denial of death, but also in the denial of darkness. I looked recently at an aerial photo of the United States at night. It was fairly bright, especially east of the Mississippi and along the coasts. Across the country there were few dark patches.

This could be an analogy of our spiritual lives. We are sometimes in denial about the darkness that is visible, the fighting within and fears without, the demons that arrive at noonday and the scourges that dehumanize so many across the world. Let us make the confession: There is darkness.

But there is more. For the scripture says, "The light shines in the darkness." Our spiritual rebirth happens when we turn down all of the artificial lights that distract us, to enter into the darkness so that we can see the true light that is coming into the world. Our Jewish friends are very good at this, using as little electricity as possible on Sabbath, so that the candles make the light visible; and at Hanukkah, insisting that the light chases away the darkness: the more we live in darkness, the greater our need for the light.

"The light shines in the darkness." So far, these are truths that are fairly evident to most people, if they are observant and attentive. There is darkness. But in the darkness, there is light. A secular radio anchor notes in passing, to no one in particular, that the holidays "bring out the worst and the best in people." That can be said without any kind of conviction or belief. The scripture, however, takes one more step, and it is a step of faith. The light shines in the darkness, and the darkness has not

407

overcome it. This is the promise of Christmas faith. The darkness has not overcome it. Light is stronger than darkness.

A member of our church, a friend, struggles over a long term with a persistent and painful form of cancer. He and his wife are always gracious, always welcoming. We pray and then we shake hands, and as I am leaving, I hear these words: "We thank God for every day," she says. "God has been good to us."

Let us not be silent about the darkness. It is real. Let us pay attention to the light. It is present. But let us believe deeply in the promise of our faith. When we light the candle at Christmas, it represents the hope of the world, a Savior, who is Christ the Lord. Even for those of us who have held these candles in our hands before, it is always new. Even for those of us who could recite the Christmas scripture from memory, the good news is always a needed word, an honest word, a hope-filled word. "The light shines in the darkness, and the darkness did not overcome it." (Kenneth H. Carter Jr.)

Lectionary Commentary
Isaiah 52:7-10

This brief selection of poetry from Isaiah echoes an earlier writing in Isaiah 40:9-11. The messenger (could this be Isaiah?) announces good news of peace and salvation, and the response to this evangel is the praise of God's people in song. The inclusive message of the prophet—"all the ends of the earth shall see the salvation of our God" (52:10)—flows into the Christian proclamation of the Savior who is for all people. This text has also been interpreted by a number of composers, including G. F. Handel.

Hebrews 1:1-4 (5-12)

Corresponding to the epistle lesson of the Fourth Sunday of Advent (Romans 16:25-27), the Hebrews text places the incarnation within the whole history of God's purpose, as articulated through the "ancestors" and prophets. In the last days, God communicates through the presence of the divine Son, who reflects God's glory and is the "exact imprint" of God's very being (Hebrews 1:3). If we want to know what God is like, we look to Jesus. Further, the Hebrews text connects the Incarnation with the later events in Jesus' life (death, resurrection, and ascension). (Kenneth H. Carter Jr.)

Worship Aids

Call to Worship

How beautiful upon the mountains
  are the feet of the messenger who announces peace.
Who brings the good news, God's word of salvation?
Let us break forth into singing.
For God is with us. Praise the Lord!

Invocation

O God, who was and is and is to come, we gather in the name of Jesus Christ—Word of the Father, now in flesh appearing. Let us be receptive to hear the good news that is your gift to all people, and let us worship you in spirit and in truth. Amen.

Benediction

Go into the world in peace. For the one who is the light of the world, Jesus Christ, now says to every one of us: "You are the light of the world!" Go in peace. You are the light of the world. In the name of the Father, the Son, and the Holy Spirit. Amen. (Kenneth H. Carter Jr.)

Physician's Word

Fourth in a Series of Four on Advent/Christmas

Matthew 1:18-25

I am constantly amazed at the variety of ways that pastors pastor, somewhat like a parent who repeatedly experiences the revelation that no two children are alike. Children born to the same parents with the same house and the same routine will not necessarily have any similar personality traits. One pastor preaches with a manuscript; another uses index cards for prompting points; while still another carries nothing to the pulpit except a Bible. One pastor directs and informs. Another facilitates and listens. One pastor arrives early and leaves early. Another comes late and stays late. Even the simple act of visiting is nuanced by the personal tastes of each pastor.

I remember a pastor who gave me his own sage advice as it pertained to visiting. He said, "You need to enter the room leaving." When approaching the shut-in visit, he advised me, a young inexperienced pastor, to make sure that I noted just how much time I had to visit, before the visit even began. What a vastly different experience from the pastor who came to the bedside of a dear relative of mine in the hours before his death. That pastor, whom I had never met, came quietly into the room, in a soft voice greeted us, a grieving family, and then silently and solidly found a place in the corner of the room to watch and wait with us. Rarely saying a word, yet standing with us, praying for us, his unmitigated presence assured us that those moments of waiting were sacred.

If the church family has a difficult time waiting, if the pastoral leadership finds itself impatient with its congregation's impatience, one might begin to question what kind of example we as pastors are setting for those whom we lead. If we, the pastors, do not have time to wait and stay, if we do not have the ability to embrace a hard chair, sip strong coffee, and hold up the call of hope, then what can we really expect from our people?

The scripture for this Christmas Sunday is preceded by twenty-eight generations of a people who waited for the Messiah to come (Matthew 1:1-17). Tenacious, attentive, enduring—these words describe the witness of generation after generation of God's people who stood quietly in the corner of humanity's sick room, bidding the patient not to die, not to give up hope, to place her feeble trust in the power and goodness of a great physician. Even Joseph himself is called upon by God to stay and wait with Mary as God's healing is made real through the birth of the Christ.

The scripture reads that Joseph, "righteous" and "unwilling to expose her to public disgrace" (Matthew 1:19), was not seeking an end to Mary's life because of her unfaithfulness. Instead, a seemingly compassionate and well-intentioned Joseph "planned to dismiss her quietly" (v. 19). One might wonder, "Did Joseph intend to enter the engagement leaving?" Like the pastor who enters the room leaving, Joseph defines the conditions for his staying with Mary before the marriage is even begun. God has other expectations for the relationship between Joseph and Mary. God pronounces the waiting and staying as holy work, informing Joseph that the fruit of Mary's womb "will save his people from their sins" (v. 21).

At the local hospital, the final moments spent in the waiting room are usually preceded by a visit from the surgeon. Now that the unseen work is finished, now that the patient is being wheeled to recovery, the surgeon arrives to convey a final word to those who wait. The surgeon relays the overall success or failure of the operation, the challenges and surprises of the ordeal, the expected recovery time, and the prognosis for the days ahead. For family or loved ones who are waiting, who are unsure about what the days ahead will hold, the visit from the doctor provides an anchor of next steps and outcomes. In the previous hours, those who waited dealt only in possibility; but now, the physician's word gives guidance and direction, a way forward. Whether the healing is imminent or delayed, whether the news is optimistic or dreaded, the final word is spoken. The uncertainty that plagues those who wait is held at bay for a moment. The physician has spoken.

The Great Physician's word to Joseph is to stay with Mary. "Joseph, you can't see yet what I am doing. You don't know what I am up to. All is not as it seems. Take my word for it—stay with her." The Great Physician's word to the church family and to the world is "Emmanuel, God is with us." God does not enter relationship with humanity planning an exit. When has God ever had enough of us? At what point has God been so disgusted with our unfaithfulness that the Holy One dismissed us quietly? Clearly, Matthew's intention is to reaffirm God's abiding presence with us, God's non-negotiable desire to embrace a waiting with, a waiting for, the salvation of all people.

On this Christmas Sunday in our earthly waiting room, the church family receives, with immense relief, the prognosis for what ails us. Our healing is at hand. We rejoice in the birth of Jesus, who will save us from our sins, and celebrate a God who is with us. Humanity sees a clear way forward, a next step through the muddled mess of our lives; and with grateful spirits, we rejoice that part of our waiting is over. But only one part of our waiting is over. Even as God is with us, waits with us, stands beside us, and engages us in significant meaningful relationship, so God calls the body of Christ to be with others. God expects Joseph to stay with Mary. God expects Ananias to lay hands on Saul (Acts 9:17). God expects Peter to befriend Cornelius (Acts 10). If we the church do not have time to wait and stay, if we are not willing to remain with those who have been unfaithful to us, how are we any different from the rest of a lost, hurting, dying world?

In a waiting room, the waiting is sacred. (Amy Persons Parkes)

Worship Aids

Call to Worship
A woman waits.
A dream is dreamed.

A man decides.
A child is born.
The people are saved.
The people are saved. God is with us.

Prayer

Little God baby, wrap us up in your love. Swaddle us with your forgiveness. Nurse us with your presence. Rock us in the assurance of your salvation. Little God baby, make us be like you. In your name and for your sake. Amen.

Benediction

The world is waiting for a message of hope and grace. The world is waiting for a faithful witness to a God who does not enter our world looking for the doorway out. Go forth to proclaim the truth we know: God in Christ is born today! Amen. (Amy Persons Parkes)

III. APPENDIX

CONTRIBUTORS

Chuck Aaron
First United Methodist Church
of Farmersville
216 Jouette St.
Farmersville, TX 75442-1516

Tracey Allred
2729 Mountain Woods Drive
Birmingham, AL 35216

Guy Ames
333 West Main
Suite 445
Ardmore, OK 73401

Chris Andrews
First United Methodist Church
930 North Boulevard
Baton Rouge, LA 70802-5728

Dave Barnhart
724 Saulter Lane
Birmingham, AL 35209

Thomas Lane Butts
First United Methodist Church
324 Pineville Road
Monroeville, AL 36460

Kenneth H. Carter Jr.
Providence United Methodist
Church
2810 Providence Road
Charlotte, NC 28211

Mike Childress
205 Riverbirch Drive
Salisbury, NC 28146

Will Cotton
St. Luke's United Methodist
Church
3708 45th Street
Lubbock, TX 79413

Dan R. Dick
Wisconsin Annual Conference
750 Windsor Street
Sun Prairie, WI 53590

Neil Epler
St. Luke United Methodist Church
201 Heath Street
Enterprise, AL 36330

Amber Essick
P.O. Box 8613
Waco, TX 76714

John I. Essick
Day Spring Baptist
P.O. Box 8613
Waco, TX 76714

Dan L. Flanagan
Saint Paul's United Methodist
Church
324 S. Jackson St.
Papillion, NE 68046

Roberto L. Gómez
El Mesias United Methodist
Church
P.O. Box 4787
Mission, TX 78573-4787

Drew J. Gunnells Jr.
1205 Dominion Drive E
Mobile, AL 36695

David C. Hockett
Forest Hill United Methodist
Church
265 Union Street, N.
Concord, NC 28025

Cameron Jorgenson
2617 Cole Avenue #8
Waco, TX 76707

Wendy Joyner
Fellowship Baptist Church
P.O. Box 1122
Americus, GA 31709

Gary G. Kindley
3906 Lemmon Ave, Suite 207
Dallas, TX 75219

Andrew D. Kinsey
Grace United Methodist Church
1300 East Adams Drive
Franklin, IN 46131

Mike Lowry
464 Bailey
Fort Worth, TX 76107

David N. Mosser
First United Methodist Church
313 N. Center St. @ Division
Arlington, TX 76011

Raquel Mull
Saint Paul's United Methodist
Church
1015 Goad Avenue
Socorro, NM 87801

Timothy Owings
902 Big Oak Circle
Augusta, GA 30907

Amy Persons Parkes
P.O. Box 463
Hurtsboro, AL 36860

Carl L. Schenck
Manchester United Methodist
Church
129 Woods Mill Rd
Manchester, MO 63011-4339

Victor Shepherd
91 Swanhurst Blvd
Mississauga, Ontario
Canada, L5N 1B8

Thomas R. Steagald
First United Methodist Church
217 N. Main Street
Stanley, NC 28164

Mark White
215 Wilkinson Road
Richmond, VA 23227

Victoria Atkinson White
9015 Birdsong Creek Court
Mechanicsville, VA 23116

Sandy Wylie
University United Methodist
   Church
4652 S. Jameston
Tulsa, OK 74135

Brett Younger
McAfee School of Theology
3001 Mercer University Drive
Atlanta, GA 30341

SCRIPTURE INDEX

Page numbers refer only to the print text.

Old Testament

New Testament

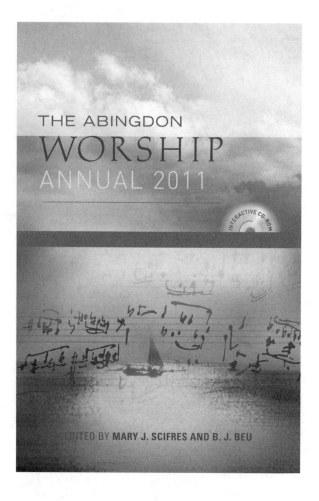

THE ABINGDON

WORSHIP

ANNUAL 2011

EDITED BY MARY J. SCIFRES AND B. J. BEU

The *Abingdon Worship
Annual 2011* offers fresh
worship planning resources fo
pastors and worship leaders.

**"Commendations to
Abingdon Press for
offering two fresh
ecumenical resources
for pastors."**
For *The Abingdon Preaching
Annual*—"Anyone who
dares proclaim a holy word
week in and week out soon
realizes that creative
inspiration for toe-shaking
sermons quickly wanes.
Multitasking pastors who
are wise seek out resources
that multiply their own
inductive initiatives."

For *The Abingdon Worship
Annual*—"Not only the
sermon but also the whole
service dares to be toe-
shaking... and the *Worship
Annual* is a reservoir of
resources in that direction.'
**—The Reverend Willard
E. Roth,** Academy of
Parish Clergy President,
*Sharing the Practice: The
Journal of the Academy of
Parish Clergy*

Abingdon Press